LA LEGA: THE MAKING OF A SUCCESSFUL COOPERATIVE NETWORK

To all those men and women of La Lega who through their ideas and commitment have created an alternative way of working.

La Lega: The Making of a Successful Cooperative Network

PIERO AMMIRATO

Dartmouth

Aldershot • Brookfield USA • Singapore • Sydney

Published by
Dartmouth Publishing Company Limited
Gower House
Croft Road
Aldershot
Hants GU11 3HR
England

Dartmouth Publishing Company
Old Post Road
Brookfield
Vermont 05036
USA

British Library Cataloguing in Publication Data
Ammirato, Piero
La lega : the making of a successful cooperative network
1.Cooperation - Italy 2.Cooperation - Europe - History -
3.Cooperative societies - Italy 4.Cooperative societies - Europe - History
I.Title
334'.0945

Library of Congress Cataloging-in-Publication Data
Ammirato, Piero
La Lega : the making of a successful cooperative network / Piero Ammirato.
p. cm.
Includes bibliographical references and index.
ISBN 1-85521-839-9
1. Lega nazionale delle cooperative e delle mutue.
2. Cooperation–Italy. 3. Cooperative societies–Italy.
4. Friendly societies–Italy. I. Title.
HD3505.A1L342 1996
334'.0945–dc20 96-16541
CIP

ISBN 1 85521 839 9

Printed and bound in Great Britain by
Hartnolls Limited, Bodmin, Cornwall

Contents

List of Figures

List of Tables

List of Abbreviations

ACAM	National Consortium for Purchases/Supplies
Associazione	Associazione Generale delle Cooperative Italiane (General Association of Italian Cooperatives)
BNL	Banca Nazionale del Lavoro (National Labour Bank)
CCC	Consorzio Cooperative Costruzioni (Consortium for the Construction Cooperatives)
CDA	Cooperative Development Agency
CGIL	Confederazione Generale Italiana del Lavoro (Confederation of Italian Labour)
CISL	Confederazione Italiana dei Sindacati dei Lavoratori (Confederation of Italian Workers Union)
CLP	Caja Laboral Popular
Confederazione	Confederazione Cooperative Italiane (Confederation of Italian Cooperatives)
DC	Democrazia Cristiana (Christian Democratic Party)
EEC	European Economic Community
ENI	Ente Nazionale Idrocarburi (National Hydrocarbon Corporation)
ERVET	Economic Development Board of Emilia Romagna
ESOP	Employees Stock Ownership Plans
ICA	International Cooperative Alliance
ICIE	Istituto Cooperativo per l'Innovazione (Cooperative Institute for Innovation Transfer)
La Lega	National League of Italian Cooperatives and Mutual Aid Societies
NCL	National Committee of Liberation
PCI	Partito Comunista Italiano (Italian Communist Party)
PSI	Partito Socialista Italiano (Italian Socialist Party)
UIL	Unione Italiana del Lavoro (Union of Italian Labour)
USL	Unitá Sanitarie Locali (Local Health Authorities)

Preface

The celebration of the *End of History* is undoubtedly premature. The term is, in fact, a euphemism for the presumed end of socialism. It is obvious that a major staging point in history has been reached, but to assume that this is the culminating point in economic and political development is myopic in the extreme. It defies the logic of history and greatly overrates the achievements both of private enterprise capitalism and liberal democracy.

It is still too early to relegate China and the remaining Asian socialist regimes to the same historical dustbin as their European counterparts. The expectation that there will be a similar pattern of events there, or that it will only be avoided by a rapid convergence with the western model, is founded more on hope than evidence. Undoubtedly there is radical economic change underway but the relaxation of political control is not in evidence.

What is disregarded in this debate is the potential for development within the western model itself. Because its closest rival is defunct does not mean that it can now ossify. Release from fears of political subversion and military confrontation may well relax constraints on reform of the existing system. Both its economic and political components demonstrate considerable variations across its constituent countries and the accentuation of any differences may well produce a radical departure.

State ownership of industry in most western countries remains considerable, despite the tide of privatisation. The consequences of privatisation are already causing an adverse reaction in several instances and there could well be a reversionary trend. The same conditions which provoked State control in the past may well produce a radical departure.

What has been neglected as an option is the cooperative alternative, despite its one and a half centuries of existence. A major problem has been that, in the country of its origin, England, the cooperative movement was quite deliberately steered away from the extension into industry. Its chosen bastion, the retail cooperative, has been debilitated in the face of the supermarket revolution. In an English context, the cooperative movement has become an historical curiosity and its operational survival is in a much truncated and modified form.

The main objection to industrial cooperatives was their supposed tendency to "degeneracy" or reversion to the same undesirable practices as capitalism. They were also claimed to have no incentive to expand, since re-investment would diminish immediate earnings. It was believed that they had inferior access to loan capital since their unconventional character made them suspect to banks. Control often fell into the hands of a few members, who might not even work in the enterprise, while most of those who were workers were not members. For whatever reason, industrial cooperatives did not flourish in England.

There was a revival of interest in cooperatives in the 1970s, mainly instigated by the broader campaign for industrial democracy through increased worker participation in management, and stimulated by the discovery of the thriving complex of industrial cooperatives in the Basque country of Spain with its headquarters at Mondragon. Some observers attributed its singular success to the specific character of the Basques and not therefore replicable. Others, including its English publicist, Robert Oakeshott, believed its success to be the result of applying the correct formula - a high degree of correspondence between membership and the workforce; a capital stake by worker-members; a distributive formula which insured a high level of re-investment; and the construction of its own infrastructure in the form of a bank with entrepreneurial division; collaborative production and marketing arrangements; a research and developing wing and a training programme. However, despite a continuous stream of visitors to Mondragon, keen to inspect its workings at source, and anxious to reproduce it at home, it has yet to be replicated.

None of the other discoveries provided a better model. The plywood cooperatives of the north-western USA were deemed operationally efficient and financially profitable, but the latter factor and the lack of an ideological commitment meant that they were prone to sell out but not to seek an extension of the coverage. Their credentials were already suspect because of their propensity to use a substantial number of hired workers.

The Scott-Bader Partnership in England offered another variant on the cooperative theme and again generated a good deal of interest. It rejected the stakeholder philosophy of the Basque cooperatives but adopted a similar formula for profit distribution and developed a finance wing in ICOF and an umbrella organisation in ICOM. However, this also failed to provide the philosophers' stone which would provide for the wholesale conversion of private enterprises to cooperatives since the transition basically depended on the benevolence of existing owners and the finance available for start-ups was extremely limited.

As the survey of viable cooperative operations continued, it was observed that the cooperative movement, despite having its roots in England, had prospered better overseas, both in the developing countries and Continental Europe. Foremost among the European examples was Italy, given some coverage by Jenny Thornley and others, but still relatively obscure to the English-speaking world because most publications and documentation were in Italian.

Piero Ammirato is a native Italian speaker who has obtained his academic qualifications through the medium of English. He is ideally placed to reveal the Italian cooperative movement to an Anglophone audience. His book is grounded in both an assiduous search of the existing literature and extensive fieldwork in Italy. He has identified those elements of the Italian experience which he believes have contributed to its success, both in terms of its size and survival.

His main conclusions concur with those of Oakeshott in his observations of the Basque case, in so far as they indicate that success lies in an appropriate organisational structure rather than in some curious cultural alchemy. However, it is salutary that the Italian cooperatives have operated within the framework of the ICA rules which Oakeshott regards as an impediment to its success. They have contrived to formulate an operational pattern within these rules which has delivered not only survival but expansion on a scale that dwarfs the much better recognised Basque cooperatives. Most of the components are the same - the generation of an infra-structure particularly in the provision of finance, the re-investment of surplus funds, and the close collaboration of the member organisations, both geographically and sectorally.

The major difference in these two southern European success stories is the role of politics. Certainly in the Basque cooperatives have benefited from an advantageous legal situation but they have not been closely integrated with any political party. They had their genesis and initial expansion under the Franco regime and have continued to thrive in the new democracy.

The Italian cooperative movement is very much politicised and it is segmented along party lines. This book deals with La Lega, the largest of them and an associate of the Italian Communist Party.[1] The connection brings both advantages and disadvantages. The ability of La Lega to obtain policy concessions depends to an extend on the political situation of the Communist Party. During the Fascist era, this brought repression and with the return of democracy, the fluctuating fortunes of electoral outcomes. A saving feature has been the domination of many local and regional governments by the Communist Party which gave it a solid base and continuing favour, whatever the political situation nationally.

The national arena is necessarily crucial in the provision of the legal setting in which cooperatives operate and the extraction of desired legislative amendments has contributed to their success. The fact that support for the cooperative movement extends across the political spectrum obviously helps in this respect if there is a unified demand for legislative reform.

Apart from the intrinsic interest of a national case study, there is the underlying question of whether the success of the Italian cooperatives is capable of replication elsewhere. While claims of cultural specificity can be overcome by a demonstration of organisational factors, there is always the possibility, perhaps even the probability, that these had their genesis in particular historical circumstances which are unlikely to be repeated.

This returns us to the starting point of declarations of the *End of History*. While history may not repeat itself, it is certainly unlikely to come to a halt. There are inbuilt factors in the current economic situation which will necessarily generate crisis and provide the possibility of change. Having discarded the Marxist prescription for how this might occur does not mean that none other exists.

The situation in the post socialist countries themselves provides the opportunities for constructive change. While the initial assumption has been of a headlong rush into pure capitalism, this has only been patchily achieved and there is a growing resistance to wholesale privatisation. Particularly in the ex-Yugoslavia, despite its derailment by inter-ethnic conflicts, the long experience of worker-management, despite its flows, has produced objections to the transfer of control to external, concentrated ownership. A cooperative formulation would meet the requirements of a market economy.

Piero Ammirato's interest is fuelled by commitment rather than mere curiosity and this raises the question of whether Italian circumstances can be replicated in a different national and temporal context.

It is clearly true that, as in many other cases, success begets success. The existence of an extensive movement with its own financial resources and the capacity to create market opportunities means that the Italian cooperative movement has the capacity to expand. In countries where the cooperative movement is rudimentary it will be difficult to reach this regenerative level.

The political connection which has been an important factor in the growth of the Italian movement would be particularly difficult to emulate. There is no groundswell of a cooperative ideology which would attract co-option by an existing political party or the generation of a new one, as occurred with the environmentalist movement.

In the European context the most likely vehicle for a cooperative resurgence is the European Union itself. The reduction of economic frontiers places nationally-specific operations under threat but offers expansionist possibilities. The cooperative movement can benefit from its existing international framework and use its more successful operations as the springboard for enlargement. The extension of the European Union into Eastern Europe would offer particularly fertile territory. The Italian movement could be the hub of such development if it were recognised that it is an international leader. This book will help to provide that recognition.

John Robbins

Department of Politics
University of Adelaide

Notes

1 In 1992 the Communist Party has dissolved into two parties namely the Democratic Party of the Left and Communist Renewal Party.

Acknowledgments

This book has grown out of my Ph.D work which I commenced in 1989 and completed in 1994. There are many people who have supported me during that period. I am deeply grateful to my supervisor Dr John Robbins who provided me with the right intellectual and moral support when I most needed it. His careful reading of my work and insightful comments stimulated my interest in the topic and gave me renewed enthusiasm. I was most fortunate to have established an open and honest relationship with John at both the human and intellectual level. To me this was as satisfying as finishing the thesis.

During my stay in Bologna between February and June 1991 I received invaluable support from many people. I am particularly grateful for the friendly and frank discussions I had with Alessandro Skuk, Giancarlo Pasquini and Emanuel Danieli. I am also indebted to the following people for granting me an interview and for sharing their knowledge and insights into La Lega and Emilia Romagna with me: Ernesto Antonelli (Quasco a division of Ervet), Roberto Calari (La Lega-Bologna), Gualberto Cappi (Alveo), A Carpani (Corticella), Giancarlo Chiusa (Giglio), Forte Clo (Partito Democratico della Sinistra (PDS), Maurizio Cocchi (Spepcoop) Stefania Conti (Coop Italia), Franco Degli Angeli (Acam), Mr Drei (La Lega-Emilia Romagna), Carla Finessi (Regional Government of Emilia Romagna), Fabrizio Gerbella (La Lega-Emilia Romagna), Mr Giolitti (Altercoop), Mauro Giordani (Consorzio Cooperative Costruzioni), Antonella Grossi (Icie), Paolo Mattiussi (Planning Department, Region of Emilia Romagna), Marchi Moreno (Comitalia), Alieri Rodiero (Sacmi), Agostino Rota (CGIL-Emilia Romagna), Mauro Saccenti (Coop Emilia Veneto), Rino Scaglione (La Lega-Emilia Romagna), Emilio Severi (Giglio), Mario Tinelli (CMB), Claudio Tolomelli (Economics Department, Region of Emilia Romagna), Sandra Verardi (CNA), Stefano Zan (University of Bologna), Carlo Zingaretti (CMC).

I also wish to acknowledge the Department of Economic and Finance of La Lega Regionale of Emilia Romagna for organising the cooperative and consortia interviews for me. Many thanks also to Elena Romagnoli and Miss Gurioli, Directors of the Centro di Documentazione sulla Storia del Movimento Cooperativo, who provided assistance in finding the right material in their library and gave me a desk to study while in Bologna. I would like to thank Chris Cornforth, Roger Spear and Rob Paton for their hospitality and intellectual support they gave me during my visit to the Open University in the United Kingdom in February 1991.

I wish to acknowledge the University of Adelaide, and in particular the Politics Department, for providing me with a scholarship, a travel grant, and a good environment in which to conduct research. Many thanks to the Italian Government for providing me with a three month scholarship and Alitalia Airlines for making available a discounted air fare. Many thanks also to the Luzzatti Institute in Rome for the material they send me.

Many thanks also to Dino and Marina Terrusi and Alfredo and Donata Camerini for their warm friendship and kindness. A special mention must go to my uncle Michele, my auntie Liliana and my cousins Piero, Carlo and Massimo for their hospitality, their love and for making me smile on numerous occasions.

I am grateful to my sister Anna and close friends Gabby, Dino and Miriam for having read and corrected parts of the book and to Li Jun for formatting the book.

Finally, I would like to thank my family for their continuous love and affection. In particular, I would like to thank my love Li Jun whose continuous support and love has given me strength, self confidence, hope and the most fulfilling moments of my life.

1 Introduction

> In places like Imola, Italian cooperators have found something very good: a way of working together, and earning a good living, in an atmosphere of greater freedom and respect for each other's dignity and personal space than most people. This way of working is not only more fun; it makes them better, more generous, interesting and creative people. It is not Utopia, but it is a good life, here and now. Others could try it for themselves [1]

> The story of Mondragon is the most impressive refutation of the widely held belief that worker cooperatives have little capacity for economic growth and long term survival[2]

The above two quotations symbolise the realisation of the dream that co-operators have held ever since cooperatives were first formed in England at the time of the industrial revolution. However, in most cases the hopes bestowed upon cooperatives have remained dreams rather than realities. In spite of this, scholars interested in the subject have remained convinced that cooperatives can play an important role in our society today. Cooperatives have been identified as being capable of expanding democracy in the workplace,[3] improving industrial relations and productivity, creating more jobs than private enterprises with the same level of investments,[4] overcoming problems with de-industrialisation,[5] and by controlling capital they provide people with the greater opportunity to control their livelihoods and their dream of a good life.[6]

It is fair to say that thc achievements of cooperatives to date have not lived up to expectations. While they have been relatively successful in the consumer, agricultural and banking sectors they have not been as successful in manufacturing. Even where they have been successful, cooperatives have not replaced conventionally structured enterprises as the dominant form of enterprise. The well documented and continued success of the Mondragon group of cooperatives however, has offered continuous hope to all those supportive of cooperative enterprises. Their ability to continue to grow over a long period of time is proof that cooperatives can compete in the market.

This book explains and analyses another success story of the cooperative movement. This book is a study of the Italian cooperative enterprises associated to La Lega Nazionale delle Cooperative e Mutue (National League of Cooperatives and Mutual Aid Societies),[7] with particular attention devoted to studying the cooperatives established in the region of Emilia Romagna because it is in this region that La Lega is most developed.

Aims and Significance

The major objective is to examine how these cooperatives have managed to compete in the market, proving once more that a form of enterprise different to capitalist and State enterprises can survive and grow in a market economy which operates under a liberal democratic State.

There are several significant aspects of this thesis which are important to explore. First, La Lega is a large cooperative group of enterprises, much larger than that of Mondragon, comprising a variety of support structures in the areas of marketing, management, finance and research and development which have contributed to cooperatives' economic success. According to La Lega's own records, in 1989, 11,389 cooperatives were members of La Lega.[8] These cooperatives have a membership of 3.4 million and produce a turnover of 32,381 billion lire.[9] On these figures alone, in 1989 La Lega's share of the national GDP was 2.73%.[10] Furthermore, 632,869 people are either directly employed by these cooperatives (230,734) or are fully dependent on cooperatives for their livelihood (16,670 fishermen and 385,465 farmers). In 1989, this constituted 3% of the total labour force in Italy.[11]

In the region of Emilia Romagna La Lega's economic role is more visible. In 1989 La Lega associated 1969 cooperatives which employed 62,500 persons, had a membership of 950,000 and produced a turnover amounting to 13,018 Billion Lire.[12] In all, these cooperatives contribute 12.75% of the regional gross domestic product.[13] Further, 24% of the regional population either works or is a member of a cooperative associated with La Lega.[14]

The second issue is that some of these cooperatives are large, employing over 1,000 persons and have managed to survive for long periods of time, some over 80 years, many since 1945. Such cooperatives are not marginal enterprises, but have managed to become leaders in their field. Sectors in which cooperatives excel are construction, agriculture, retailing, housing, food catering, transportation, health, and many manufacturing areas such as ceramics, machineries, rubber products, furniture and hi-tech equipment.

A third aspect is that in Italy the State has generally been supportive of cooperatives. As will be discussed later, this is not the norm in the history of the cooperative movement in Europe and North America where evidence suggests that the State has mostly been indifferent or discouraging. Considering the power held by the State, in terms of power over legislation, taxes and other resources, this is an important area to explore, but one which has been mostly neglected by the field of cooperative studies.

Other scholars have already alluded to the important role played by the State and the support structures in the development of cooperatives in Italy. Oakeshott has identified the State as a major contributor of the success to the cooperative sector in Italy.[15] Thornley has also noted the contribution of the support structures in helping cooperatives compete in the market.[16] While these studies have been important, they do not provide a full explanation of the factors which have led to the success of La Lega, nor have there been in-depth studies on the subject. This study will fill this vacuum and will provide the first in-detailed analysis of La Lega. In particular some of the questions that need to be answered are the following:

- How does the network of enterprise function?
- How are cooperatives from different sectors kept together?
- How are economic linkages organised?
- How have cooperatives managed change over periods of economic growth and recession?
- Why has the State supported cooperatives?
- When is the State most likely to support or be hostile to cooperatives?

These questions will have to be answered in order to have a better understanding of La Lega's organisation and of the factors which have enabled cooperatives in Italy to compete successfully in the market.

Hypothesis and Approach

In order to analyse a complex issue like the establishment and functioning of a large cooperative group of enterprises, the study considers both the internal dynamics of a cooperative enterprise and the external environment in which it operates. This study will analyse La Lega's cooperatives by taking into consideration the political, economic, social and cultural environment in which Italian cooperatives operate. It will also be an interdisciplinary study, including the fields of history, politics, economics, organisational theory, business studies and cultural studies.

The hypothesis advanced here is that cooperatives in Italy have become successful and overcome the problems they normally face when competing in a market economy which operates under a liberal democratic State by managing to promote their interests in the economy and by being able to successfully represent their interests versus the State. In the economy their interests were promoted by organising different levels of support structures which improved their competitiveness. Their interests toward the State were successfully represented by acting as a group of enterprises through La Lega, and by benefiting from the support provided by political parties. This ensured wide ranging public support for cooperatives in the form of favourable legislation and access to a variety of public resources.

This study seeks to understand the success of cooperatives associated to La Lega by analysing the interrelationship that has developed between the cooperative enterprises, La Lega's support structures and the State. While each of these three entities will be treated separately, evidence will be provided to demonstrate that they are all interrelated. In fact, one cannot understand the success of La Lega's cooperatives by concentrating only on one of these three entities.

The Research

The research for this book commenced in March 1989. It included reading primary sources such as conference proceedings, cooperative annual budgets and internal cooperative journals, augmented by interviews from people working in cooperatives, consortia, research institutes, trade unions, political parties, local and regional governments. A major part of the research involved conducting case studies on cooperatives and consortia from different economic sectors. The interviews and the case studies were conducted between February and July 1991, during which time I stayed in Emilia Romagna, mainly in Bologna. In the same year I attended the Regional Congress of La Lega of Emilia Romagna and the Provincial Congress of the Federation of La Lega of Bologna. The research also consisted of material predominantly from Italian sources.[17]

Chapter Outline

The book is divided into ten chapters. The following chapter, chapter two is both a historical overview of the cooperative movement in Europe and North America, and a comparative study of the cooperative sector in the United Kingdom and Mondragon. It canvasses the reasons which have prompted people to set up cooperatives and identifies some of the factors which have led to their failure and to their success.

Chapter three attempts to understand further the reasons which hinder the development of cooperatives and the possible solutions to those problems. This is be done by analysing seven major problems which have been identified as hindering the formation and growth of cooperatives. These are: 1. low rate of formation - the entrepreneurial problem, 2. lack of finance, 3. lack of managerial and specialist competencies, 4. forms of discrimination, 5. internal limits to growth, 6. constraints on takeovers and 7. the place of cooperatives in the economy. An analysis of the limits of this discussion will be made. Also, examples of ways to overcome these problems will be given. The research on La Lega's cooperatives will then provide evidence of how cooperatives have managed to overcome each of these problems.

Chapter four begins to analyse La Lega. This chapter provides an historical account of cooperative development in Italy from the 1850s until 1992. It provides details regarding the character of cooperatives in Italy, their identity, their leaders, their ideology and their economic strength. It also gives information on the relationship between cooperatives, society and the State.

Chapters five to seven analyse La Lega as an organisation and the contribution that each component part has played in the economic success of cooperatives. Chapter five explains the structure and the functions of the Central Association of La Lega. This entails a study of the territorial structures and the sectoral associations. Chapter six analyses the consortia network and the level of support they provide to individual cooperatives. This is explored by analysing five case studies conducted on consortia from four different sectors including: retailing, manufacturing/construction, agriculture and research and technology. Chapter seven concentrates on the financial institutions of La Lega, with particular emphasis on the role played by the consortium Fincooper and the finance company Unipol Finance.

Chapter eight analyses how cooperatives manage change. Four cooperatives from the retail, construction, manufacturing and health sector are studied to discover out how their strategy, structure and culture changed over time. This provides evidence of the relationship that exists between the individual cooperative, La Lega and the State and how changes are made at the enterprise level.

Chapter nine deals with the relationship that has developed between the Italian State and cooperatives. The purpose of this chapter is twofold. First, the nation-specific aspects of the Italian State will be analysed to determine the way they have influenced cooperative development in Italy. Secondly, an historical analysis of the relationship between the State and cooperatives between 1945-1991 will be made to determine why and when the State is most likely to support cooperatives.

Chapter ten evaluates La Lega as an organisation. In doing so an appropriate definition of La Lega will be developed. The problems confronting La Lega are identified, followed by a discussion on the future of the organisation.

The concluding chapter will provide a summary of this study, its main findings, the contribution it has made to the field of cooperative studies and a discussion of its wider societal implications.

Notes

1 Mark Holmstrom, Industrial Democracy in Italy, Avebury, Aldershot, 1989, p.164.
2 William Foote Whyte and Kathleen Foote Whyte, *Making Mondragon: the Growth and Dynamics of the Worker Cooperative Complex,* ILR Press, New York, Second Edition, 1991, p.3.
3 Jack Quarter and George Melnyk, "Preface", in *Partners in Enterprise: The Worker Ownership Phenomenon*, Black Rose Books, Montreal, 1989.
4 Robert Jackall and Henry Levin, "Work in America and the Cooperative Movement", in Robert Jackall and Henry M Levin (eds), *Worker Cooperatives in America*, University of California Press, Berkeley, 1984, pp.6-7.
5 Keith Bradley and Alan Gelb, *Worker Capitalism: the New Industrial Relations*, Heinemann Educational Books, London, 1983.
6 T L Hill, "Publishers Note", in Len Krimerman and Frank Lindenfeld, *When Workers Decide: Workplace Democracy Takes Root in North America*, New Society Publishers, Philadelphia, 1992, pp.v-vi.
7 Hereafter it will be called La Lega.
8 La Lega's records did not include social insurance and welfare cooperatives which in 1986 amounted to 1,500 with a membership of 825,000. See Onelio Prandini, *La Cooperazione: Organizzazione, Storia e Futuri Sviluppi del Movimento Cooperativo*, Editori Riuniti, Roma, 1986, p.85.
9 Lega Nazionale delle Cooperative e Mutue, *Principali Indicatori del Movimento Cooperativo Lega*, Roma, 1991, p. 2. For information on the exchange rate of La Lira into Australian and American dollars see Table C.1, p.323.
10 This figure was arrived at by dividing the figures provided by La Lega (32,381 billion lire) divided by the national figures for 1989 provided by the OECD report on Italy (1,188,000 billion lire). For La Lega's figures see *ibid.* For the national figures see OECD Economic Surveys, *Italy*, Paris, 1991, p.7.
11 The percentage of national employment was arrived at by dividing 632,869 by the total Italian labour force which in 1989 amounted to 21,004,000. For both figures see *ibid.*
12 Francesco Boccetti, "Introduzione", in Emanuel Danieli (ed), *Le Imprese Cooperative: Trend 1982-1989*, Osservatorio Economico Finanziario della Lega Regionale dell' Emilia Romagna, Editrice Emilia Romagna, Bologna, 1991, p.6.

13 This figure was arrived at by dividing La Lega's turnover for the year 1988 which amounted to 11,338 billion lire by the regional gross domestic product which amounted to 88,939 billion lire. I suspect La Lega's quota has increased since in 1989 its turnover increased by 14.8% to 13,018 billion lire. For figures relating to the Regional Gross Product see: Confederazione Nazionale dell'Artigianato, *La Risorsa-Futuro per L'Artigianato e la Piccola Impresa*, Bologna, 1991, Table 6.6.
14 The population of Emilia Romagna was 3,921,000 in 1988. La Lega's membership of 950,000 makes up 24.23% of the total population. See Istituto Nazionale di Statistica, *Introducing Italy*, Rome, 1989, p.36.
15 Robert Oakeshott, *The Case for Workers' Co-ops*, Routledge & Kegan Paul, London, 1978, pp.145-164.
16 Jenny Thornley, *Workers' Co-operatives: Jobs and Dreams*, Heinemann Educational Books, London, 1981, pp.151-167.
17 I speak fluent Italian and all the translations that appear in the text are mine.

2 The Failed Alternative?

The purpose of this chapter is to provide a historical overview of the cooperative movement in Britain and Mondragon and to explore the central question faced by all who study cooperatives: are cooperatives a viable alternative to capitalist firms? Following on from this, if they are, then why are there so few cooperatives operating in Western capitalist countries given that cooperatives have been set up in various countries since the 1850s? Alternatively are they a failed alternative as the chapter title provocatively suggests? This becomes even more important considering that cooperatives were initially established to combat unemployment, lower food prices, provide cheap housing, create more humane and democratically managed work places where human beings contributed with their physical as well as intellectual labour. These are still objectives that cooperatives are designed to fulfil and that capitalist mixed market economies centred on privately owned enterprises have not satisfied.

This chapter will provide a historical overview of cooperatives. The discussion is mainly based on the experiences of the British cooperatives and those of the Spanish town of Mondragon. In addition, the experiences of cooperatives in other countries will be considered wherever necessary but not to the extent of the British and the Mondragon cooperatives.

There are a number of reasons for concentrating on Britain and Mondragon. The British experience has been chosen because it is the country where cooperatives were first developed, there is ample research material available which allows a thorough understanding of its history, and it is a movement which has developed very successful consumer cooperatives but which has failed to develop successful producer cooperatives. The Mondragon experience has been chosen because there is a wide range of literature available on it, and because it has been remarkably successful in the banking, manufacturing and consumer sectors. The study of these two cooperative experiences should provide some answers as to why cooperatives succeed or fail providing valuable background information for the issues explored by this book.

The first part will define what is meant by a cooperative and describe the various types of cooperatives that exist. A brief comparison is then made with private enterprises. The second part will be a historical analysis of the

British and the Mondragon cooperative experience. The third part will outline some of the experiences in other parts of the world, with particular reference to the Plywood cooperatives of the United States and to the Employee Stock Ownership Plans (ESOP) which are becoming very popular in the United States.

What is a Cooperative?

Defining a worker cooperative is difficult because the word has been used to refer to various types of enterprises which involve some form of employee or workers' ownership. While the question of ownership is important, it is not the only criterion used to define a cooperative enterprise. The most comprehensive definition of what a cooperative should be is that provided by the International Cooperative Alliance, (ICA), an international body which unites cooperatives from all over the world. In 1966, it formulated six principles, which were to provide the basic guidelines under which member cooperatives were to operate. The six ICA principles are: voluntary and open membership, democratic control, limited interest on capital, equitable distribution of capital, education and intercooperative cooperation. What follows is an explanation of each of these principles as a starting point for defining a cooperative.

The Six Principles of the International Cooperative Alliance [1]

The first principle is open and voluntary membership. Voluntary and open membership of cooperatives involves the idea that cooperatives should be open to all persons and any form of discrimination should be avoided provided members are willing to respect and support the rules of the cooperative. It is also a way of discouraging cooperatives to be controlled by a few members. The ideal is for all workers to be members, however, different countries have different rules in relation to this principle. In Italy, each cooperative must have 50% membership, while in Mondragon at least 80%.[2] Usually to protect the nature of the enterprise, a probationary period has to elapse before a worker is allowed to become a member. Non-members also provide a degree of flexibility when cooperatives have to adjust to downturns in the economy. This can be acceptable provided all workers receive the same wage and that non-members are given the opportunity to become members once full time employment can be guaranteed. What is not acceptable is the hiring of workers at lower wages and the violation of the principle of open membership.

Democratic control is the second major characteristic of cooperatives. Democracy within the cooperative is to be based on the principle of "one person, one vote". In addition, members should be given the opportunities to elect representatives, exercise control over them, and be informed about decisions taken by the board of directors. Since voting power is based on the principle of "one person, one vote" and not according to how much capital is owned, cooperatives are usually described as being a society of people and not of capital. This objective is clear enough, but the practical and technical means to achieve it is left to the cooperatives themselves.

The third principle is limited return on capital. Limiting the interest rate payable on members' shares has the task of safeguarding the social aspect of cooperatives and act as a deterrent to speculative activity. The ICA clearly affirms that remuneration on members' shares should be limited, but does not state by how much. Compliance with this provision has differed from country to country: in Mondragon, the remuneration of members' shares cannot exceed 6% per annum;[3] in France, 20%;[4] in Italy, it was 5% until 1983, then it was increased to 2.5% above the rate of interest paid on government postal bonds.[5] Considering the high inflation rate of the 1970s, the real value of the members' shares owned by Italian and Spanish cooperators was reduced during that period. Generally, a slightly higher rate of return than the inflation rate is complying with the above principle because it still places a limit on capital but it maintains the real value of invested capital.

The fourth principle is equitable distribution of surplus. This principle aims to ensure that members do not exploit other members and that the surplus is distributed according to the amount of work performed and not the amount of capital invested. Once again these are general guidelines and variations of how this principle is implemented have appeared between cooperatives from different countries. The Mondragon cooperatives divide the surplus between community activities (10%), collective reserve (not less than 20%) and individual accounts (not more than 70%). The last two figures are flexible. In a time of economic downturn more money is placed in the collective reserve.[6] In 1982, the French cooperatives associated with General Association of Producer Cooperatives (GSSCOP) distributed their surpluses by allocating 40% to members as bonus payments, 20% as remuneration of members' shares and 40% to indivisible reserves.[7] In both cases, the cooperative assets are collectively owned. Members cannot sell the assets, if they leave they are entitled to receive the nominal sum of members' shares held in their individual account. This ensures the continuity of the enterprise and the provision of employment for future generations. In addition, in the event of a dissolution, the net assets (gross assets minus members' shares and other debts repayments) will remain within the community either to be used to support other cooperatives or to support charitable and other organisations.

The fifth principle is that of education. This principle places responsibility on the cooperative to educate the public regarding the principles of cooperation. It also makes the cooperative responsible for educating and training members so that they are aware of the technical and administrative aspects of a cooperative enterprise. In addition, the cooperative should also attempt to elevate the general cultural awareness of its members through appropriate means. Some ways to achieve this is through publishing a newspaper, organising public lectures and giving workers time off for studying.

Intercooperative cooperation is the sixth principle. The ICA encourages cooperation between cooperatives at a local, national and international level. This is seen as the most appropriate way to best serve the interests both of its members and of the community. As we shall see, Spain and Italy are good examples where intercooperative trading and support takes place with good results.

The six ICA principles have provided a general description of what constitutes a cooperative. Later in this chapter, the experience of cooperatives in Great Britain and Mondragon in Spain will provide empirical evidence on the behaviour of cooperatives in those countries. This will enable an investigation of and how the general principles of cooperation are put into practice by these cooperative movements.

From this discussion the following characteristics of a cooperative enterprise have emerged:

- Cooperatives are enterprises which produce goods and services on behalf of their members and the community. The primary objective is to satisfy members' needs such as employment, cheaper goods, housing, health services, etc.
- They are democratically-managed enterprises on the basis of the principle of one person, one vote.
- The role of capital over surplus entitlements and voting power is limited. This takes place in a number of forms: remuneration on members' shares is limited, ownership of capital does not give a member more voting power over another, the assets of cooperatives in France and Mondragon are collectively owned, and distribution of surplus is based on hours worked not the amount of capital owned.

All of these features have made cooperatives enterprises where labour hires capital and not vice versa.

- Cooperatives are socially responsible enterprises. The various rules such as the constraints on the distribution of surplus, the obligation to educate the public regarding cooperative principles, solidarity towards other cooperatives, collectively owned assets ensure that investments are re-invested in the local community are all part of this cooperative enterprise culture.[8]

Forms of Cooperatives

Before the historical development of cooperatives is analysed, the different forms of cooperatives need to be discussed. Basically cooperatives can be divided into three groups: producers, consumers and support cooperatives. Producer cooperatives are formed by working people who seek to assert their control over their labour power and the benefits derived from it. Usually the main objectives of these cooperatives are to create stable employment and to improve the working conditions of their members. Industrial relations in these enterprises are quite unique since the workers are also owners and participate in the decision-making process which is based on the principle of "one person, one vote".[9]

The second form is the consumer cooperatives. The most famous of these are retail cooperatives. The main purpose of consumer cooperatives is aimed at increasing their members' purchasing power. By pooling together the purchasing power of their members consumer cooperatives achieve economies of scale. This enables them to pass on the savings to their members in the form of lower prices or by paying a dividend on the amount of goods purchased by the member throughout the year. Members of consumer cooperatives usually come from all social backgrounds. Unlike producers cooperatives the industrial relations in a consumer cooperative are traditional, in that the employees are usually not members of the cooperative.[10]

The third form of cooperative is the support cooperatives which are usually associated with the agricultural sector. The main objective of these cooperatives is to increase the marketing power of individual members. Usually members pool their produce together to achieve economies of scale in the marketing process. However, agricultural cooperatives can also perform other services aimed at reducing costs such as bulk buying of farming inputs such as manure, fertilisers, fodder and anti-parasites. They can also provide technical expertise to their members. Membership of these cooperatives can be formed by other cooperatives, individual farmers or farmers who employ other persons. Industrial relations are similar to consumer cooperatives because the people who work in these cooperatives are employees and do not have voting rights.[11]

Comparison with Private Enterprises

From the discussion so far the following three major differences can be identified between the cooperative enterprise and private enterprises: type of ownership, democratic management and rights of capital. As it has been already explained, a cooperative enterprise is collectively owned by the people who work in them or by those who use its services such as consumers who own consumer cooperatives. Private enterprises are instead owned by an individual, a group of persons, or shareholders. Ownership is important because with it comes power and control over the decision-making process.

The second major difference is that cooperatives are democratically-managed enterprises such that each member has only one vote irrespective of the amount of shares owned. In private enterprises, the decisions are made either by the owner-manager or by a management team whose authority is derived from the owners or shareholders. In private enterprises usually workers are not actively involved in the decision-making process. Although some forms of participation on the job exist such as the Japanese "quality circles" and Germany's "Co-determination Policy" which allows trade unions representation on company supervisory boards, workers themselves do not have a say over the decision-making process.[12] In both Japan and Germany control remains in the hands of those who own capital. In cooperatives, while the question of democracy is also problematic, members elect their own representatives to the board of directors and have control over the overall decision-making process through the general assembly which ultimately makes decisions relating to investments, overall planning and industrial relations.

The third major difference relates to the rights of capital. This is closely linked to the ends of the enterprise. In private enterprises, the end is to maximise profits which are then distributed to the owners and shareholders in proportion to the capital invested, and who can then dispose of them as they wish. In cooperatives, capital has limited power. Firstly, there is a limit placed on the remuneration of members' shares. Secondly, in the cases of France and Mondragon, a percentage has to be placed in the collective reserve which no individual can access. Thirdly, assets cannot be sold by individuals. These constraints on capital are closely linked to the objective of the cooperative enterprise which is not to maximise profits but to provide employment or a service to their members. Profits are a means to achieve this end and not the end in itself, as it is in private enterprises.

Britain and Mondragon: A Comparative Analysis

Having established what a cooperative is, described the different types of cooperative enterprises and how they differ from private enterprises, Part Two of this Chapter will endeavour to analyse and evaluate the history of cooperatives in the United Kingdom and Mondragon. It is hoped that this examination will identify some of the causes explaining the successes and failures of cooperative enterprises when competing in capitalist economies.

The British Experience

The birth of cooperatives in Britain was a response to the turmoil caused by the Industrial Revolution. The nascent factory system alienated human beings. The workers were dependent on the master, the owners of the factories. With little or no protection from the State and a weak trade union movement entailed that workers had to work long hours for little pay.[13] The lack of welfare provisions made matters worse. In response to this, both workers and wealthy philanthropists created producer and consumer cooperatives to alleviate the problems caused by the capitalist system. This section has been divided in three distinct periods. The first period was mainly dominated by Robert Owen and his followers and spanned from 1820s until the early 1840s. The second period commences with the Rochdale Pioneers in 1844 and lasts until the beginning of the First World War. The last period commences in the 1970s and is continuing to this very day.

Early Years. The first cooperative was formed in 1760 by dockside workers who ran a corn mill at Woolwich. A flour mill was run as a cooperative at Hull in 1795. Both of these cooperatives were set up as a response to high food prices. In 1769, the first cooperative store was set up by the Weavers Society at Fenwick in Ayrshire. However, these were isolated incidents. The ideals of cooperation became better known through the work of Robert Owen in the 1820s and 1830s.[14]

Owen was an industrialist concerned about the appalling conditions of workers in the factory system and the effect it was having on human beings. He blamed the rising capitalist system for the level of poverty, crime and immorality present in society. In response to this, he wanted to create a new moral order in which human beings would achieve happiness. The solution to this problem was to be found in the creation of self-sufficient communities.

These communities were to provide better working conditions, welfare measures, education for all. This would eventually create an environment in which morally superior persons would be able to develop.[15] A number of communities were established in England and even in America on Owen's principles, but they all failed. Bad management, unsuitable colonists, insufficient capital and poor sites have been identified as some of the reasons for their failure.[16]

Such cooperative communities were difficult to establish. Owen tried, but failed to get the support of philanthropists and governments. In 1827, William Byron, a Christian, moved by the level of poverty, disease and crime caused by the economic and social system, proposed to form retail stores whose profits were then to be used to set up communities. Trade unions were another source which formed cooperative societies. Legalised in 1824, unions supported cooperative societies formed by the unemployed and by workers during lockouts. Some of these cooperative societies were known as labour exchanges, which priced goods on the amount of labour time taken to produce them. Once again, these attempts met with little success.[17]

After the passage of the Reform Act, 1832, which denied the working class the right to vote, Owen attempted to form an alliance between the cooperative and the trade union movement. He had a vision of trade unions forming national production companies comprised of individuals from a particular trade.[18] Later these were to unite with master traders, manufacturers and even the government. This plan met with resistance from those inside the trade union movement who favoured class conflicts, and also from business and government. The Grand National Consolidated Trade Union formed in 1834, collapsed in 1837. This also brought down and weakened many cooperative societies.[19]

There was also an attempt to form a national cooperative movement. At the first congress held in Manchester in 1831, two major differences soon emerged between Owen and the Christian Socialists. The first concerned religion. Owen denied that he was an atheist, but he had a distrust of religion and was critical of the family. In contrast, the Christian Socialists believed that the principle of cooperation was in accordance with the Gospel. The second problem was political. Owen sought the support of the State regardless of its form of government. The Christians had no confidence in the State. One of their leaders, Dr King, believed that the State would do more harm than good.[20]

This first phase of the cooperative movement produced mixed results. It was important because it provided a critique of the emerging capitalist system and sought to overcome the problems caused by it by promoting communities and cooperative societies. Whilst the actual experiments failed, the ideals which promoted them, such as egalitarianism, fraternity, education and human kindness have remained. The lack of economic success, however, turned many persons away from cooperatives. Throughout the 1840s, the majority of the population concentrated on political demonstrations and political goals rather than the cooperative movement.[21]

The events of this first phase are important for understanding the later problems confronted by the movement. The failure to unite with the trade union movements in a national movement weakened the potential of the cooperative sector. The lack of an understanding of what role the State could play in the development of cooperatives limited the movement's options for development. Finally, the failure of the cooperative communities and societies tarnished the image of cooperatives and raised questions as to their ability to provide an alternative form of employment to private enterprises.

Rochdale: the Birth of the Modern Cooperatives. In spite of the early setbacks, cooperators persisted with their ideas. In 1844 the Rochdale Cooperative Retail Store was formed. The immediate purpose of the store was to provide food at low prices. However, the Rochdale Pioneers also believed in the emancipation of labour and wanted to develop a community of cooperatives. The Rochdale Cooperative Store laid down the principles and foundations which were later adopted by the International Cooperative Alliance. The major principles were as follows: goods were to be sold at market prices; the stores were to be managed democratically based on the principle of one person one vote; profits were mostly reinvested in the store; some profits were used to remunerate members' shares (3.5%); a dividend was paid to each member as a proportion of the amount purchased in the store; and a percentage was also spent on education.[22]

The Rochdale retail store was very successful. The rising living standard experienced during the economic boom of the 1850s and 1860s increased members' purchasing power. Most importantly, the dividend played a large part in attracting new members and in fostering members' loyalty to the store. However, the dividend also attracted persons with different ideals and in time the cooperative became more economically oriented, abandoning the original goal of creating a community of cooperatives.[23]

The experience of the Rochdale Cooperative Manufacturing Societies reflected the influence that new members were having on the cooperative. These societies were mainly owned by the consumer cooperatives but included employees and outside shareholders. Initially, employees were paid a dividend and participated in decision making. Later, as the external members increased in number, the employees' dividends were abolished. In 1862, the cooperative was transformed into a capitalist enterprise controlled by external members. This experience is one of degeneration. Other cooperative societies had similar experiences equating cooperation with profit sharing alone.[24]

During the same period the Christian Socialists formed cooperative workshops independently of the consumer sector. These were influenced by the ideas of French Socialists who advocated the formation of workers' workshops following the 1848 revolution. In England a number of workshops were formed but soon failed. They suffered from a number of internal and external problems. Since the workshops were mainly managed by managers not appointed by the work-force conflicts arose between them. Other problems were caused by lack of discipline and lack of cooperative training. These workshops also suffered both from discrimination by suppliers who refused trade credit and from the economic recession which made it difficult for new enterprises to succeed.[25] What the Christian Socialists did do was to persuade the government to pass the Industrial and Provident Societies Act (1852), which gave cooperatives a proper legal status and granted them Propriety Limited status.[26]

In the 1860s and 1870s, many of the successful consumer societies continued to support producer cooperatives. Thornley notes that between 1860 and 1880 some 200 cooperatives were formed. By 1882, only 20 remained.[27] This constant failure of producer cooperatives led the consumer cooperative societies to promote their own enterprises. In 1882, Neale established the Cooperative Producers Federation with the aim of promoting producer cooperatives. For a while they succeeded but few have remained after 1914. Once again the cooperators failed to create a united movement.[28]

Contrary to the experience of producer cooperatives, consumer cooperatives were very successful. By 1914 the consumer cooperatives numbered over 3 million members, held £44 million of shares and loan capital, and boasted sales of £87 million. Part of the success of consumer cooperatives could be attributed to working people's spending power and the high level of membership which enabled consumer cooperatives to raise capital. However, they also became successful by selling goods at market prices, by paying a dividend to members, by the higher living standards which increased the purchasing power of individuals and by legislative measures which did not tax profits made by consumer cooperatives.[29] In addition, a successful policy of mergers was implemented between 1919 and 1940 which, while it reduced the number of cooperatives from 1,357 to 1,065, managed to increase membership from 4 to 8.7 million.[30]

The other success story also linked to the consumer movement was the Cooperative Wholesale Society Bank (CWS). The CWS Bank commenced operating in 1872, by 1939 it held 75,084 accounts and had a turnover of £832 million. It also managed to attract as members many of the municipalities, trade unions and churches.[31]

The status of the consumer movement was further enhanced by the support given by Beatrice and Sydney Webb. The Webbs generally supported consumer cooperation and disapproved of producer cooperation. They believed that consumer cooperatives were superior because they had universal values, were democratically controlled and because they provided immediate benefits to the whole of the community by distributing part of their profits and by selling goods at low prices. They also supported them because they were successful.[32] Producer cooperatives were criticised by the Webbs because members exploited non-members, they only benefited those who worked in them and because they cut wages and the overall standard of living in order to compete in the market. In addition, they were unsuccessful. In support of their criticism, the Webbs identified a number of problems associated with producer cooperatives. They found that the causes for their economic failure were inefficient management, an undisciplined work-force and a reluctance towards industrial change.[33]

The Webbs' arguments were very forceful and widely accepted.[34] By the turn of the century producer cooperatives were no longer seen as an alternative form of enterprise. The Labour Party too was greatly influenced by the Webbs. Formed in 1900, the Labour Party supported the common ownership of the means of production. However, this did not imply cooperative ownership but mainly social ownership through municipal enterprises and nationalised public enterprises as a way to advance to Socialism.[35] The idea to use the State to ameliorate the conditions of working people was reinforced during the First World War when the State in Britain virtually regulated every sector of the economy. In addition, laws were passed which limited rent increases and the price of coal and which also granted workers a minimum wage.[36] The Russian Revolution of 1917 provided another impetus to the idea of using the State to solve the problems of working people. Even the Webbs began to support this yet untried form of State Socialism as it was being constructed in the Soviet Union.

This second phase (1844-1910s) of the cooperative movement in Britain confirmed the success of the consumer cooperatives over those of producers.

These two sectors remained separate and during this period the movement never united. Considering the power of the consumer sector and the financial strength of the CWS bank, a united movement could have succeeded in promoting a more diversified sector by providing retailing space and finance to producer cooperatives.

However, this did not occur. As noted, the consumer cooperatives did promote secondary cooperatives, but their legal structure was that of a public company with shareholders rather than workers being in control. Indeed, the lack of a legislation which protected the cooperative from degenerating into a capitalist firm was a major downfall of the producer cooperatives. Finally, the cooperative movement also failed to get the support of the trade union and the labour movement. This further weakened its potential, especially when dealing with the State, which apart from tax concessions to consumer cooperatives and the Industrial and Provident Societies Act (1852), provided little support.

As already stated, Britain is the place where the modern principles of cooperatives were first formulated and sought to be implemented. However, as the process of industrialisation swept throughout Europe, working people in those countries also began to experiment with the idea of cooperation. The examples of France and Germany stand out because they gave birth to producers and banking cooperatives respectively.

Cooperatives in France and Germany. France has been regarded as the birthplace of producer cooperatives. In 1832-1834, Buchez founded an association of cabinet makers and goldsmiths managed along cooperative lines. Some of the governing rules of the cooperative included the following: democratic election of one or two workers to hold the signature of the company; payments were based on skill and the traditional rates of pay of that particular craft; profits were to be divided equally among members; members had no right to the capital of the cooperative even if it was dissolved; all workers became members after one year. These rules encouraged equality among members, an open door policy and it protected the cooperative form of enterprise by not allowing members to sell the cooperative's assets.[37]

In Germany two types of banks were formed. In the urban areas, the peoples' banks were established to provide capital to craftsmen and urban property owners. In the rural areas, rural banks were created to help the small farmers have access to cheap capital. Both banks were created as a response to industrialisation and to the difficulty small farmers and craftsmen were having in getting loans from conventional banks. The small farmers in particular, were greatly disadvantaged because the banks would normally lend money to large landowners leaving the small farmers at the hands of profiteers who charged as much as 100% interest on loans. Both banks operated along cooperative lines: they were democratically managed on the principle of "one person, one vote", the return on shares was limited and loans were provided on the basis of character instead of collateral. These forms of banks became very popular. By the 1910s there were as many as 1,000 peoples' banks and 16,000 rural banks operating in Germany.[38]

The Revival of the 1970s. It seemed that since the turn of the century consumer cooperatives were the only form of cooperation in Britain. Especially since 1945, the continuous economic growth, the nationalisation of key industries and the development of the Welfare State seemed to resolve all of working people's problems. However, since the 1970s a number of economic, political and cultural factors have led to a resurgence of producer cooperatives. First, the end of the long economic boom swept through the whole of the industrialised world creating a high level of unemployment. In the United Kingdom unemployment reached 10.5%, with youth being the hardest hit reaching an unemployment rate of 19.8% by 1982.[39] Cooperatives once again were formed as a response to unemployment. Second, demand for different forms of enterprises came from persons who had been part of the sixties youth culture and who generally wanted to work in a non-hierarchical work environment.[40] Third, support also came from the Labour party who began to reconsider its nationalisation programme and started to look favourably to cooperatives. Support for cooperatives was especially provided through the Labour controlled local councils, especially the Greater London Council and the West Midlands County Council. Fourth, the 1970s were also a period when industrial democracy was again on the agenda. Basically, the proposals sought business and unions to work together in a similar fashion as the German Co-Determination model.[41]

During this period cooperatives were also sought to solve wider societal problems. Robert Oakeshott supported cooperatives along the Mondragon model because this model could encourage a better working relationship between workers and management.[42] Jay supported the development of a "cooperative economy". He supported cooperatives because they could implement a flexible wages system which could overcome problems of inflation and unemployment.[43] Both Jay and Oakeshott viewed the power of trade unions and inflexible wages as part of the problem confronting British business in the 1970s; to them cooperatives were also a way to overcome trade union power. Further support for worker cooperatives and other forms of employee ownership came from Bradley and Gelb. In response to the economic crisis of the late 1970s and the numerous plant closures, they proposed the conversion of private enterprises into cooperatives as a way to combat the political, social and economic problems caused by de-industrialisation. In particular, they advocated that cooperatives could maintain production and employment, stop regional decay and as a consequence strengthen the democratic system of government.[44]

This period was accompanied by the birth of various independent support organisations which provided a number of services to cooperatives in their early formative phase. The largest organisation is the Industrial Common Ownership Movement (ICOM), founded by Ernest Bader, a Quaker. ICOM aims to create a better society. It supports the ICA principles of cooperation and common ownership. ICOM rules which limit the maximum amount of members shares to one pound make it particularly easy for members to join, however this clause increases the reliance on external credit. The second largest is Job Ownership Limited (JOL). This is led by Robert Oakeshott and supports the Mondragon model where members have a substantial capital stake in the enterprise. Contrary to ICOM's policy, JOL's cooperatives do not support trade union membership. Other organisations are Commonwork set up in 1976, the Mutual Aid Centre established in 1979 and SERA (Socialist Environment and Resources Association).[45]

The most successful of these support associations was ICOM. ICOM supported the Industrial Common Ownership Act, which gave legal recognition to common ownership enterprises. It also set up Industrial Common Ownership Finance (ICOF), which was funded by the State and individuals, for the purpose of providing cheap loans to cooperative enterprises. ICOF was also instrumental in providing a set of rules for cooperatives.[46]

However, a greater impetus to cooperative formation was provided by the State. The government's support for cooperatives became prominent in the mid-1970s when the then Labour minister Tony Benn, financed the conversion of three ailing private enterprises into cooperatives. The three enterprises were the Scottish Daily News, Kirkby Manufacturing and Engineering and the Meridian Motor Cycles. They all collapsed, lasting between six months and ten years. These cooperatives suffered from inadequate planning, lack of finance, and lack of training in the principles of cooperation.[47] Although these cooperative experiments should be praised for their attempt to maintain employment, their failure created a negative public image for the cooperative movement in Britain.

In 1978 the Labour government established a National Cooperative Development Agency (CDA). This body was given the task of promoting industrial and service cooperatives. The CDA has since promoted cooperative legislation, has helped to coordinate statistics and has supported the funding of Local Cooperative Development Agencies. In spite of these achievements, the CDA was managed by persons appointed by the government who had no previous cooperative experience. Furthermore, its lack of accountability to the cooperative sector and the fact that it promoted cooperatives with access to external shareholders were matters of concern for the cooperative movement.[48]

In addition to the National CDA, many local CDAs were also established and successfully promoted new cooperatives. The first local CDA was formed in 1976. Ten years later 80 were spread throughout Britain. Most of these were funded by the local councils but were independently managed. Only 19 were under council control. They employed an average of 3 persons and were engaged in promoting cooperatives, in providing marketing and group skills and also some training. The largest local CDAs were those of London and the West Midlands. The Greater London Council spent some £5 million between 1983 and 1986 for the promotion of cooperatives.[49] In all, between 1976 and 1986, the public sector provided a total of £28.7 million. From this amount £17.9 million was spent on independent and State support structures and £10.8 million was allocated to various State and independent cooperative funding bodies. The success of local CDAs is unquestioned. Between 1976 and 1988, the number of cooperatives established in Britain increased from 48 to 1025.[50]

In spite of their success, a number of factors limited the effectiveness of the local CDAs. It was found that they were usually understaffed, were staffed mainly by generalists from a community work background and that they spent most of the time establishing new cooperatives. There was also a lack of coordination among the local CDAs.[51] In addition, many experienced pressure from local authorities to increase employment.[52] This aside, the experience of local CDAs has been an important one.

This recent phase in the development of the British cooperative movement has been more successful than the past. The major change has been the greater support it has enjoyed from the central and local authorities, in particular from Labour-controlled local governments. However, many problems remain. The uncoordinated approach between the central and local government, and between government and the cooperative movement, are major flaws. The cooperative movement is also divided and the different associations have failed to develop a common strategy. The differences between ICOM and JOL are a testimony to this, as is the continuing division between the consumer and other sectors.

Another major problem is the size of cooperative enterprises and the cooperative movement. Cooperatives employ on average four persons, offering limited potential for economic policy makers. They are also dispersed throughout the country in many sectors thereby making it difficult to develop interfirm cooperation and create synergies within a particular sector. The lack of economies of scale, their vulnerability as small firms and the failure of the three Benn cooperatives make it difficult for the cooperative movement to overcome the image of failure and smallness. This makes it difficult to promote cooperatives and establish a viable sector.

The British movement faces the 1990s with little optimism. The small scale of the producers cooperatives and the lack of strong well staffed support organisations will make it difficult for them to survive in a highly competitive market. What is left is still a large, but declining consumer sector. This sector still held 10.9% of the British food market in 1990, a 6% lower share than it held in 1980.[53]

Summary of the British Experience. The British experience has been very influential in the Western world. The ideas developed by Robert Owen and others influenced cooperative movements all over the world. The Rochdale Pioneers can rightly claim to have laid down the principles of the modern cooperative enterprise. However, it has also left a legacy, particularly influential in countries with strong British influence, of not been able to create a successful producers' movement. What the analysis has shown is that there are various internal and external factors which have caused this. First, the cooperative movement has not had continuous development. It has had to rebuild on three occasions. Secondly, the early legislation did not prevent cooperatives from degenerating, while the ICOM rules are a barrier to self financing. Thirdly, cooperatives have faced discrimination from private firms and banks. Fourthly, it has had little support from the State. This can partly be attributed to the various governments' indifference to cooperatives and partly to the cooperative movement's inability to evaluate fully the important role the State could have performed for cooperative development. Fifthly, when the movement did look to the State for help, its divisiveness and small economic weight in the economy limited its lobbying capacity. Sixthly, the Webbs' research has shown that cooperatives have internal problems such as lacking managerial expertise, unwillingness to introduce technology and undiscipline all reducing their ability to compete in the market. Seventhly, the various support structures are numerous, decentralised, poorly funded and uncoordinated thus reducing their effectiveness. Finally, the actual cooperative enterprises are small in size and, with no evidence of interfirm collaboration, they compete in the market in isolation, and, as a consequence are very vulnerable to market fluctuations and competition from larger enterprises.

The Case of Mondragon

The second historical analysis of a cooperative movement is that which originated in the small town of Mondragon, situated in the Basque region of Spain. The first cooperative was established in 1956 and by 1992 the Mondragon group comprised of 172 cooperatives employing 25,322 persons. It has now become the largest group of companies in the Basque region and the fifteenth largest in Spain.[54] The majority of cooperatives are industrial cooperatives, followed by agricultural, fishing, catering, retail and educational. The success of these cooperatives is unquestioned. They have continually outperformed their private enterprise counterparts. They boast an absenteeism rate which is 50% lower than private enterprises.[55] Their employment record is equally impressive: between 1974 and 1984 the number of persons employed increased from 11,417 to 18,795 at a time when the rest of Spain lost 252,000 jobs and the Basque region lost about 23,800.[56] In 1985, only 20 persons were unemployed in Mondragon compared to the 20% unemployment rate in the rest of the Basque region.[57]

There are many reasons behind the success of Mondragon. These can be divided into external factors, the leadership qualities of Father Jose Maria Arizmendi, cooperative legislation, support structures, the role of the State and the ability of cooperative enterprises to manage and adapt to change.

External Factors. A major reason which explains the success of the Mondragon cooperatives is that they have developed within a supportive environment. It was not uncommon in the Basque region to find fishing, farming and forests managed in common by the people.[58] The Basque community also placed a lot of emphasis on trust and solidarity.[59] In addition, as early as 1930, the Basque trade union movement supported all types of cooperatives.[60]

Another external factor is Basque nationalism. The Basques have their own language and culture. They suffered greatly during Franco's dictatorial regime because they supported the Republicans during the Spanish Civil War. The tension that developed between the Basques and Madrid has been a source of strength and unity for the movement.[61] However, the effect of nationalism on the success of the Mondragon cooperatives should not be overemphasised. As it will be pointed out later in this chapter, other factors were just as important.

Nevertheless, the Basque culture's support of associations and nationalism is a source of community support. Mondragon's technical school was established because of the financial support given by 25% of the town's families. The first cooperative, Ulgor, received financial support from 100 persons from Mondragon. When the cooperative bank, Caja Laboral Popular (CLP), was formed in 1959, the people from Mondragon once again showed their support by investing their savings in it.[62]

The economy is another important factor. The first cooperatives were industrial in nature producing consumer goods such as washing machines, heaters and industrial components. These industrial goods experienced external and domestic demand. External demand came from European countries which had experienced economic growth throughout the 1950s and 1960s. Domestic demand was encouraged by the government's protective tariff policy and the rising standard of living. In addition, the area where these cooperatives were formed had a good supply of skilled labour.[63]

Father Jose Maria Arizmendi. The inspiring force behind the Mondragon experience has been the leadership provided by Father Jose Maria Arizmendi. Until his death in 1977, his objective had always been that of creating employment opportunities for the people of Mondragon. He provided a vision of what could be achieved and persuaded first, the people of Mondragon to support a technical school, and, later, the cooperators of Mondragon to establish the CLP bank and other cooperative support structures. He also formulated the ideals for the movement. Arizmendi was anti-capitalist, anti-collectivist and disliked Tayloristic methods of production.[64] He saw cooperatives as being capable of creating a new conscience and a new culture which encouraged solidarity and egalitarianism without suppressing the needs of the individual. He was a pragmatist. He always supported economic growth, but not at the expense of democratic management. From the beginning he always sought to establish a relationship of trust with the local community. This culture of equilibrium between pragmatism and idealism, economic growth and democracy, an enterprise's needs and an individual's needs, between the enterprise's needs and the community's needs, form the backbone of the culture which permeates the cooperative movement in Mondragon.[65]

Legislation. The British experience demonstrated the problems confronted by the early producer cooperatives because of a lack of suitable legislation. In the Mondragon experience, cooperative legislation is one of its strengths, protecting both the individual, the enterprise and the community. The major aspects are the following: membership rules, wages system, distribution of surplus and democratic management.

Membership rules are very strict. Membership must be open and at least 80% of workers must be members. Each member is required to make a substantial investment in the enterprise equivalent to 12 months' salary. If the members do not have this amount of money, they can borrow it from the CLP or pay by instalments.[66]

The wages system is set by the CLP bank. Basically wages are similar to those paid within the Basque region. However, cooperative payments can fluctuate between 80% to 110% of the set rate depending on the performance of the enterprise.[67] In addition, the enterprise pays social security payments covering sickness benefits, pension and unemployment benefits. The other aspect is the low wage differentials which were limited to a maximum of 4.5:1. Since this low differential led some managers to search for higher paid jobs with private enterprises, the wage differential has now been increased to 6:1.[68]

A major characteristic of Mondragon is the manner in which surplus is distributed. The surplus is usually divided between the community's needs (10%) and enterprise's needs (90%). However, the 90% is divided between the enterprise's indivisible reserves account and the members' individual accounts. The amount divided between these two accounts varies according to the enterprise's performance and needs. If the enterprise requires more money for investments, then a greater proportion is accredited to the reserve account. In the 1970s up to 70% was paid to individual capital accounts. In the 1980s, because of the recession, the amount paid was reduced to 40%.[69] In addition, the enterprise may use the members' capital accounts for investment purposes if required. Each year a dividend is paid to the individual capital account which cannot exceed 6%. When a member retires he or she can withdraw their individual capital accounts which must be re-paid within two years. If they leave the firm before retiring, a penalty may apply.[70]

Democratic management is another major element of the cooperative enterprise. Voting rights are based on the "one person one vote" value system. A mixture of direct and indirect democracy is practised. Direct democracy is practised in the general assembly. This body meets once a year to discuss the budget and overall planning. The general assembly elects an executive of 12 persons whose role is to control management. The management of the cooperative is a separate body, formed by persons who are not members of the executive. The members also elect representatives to the social council which is a body concerned with workers' rights such as health, safety, working conditions and payment system.[71] Studies have shown that the level of worker participation is generally higher than that experienced in private enterprises. However, participation is more reactive to already designed management plans.[72]

Ularco: Interfirm Collaboration. One important aspect of the Mondragon model is the level of interfirm collaboration. The first cooperative, Ulgor, was the centre out of which many other cooperatives were formed. In order to maintain its flexibility and the democratic nature of the enterprise, Ulgor decided to promote new enterprises once it reached a certain size. Arrasate, a machine tool manufacturer, and Copreci, a producer of valves and thermostats, were two cooperatives created by Ulgor. Initially they sold all their products to Ulgor, until they managed to expand and diversify their market.

In 1965, another form of interfirm collaboration took place. Ulgor, Copreci, Arrasate and other cooperatives from the area of Guipuzcoa formed Ularco. All member cooperatives were required to pool their resources. Ularco is governed by a general assembly, a governing board, a general management, with all the member cooperatives being represented on the various boards. Through Ularco, cooperatives have achieved economies of scale in relation to legal, administrative work and the financing of their activities. Ularco also developed forms of solidarity such as the transfer of employees from one firm to another. This form of collaboration promoted new enterprises, has reduced costs by achieving economies of scale and supported cooperatives in times of economic downturn.[73]

Support Structures. A major reason for the success of Mondragon's cooperatives is the well established network of support structures. These support structures offer vital services and skills which are essential for the survival of new and established enterprises. The first support structure formed in Mondragon is the well-respected technical training school whose role has been to provide engineering talent for cooperatives. While at school students can practise their business and manufacturing skills in the cooperative Alecoop, which is owned and managed by them.[74]

Since cooperatives are not covered by the national social security system, Mondragon has organised its own. Until 1967, this fund was managed by the CLP bank. Now it is independently managed by the insurance cooperative Lagun-Aro. Cooperatives pay payroll tax equivalent to 2.35% of their pay, in return workers receive unemployment benefits (up to 80% of one's pay), pension (60% of one's pay), health cover and indemnity payments for early retirees.[75] The system is well managed and it has been calculated that it is $800 per person cheaper compared to that managed by the State.[76]

To improve cooperatives' economic competitiveness other support structures have been established. Ikerlan conducts the groups' research and development projects. Lankide Export provides expertise in export.[77] However, by far the most important support structure is the CLP bank.

The CLP is the bank of the cooperative movement. It performs a banking role and an entrepreneurial role. The banking division collects deposits which are then used to provide finance to cooperatives. The interest rates charged are lower than the market rate. In 1985, the CLP bank charged 13% for normal loans and 8% for special loans. Sometimes for very special cases it charged no interest. This compares with the national average of 18%.[78] New cooperatives usually receive loans without having to pay interest for the first couple of years. In addition, the bank is very sensitive to cooperative needs in times of economic downturn or enterprise restructuring. During the recession of the 1980s, "the bank wrote off more than USA $1 million in cooperative loans and declared an interest moratorium on about 40% of the rest".[79]

CLP's Entrepreneurial Division plays a central supportive role on behalf of cooperatives. It promotes new cooperatives and provides consultancy and auditing services to all cooperatives. In 1982, it employed 116 persons and provided up to 60% of the funding needed by new cooperatives.[80] Other services include feasibility studies, training and advance payments for future cooperative managers who seek to establish new cooperatives. Establishing a new cooperative usually takes two years, but the services are provided throughout the life of the enterprise. Since the recession of the 1980s, the entrepreneurial division has been called on to make recommendations to a number of cooperatives regarding their strategy and managerial personnel. In 1983, 34% of the cooperatives sought support from the CLP's financial and entrepreneurial services.[81]

In return for these services, cooperatives are obliged to enter into a "Contract of Association" with the CLP. This is a binding agreement which obligates cooperatives to: comply with cooperative legislation, provide the CLP with access to their company records and audit the cooperative's financial and accounting records. Further, cooperatives are required to deposit their earnings with the CLP.[82]

The State. An important influence on the success of Mondragon, often bypassed by experts, is the role of the State. The State in Spain has not been hostile to cooperatives. During Franco's regime, cheap government loans and favourable legislation were already in existence.[83] Especially since 1969, in return for the 10% of the profits channelled by all cooperatives to the social fund and for the absence of a State social security system, a favourable tax structure has supported cooperative development.[84] This includes cooperatives not paying corporate tax for the first ten years from establishment and paying only 50% of the standard rate thereafter.[85] Today the State provides medium term loans at 10% per annum,[86] and 20% of the start up capital for every cooperative created.[87] The central government has also accredited and funded the technical school at Mondragon.[88] At the regional level, the Basque government has funded 50% of the costs incurred by Ikerlan, the cooperatives' R & D institute.[89] In addition, it gives USA $2,000 for every new job created.[90] Cooperatives have also benefited from other job creation schemes initiated by the Basque government to stimulate investment in new and competitive technologies. Between 1985 and 1987, 31 cooperatives received USA $15.6 million in grants and USA $13 million in guarantees from the Basque Government.[91]

However, it is important to place the role of the State in perspective. The 20% of "start up capital" it provides for each new cooperative formed is much less than the 60% provided by the CLP. Second, the technical school and Ikerlan play a regional role. The school is open to all students, while the research centre is also open to private enterprises. Third, the Mondragon cooperatives export 35% of their production making them a vital part of the national economy. Thus, while the State has supported cooperatives it has also benefited from the role the Mondragon cooperatives play in the regional and national economy.

Managing Change. The ability to respond to changes is another important ingredient in Mondragon's economic success. The first major crisis which occurred in Mondragon was internal. In 1974, a strike took place at Ulgor, the largest cooperative, because of workers' dissatisfaction with the new pay and merit system about to be introduced. After a lengthy debate lasting a couple of years, the cooperative decided to replace Tayloristic methods of production with "group activity" within the firm. It also encouraged better relations between shopfloor and management mediated through the members' representational body, the social council. In addition, the Mondragon cooperatives decided to limit the size of new cooperatives to 500 persons or less. By 1978, excluding Ulgor, 53% of the Mondragon cooperatives employed between 100 to 500 persons, 31% over 500 persons and only 12.5% employed 99 persons or less. Excluding Ulgor, the average cooperative employed 304 persons.[92]

The recession in the 1980s and Spanish integration with the EEC posed cooperatives with new problems. In particular, joining the EEC placed Spanish companies under increased competition. To improve their competitiveness, cooperatives had to make important strategic decisions regarding pay levels, labour mobility and gaining access to new technology. Pay levels were reduced by 14% between 1978-1984.[93] In addition, flexible working hours were introduced so that workers were available to work between six to ten hours per day instead of the usual eight hours. Both decisions increased profitability.[94]

The cooperatives also experienced an oversupply of labour which was dealt with in a number of ways. Most of the work-force were able to find employment in other cooperatives. Some underwent extensive retraining programmes. Those who could not find employment were eligible for unemployment benefits paid mostly by Lagun-Aro (70%) and their cooperative (30%). Others were given the opportunity to retire and were offered indemnity payments and a pension.

It is important to note how these changes have been managed at a group level facilitated by interfirm cooperation and by the cooperative's support structures. The search for markets and technological innovation is also conducted at a group level through support structures like Ikerlan and Lankide Export. The fourteen cooperatives which make up the Ularco group have decided to sell their products by using one brand name as a means to reduce marketing costs.[95] Both of these measures reduce costs and improve cooperatives' competitiveness. The CLP also offers financial support by providing loans or reducing the interest rates charged on existing ones. Furthermore, through its Entrepreneurial Division, it provides managerial assistance to cooperatives. As already stated, in addition to the group's support structures, the Basque government has also contributed to the restructuring process by offering grants and guarantees.

Comparison Between Mondragon and Britain

Table 2.1 Mondragon and the United Kingdom: A Comparison

	Mondragon	United Kingdom
Cooperative Size	Average 304 people	Average 4 people
Support Structures	Few, well funded specialist staff	Many, under funded, generalist staff
Relation between Enterprise & Movement	Very cohesive	Divided
State	Supportive	Some support after 1970
Community	High support	Low support
Economic Performance	Successful	Unsuccessful

A number of important observations can be drawn when comparing Mondragon and Britain (see Table 2.1). Influenced greatly by Father Jose Maria Arizmendi, Mondragon's cooperatives were governed by clear rules from the beginning. These rules created a balance between rewarding individuals, maintaining the enterprise economically viable and supporting the community. Secondly, the enterprises developed into medium to large size enterprises, much larger than those in the United Kingdom. Third, interfirm cooperation promoted cooperatives and achieved economies of scale strengthening further their position in the economy. Fourth, centred around the CLP cooperatives are united. This unity has enabled them to establish many support structures vital for their success. Contrary to the British CSOs, these support structures are specialists in their own field, work together and are well staffed. The Entrepreneurial Division alone employed 116 persons in 1982. Most importantly, the CLP provides finance and managerial expertise for new and established cooperatives. Fifth, community support, partly because of Basque nationalism, and partly because of cultural affinity with the idea of cooperation, played a major role, especially in the early stages of development. This support is continually fostered by cooperatives which invest 10% of their profits toward social and cultural activities and in the local economy. Finally, the State, at the regional and national level, was supportive of cooperatives.

Cooperative Development in the Rest of Europe and North America

The 1970s and 1980s have been a period of cooperative growth all over the world. A number of factors contributed to this growth. The level of economic integration and of communication technology have ensured a degree of homogeneity in the economic history of Western countries. Thus many of the reasons which led to a revival of interest in cooperatives in the United Kingdom were also present in other countries. The economic recession which began in the 1970s has led to a continuous high level of unemployment throughout Western industrialised countries. The alternative youth culture of the 1960s so prevalent in the UK, was also present in other countries and they too turned toward cooperatives as a work alternative. The belief that neither free markets nor State ownership (especially after the demise of the Communist countries since the late 1980s) can solve all the economic problems has prompted people and governments, in various degrees, to look toward cooperatives as a way to alleviate unemployment problems. In addition, by the 1980s, the experience of Mondragon became known throughout the world and was often cited as an example of what cooperatives could achieve.

The statistics revealing the level of cooperative activity world wide are quite staggering. The International Cooperative Alliance estimates that by the late 1980s there were over 500 million persons who were members of a cooperative.[96] The French President François Mitterrand, in his opening speech made at the European Conference on the Social Economy held in Paris in 1989, stated that in Europe alone the social economy has a total of 60 million members and provides employment to 3 million persons. In addition, he also noted that the social economy attracts 17% of peoples' savings, provides health insurance to some 27 million families and agricultural cooperatives control 60% of the agricultural market.[97] The consumers' movement is equally strong with market shares ranging from 10% in Britain, 20% in Sweden[98] and 30% in Denmark.[99]

The success of retail, agricultural and health insurance cooperatives is not suprising as these sectors since their formation have had continued success. What is important about this period is the rebirth of producer cooperatives or worker cooperatives since the 1970s. While the statistics are not as impressive as the previous sectors, they are encouraging: in France, by 1983, there were 1,269 cooperatives employing 40,423 persons;[100] in Holland, 311 cooperatives employed 6,300 by 1984; in the Scandinavian countries there were at least 164 cooperatives employing 5,200 persons in

1985-86;[101] In Canada, by 1987, 400 worker cooperatives had 15,000 members;[102] In the United States there are 1,000 worker cooperatives.[103]

A major boost to cooperative formation in Europe was provided by governments at the national and local level extending finance and incentives to workers to take over private enterprises in crisis. A study of seven European countries has revealed that between 1975 and 1985 approximately 3,000 cooperatives were formed in this way. In Spain alone, 1,300 worker cooperatives and labour societies, the latter based on individual ownership, were formed during this period employing a total of 50,000 people.[104]

The forms that cooperatives have taken over the years have not been homogeneous. Indeed, Jack Quarter asks whether there is only one type or more of cooperative movements.[105] The discussion on the British and the Mondragon experience has already highlighted the differences between cooperatives in these two countries. For the remainder of this section, two more types of cooperative will be discussed to further highlight the heterogeneity of enterprises often characterised as cooperatives.

Plywood Cooperatives

One form of cooperative which has received a lot of attention is embodied by the Plywood cooperatives of the United States. The first of these cooperatives was formed in 1921. They reached the height of their success by the mid-1960s when 24 cooperatives were in operation controlling between 20%-25% of industry production of plywood. In these cooperatives workers buy one share in the enterprise and are entitled to one vote. Unlike the rules governing the ICA cooperatives and Mondragon, this share entitles workers to the assets of the enterprise which can be sold to outsiders. Shares increase in value according to the performance of the enterprise. Other features include distribution of profits according to hours worked and equal pay for equal work for both members and non-members.[106]

The governance of these enterprises is based on the principle of "one person, one vote" and a blend of direct and indirect democracy. The members usually all meet in a general assembly which then elects the board of directors who in turn elect a general manager. The management is hired and is accountable to the board of directors. Evidence also suggests that there was a strong commitment to the firm by shareholders, information is readily available to members and member participation in meetings is quite high. However, some common complaints were that there were too many decision makers and that their representatives lacked the necessary skills.[107]

However, the Plywood cooperatives can be criticised on a number of grounds. First, the fact that non-members are not eligible to receive a portion of the surplus is a form of degeneration. Secondly, these cooperatives do not meet any of the ICA prerequisites in full except for the principle of "one person-one vote". Thirdly, because the individual shares are linked to the assets of the firm their value rises as the firm's assets rise. This has led some shares being worth up to USA $25,000 and because of this, members are difficult to replace. This state of affair violates the open door principle promoted by the ICA. Fourthly, because members can sell their assets in the open market, whenever a buyer or buyers cannot be found, members have often decided to sell their enterprise to private owners to recuperate their investments, thus turning the enterprise into a conventional one. This is a frequent recurrence. Under this form of ownership it is difficult to find new members and maintain the enterprise as a cooperative.[108] Indeed, by 1984 only 14 Plywood cooperatives remained in operation.[109]

Worker Capitalism

"Worker Capitalism" is used to refer to enterprises which offer their work-force the opportunity to become shareholders. There are a number of different schemes. For example, "profit sharing plans" which offer workers company stock instead of cash and "gain sharing" which offers shares if productivity targets are met.[110] Other schemes available to working people in the USA include the "Employees Stock Purchase Plans" where employees are offered company stock at a discount rate and the "401k scheme" where employees buy shares and in return the company makes matching contributions to them. These forms of employee ownership have become widespread in the United States. Blasi and Kruse note that some 10.8 million Americans or 12.5% of the American private sector work-force own shares through these schemes. Considering that only 12.2% of American workers are members of a union, a dramatic change is taking place in the attitude of workers towards their enterprises.[111] In Canada, Quarter informs us that 63.3% of the companies listed on the Toronto Stock Exchange offer some form of employee ownership scheme to their work-force.[112]

Bradley and Gelb have proposed the employee share alternative to rescue ailing capitalist enterprises by attracting capital from the work-force, by improving industrial relations and by increasing productivity. The three elements are interlinked because it is hoped that if workers have a stake in the enterprise then the other two requirements will follow.[113] In these enterprises, voting power is based on the amount of capital owned and there is little evidence of workers' participation in management. Profits are not distributed according to the amount of labour hours worked as in the Mondragon and other ICA cooperatives, but according to the quantity of capital owned.[114] "Worker Capitalism" is an apt term because these schemes are provided in companies which are profit-making, conventional firms without any of the social objectives characterising ICA cooperatives.

The most talked about American version of worker capitalist enterprises are "Employees Stock Ownership Plans" (ESOP). ESOPs came into life in 1974 thanks to the vigorous work of their two main promoters: Louis Kelso, an investment banker and Russell Long, a former Senator. They wrote an influential book called *The Capitalist Manifesto* in which they promoted ESOPs with the aim of making every worker a capitalist. Their goals were to provide companies with much needed capital and at the same time promote social stability by giving workers a stake in the company in which they worked.[115] This was most appropriate since the 1970s were a period of economic crisis for America. Indeed, in 1971, for the first time since 1945 the United States Government devalued the dollar to improve the competitiveness of American companies. In addition, to Kelso and Long, some academics also advocated the establishment of ESOPs for the purpose of giving more power to local government, overcoming social dislocation caused by plant shutdowns and stopping small businesses being taken over by large ones. Blasi argues that it was this overall approach which won the support of both the Republicans, who supported worker capitalism and were concerned with family breakdowns, and from the Democrats, who supported the idea of giving local administrations more power and redistributing wealth in favour of employees.[116]

ESOPs "are a type of employee-benefit plan through which a company either makes tax deductible contributions of new issues of stock to a trust fund for the employees or it uses cash to buy existing shares. Alternatively the ESOP can be used to borrow money to buy shares".[117] In the latter arrangement, also referred to as a leveraged ESOPs, an Employee stock Ownership Trust (ESOT) is set up which borrows money to buy stock for employees. The loan is then paid back through operating profits. Once the loan is re-paid the shares are allocated to the individuals' investment accounts.[118] However, the employees only acquire direct ownership when they leave the firm or when they retire.[119]

A major reason why these schemes have been successful is because of the tax concessions companies, owners, banks and employees receive from the State. The companies receive tax deductions on the loan repayments they have to make. They also receive tax deductions on the dividends paid to employees held stock. Banks are also encouraged to lend money to ESOPs by allowing them a 50% tax deduction on interest received from loan repayments. Owners who sell their business to an ESOP and re-invest their capital in another business will have their capital gain tax deferred until the new securities are sold. Employees also benefit because they do not have to pay any taxes on ESOP benefits until they leave the company.[120]

While ESOPs can provide advantages such as a supplementary income for workers, (when the company is successful), and low cost capital for firms, which improves their financial state and consequently improve the workers' job security, they fail short of satisfying the requirements of the ICA or Mondragon type cooperatives. First of all, these are conventional profit-maximising firms where managers have full control of the workplace. Secondly, the workers rarely elect their representatives in the Employee Stock Ownership Trust. Indeed Blasi and Kluse found that only 1% of the firms they researched had employee representatives on the boards of directors.[121] Thirdly, in 85% of ESOPs where employees are minor shareholders and in about 60% of the majority owned ESOPs (approximately 1,500), employee shares are not accredited full voting rights.[122] Finally, there are no provisions made in ESOPs to encourage workers' participation in the decision-making process. It would seem that on the basis of the evidence so far, the main basis for ESOPs has been to raise low cost finance for the company.[123] Whether in the future they can become democratic allowing the employees to elect their representatives on the basis of "one person one vote" remains to be seen. In any case, as long as the individual shares are linked to the assets of the company and profits are distributed on the basis of capital ownership rather than amount of hours worked, they will remain worker capitalist enterprises radically different to ICA and Mondragon cooperatives. Further differences emerge if one considers that ESOPs do not have any provisions to support social goals.

Summary

The research so far has provided a number of important findings. First, it has identified that the type of ownership, the form of democratic management and rights of capital are major elements distinguishing cooperatives from conventional enterprises. Second, it has also identified different types of worker cooperatives, arguing that those which comply with ICA principles and Mondragon provide a clear alternative to conventional forms. Worker capitalist firms and ESOPs, while they can be regarded as an improvement on the traditional private firms by allowing employee ownership, do not abide by the principle of "one person, one vote", but rather accept the right of capital to control labour and do not support social goals.

The third finding is that the character of each cooperative movement is nation specific. Each movement's character has been influenced by economic, political, social and cultural factors. One needs only to compare the ideas and ends of Robert Owen's thought to that of Kelso and Long, the founders of ESOPs, to realise that he was promoting a different enterprise in a different historical period and in a different political and social context.

Fourth, the comparative analysis between the British and the Mondragon experience has clearly shown that explanations of cooperative development cannot be universalised. Thus, the answer to the question have cooperatives failed is quite a complex one. The evidence gathered on the British and Mondragon cooperative movement has shown that factors within and external to the enterprise are responsible for the demise or success of a cooperative. The British case study has identified lack of capital, lack of managerial expertise, discrimination by private firms, indifference by the State prior to the 1970s, reluctance to initiate technological change and a poor image caused by inability to compete in the market as the main reasons for their low presence in the economy. It has also identified that since the development of support structures and the provision of State support the number of cooperatives has increased.

In contrast, Mondragon experience is an example of a successful cooperative movement. Its success is due to a number of factors which include: a general culture supportive of cooperatives; the Basque culture provided a source of unity among the cooperatives; tariff barriers which protected the Spanish economy; the ideological and motivational leadership of Father Arizmendi; the cooperative rules; the high quality of its support structures, especially the CLP; the supportive role played by the State at the national and regional level, and the ability of cooperatives to manage change.

Has the cooperative alternative failed? The evidence so far suggests that generally speaking producer cooperatives have not fared well and, as the UK experience has shown, there are a number of reasons for this. However, the Mondragon experience has shown that cooperatives can successfully compete in the market. Furthermore, the greater number of cooperatives being formed since 1975 and the promotion of cooperatives being formed from private enterprises in crisis seems to suggest that producer cooperatives have become more popular and can still be regarded as an alternative form of enterprise.

Notes

1 A good discussion of the six ICA principles are contained in the following: Stefano Zan, La Cooperazione in Italia: Strategie e Sviluppo della Lega Nazionale delle Cooperative, De Donato, Bari, 1982, pp.21-26., Chris Axworthy and Terry Phalen, Cooperative Growth and Survival: Two Viewpoints, Cooperative College of Canada, Volume 4, Number 5, pp.1-30.
2 David Morris, "Mondragon: Cooperative at Work", *Co-op America Quarterly*, Winter 1992, p.6.
3 Roberst Oakeshott, *The Case for Workers' Cooperatives*, Routledge and Kegan Paul, London, 1978, p.192.
4 Christopher S Axworthy, *Worker Cooperatives in Mondragon, The U.K. and France, Some Reflections*, Occasional Papers, Centre for the Study of Cooperatives, Saskatchewan, Canada, 1985, p.31.
5 Renato Midoro, *Gli Strumenti per il Finanziamento delle Cooperative,* Editrice Cooperativa, Roma, 1984, p.16.
6 William Foote Whyte and Kathleen King Whyte, *Making Mondragon: The Growth Dynamics of the Worker Cooperative Complex*, New York, ILR Press, 1988, p.43.
7 Axworthy, *op.cit.*, p.31.
8 Zan, *op.cit.*, p.39.
9 Howard Aldrich and Robert Stern, "Resource Mobilisation and the Creation of US Producer Cooperatives, 1835-1935", *Economic and Industrial Democracy*, Volume 4, 1983, p.373. See also Emanuel Danieli, "L'Impresa Cooperativa Definizione e Tipologia", in Francesco Garella (ed), *Il Movimento, Il Sistema, la Rete: Un Decennio di Cambiamenti nelle Imprese Cooperative*, Editrice Emilia Romagna, Bologna, 1991, p.23.
10 Aldrich and Stern, *ibid.* See also Zan, *op.cit.*, pp.138-139.
11 Zan, *ibid.*, pp.170-176.
12 Mark Holmstrom, *Industrial Democracy in Italy*, Avebury, Aldershot, 1989, pp.8-10.
13 Arnold Bonner, *British Cooperation: the History, Principles, and Organisation of the British Co-operative Movement*, Cooperative Union Limited, Manchester, 1961, p.2.
14 Jenny Thornley, *Workers' Co-operatives: Jobs and Dreams*, Heinemann Educational Books, London, 1982, pp.12-13.
15 See Robert Owen, *A New View of Society and Other Writings*, JM Dent and Sons, London, 1927. In particular see "A New View of Society" and "Report to the County of Lanark". For a quick summary of Owen's ideas see Bernard Crick, *Socialism*, Open University Press, Milton Keynes, 1987, pp.42-43.
16 Bonner, *op.cit.*, p.15.
17 Chris Cornforth et al., *Developing Successful Worker Cooperatives*, Sage Publications, London, 1988, p.11.
18 Bonner, *op.cit.*, p.36.
19 Cornforth, *op.cit.*, p.13.
20 Bonner, *op.cit.*, pp.19-39.
21 Ibid., p.40.
22 *Ibid.*, pp.47-48.
23 Peter Milford, "Worker Cooperatives and Consumer Cooperatives: can they be Combined?", in Sune Jansson and Ann-Britt Hellmark (eds), *Labor-Owned Firms and Worker Cooperatives,* Gower, Aldershot, 1986, p.123.
24 Cornforth, *op.cit.*, p.13.
25 Bonner, *op.cit.*, p.64.

26 Thornley, *op.cit.*, p.21.
27 *Ibid*, p.22.
28 Cornforth, *op.cit.*, p.16.
29 Bonner, *op.cit.*, p.143.
30 *Ibid.*, p.160.
31 *Ibid.*, p.170.
32 Sydney and Beatrice Webb, "Special Supplement on the Cooperative Movement", *The New Statesman*, May 30 1914, pp.25-30.
33 Sydney and Beatrice Webb, "Special Supplement on Co-operative Production and Profit Sharing", *The New Statesman*, February 14 1914, p.30.
34 Thornley, *op.cit.*, p.27.
35 Robin Murray, "Withering Heights: Social Ownership in a Changing World", *New Socialist*, April 1987, p.41.
36 G.D.H. Cole, *A Short History of the British Working Class Movement 1789-1947*, George Allen and Unwin Ltd, London, 1948, pp.363-366.
37 Mary Mellor et al, *Worker Cooperatives in Theory and Practice*, Open University Press, Milton Keynes, 1988, pp.12-13.
38 J Carroll Moody and Gilbert C Fife, *The Credit Union Movement: Origins and Development 1850-1870*, University of Nebraska Press, Lincoln, 1971, pp.1-24.
39 Philip Armstrong et al., *Capitalism Since World War II: the Making and Breaking of the Great Boom*, Fontana, London, 1984, p.330.
40 Keith Jefferis and Chris Cornforth, "Worker Cooperatives in Britain: a Review of the Literature", unpublished paper, Milton Keynes, *1988*, p.3.
41 Mark Holmstrom, *op.cit.*, pp.8-10.
42 Robert Oakeshott, *op.cit.*, Chapter One.
43 Peter Jay, "A Cooperative Economy", in Alasdair Clayre (ed), *The Political Economy of Cooperation and Participation*, Oxford University Press, Oxford, 1980, pp.9-12.
44 Keith Bradley and Alan Gelb, *Worker Capitalism: the New Industrial Relations*, Heinemann Educational Books, London, 1983.
45 Thornley, *op.cit.*, pp.36-52.
46 ICOM, *ICOM: a Description of the Industrial Common Ownership Movement*, London, 1975.
47 Mellor et al., *op.cit.*, pp.46-47.
48 Cornforth et al., *op.cit.*, pp.19-20.
49 *Ibid.*, pp.175-176.
50 Chloe Munro, *The Financing of Worker Co-operatives: A Comparison with Conventional Small Businesses and Evaluation of Proposed Mechanisms for Investments*, CRU Monograph Number 8, Open University, Milton Keynes, 1988, pp.9-10.
51 Mellor et al., *op.cit.*, pp.101-104.
52 Chris Cornforth, "The Role of Support Organisations in Developing Worker Cooperatives: A Model for Promoting Economic and Industrial Democracy?", in Gyorgy Szell et al., *The State, The Trade Unions and Self Management*, Walter De Gruyter, Berlin, 1989, p.121.
53 Keith Thompson, "The Serpent in the Supermarket's Paradise", *European Management Journal*, Volume 10, Number 1, March 1992, p.114.
54 Gary Mead, "Profile: Mondragon Co-operative Movement", *Financial Times*, 24 November 1993, p.29.

55 Bradley and Gelb also note that between 1976-1983 industrial output in Mondragon increased by 6% compared with the 1.5% increase registered by Spanish industry. See Keith Bradley and Alan Gelb, "Cooperative Labour Relations: Mondragon's Responses to Recession", *British Journal of Industrial Relations*, Vol XXV, Number 1, March 1987, pp.84 and 93.
56 Jack Quarter, "Starting Worker-Owned Enterprises: Problems and Prospects", in Jack Quarter and George Melnyk (ed), *Partners in Enterprises: the Worker Ownership Phenomenon*, Black Rose Books, Montreal, 1989, p.38.
57 Axworthy, *op.cit.,* p. 11.
58 Whyte and Whyte, *op.cit.*, p.18.
59 Robert Oakeshott, *op.cit.,* p.173.
60 Henk Thomas and Chris Logan, *Mondragon: An Economic Analysis*, George Allen and Unwin, London, 1982, p.16.
61 Ma Jesus Zabaleta, "Mondragon: Un'Esperienza Integrata", in Anna Avitabile et. al., *Cooperare e Competere*, Giangiacomo Feltrinelli Editore, Milano, 1986, p.22.
62 Oakeshott, *op.cit.*, pp.170-185.
63 Zabaleta, *op.cit.*, p.21.
64 Tayloristic methods refers to a system of production divided into specific tasks performed continuously by the same person. See FW Taylor, 'Scientific Management", in D S Pugh (ed), *Organisation Theory: Selected Readings*, Penguin Books, London, pp.157-176.
65 Whyte and Whyte, *op.cit*, pp.237-248.
66 Axworthy, *op.cit.*, p.8.
67 Bradley and Gelb, *op.cit.*, "Cooperative Labour Relations: Mondragon's Responses to Recession", p.88.
68 Whyte and Whyte, *op.cit.*, p.216-217.
69 *Ibid.*, p.43.
70 Oakeshott, *op.cit.*, pp.191-192.
71 *Ibid.*, pp.187-188.
72 Whyte and Whyte, pp.209-210.
73 *Ibid.*, pp.58-61.
74 Christopher B Meek and Warner P Woodworth, "Technical Training and Enterprise: Mondragon's Educational System and its Implications for Other Cooperatives", *Economic and Industrial Democracy,* Sage, London, Volume 11, 1990, pp.505-528.
75 Whyte and Whyte, *op.cit.*, pp.150-151.
76 *Ibid.*, p.53.
77 Zabaleta, *op.cit.*, p.23.
78 Axworthy, *op.cit.*, p.6.
79 Roy Morrison, *We Build the Road as We Travel,* New Society Publishers, Philadelphia, 1991, p.114.
80 Whyte and Whyte, *op.cit.*, p.72.
81 *Ibid.*, pp.,170-171.
82 *Ibid.*, pp. 67-70.
83 John Robbins, "The Cooperative Alternative: The Revival of a Democratic Ideal in Industry", *The Journal of Industrial Relations*, March 1982, p.15.
84 Alasdair Clayre, "Some Aspects of the Mondragon Co-operative Federation", in Alasdair Clayre (ed), *The Political Economy of Co-Operation and Participation*, Oxford University Press, 1980, p.172.

85 Cooperatives Research Unit, *Mondragon Co-operatives: Myth or Model*, The Open University, Milton Keynes, 1982, p.6.
86 Whyte and Whyte , *op.cit.*, p.80.
87 Oakeshott, *op.cit.*, p.209.
88 Meek and Woodworth, *op.cit.*, p.518.
89 Axyworthy, *op.cit.*, p.8.
90 Whyte and Whyte, *op.cit.*, p.79.
91 Morrison, *op.cit.*, p.201.
92 Thomas and Logan, *op.cit.*, p.117.
93 Zabareta, *op.cit.*, p.24.
94 Whyte and Whyte, *op.cit.*, p.144.
95 *Ibid.*, p.163.
96 This statistic refers to all type of cooperatives including Credit Unions. See Mario Gabbi and Alberto Terzi, *Il Manager Cooperativo: Il Modo di Partecipare e Dirigere*, Edizioni Spiel, Milano, 1989, pp.19-21.
97 François Mitterrand, "Un'Idea Antica di cui l'Europa ha Bisogno", in *La Cooperazione Italiana*, Dicembre 1989, pp.16-17.
98 Victor Pestoff, "The Dilemma Facing Swedish Consumer Cooperatives: Can Members, Markets, Authorities and Employees all be Optimised", in Colin Crouch and Frank Heller (ed), *Organisational Democracy and Political Processes*, John Wiley and Sons Ltd, Chichester, 1983, p.433.
99 Paola Bergonzoni, "Una Scelta Europea per Crescere Ancora", *La Cooperazione Italiana*, Giugno-Luglio 1991, p.38.
100 Axworthy, *op.cit.*, p.30.
101 Lars Lindkvist and Ann Westenholz (eds), *Employee Owned Companies in the Nordic Countries: An Historical Parenthesis or a Future Possibility? (a Summary),* Nordic Council of Ministers, Copenhagen, 1987, p.9.
102 Jack Quarter, "Worker Ownership: One Movement or Many?", in Jack Quarter and George Melnyk (eds) *Parteners in Enterprise: the Worker Ownership Phenomenon,* Black Rose Books, Montreal, 1989, p.12.
103 Len Krimerman and Frank Lindenfeld,"Changing Worklife: Grassroots Activism Takes a New Turn", in Len Krimerman and Frank Lindenfeld (eds), *When Workers Decide: Workplace Democracy Takes Root in North America*, New Society Publishers, Philadelphia, 1992, pp. 5-8.
104 Rob Paton, *Reluctant Entrepreneurs*, Open University Press, Milton Keynes, 1989, Chapter 2.
105 Jach Quarter, *op.cit.*, "Worker Ownership: One Movement Or Many", pp.1-32.
106 Katina V Berman, "The United States of America: A Cooperative Model for Worker Management", in Frank H Stephen, (ed), *The Performance of Labour Managed Firms*, MacMillan Press, London, 1982, pp.76-81.
107 Edward S Greenberg, "Producer Cooperatives and Democratic Theory: The Case of the Plywood Firms", in Robert Jackall and Henry M Levin (eds), Berkeley, 1984, pp.171-214.
108 Christopher S Axworthy and David Perry, *Worker Cooperatives and Worker Ownership: Issues Affecting the Development of Worker Cooperatives in Canada*, Occasional Papers, Centre for the Study of Cooperatives, University of Saskatchewan, Canada, 1988, pp.6-7.
109 Greenberg, *op.cit.*, p.175.

110 Quarter, *op.cit.*,"Worker Ownership: One Movement or Many", p.2.
111 Joseph Raphael Blasi and Douglas Lynn Kruse, *The New Owners: The Mass Emergence of Employee Ownership in Public Companies and What it Means to American Business*, Harper Collins, USA, 1991, pp.12-29.
112 Jack Quarter, *op.cit.*,"Worker Ownership: One Movement or Many", p.2.
113 Keith Bradley and Alan Gelb, *op.cit.*, *Worker Capitalism: The New Industrial Relations*, pp.1-61, esp. pp.53-55.
114 For a good Discussion see David Ellerman, *Worker Ownership: Economic Democracy or Worker Capitalism?*, Industrial Cooperative Association-School of Management, Boston College, Boston, March 1985.
115 Henry M Levin, "ESOPs and the Financing of Worker Co-operatives", in Robert Jackall and Henry M Levin (eds) *Worker Cooperatives in America*, University of California Press, Los Angeles, 1984, p.247.
116 Joseph R Blasi, (et al.),"The Politics of Worker Ownership in the United States", in Colin Crouch and Frank Heller (eds), *Organisational Democracy and Political Processes*, John Wiley and Sons, Chichester, 1983, pp.638-644.
117 Quarter, *op.cit.*, "Worker Ownership: One Movement or Many", p.5.
118 Blasi and Kruse, *op.cit.*, p.23.
119 Ellerman, *op.cit.*, *Worker Ownership: Economic Democracy or Worker Capitalism*, p.7.
120 Peter R Pitegoff and Deborah Groban Olson, "ESOP Tax Benefits", in Len Krimerman and Frank Lindenfeld (eds), *When Workers Decide: Workplace Democracy Takes Root in North America*, New Society Publishers, Philadelphia, 1992, pp.288-289.
121 Blasi and Kluse, op.cit., p.245.
122 Corey Rosen, "ESOPs: Hype or Hope", in Len Krimerman and Frank Lindenfeld (ed), *When Workers Decide: Workplace Democracy Takes Root in North America*, New Society Publishers, Philadelphia, 1992, pp.186-187.
123 Quarter, op.cit.,"Worker Ownership: One Movement or Many", p.8.; Levin, *op.cit.*, p.250.

3 Cooperative Development: Problems and Solutions

The Mondragon experience has demonstrated that cooperatives can successfully compete with conventional private firms in the open market. At the same time, the previous chapter also highlighted the fact that, other than in the agricultural, retailing and social welfare areas, the number of cooperatives in capitalist countries are few and rarely hold a position of great significance in their economies. Both the success of Mondragon and the failure of cooperative movements in other parts of the world has captured the attention of many scholars. The purpose of this chapter is to engage in some of the wider debates which have sought to identify the reasons behind the failure of cooperatives in Western industrialised countries. In doing so, the solutions offered by various cooperative movements to overcome these obstacles will also be explored. This discussion will be vital for a proper understanding of the complexities involved in creating a successful cooperative movement and will provide a valuable comparative tool of analysis when describing and analysing the experience of La Lega's cooperatives in later chapters.

Problems of Cooperative Development

The British experience has already identified a number of problems faced by cooperatives in that country: insufficient capital, inefficient management and discrimination by private businesses have been mentioned as causes of cooperative failure. Drawing on research from many countries, some authors have attempted to categorise cooperative problems. Fanning and McCarthy have divided these problems under into the following main groupings: founding, administrative and finance.[1] A more comprehensive categorisation was developed by Cornforth et al., who have identified seven major problems faced by cooperatives. These are as follows: low rate of formation - the entrepreneurial problem; lack of finance; lack of managerial and specialist competencies; forms of discrimination; internal limits to growth; constraints on takeovers and the place of cooperatives in the economy.[2] All of these problems, in various degrees, have hindered the growth of cooperatives. Cornforth et al., drawing mainly on the British experience, have actually classified them as barriers to cooperative development. The preferred term used here will be problems for the simple reason that the word barriers implies the existence of insurmountable obstacles whereas the word problem implies something which can be overcome, as the experience of Mondragon has shown. What follows is an analysis of each problem and an outline of possible solutions drawn from the experience of existing cooperative movements from Europe and North America.

Cooperative Formation - The Entrepreneurial Problem

A number of authors have suggested that a low rate of cooperative formation rather than poor performance explains the relatively small size of the cooperative sector in capitalist economies. Support for this proposition comes from Canada where, for every 100 new cooperatives formed annually there are 10,000 conventional businesses formed each month.[3] This is further supported by evidence which indicates that the survival rate of cooperatives is comparable to that of similar size private enterprises.[4]

So why are people forming private enterprises and not cooperatives? Abell argues that it is not in the material interest of the entrepreneur to set up a cooperative because control of the enterprise will have to be shared, the return on capital will be limited and the right to sell or redeem any capital investment will be restricted. He concludes by saying that only when individuals have equal capital and a common marketable idea will a cooperative begin to prove at all attractive.[5] Aldrich and Stern, after having conducted research on producer cooperatives in the United States between 1835-1935, concluded that cooperatives may be materially attractive to workers only in times of economic crisis such as during a period of high unemployment. They further suggest that cooperatives may be formed when incentives other than material ones are considered important:

> If people are committed to cooperation as an ideal, or if they believe cooperation is a means to some larger political objective, they might be willing to ignore the obvious disincentives involved in creating cooperatives and instead provide the resources required.[6]

A study by Lindkvist, Westenholz et al., of Nordic countries revealed the absence of a collective entrepreneurial culture. They found that Nordic countries had a wage earner culture, career culture, individual entrepreneur culture and the professional employee culture. They traced this to the history of working people in their countries which through the trade union movement and political parties, had managed to create successful economies with low unemployment rates supported by an elaborate unemployment relief and social security system.[7]

The low formation rate of cooperatives could also be a consequence of cooperatives being viewed negatively or not being well known. That cooperatives in some countries pay low incomes and are in marginal sectors of the economy may also act as a deterrent.[8] In addition, the media and the education system rarely discuss cooperatives, thus people do not know of their existence. The reason for this may be either ideological or practical. In the latter case, cooperatives are not given sufficient coverage because they are not perceived as a viable alternative to conventional enterprises as they have not proved themselves to be capable of solving unemployment problems on a large scale.

There have been a number of ways that cooperative movements have attempted to overcome the entrepreneurial problem. The formation of cooperatives from private enterprises in crisis is one way of alleviating the problem. The results from a European study reveals that close to 3,000 cooperatives have been formed in this way between 1975 and 1985. Their success rate after three years is fairly high, with a 63% success rate in France and 70% in Spain. The research further revealed that when the cooperative movement has managed to get a favourable support from the State, the trade unions and from their own support structures, both the number of cooperatives formed from ailing private enterprises and their success rate has been higher.[9]

Another way of solving this problem is by developing support structures which promote cooperative formation. A successful example of this is CLP's Entrepreneurial Division. It provides feasibility studies, training and funds for potential entrepreneurs who wish to start a new cooperative.[10]

Providing an attractive salary can also attract potential entrepreneurs. It is often assumed that cooperatives provide low wages or equal wages between workers and management.[11] This need not be the case. In Mondragon, wage differentials within the work-force have always existed. Recently they have been increased from 4.5 to 1 to 6:1.[12] This may attract more potential entrepreneurs. However, the wage differentials should be contained, otherwise the cooperative risks developing wage differentials which are similar to those existing in conventional firms.

Finance

Finance is very important for the success of cooperatives. It is needed to have access to plant and equipment, to purchase raw materials and to provide income to its work-force in advance of sales revenue.[13] It is also vital for business expansion, research and development, staff training and marketing. Three major reasons have been identified which cause cooperatives financial problems: cooperative principles, high gearing and a tendency to under-invest.

ICA cooperative principles and cooperative rules constrain a cooperative's capacity to raise finance. Unlike private enterprises, cooperatives cannot issue bonds or raise finance through external shareholders. Under these circumstances, cooperatives are reliant on members' shares, members' loans and private bank loans. The limited remuneration on members' shares means that this form of finance raises little money. The problem is further exacerbated by the fact that cooperatives are usually formed by working people in search of employment with little money to invest.[14]

As a result, cooperatives rely on external borrowing and suffer from high gearing in a similar fashion as small businesses. Since bank repayments have to be met regardless of whether the cooperative is profitable or not, external debt hinders their economic success. In addition, if a cooperative relies mostly on external finance from its inception, their chances of getting further finance in the future may be reduced since their collateral may have been used to secure the first loan.[15]

Neo-classical economists such as Ward and Vanek have suggested that cooperatives have a tendency to under-invest, causing financial problems for cooperatives. The findings of these authors are based on a theoretical model and not empirical evidence. The model is based on a number of assumptions. The first assumption is that individuals are basically selfish, and interested only in maximising their income. The second assumption is that cooperatives are to be financed exclusively from retained earnings. The third assumption is that, other than wages, workers receive only a limited return on capital (the percentage paid annually is not specified). Fourth, all profits that are re-invested are part of the collective reserves which are themselves collectively owned. The argument concludes that because members do not get any immediate rewards from profits re-invested in the firm, cooperatives have a tendency to under-invest because of the inclinations of members to maximise income per worker leading to a distribution of profits as wages.[16]

There is ample evidence to suggest that the validity of the assumptions made by Ward and Vanek should be doubted. These authors have not taken into consideration that cooperative rules can prohibit such action. The Mondragon rules ensure that members receive standard wages set by the CLP. The rules also ensure that the surplus is distributed into individual accounts, collective reserves and community support. In France, the surplus is distributed as follows: 40% were distributed to members, 40% to reserves and 20% as remuneration on capital.[17] In both instances, cooperative rules ensure that a balance has been struck between individual and collective goals. Secondly, in his study of eight cooperatives in Denmark, Mygind found that the members' objective was not one geared toward maximisation of their income. Instead, their priorities were the long term survival of the cooperative and the maintenance of employment.[18] Therefore these assumptions are not correct given the practise and experience of existing cooperatives.

A number of possible solutions have been suggested to overcome the financial problems deriving from cooperative principles and high gearing. One of these proposes the idea of allowing non-voting preferential shares to be issued to members which can receive a limited return of variable interest and cannot be traded except back to the cooperative when the member decides to leave. This is to offset the disadvantages that cooperatives have when compared with conventional enterprises, which have a market for debentures providing them with a source of much needed capital. However, this solution may introduce capital rights which may influence the workings of a cooperative. As Chloe Munro points out: "if the distinction between trading for the benefit of labour is abandoned completely, the meaning of worker cooperative is also lost".[19]

Another approach is to increase the amount invested as members' shares which can be used throughout the member's permanence in the cooperative. In the UK, an amendment to the Finance Act, 1986, allows cooperatives to have tax concessions on a certain amount of pre-tax profits passed onto employees. The scheme operates in the following way. The cooperative transfers a portion of its pre-tax profits to a trust which then purchases shares in the cooperative on behalf of employees. The shares are transferred to the member after five years and upon redemption or retirement, the member receives a tax free lump sum. This is a form of profit sharing which allows the firm to retain capital within the enterprise.[20]

A further attempt in the UK at promoting investment has been made by the Scottish Cooperative Development Committee and ICOM. They have sought to attract external shareholders to invest money in their funds. Although money in the sums of £250,000 and £500,000 respectively has been raised, the lower rate of return compared to private banks and institutions means that only sympathetic investors can be attracted thus limiting the amount of capital that can be raised.[21]

The Mondragon cooperatives have attempted to overcome the problem by promoting a high level of initial personal investment and the promotion of individual accounts. Each worker has to deposit a sum equivalent to one year's income upon joining the cooperative. This is remunerated at the fixed rate of 6% per annum. Furthermore, 40% of the enterprise's profits are distributed to each account. This sum is held in the cooperative until the worker leaves the firm. If the firm suffers a loss, money is subtracted from the individual account as well as the collective reserves.[22] The major criticism of this type of arrangement is that if many workers leave the firm at once, then the enterprise may have financial difficulties. The other criticism is that if the enterprise fails, then workers risk losing their jobs plus a substantial sum of money.[23] The Mondragon cooperatives have already taken precautionary measures to limit these potential problems. For instance, penalties apply to those who leave the firm without a good reason. In addition, the money owed to individuals can be paid within two years, thus alleviating the financial burden of the enterprise.[24] Evidence also suggests that workers at Mondragon can usually be placed at other cooperatives if they lose their job.[25] However, an element of risk is always present, and worker-entrepreneurs, like private entrepreneurs, must assume this risk if they are to own and manage an enterprise.

The other example to come from Mondragon is the role played by the CLP bank. In 1985, the CLP was offering member cooperatives loans at a maximum rate of interest of 13% for regular loans, 8% for special sectors the bank wished to encourage and loans free of interest for very special cases. This compared very favourably with the prevailing market rate of 18%.[26] The CLP can also further reduce interest rates and forgive a portion of the outstanding debt of cooperatives which are experiencing difficulties in repaying loans. The role played by the CLP is further highlighted by the fact that it provides all of the financing needs of the Mondragon cooperatives.[27]

In France, the Institute for the Development of the Social Economy (IDES) was formed in the mid-1980s with half of its funds provided by the State and the other half by cooperatives. The Institute lends money to cooperatives at a fixed rate of interest around 7-8% in 1985, plus it retains a percentage of the profits. It has no participation in a cooperative's assets, reserves or decision making. The return from loans are used to provide loans to other cooperatives. Overall, the objective is to get cooperatives to invest in IDES and for IDES to provide loans for cooperative development.[28]

Management

Lack of managerial skills have always been identified as a major problem faced by cooperative enterprises. The Webbs identified the major reasons for producer cooperatives' failure in their lack of knowledge of the market, an unwillingness to keep up with technological change and an undisciplined work-force.[29] Mead also raised questions whether the cooperatives could operate with sufficient discipline to enable a large enterprise to function efficiently.[30] Cornforth et al., found that cooperative members generally undervalue the role of managers. There are a number of reasons for this. Cooperatives born out of the "alternative movement" see management as being part of the hierarchy of conventional firms. Socialists may regard management as agents of capital, while ex-trade unionists have a long history of struggles against management which may have led to them having a low opinion.[31] This has contributed toward a lack of expertise in cooperatives in the fields of marketing, financial management and planning. It has also been found that once these weaknesses are recognised, the need to work may prevent cooperative members from taking time off to acquire suitable managerial skills.[32]

One way to overcome this problem is to recruit managers and specialists externally, as has been practised by the Plywood cooperatives in the United States.[33] This may not be easy. The UK experience shows that, at least initially, cooperatives cannot afford to offer market wages. Secondly, a small business requires general management skills and usually people with these tend to run their own businesses. Thirdly, the cooperative has no guarantee of loyalty from a professional manager. This view is supported by a number of cases where managers have tried to take over cooperatives or to open up businesses in the same market.[34] However, this is not be a problem exclusive to cooperatives as private enterprise may suffer the same fate. Cornforth further states that large cooperatives too will face difficulties because the cooperative movement has not yet developed an internal market for managers and because of its commitment to low wage differentials.[35]

This shortage of managerial expertise can be overcome by following the example of Mondragon which created its own management and technical school, (Professional Polytechnic School-Escuela Polytecnica Profesional). The school is funded by the State and by cooperatives, with some support also coming from private firms. It is democratically managed by students, the faculty staff, cooperatives and private enterprises. In addition, nearly 50% of its students have the opportunity to apply their skills in a student-owned cooperative. This provides them not only with earnings but also practical experience in working in a democratically managed enterprise. Training includes the following components: basic business competencies (accounting, marketing, business strategy), technical work processes and manufacturing methods and working experience in a cooperative.[36]

The Mondragon cooperatives also pay reasonable salaries. As stated previously, the Mondragon cooperatives have long had a policy of wage differentiation, and while this is limited when compared to private firms, a 6:1 ratio applies making it attractive for managers to remain in the cooperative.

Cornforth also provides ideas on how to manage conflicts between management and the work-force. He has placed a lot of emphasis on managerial practises and has attempted to find ways to avoid managers becoming dominant in a cooperative. He suggests that managers should not only be concerned with economic growth but also with the realisation of internal democracy. The author concludes that part of the managers' job should be to provide information to members, help workers to develop their skills to the full, to face and deal constructively with criticism, to develop skills as an educator and, finally, to be masters as well as servants.[37]

Internal Limits to Growth

Arguments have been raised that cooperatives remain small because of their members' culture and because of their tendency to under-employ. Growth could be limited by those cooperative members who value the informal 'family type' atmosphere of a small enterprise. Others may limit growth because they are committed to maintain democracy in the workplace. Joyce Rothschild-Whitt's study of alternative organisations in the USA discussed how the need to create organisations without hierarchical controls, with a consensus type approach to decision making, with limited rules, with decentralised controls and homogeneity of political and social goals among its members, "may constrain the social base of collectivist organisation" thereby making it difficult to grow.[38] An example of the difficulties encountered by a large cooperative is provided by the experience at Ulgor, Mondragon's largest cooperative. Ulgor employed 3,250 persons and experienced a strike because of inadequate communication and worker alienation caused by the cooperative's large size. In response to this, the Mondragon cooperatives decided to keep the size of future cooperatives down to 500 members wherever possible.[39]

Ward and Vanek using the same model as that which suggested that cooperatives have a tendency to under-invest, also suggested that another reason for cooperatives remaining small is because, in times of increased demand, they would tend to increase prices instead of increasing production and employment as this would maximise income per worker. The argument goes like this: during times of increased demand, cooperative members would not increase productivity and employment because they would have to share their profits, thus reducing income per member. Instead, they would tend to maintain the same productivity and employment levels and increase prices, thus maximising the income per member by sharing larger profits between a constant work-force.[40] Once again, the case of Mondragon challenges this argument on a number of grounds. First, cooperative rules regulate wages as well as the distribution of surpluses. Secondly, Mondragon cooperatives have pursued a strategy of growth and, consequently, have increased production as well as employment. It has also been found that new members have not threatened the wage levels of the existing membership.[41] Mygind's research in Denmark also revealed that, in times of increased demand, cooperatives increased their output and employment in order to maintain market share and ability to compete.[42]

From a different perspective to that of Ward, Cornforth suggests that because cooperative shares are not linked to the value of the enterprise and cannot be traded, cooperatives lack the same incentive to grow as private businesses.[43] This argument too can be challenged because growth may mean getting a larger share of the market or becoming more competitive and thereby creating conditions for employment stability.

One way for cooperatives to compete in the market while remaining small or medium in size is by achieving economies of scale through interfirm collaboration. Once again, the Mondragon case, with the CLP at the centre of its activities, provides a good example of what can be achieved through a process of interfirm collaboration. Jordan also suggests the creation of cooperative support structures citing the consumer movement in Canada as a good example of economically successful cooperatives.[44]

One other way to overcome this problem is to encourage a cultural rethink of what democracy means in the workplace. Members have to decide whether they want their enterprise to grow and develop a decision-making process based on a mixture of direct and indirect democracy with a professional managerial team to provide guidance and expertise; or whether they wish their enterprise to remain small and choose direct democracy, possibly at the expense of economic stability. In the future, cooperatives may have to grow in size in order to compete effectively in the market and, simultaneously, may have to find new ways to improve participation in the workplace so that members do not feel alienated from the decision-making process. A cultural change in this direction may overcome the internal limits hindering growth.

Place of Cooperatives in the Economy

Most cooperatives are seen as having to face similar problems to those of small businesses. Cornforth has stated that, because cooperatives usually operated in sectors dominated by large firms or those which serve highly fragmented competitive markets, it was extremely difficult for them to expand beyond the small firms sector.[45]

The concentration of economic power can also be regarded as an obstacle for cooperative development. Bennett argues that one reason for Mondragon's success is that it had to compete against relatively small industrial firms.[46] Indeed, by the 1970s Mondragon cooperatives were slightly bigger in size than their private counterparts.[47] However, it would be too simple to equate cooperative success with an environment dominated by small firms. Having a local economy based on small firms may help the initial stages of cooperative development, but successful cooperatives have also shown that they can compete in the national and international markets. In the case of Mondragon, as has been shown, there have been a number of reasons for their success.

A number of suggestions have been made to improve the position of cooperatives in the economy. Thornley proposes that a quota system be applied like that operative in France which allocates a portion of public works to cooperatives provided that they are competitive.[48] Cornforth suggested that cooperatives should find niche markets within their sectors which enable them to produce high value-added products. For instance, in the textile sector they can produce high quality and specialist garments.[49]

Constraints on Takeovers

A further problem to the growth of cooperatives is the constraints imposed on them when taking over other firms, a major method of expansion practised by private firms. There are a number of such constraints. The financial and legal structure of cooperatives may limit their ability to grow or to take over other firms. In addition, problems may arise if they take over an enterprise with workers who have had no prior experience in working in a cooperative or knowledge of cooperative principles.[50] Joan Bennett suggested this to be a major reason for the demise of cooperatives. Her major study compared 32 cooperatives which were members of the Producers Federation with a similar sample of small businesses between 1950 and 1979. By 1979 she discovered that only 12 cooperatives were still in operation.[51] The remainder failed to survive not because they were inefficient but because:

> ...they have been squeezed out of the market because their potential outlets have been acquired by competitors, and because they are unable to grow to a sufficient size (being unable to acquire other firms) either to set up their own outlets; to have the strength to obtain a decent bargain with monopolistic buyers and to provide the range and flexibility of production available from large competitors.[52]

She concludes that cooperatives should have access to a protected market. Market protection, however, need not be the only remedy for cooperative growth. Nor should one assume that cooperatives must compete in the market as individual enterprises such as the producers cooperatives have done in the United Kingdom. Other ways to compete are available. In Canada, 350 retailing cooperatives have formed a Federation (Federated Cooperatives Limited). The federation helps local consumer cooperatives to plan and implement expansion by providing a range of services including: market assessment, labour planning and management development, product development and testing, advertising and promotion, manufacturing, computer system development and operation, government relations and coordinated planning for the whole consumer sector.[53]

The Mondragon experience also indicates that a number of support structures have helped cooperatives compete in the market. The CLP bank provides support services in the area of finance, management, engineering and marketing. Further support is also provided in respect of education (Hezibide Elkartea), research and technology (Ikerlan), social security (Lagun-Aro) and export promotion (Lankide Export).[54]

In addition, the Mondragon cooperatives have also managed to buy out private firms. In 1989, Ulgor acquired the Basque firm, Fabrelac, in the hope of maintaining its market leadership over its rivals. A year later, Fagor, became a major shareholder in the private foundry, Victorio Luzuriaga. In this latter instance, the national government, the Basque regional government and the provincial government of Navarre supported the transaction by paying early retirement compensation to some 447 workers.[55] The important point here is that a large cooperative has been able to take over a private firm either with its own finances, or, with the support of three tiers of government.

Discrimination

There are many forms of discrimination faced by cooperatives. Vanek has stated that cooperatives are seen as a threat by corporations, unions and bankers. Thus, bankers may not lend money to cooperatives and businesses may withhold supplies or not sell cooperative products.[56] The State is another institution which has discriminated against cooperatives. Laylock has stated that a reason why the national government in Canada has not actively supported cooperatives, when compared to its support of private businesses, is because the ministers and the bureaucrats who control public policy making and its implementation, are not familiar with cooperatives.[57] Cornforth argues that in Britain the taxation system and the law have discriminated against the cooperative system. In particular, the financial system has evolved to meet the needs of large private companies.[58]

While discrimination has occurred, it is also important to acknowledge that this need not be the case. If a cooperative is a viable enterprise then it will be in a bank's interest to lend it money. Private enterprises also need not be antagonistic toward cooperatives. If cooperative enterprises can provide raw materials or components at a cheaper rate than private competitors, then it will be in the economic interest of private enterprises to trade with cooperatives. If cooperatives produce products which are in high public demand and at competitive prices, then it is in the interest of private retailers to stock them. Similarly, cooperative retailers have long sold products made by private enterprises. Once again the Mondragon experience offers some examples. Ulgor's white goods products are sold throughout Spain and abroad by private retailers. The cooperative Guria sells equipment and produces components for Kawasaki of Japan. The cooperative Sorulace, in a joint venture with a Basque private firm which is 45% owned by Rolls Royce, produces a flexible manufacturing cell for jet engines.[59] Another example of cooperative-private firm collaboration is provided by the cooperative Oinakar which has purchased a licence to manufacture fork-lift components from Mitsubishi. Initially the cooperative is merely assembling components but with a view to manufacturing the whole product in the not too distant future.[60]

Evidence also suggests that the State may not necessarily discriminate against cooperatives. The State in the UK provided over £28.7 million between 1976 and 1986, which was used to fund various support structures and to provide loans for cooperatives. Mondragon has also benefited from the national, regional and local governments who have provided favourable legislation, tax concessions, loans, and funds for a number of projects. In France, the State provides loans and public works projects. In Quebec, the provincial government has provided $10 million to the Cooperative Development Society which has used it in providing loans, grants and managerial and planning assistance.[61] On the basis of this information, it is important not to judge the State *a priori*, but instead determine when the State is most likely to support cooperatives and how can the cooperative movement influence State policies to increase or enhance State support.

Some authors have attempted to understand the reasons why States have supported cooperatives. The cooperative experience in the United Kingdom has shown that the State at the national and local level supported cooperatives because it wanted to reduce unemployment. This was made possible by a supportive national Labour government in the 1970s and by Labour controlled local councils in the 1980s. David Laylock suggests that the Quebec government, unlike the national government of Canada, supported cooperatives because first, the government wanted to create employment through them, and, secondly, a number of ministers and government bureaucrats supported the idea of cooperation.[62]

Considering the important influence that the State can have on cooperative development through its power to regulate the market, provide finance, enact favourable tax legislation and give access to its resources and public works, it is important for cooperative movements to find ways to influence the State. A major study in this area has been conducted by Laylock. He has tried to understand government-cooperative relations by looking at the ways the cooperative movement in Canada has tried to influence governments. He found that a number of factors minimised the impact cooperatives have had on national public policy. First, the cooperative movement in Canada has generally held an anti-State attitude. Second, the different sectoral interests within the cooperative sector has ensured that the cooperative movement has not developed a clear policy regarding the role the State should play both in the economy and in cooperative development. Third, the cooperative movement has not developed substantial and continuous relations with politicians and government departments and bureaucrats. Usually lobbying has been *ad hoc* to seek support for cooperatives in crisis or for taxation concessions, but little has been done to influence the overall orientation of government policy. In this study, Laylock also identified that the federalist nature of the Canadian State increases the financial burden of lobbying. In addition, four key ministries were identified as having most of the power over public policy making. These were: the Privy Council Office, the Prime Minister's Office, the Treasury and the Department of Finance.[63]

The findings made by Cornforth, and, to a greater extent, by Laylock, are of immense importance because they identify a need to lobby and influence the State in the interest of cooperative development. In doing so, it is important for cooperatives to have a unitary policy, identify agencies of representation (Ministers and political parties), understand the specific character of the nation States (federalism), the manner and process of how decisions are made and influence the ministries and bureaucrats who contribute to government policies.

They also identified that the State is more likely to support cooperatives in times of economic recession. This poses a number of challenges to cooperative movements in getting the State to recognise their legitimate interests. First, they must become economically viable movements capable of creating employment. Second, they must have a large membership capable of influencing elections. Third, they must create alliances with political parties which support a strong cooperative role in the economy. Fourth, they must become influential in the discourse of ideas and policy debates so bureaucrats and politicians will consider their interests when formulating government policies.

Limits and Validity of the Discussion on Problems Faced by Cooperatives

The main point to emerge from this discussion is that extreme caution should be taken in applying any conclusions from a previous study to a new situation given that the studies cited have been conducted in various countries at different times. Caution should also be taken when analysing research conducted by authors using a single disciplinary approach, such as economists, as they are inadequate to explain a complex phenomenon such as cooperatives. In all, five major concerns have emerged from this discussion. First, the hypothesis advanced by Ward, Vanek and Mead is based on a pure theoretical model and it has little relevance to cooperatives as they actually operate. Second, it is important to note when the research was conducted and place it in its proper temporal and historical setting. For instance, the Webbs conducted their research early this century and reported it in 1914. While their findings may be true for that period, the conditions under which cooperatives operate today are different: for instance, working people are more educated than they were then and have more access to knowledge and information.

Third, when discussing forms of discrimination, it is assumed *a priori* that the State and private enterprises discriminate and are hostile to cooperatives. Underlying this assumption is a tendency to see private business as having irreconcilable differences with cooperatives. Similarly, the State is seen as being an institution supportive of capitalism and hostile or indifferent to cooperatives. Empirical evidence suggests that in both cases this is not always true.

The fourth major point is that most of the problems identified have derived from studies conducted mainly on small cooperative enterprises competing in the market as individual entities. The majority of examples have been taken from the British experience where the average size of cooperatives is less than 10 employees and there is little linkage between them. The smallness of these cooperatives is a major reason for cooperatives not being able to overcome problems associated with cooperative development.

Finally, this discussion once again highlighted the nation specific aspects of cooperative development. Lindkvist and Westenholz' study of the Scandinavian cooperative sector should be viewed in the light of cooperatives having to operate within a culture hostile to the collective entrepreneur and a society which has been accustomed to low unemployment and a strong Welfare State system. Thus, it is important to consider the relationship that has evolved between the State, society and the economy and how this has effected cooperative development in each country, without generalising, because the conditions between countries are different.

In spite of the above qualifications, the various obstacles which many authors have identified to explain the low level of cooperative activity in an economy are relevant to analysing the viability of a cooperative sector. These problems, although not attributable only to cooperatives, are factors which influence every stage of cooperative development and which must be overcome if cooperatives are to survive and grow in a market economy. Therefore, it is important to discover how successful cooperative movements have managed to react to and overcome these problems.

As already identified, cooperative support structures and the State are two major means which cooperatives have used to overcome these problems. The role of support structures is a widely developed theme by authors of this field. The various experiences already cited, in particular that of Mondragon, have shown that, through support structures, cooperatives can have access to finance, managerial expertise, entrepreneurial talent and improve their economic position by seeking economies of scale through interfirm collaboration. Thus, it is vital that various support structures be created to support the individual cooperatives.

The State has also been identified as an institution which can aid cooperative development by providing tax concessions, access to public works and other forms of financial support. The important role that the State can play must be understood by cooperative movements as well as when the State is most likely to support cooperatives, which departments hold power, how to lobby successfully ministers and bureaucrats and how to get parliamentary support from political parties. It has been suggested that to influence successfully the State, cooperative movements must develop a unitary policy, become large enough to be able to influence the election results, form alliances with political parties and develop the capacity to create employment.

Conclusion

Chapter one established that cooperatives could not be considered as having failed because of the experience of Mondragon and the resurgence of cooperatives since the mid-1970s. This chapter sought to analyse the factors which have prevented cooperatives from becoming economically viable and from developing into strong sectors of their local or national economies. Seven major obstacles were discussed and while some of the reasons given to describe cooperative failures are inappropriate or of limited effect, Cornforth's categorisation has been found to be a good tool of analysis regarding the viability of cooperative enterprises in a market economy. The research that follows will provide details of how La Lega's cooperatives have managed to overcome these obstacles by exploring the relationship that has developed between the individual cooperative enterprise, cooperative support structures and the State.

Notes

1 Connell M Fanning and Thomas McCarthy, "A Survey of Economic Hypotheses Concerning the Non-Viability of Labour-Directed Firms in Capitalist Economies", in Sune Jansson and Ann-Britt Hellmark (eds), *Labor-Owned Firms and Workers' Cooperatives*, Gower, Aldershot, 1986, pp.7-50.

2 Chris Cornforth, "The Role of Support Organisations in Developing Worker Co-operatives: A Model for Promoting Economic and Industrial Democracy?", in Georgy Széll et al., (eds), *The State, Trade Unions and Self Management: Issues of Competence and Control,* Walter De Gruyter, Berlin, 1989, pp.109-115.

3 George Melnyk, "Future Directions for Worker Cooperatives: a Postscript", in Jack Quarter and George Melnyk (eds), *Partnership in Enterprise: The Worker Ownership Phenomenon*, Black Rose Books, Montreal, 1989, p.194.

4 Peter Abell, "The Viability of Industrial Producer Co-operation", in Colin Crouch and Frank Heller (eds), *International Yearbook of Organisational Democracy*, John Wiley and Sons, London, 1983, p.83.
5 *Ibid.*, p.88.
6 Howard Aldricht and Robert Stern; "Resource Mobilization and the Creation of US Producer's Cooperatives, 1835-1935", *Economic and Industrial Democracy*, Volume 4, London, 1983, p.387.
7 Lars Lindkvist and Ann Westenholz (ed), *Employee Owned Companies in the Nordic Countries: An Historical Parenthesis or a Future Possibility*, Nordic Council of Ministers, Copenhagen 1987, p.21.
8 Jack Quarter, "Starting Worker-Owned Enterprises: Problems and Prospects", in Jack Quarter and George Melnyk (eds), *Partnership in Enterprise: The Worker Ownership Phenomenon*, Black Rose Books, Montreal, 1989, p.37.
9 Rob Paton, *Reluctant Entrepreneurs*, Open University Press, Milton Keynes, 1989, pp. 107-108.
10 For more details see section on Mondragon's Support Structures in Chapter 2.
11 Aldrich and Stern, *op.cit.*, p.387.
12 William Foote Whyte and Kathleen King Whyte, *Making Mondragon: The Growth and Dynamics of the Worker Cooperative Complex,* ILR Press, New York, Second Edition, 1991, pp. 216-217.
13 Fanning and Mc Carthy, *op.cit.*, p.23.
14 Chris Cornforth, *op.cit.*, pp.112-113.
15 Alan Thomas, "Financing Worker Cooperatives in EC Countries", in *Annals of Public and Cooperative Economics*, Volume 61, Number 2-3, April-September 1990, pp.179-180.
16 Benjamin Ward, "The Firm in Illyria: Market Syndicalism", *The American Economic Review*, Volume XLV11, June 1958, Number 3, pp.570-571. Jaroslav Vanek, "The Basic Theory of Financing Participatory Firms", Working Paper Number 27, Cornell University, Department of Economics, Ithaca, July 1971, in Jaroslav Vanek (ed), *Self Management: Economic Liberation of Man*, Penguin Books, Harmondsworth, 1975, pp.445-455.
17 Christopher S Axworthy, *Worker Co-operatives in Mondragon, the U.K. and France; Some Reflections*, Occasional Paper, Centre for the Study of Cooperatives, University of Saskatchewan, Saskatoon, 1985, p.31.
18 Niels Mygind, "From the Illyrian Firm to the Reality of Self-Management", in Sune Jansson and Ann-Britt Hellmark (eds), *Labor-Owned Firms and Workers' Cooperatives*, Gower, Aldershot, p.99.
19 Chloe Munro, *The Financing of Worker Cooperatives*, CRU Monograph Number 8, Open University, Milton Keynes, 1988, p.30.
20 *Ibid.*
21 Chris Cornforth et al., *Developing Successful Worker Cooperatives,* Sage Publications, London, 1988, p.217.
22 Axworthy, *op.cit.*, p.8.
23 Cornforth et al., *Developing Successful Worker Cooperatives*, *op.cit.*, p.215.
24 Robert Oakeshott, *The Case for Workers' Cooperatives*, Routledge and Kegan Paul, London, 1978, p. 191.
25 Whyte and Whyte, *op.cit.*, pp.159-160.
26 Axworthy, *op.cit.*, p.6.

27 Melissa A Moye, "Mondragon: Adapting Co-operative Structures to Meet the Demands of a Changing Environment", *Economic and Industrial Democracy,* Volume 14, 1993, pp.264-268.
28 Axworthy, *op.cit.*, p.38.
29 For general overview see Fanning and McCarthy, *op.cit.*, pp.30-39.
30 James Edward Mead, "The Theory of Labour-Managed Firms and Profit Sharing", *The Economic Journal*, Volume 82, March 1972, p.426.
31 Cornforth et al., *op.cit., Developing Successful Cooperatives*, p.91.
32 Cornforth, *op.cit.*, "The Role of Support Organisations in Developing Worker Co-operatives: A Model for Promoting Economic and Industrial Democracy?", pp.111-112.
33 Edward S Greenberg, "Producer Cooperatives and Democratic Theory: The Case of the Plywood Firms", Robert Jackall and Henry Levin (eds), *Worker Cooperatives in America*, University of California Press, Berkeley, 1984, p.178.
34 This happened at the Clothing Co-op in the U.K. See, Cornforth et al., *Developing Successful Cooperatives*, p.86.
35 *Ibid.*, p.219.
36 Christopher B Meek and Warner P Woodworth, "Technical Training and Enterprise: Mondragon's Educational System and its Implications for Other Cooperatives", *Economic and Industrial Democracy*, Volume 11, 1990, pp.511-525.
37 Chris Cornforth, "The Role of Managers in Worker Co-operatives", in *Yearbook of Cooperative Enterprise 1989,* Plunkett Foundation, Oxford, 1989, pp.13-22.
38 Joyce Rothschild-Whitt, "The Collectivist Organisation: An Alternative to Rational Bureaucratic Models", *American Sociological Review*, Volume 44, 1979, p.521.
39 Thomas and Logan, *op.cit.*, p.35.
40 Ward, *op.cit.*, p.575. Vanek, *op.cit.*, p.448. Mead, *op.cit.*, p.409.
41 Moye, *op.cit.*, p.255.
42 Mygind, *op.cit.*, p.83.
43 Cornforth, *op.cit.*, *Developing Successful Cooperatives*, p.223.
44 John Jordan, "A System of Interdependent Firms as a Development Strategy", in Sune Jansson and Ann-Britt Hellmark (ed), *Labor-Owned Firms and Workers' Cooperatives*, Gower, Aldershot, 1986, p.109.
45 See Cornforth et al., *op.cit.*, *Developing Successful Cooperatives,* pp.24-39; and Cornforth., *op.cit.*, "The Role of Support Organisations in Developing Worker Co-operatives: A Model for Promoting Economic and Industrial Democracy?", p.114.
46 Joan Bennett, *Producer Cooperatives: A Case for Market Protection,* Centre for Research in Industrial Democracy and Participation, University of Glasgow, 1984, pp.22-23.
47 Thomas and Logan, *op.cit.*, p.117.
48 Jenny Thornley, *Workers' Co-Operatives: Jobs and Dreams*, Heinemann Educational Books, London, 1982, p.146.
49 Cornforth, *op.cit.*, "The Role of Support Organisations in Developing Worker Co-Operatives: A Model for Promoting Economic and Industrial Democracy?", p.115.
50 Chris Cornforth and Alan Thomas, "Cooperative Development: Barriers, Support Structures and Cultural Factors", Editorial Introduction, *Economic and Industrial Democracy*, Volume 11, 1990, p. 456.
51 Bennett, *op.cit*, p.11.
52 *Ibid.*, pp.24-25.
53 Jordan, *op.cit.*, p.109.

54 Ma Jesus Zabaleta, "Mondragon: Un'Esperienza Integrata", in Anna Avitabile et al., *Cooperare e Competere*, Feltrinelli, Milano, 1986, pp.20-25.
55 Whyte and Whyte, pp.209-210.
56 Jaroslav Vanek, *The General Theory of Labour Managed Market Economies*, Ithaca, Cornell University Press, New York, p.38, in Cornforth, *op.cit.*, "The Role of Support Organisations in Developing Worker Cooperatives: A Model for Promoting Economic and Industrial Democracy?" p.113.
57 David Laylock, *Co-operative-Government Relations in Canada: Lobbying, Public Policy Development and the Changing Co-operative System*, Centre for the Study of Cooperatives, University of Saskatchewan, Saskatoon, 1987, pp.155-156.
58 Cornforth, *op.cit.*, "The Role of Support Organisations in Developing Worker Co-operatives: A Model for Promoting Economic and Industrial Democracy?", p.113.
59 Whyte and Whyte, *op.cit.*, pp.208-209.
60 Greg MacLeod, "Worker Co-Ops and Community Economic Development", in Jack Quarter and George Melnyk (eds), *Partnership in Enterprise: The Worker Ownership Phenomenon*, Black Rose Books, Montreal, 1989, p.187.
61 Laylock, *op.cit.*, p.140.
62 *Ibid.*, pp.140-142.
63 *Ibid.*, pp.155-156.

4 La Lega, an Historical Account: 1850-1992

This chapter will analyse the birth and the evolution of La Lega. It will also show the development of the relationship between La Lega, cooperatives and the State and identify factors that have helped the Italian cooperatives overcome some of the problems they face in a market economy operating within a liberal democratic State. The overall purpose is to introduce La Lega and the political, economic and social environment in which it operates and set the scene for the elaboration of the main themes in subsequent chapters.

This chapter has been divided into seven parts. The first part deals with the period between 1850 to 1900. This is followed by what is generally regarded as the golden years of cooperation in Italy spanning from 1901 to 1921. The next period (1921-1943) analyses cooperatives under Fascism, generally regarded as the dark years of cooperation in Italy. The fourth part explains the rebirth of cooperatives after the fall of Fascism covering the years 1943-1947. The "Cold War" years of 1948 to 1962 will be analysed next. The sixth part covers the period between 1963 to 1979 during which La Lega's cooperatives experienced continuous growth. The final period (1980-1992), investigates how La Lega's cooperatives have managed the turbulent changes with the European and world economy.

The Birth of Cooperatives 1850-1900

The Italian cooperative movement, like its counterparts in Britain and the rest of Europe, was born in response to the upheavals caused by the industrial revolution and urbanisation. This new economic order created economic insecurities for working people and dissatisfaction with a political and economic system that did not provide for their basic needs such as an adequate wage, food and shelter. Cooperatives were formed to overcome these basic problems.

Early Years

The first forms of associations formed by workers were Mutual Aid Societies. These were often promoted by philanthropists, aristocrats and notables in response to the problems caused by industrialisation in the cities. Since the State had not yet developed welfare provisions for its citizens, mutual aid societies were formed to provide members with a series of social security support measures such as health cover, unemployment benefits, pension and shelter. These mutual societies were the embryonic stage of what later became known as the Welfare State. They also were breeding grounds for trade unions and cooperatives.[1]

The first cooperatives were formed in the cities most affected by industrialisation. In response to high food prices, the first consumer cooperative was formed in Turin in 1854. The cooperative was managed by a mutual aid society which got the idea from a similar experience taking place in Switzerland. After one year of operation it had attracted 7,000 members and was selling food 30% to 40% below the market price.[2] Consumer cooperatives soon became very popular and spread throughout Italy, but with uneven pricing outcomes. Some sold food at cost prices without making any profit. Others set aside part of the profits for a social security fund. However, most cooperatives soon adopted the Rochdale model of selling at market prices and paying members a yearly dividend.[3] The early promoters of consumer cooperatives were mainly artisans who feared being marginalised by large businesses. Later workers and peasants also began to form consumer cooperatives.

The cities were also the hosts for the first popular banks. The founder of these banks was Luigi Luzzatti who, after having visited Germany in 1864, began to set up banks in Italy based on the Schulze-Delitzsch model with minor modifications. Contrary to the Schultze-Delitzsch model, Luzzatti adopted limited liability, small numbers of shares per member, and supported the development of popular banks into all purpose banks.[4] The purpose was to help small businesses by providing them access to cheap loans to improve their economic competitiveness. The first popular bank was formed in 1864, and by 1902 there were 736 present throughout Italy.[5]

The first producer cooperative was formed in 1854 by the glass blowers of Altare, a town in the region of Liguria. These were collectively owned cooperatives. Many other artisans such as printers, stone masons, carpenters and local carvers soon followed. As with consumer cooperatives, the characteristics of these cooperatives differed. The Altare glass blowers cooperative was dominated by a few families who did not allow people from other municipalities to be admitted as members. The Cooperative Society of Crockery and Majolica of Imola, near Bologna, had an open membership and distributed profits also to casual workers. The Construction Cooperative of Cesena (in the region of Emilia Romagna) distributed its profits as follows: 50% to shareholders; 35% reserve fund; 10% to a pension fund for retired workers and their widows and children; and 5% for health cover. Others allowed external shareholders to invest in cooperatives. In many cooperatives the number of shareholders exceeded the member-workers by 10:1. This was clearly reflected in the distribution of profits which mostly went to remunerate capital. Indeed, a study of 15 cooperatives conducted in 1887 found that 54% of profits were assigned to capital while worker members only received 14.18% on average.[6] There is no doubt that some of these early forms of cooperatives were not open to all citizens, some resembled joint stock companies while others showed signs of social responsibility.

A different type of worker cooperative was formed in the countryside by landless labourers of the Po Valley in Northern Italy. In the 1880s, as a result of wheat imports from the United States and Russia and the high tariff barriers which protected industries, there was a flow of investments from the rural areas to the cities. In addition, labour extensive agricultural production began to appear and in the process it created a large number of unemployed or casually employed landless labourers. The lack of industries in nearby areas and the labourers' unwillingness to emigrate exacerbated the unemployment problem.[7] By 1900, in Emilia Romagna alone, landless labourers comprised 55% to 60% of the population.[8] To overcome unemployment, labourers formed building cooperatives to perform public works such as clearing swamps, building roads and public buildings. These were the cooperatives which were the most radical and later supported the trade union movement and the Socialist party.

Along with labour cooperatives, Socialists also formed cooperatives known as "Affittanze Collettive". Literally it translates as "Collective Rental". These were cooperatives formed by landless peasants whose purpose was to buy or rent property from private owners and the local councils. These properties were then managed collectively and the work was evenly distributed among its members. The first of these cooperatives was formed in 1888 by the landless labourers of Ravenna. One cooperative from Fabbrico, in Reggio Emilia, had 500 members and managed to increase the hours worked by each member in a year from 800 to 3,000-4,000. Each member had one non-transferable share. The profits were distributed as follows: 20% to members' shares, 40% according to members in proportion to their work, and 40% in reserves. The most famous of this type of cooperative was the Federcoop of Ravenna which by 1915 managed 3,150 hectares of land.[9]

In the rural areas, the Conservatives and Catholics were also prominent supporters of cooperatives. The Conservative Leone Wollemberg created the first rural bank in 1883 based on the German Raiffeisen model. The purpose of these was to lend money to rural farmers at low interest rates. There were no shareholders and profits were ploughed back in the reserve funds. Following Wollemberg's example, the Catholics too promoted rural banks. By 1915 there were 2,594 rural banks in Italy, 2,002 of which were set up by Catholics.[10]

In addition to the rural banks Conservatives and Catholics supported farmers in other ways. Since 1856 Conservatives promoted consortia in the countryside to bulk-buy seeds and fertilisers and reduce costs for the farmer. Catholics created service cooperatives such as dairy cooperatives or wine making cooperatives and bakeries. The dairy cooperatives in particular became very popular. Farmers either used the cooperative's facilities to process milk into cheese or would sell the produce to the cooperative which in turn would process and sell it.[11]

Ideologies and Cooperatives

The history of the cooperative movement has always been influenced by political parties and ideologies. The role that cooperatives were to play in society was hotly debated between different traditions representing social classes and different political projects. Four major ideologies can be identified: the Conservatives, Republicans, Socialists and Catholics.

As has been stated, the first to promote cooperatives in the cities were the enlightened Aristocracy and Conservatives. They had been greatly influenced by the French upheavals of 1848 and 1870, consequently they viewed cooperatives as a way to reduce social tensions. Their promotion of mutual aid societies, consumer cooperatives, popular banks and later, housing cooperatives, was geared to increase the support of working people for the liberal State and capitalist system. Their actions were mainly directed at those sectors of the population which were better off, such as artisans, public servants and retailers. The major figure of the Conservative camp was Luigi Luzzatti, the founder of popular banks. As it will be seen later, when he became Minister of Treasury he promoted many laws in favour of cooperatives. The Conservative forces were dominant in the mutual aid societies and remained influential in the cooperative movement until 1896. The first challenge their power came from Mazzini's Republicans.

The second major ideology comes from the Republican Mazzini. Mazzini had been living in exile in Britain during the 1840s and was aware of the achievements of the Rochdale pioneers and of Robert Owen's ideas. When he returned to Italy he continued to keep in contact with Holyoake, one of the leaders of the English cooperative movement. Mazzini believed that human beings should have access to the fruits of their labour and cooperatives were a means to achieve this. He viewed cooperatives as forming the basis of a new economic system and a new democratic society. The State was to play a central role in this transformation by providing cooperatives with loans, by distributing land, by allowing them access to public works and by changing the taxation system. He was against class struggle and believed instead in a gradual transformation of society through the consensus of all social classes within a democratic State.[12]

Mazzini believed that mutual aid societies (in which the Mazzinians were the dominant party since 1862), and cooperatives, because of their large membership, were also a political force which needed to contribute to the unification of Italy and to the democratisation of Italian society. The objective was to replace the Liberal/Monarchical State based on limited suffrage with a Republican/Democratic State based on universal suffrage.[13]

The third group is the Socialists. On the whole the Socialists agreed with Mazzini, but questioned whether change could come through social consensus. The repression of the Paris Commune, the undemocratic character of the Liberal State, and the repressive measures often used by the Italian State toward workers confirmed the Socialists' scepticism. However, this group was not homogeneous in its views toward cooperatives. Party leaders like Turati and Labriola were mainly concerned with political action and revolutionary activity though the Socialist party. To them cooperatives were a means to distract workers from the class struggle and a means used by Conservatives to defeat the Socialists.[14] Andrea Costa of Imola offered a different view. He was in favour of cooperatives and proposed collaboration between cooperatives, trade unions and the party to win local and national elections and then use the available resources from the national State and, mainly from the local councils, to help improve people's working and living conditions. It is not surprising that the first local council to be administered in Italy by Socialists was that of Imola.[15] Prampolini of Reggio Emilia proposed another version of cooperative development. He wanted to create cooperative republics centred around consumer cooperatives, producer cooperatives and cooperative banks.[16] In spite of these differences, all

Socialists supported cooperatives, acknowledging that these were an anti-capitalist form of organisation; educated workers in the management of their own enterprises; and supported ideas of liberty and equality.[17]

The fourth major influence on the Italian cooperative movement were the Catholics who, since 1874, concentrated their cooperative activities in the rural areas, especially in the region of Veneto. Hence the major contribution by Catholics was to create agricultural cooperatives which tended to reduce costs and market farmers' products. This was supported by rural banks which provided the small farmer and artisans with cheap loans.[18] In this strategy the protection of private property was directly linked to the preservation of the family unit which was being threatened by capitalism. The action of the Catholics toward cooperatives and working people increased after 1891 when Pope Leo the 13th launched the *Encyclica Rerum Novarum* which encouraged Catholics to take an interests in social issues and to participate in parliamentary elections. Fearful of the Socialists, the Encyclica stated that private property was part of the natural order and denounced class struggle. Within this context Catholics have seen cooperatives as a way to correct the inequalities and imbalances caused by the capitalist system. Their strategy was to create an interclass alliance to curb Socialist influence in the countryside.[19]

The Birth of La Lega Nazionale delle Cooperative

In 1886, a group of Lombard notables led by Luzzatti promoted the Federation of Italian Cooperatives. In all, 248 cooperatives from various sectors of the economy representing 74,000 members attended the first congress.[20] In 1893, at the fifth congress, the name was changed to the National League of Cooperatives (La Lega Nazionale delle Cooperative usually known as La Lega) which it still holds today. The early history of La Lega was dominated by the Conservatives and the followers of Mazzini. They concentrated mainly on influencing the State to pass legislation in favour of cooperatives. In particular they sought tax concessions, access to public works and financial support. They saw cooperatives as an end in themselves and did not see them as part of a wider social movement intent on changing the political and economic system. This often placed them at odds with the Socialists who were a minority.

During this early stage of cooperative development La Lega successfully influenced the State to pass legislation favourable to cooperatives. Cooperatives had been legally recognised in 1882. Luzzatti, then member of parliament, promoted and drafted this legislation. The 1882 law granted cooperatives which were less than five years old and that had less than 30,000 lire as capital, exemption from stamp duty. In addition, it stipulated that: the election of the board of management had to be based on the principle of one person one vote; the manager had to be a member of the cooperative and members' shares could vary between 100 to 5,000 lire.[21]

The major legislation in favour of cooperatives was the law relating to public works passed in 1899. This law was made in response to the high unemployment in the countryside and once again was promoted by Luzzatti who was then the Treasurer in the national government.[22] This law allowed cooperatives to bid for public contracts directly with the State and local authorities by-passing the intermediaries. It permitted the public authorities to sign contracts without recourse to competitive tender for sums not exceeding 100,000 lire and exempted cooperatives from the usual requirements of putting up bonds. Further requirements included: a periodic deduction of 10% from the payments to be used as bond; cooperatives had to be registered with the local prefecture; the majority of members had to be workers; no subcontracting was allowed; interest paid on members' shares was restricted to a maximum of 5%; the surplus was to be redistributed according to the amount of work done; non members could be hired under exceptional circumstances and they too had a right to receive part of the surplus according to work performed.[23] This policy of creating employment through public works helped the formation of Labour cooperatives in rural areas especially in Emilia Romagna and Veneto. Indeed, in the first two years these two regions obtained 70% (Emilia Romagna 33%, Veneto 37%) of all the work allocated to cooperatives which amounted to 4.8 million lire. By 1896, 180 cooperatives had access to public works worth 13 million lire.[24]

The policy of public works was implemented to appease conflicts in the countryside which was undergoing a period of crisis and transformation. In doing so it created many cooperatives influenced by Socialists which in turn began to influence La Lega. The Socialist influence was also growing in the rest of society. The Italian Workers' Party was formed in 1892 which three years later was renamed the Italian Socialist Party. In 1891 the first Camera del Lavoro (Workers' Association) was formed in Milan. These Workers' Association preoccupied themselves with every aspect of workers' needs such as employment, food, housing, and democratic rights. Usually they became the meeting place for unions, the Socialist party and cooperative organisations. Individual workers and peasants were members of all three.[25]

The industrialisation of the Italian economy and the rise of an industrial and rural proletariat influenced the composition of La Lega. In 1896, 254 cooperatives were affiliated to La Lega of which 111 (44%) were consumer cooperatives and 98 (38%) were producer and labour cooperatives (33 of which were landless labourers' cooperatives). Within the consumer and the producer and labour cooperatives, the influence of blue-collar workers and landless labourers was increasing at the expense of public servants and artisans. As a consequence, in 1896 the Socialists almost formed the majority of the elected members to La Lega's executive. Another interesting statistic to emerge is that most cooperatives (72%) were situated in Northern Italy, while 23% were present in Central Italy and only 5% in Southern Italy. The regions with the highest numbers of cooperatives were Lombardy (34%), Tuscany (14.3%), Piedmont (13%) and Emilia Romagna (10.2%).[26] These characteristics made La Lega an association representing mainly Northern Italian cooperatives, in particular those in the consumer and construction sector. Another factor which emerged is that only a minority of cooperatives had joined La Lega. Indeed, by 1896 there were some 3,698 cooperatives present throughout Italy and only 254 had joined La Lega.[27]

In the late 1890s the State became authoritarian and halted the democratisation of Italian society which had begun in 1854 when freedom of association was granted to the population. A banking scandal, conflicts with France over tariffs, a humiliating war defeat in Ethiopia, and a dramatic increase in the price of wheat led to rioting in Milan and in particular Sicily. In 1894, the State responded by banning the Socialist party and the workers' associations. During the rioting in Milan, the police fired on the crowd killing 80 and wounding another 450. Many cooperatives were closed. Consumer cooperatives were singled out because the authorities thought they were encouraging subversive activity.[28]

The Golden Years 1900-1920

A New Political Climate

The repression of the 1890s further radicalised La Lega. It became clear that the development of cooperation had to be linked with democratic rights. This led to La Lega taking a greater interest in parliamentary elections and to work closer with the Socialist party and workers' associations. As the industrialisation continued, the workers' movement became the focal point of the left and replaced the Mazzinian Republicans as the representatives of the aspirations of working people. Proof of the Socialists' growth in popularity was the fact that they successfully led a number of strikes in the cities and the countryside. In 1900 the first general strike was called in Genoa. In the urban areas, the Socialists called 1,034 strikes in 1901 in which 189,000 turned out and 801 in 1902 which had the support of 196,000 strikers. In the rural areas, for the same years, 222,000 and 189,000 respectively turned out. Workers' associations were spreading throughout the country and in 1902 they had over 270,000 members.[29] With industry increasing its share of the country's Gross Domestic Product (GDP) from 19% in 1901 to 23% in 1911 and agriculture declining from 48.2% to 42.8%, the industrial proletariat was increasing in numbers. In response to this, the trade union organisation Confederazione dei Lavoratori Italiani (National Confederation of Italian Labour) was formed in 1906 and was prominent in organising strikes throughout the 1910s.[30]

The growing influence of the Socialists was also felt at national and local elections. At the 1882 elections even though only 2,017,829 (6.9% of the entire population) were eligible to vote, Andrea Costa became the first Socialist to be elected in parliament. In 1913, universal male suffrage was introduced and the number of eligible voters had reached 8,443,205. In this election left candidates won 169 out of 473 seats in parliament. However, the voting pattern showed that while on a national scale the Socialists received 13% of the vote, in Emilia Romagna their share of the vote rose to 45%. The Socialists obtained more than 13% of votes also in Lombardy, Tuscany, Liguria and Piedmont.[31] At the local level, Socialists also began to win local elections. In 1899 many local councils were governed by left coalitions. In 1914, the local councils of Bologna and Milan were governed by the Socialists, indicating an increasing level of power in Italian society. In the same year 34 out of 65 local councils in the province of Bologna were governed by Socialists.[32]

The inability of the State to stem the rise of the workers' movement and Socialism led to the formation of a more accommodating government led by the liberal Giolitti. Giolitti conceded that the influence of the Socialists was bound to increase as Italy industrialised. He began to acknowledge the legitimacy of the aspirations of the Socialist party and the working people and offered them the opportunity to influence the government's economic and political decisions, hoping that by this concession they would turn away from revolutionary activity. His overall aim was to promote economic growth in which business would make profits and workers would improve their wages and working conditions under the leadership of the Liberals.[33] His years in office between 1903 to 1914 led to the enactment of progressive legislation in favour of working people, the introduction of universal male suffrage in 1912 and many laws in favour of cooperatives.

The Triple Alliance

Within this emerging new political and economic reality, La Lega adopted a new strategy. In the past it relied on the support of parliamentarians, mainly Liberals and Republicans, to get State support. La Lega now became part of a broad alliance which included the trade union movement and the mutual aid societies. The overall aim of these three organisations was to improve the living conditions of working people. This resulted in these organisations forming the Triple Alliance in 1907 with a political programme aimed at improving working conditions in the work place, reducing working hours, introducing social security measures, especially the old age pension, and supporting cooperatives through public works, tax concessions and credit. Through this broad alliance and the support La Lega could get from Socialists, Liberal and Republican parliamentarians it sought to influence the State at the local and national level. As a consequence, it became more and more active in local and national elections. From the local councils it sought public works, land for agricultural cooperatives, housing and lower taxes. In areas like Emilia Romagna it relied on Socialist-run local councils to deliver these policies. At the national level it sought to influence the State through a lobby group called "Friends of Cooperation" formed by parliamentarians who supported cooperatives. This group was officially formed in 1905 and by 1909 it boasted 60 members from various parties. Further, La Lega had a representative on three major State commissions. In 1896 it had already been invited to be part of the Commission for Industry and Commerce, in 1901 it joined the Commission on Emigration and two years later it became a member of the Commission on Labour Reform.[34]

Cooperative Legislation

During Giolitti's reign the government passed some 12 laws which supported cooperative activity. Some were specific to certain sectors such as fishing, wine making and agriculture. Others were directed at disadvantaged regions such as Sicily and Basilicata. One law was passed in relation to cooperatives' bidding for railway works. Another increased the maximum value of public works which could sign with cooperatives without recourse to competitive tender from 100,000 to 200,000 lire. In 1903, a law was passed which provided cheap loans and tax concessions to housing cooperatives. In 1909, a very important law was passed which enabled cooperatives to set up consortia when bidding for public contracts thus increasing their economic competitiveness.[35] In 1913, the National Institute of Cooperative Credit was formed with 7.75 billion lire of capital at its disposal. It is estimated that between 1914-1924 this Institute provided 10 billion lire worth of credit to cooperatives.[36]

During this period the public works concessions continued. It was estimated that between 1889 and 1909 a total of 4,426 public works were assigned to cooperatives worth a total of 89 million lire. Once again, statistics show that 86.2% of the total were assigned to cooperatives from Northern Italy, of which 50.1% went to Emilia Romagna.[37] Between 1910 and 1912 Emilia Romagna's share had increased to 58.34%. In some provinces the percentage of public works assigned to cooperatives between 1910-1912 was higher than the average, for instance: Ferrara (89%), Ravenna (85%), Bologna (76%).[38] As stated earlier, these were areas where unemployment was very high and where workers and landless peasants were best organised, prompting a response by the State to appease tensions. It is also important to note that most of the public works in Italy were being performed by private enterprises. Galasso notes that between 1889 to 1907 only 5.6% of the total public works were assigned to cooperatives.[39]

The growth of the Socialists and the closer relations between them and La Lega led to a changed balance of power within La Lega in favour of Socialist forces. In 1912 the Socialist Vergnanini was elected secretary. In 1914 Italy was about to enter the war against the Austrians. There was a lively debate within the left whether to support or not to support the war. La Lega chose neutrality, but once Italy entered the war it chose to cooperate with the Italian State. Consequently it developed a programme to create welfare institutions, child care centres to enable women to join the work-force, and sought public works from the Ministry of Defence and other public ministries.[40]

La Lega restructured its organisation in response to the war economy. In 1908 it moved its central office from Milan to Rome. It had restructured vertically by forming a National Federation of Producer and Worker Cooperatives with a central office in Rome; a National Federation of Consumer Cooperatives with its head office in Milan and a similar organisation for the agricultural cooperatives with its central office in Bologna. The federation of producer and worker cooperatives was most successful in obtaining public works totalling 10 million lire in 1916 alone. In addition, consortia for the consumer, agriculture and producer sector were already set up. The best organised was the consumer sector. Modelled on the English Wholesale Society it had formed 13 consortia to cater for 1,311 consumer cooperatives.[41]

Growth and Divisions Within the Cooperative Movement

The size of the cooperative movement increased dramatically during the first twenty years of the 20th century. The number of cooperatives operating in Italy increased from 2,199 in 1902 to 7,429 in 1914, reaching a high of 15,099 in July 1920.[42] Those affiliated to La Lega jumped from 639 in 1902, to 2,132 in 1914 to 8,000 in May 1920.[43] The 8,000 cooperatives were comprised of 3,600 consumer cooperatives, 2,700 producer and labour cooperatives, 700 agricultural cooperatives and 1,000 cooperatives operating in other sectors. The total membership was 2 million. As in previous years, most cooperatives were situated in Northern Italy. The statistics indicate that in 1914, 23% of La Lega's cooperatives were in Emilia Romagna, 19.9% in Lombardy and 10.1% in Tuscany. Only 15.5% were situated in Southern Italy.[44]

A major event which had great ramifications for the Italian cooperative movement was the formation of the Catholic National Confederation of Italian Cooperatives (Confederazione). As stated previously, the Catholics had encouraged the formation of cooperatives assiduously since the Papal Encyclical of 1891. The differences with La Lega increased further when La Lega continually refused to support Catholic participation in the various government commissions on which it had a representative. By 1907 it was estimated that Catholic cooperatives had up to 400,000 members. They were present in most sectors, particularly in insurance and banking. In 1919, in addition to the Confederazione, the Catholic movement organised itself through a political party "Partito Popolare" and the Catholic trade union movement. At the 1921 congress 7,735 cooperatives were members of the Confederazione which included: 2,116 rural banks, 3,200 consumer cooperatives, 694 producer and labour cooperatives, 800 agricultural cooperatives, 400 fishing cooperatives and 525 cooperatives formed by ex soldiers. The major difference between La Lega and the Confederazione was that the latter had also access to finance through the rural banks, where as La Lega not having banks of its own, had to rely mostly on the State for finance.[45]

While La Lega and the Confederazione were the largest cooperative associations of the Italian cooperative movement, others soon followed. The Sindacato Nazionale delle Cooperative (National Union of Cooperatives) was formed by some Republicans and trade unions in 1919. In the same year the Federazione delle Cooperative fra Combattenti (Ex Servicemen Cooperative Federation) was formed. More importantly in 1921 the Fascists established their own Sindacato Italiano delle Cooperative (Italian Union of Cooperatives), SIC, which marked the beginning of the end for non-Fascist cooperative associations.

The Dark Years: Fascist Italy 1921-1943

Economic and Political Crisis and the Rise of Fascism

The year 1919 was one of the most important in Italian post-unity history. It was a year of high unemployment. There was a high level of discontent among the 600,000 people who had served in the army. The cost of living was rising, and both in the cities and the countryside workers and peasants went on strike. The most radicalised movement was led by 500,000 workers who occupied their factories in Turin and other industrialised cities in Northern Italy.[46] La Lega too became more radicalised and it, along with the trade union movement, supported the socialisation of land. By this time the Socialist movement had become a mass movement; the Socialist party had 216,000 members, the left trade union movement had over two million and La Lega also had two million members. This popularity was confirmed at the 1919 national election.

In the 1919 election, 10,239,326 persons voted and for the first time the liberals did not have the parliamentary majority. The majority was held by the combined populist forces of the Socialists (156 deputies) and the Catholic Popular Party (100 deputies). The Socialists obtained 60% of the votes in Emilia Romagna and over 40% in Piedmont, Lombardy, Umbria and Tuscany.[47] In the province of Bologna 55 out of 61 local councils were now governed by Socialists.[48] What is also important is that 16 cooperators were elected to parliament.[49] However, the 1919 result led to a stalemate because the differences between three major parties made it difficult to form alliances. This led to a power vacuum soon to be filled by the Fascists.

The Fascist party was formed in Milan in 1919 and began to gather support from various sections of Italian society. The economic crisis and the continuous radicalisation of the workers and peasants had galvanised the industrialists in the North and the agrarian class of North and Southern Italy in support of Fascism. Support also came from the military who not only wanted law and order, but also felt cheated that Italy had been treated as a second rate power at the Treaty of Versailles. From 1922, the Catholic church too began to support openly a Fascist regime after it was reassured by Mussolini that the Fascist State would not be anti-clerical. The Fascist party soon developed into a mass movement attracting teachers, technicians, artisans, retailers, small landowners and public servants.[50] Already in 1921 it had 200,000 members and had 35 deputies elected to parliament.

Along with its strategy of working within legality, Fascism also adopted violent means as a way of getting to power. The years 1920 to 1921 were particularly violent as Fascist squads, with the tacit approval of the State, raided Socialist party headquarters, trade unions organisations and workers' associations. The State was also active against the workers' movement: in 1921, in the province of Bologna 550 workers were arrested, 1,936 were injured and 19 died.[51] In response to Fascist violence, the Socialists called a national strike in March 1922, but it failed. This should come as no surprise since by that time the Socialist party had split twice, (one faction formed the Communist Party in 1921 and a reformist faction left in 1922), and had ended its ties to the trade union movement. The church had by this time also withdrawn its support of the Catholic Popular Party founded by Don Sturzo.

Taking advantage of the unstable political situation and the disarray of the opposition, Mussolini decided to take political power by force. On the 28th of October, the Fascists marched on Rome and the day after the king Victor Emanuel gave Mussolini the authority to form government.[52]

Fascism and Cooperatives

Fascism's position toward cooperatives was one aimed at making the cooperative sector a passive actor within a totalitarian State.[53] This was achieved by the using the following methods: violence, control, degeneration, and using cooperatives as a tool for obtaining consensus for the regime.

Violence. The first strategy used toward cooperatives was violence. Fascists viewed La Lega's cooperatives as being supportive of Socialism thus, politically, weakening the cooperative movement meant weakening Socialist and democratic forces in Italian society. Anti-cooperative feeling was particularly high among: small and large farmers who feared the challenge coming from collectively-owned agricultural cooperatives; small retailers had been campaigning against consumer cooperatives since 1902, attempting to restrict their trade to members only, thus diminishing their capacity to grow; builders and constructors who resented the fact that public works had also been assigned to cooperatives.[54]

Fascist violence was mostly felt in Emilia Romagna, Lombardy and Tuscany. Methods such as fire, physical destruction of cooperatives in raids and various forms of intimidation were used. Galasso claims that 150 cooperatives were attacked between May and July 1921.[55] Earle states that between January and June 1921, 198 were attacked in the Po Valley.[56] In Bologna, 73 cooperatives were destroyed.[57] One consumer cooperative in Masi, near Ferrara, was attacked by a squad of 400 Fascists.[58] What is important to note is that other than particular localities, certain types of cooperatives were attacked. Those mostly targeted were agricultural cooperatives which were collectively owned, labour cooperatives which had a strong Socialist culture and consumer cooperatives which provided support to workers during strikes and which had become meeting places for the dissemination of Socialist ideas.[59] These continuous attacks led to an exodus of cooperatives from La Lega, while some ceased to exist. It also led some cooperative members to emigrate. The end result was that from the 8,000 members of 1920, La Lega numbered only 600 cooperatives in 1926. By 1926, the Catholic cooperatives were also targeted for mistreatment by the Fascist forces. That same year all cooperative associations were dissolved.[60]

Fascist Control. Fascist control over the cooperative movement took place between 1922 and 1926, simultaneously taking control of cooperative enterprises, cooperative support structures and State controlled cooperative institutions. In 1921, the Fascist Italian Union of Cooperatives, SIC, was formed in Milan. Initially it hoped to attract cooperatives through violence and intimidation. This partly succeeded as in 1923 the Ex Servicemen Cooperative Association joined SIC.[61] In 1923, a Fascist was placed as head of the Cooperative Institute of Credit. This gave Fascists control over credit supply and their position was often used as a weapon to persuade cooperatives to join SIC or to force them into liquidation. In the latter case, the institute would force them into liquidation by asking them to make quicker loan repayments. The final blow to the independent cooperative sector came in 1926 when a government decree dissolved all cooperative associations and their newspapers. The same decree also established the National Agency for Cooperation (Ente Nazionale della Cooperazione -ENC) as the sole representative body of the cooperative movement. The ENC was given the power to dissolve any cooperative which was thought to be subversive or expel any person from cooperatives for the same reasons. To complete its takeover, the ENC also changed the status of consortia to government institutions taking away from them any direct link to cooperatives.[62]

Fascist control of cooperative enterprises also took place in a number of ways. It has been mentioned that Fascists controlled the National Institute of Cooperative Credit. In addition to this, they also controlled the allocation of public works, local council land and legislative measures. This power was used to force cooperatives to join the Fascist cooperative organisation before ENC was created, and for their members to join the Fascist trade union. Fascist members were placed on the board of directors of cooperatives. Once in this position, they proceeded in purging cooperatives of left wing members replacing them with loyal Fascists. In the last instance, the Prefect could intervene and dissolve the cooperative or force it to join the ENC.[63]

A clear indication of how the Fascists behaved is provided by the history of the construction cooperative CMC of Ravenna. The assault of Fascists on CMC came after they had marched on Ravenna and seized political control of the city as they had done in Rome. From the outset members of cooperatives who were openly anti-Fascist had to emigrate, most of whom went to France. Secondly, the local Fascist hierarchy told the cooperative that unless Fascist technical staff were appointed, the cooperative would not get any public works. Once in the cooperative, Fascists expelled anti-Fascists and replaced them with a work-force loyal to the regime, thus changing the political composition of the membership. They also stopped the cooperative from making solidarity payments to ex-members and to those members who had emigrated. Third, at the next cooperative election Fascists were nominated as members of the board and organised mock elections[64] to ratify the nomination. Fearing a loss of public works and credit, their nominations were accepted. Fourth, the cooperative was forced to: make donations to various Fascist organisations and institutions; allow workers paid days off to work for Fascist associations; sign up all cooperative members in the Fascist trade union organisation and pay members' fee directly to the union. Furthermore, CMC was forced to deposit all of its funds with the Fascist controlled Institute of Cooperative Credit. This led people to leave the cooperative and once again they were replaced with Fascists. Fifth, members were told to join the Fascist party. However, in spite of the purges and the emigration that followed, it was estimated that one quarter of the remaining work-force of 400 never joined the Fascist party. Finally, the government appointed a commissariat to take over on the pretext that, for the benefit of workers, it was merging CMC with the cooperative "Nuova Muratori" formed by some ex-Republican members of CMC in 1910.[65] In reality, it was a political act designed to take full control of CMC and to prove to the people that ideological differences no longer existed under the new totalitarian regime.[66]

Degeneration and Limitations Faced by Cooperatives. Once in full control, the Fascists set about removing some of the most important characteristics of cooperatives. Cooperatives slowly lost their democratic nature. Initially a multiple voting system was introduced in place of the principle of one person, one vote. Later, cooperatives were managed in a hierarchical manner by the Fascists virtually making the general assembly redundant. Consumer cooperatives were encouraged to sell to members only and were prohibited from supporting cultural and social activities. The latter now were under the control of Fascist organisations and only they could provide these services. In 1929, the Institute of Cooperative Credit was replaced by the Banca Nazionale del Lavoro (National Labour Bank) which, while it still provided credit to cooperatives, it was no longer solely a Cooperative Credit Institution.[67] The consortia were turned into State institutions, and those which possessed land had to sell it to private enterprises.[68] These policies caused cooperatives to degenerate into undemocratic enterprises concerned only with economic matters devoid of any social content.

Cooperatives as a Form of Consent and Interest Group Support. The fact that the cooperative sector had a large membership, was seen by Fascists as being a useful tool of consent for the regime.[69] Basically, as long as Fascists controlled them, the role cooperatives could play in creating jobs or reducing food prices was acknowledged. It is for these reasons that the Fascist government allowed the coexistence of cooperatives in a capitalist economy.

Cooperatives were also used to win support from particular interest groups. The regime set up consumer cooperatives within State departments on behalf of employees and housing cooperatives for the purpose of building housing for members to buy.[70] This policy clearly indicates two important points: first, the support of cooperatives building private housing was ideologically motivated since their purpose was to increase private ownership among the middle class. Second, setting up consumer cooperatives for members only was done to compete against cooperatives selling in the open market and to protect the interests of small businesses.

Surviving in a Totalitarian State. The cooperative experience clearly illustrates how Italian society was governed by a totalitarian State in which the party controlled the State and society through Fascist controlled institutions and organisations, supported by restrictive laws which prohibited non-Fascist organisations.[71] Within this environment cooperatives did manage to survive. Statistics indicate that in 1927 there were 6,124 cooperatives and 827 mutual aid societies, many fewer than the 20,000 operating in 1921. Subsequently, however, more cooperatives were set up and by the end of the Fascist reign 11,600 cooperatives were in existence.[72] On the positive side, some of the cooperatives that did survive, like the construction cooperative

CMC, had accumulated a great deal of experience vital for their growth after 1943.[73] Nonetheless, the period must be seen as a lost opportunity for the cooperative movement which in 21 years was more than halved.

Rebirth of Cooperatives 1943-1947

Fascist rule in Italy formally ended in 1943. That year the allied forces had landed in Southern Italy and King Victor Emanuel replaced Mussolini with General Badoglio and decided to collaborate with the allied forces to defeat the German army. In that same year the Resistance forces formed by the Communist, Socialist, the Mazzinian Action Party, the Liberals and the Christian Democrats formed the National Committee of Liberation (NCL). Of these, only the Communists maintained an active organisation within Fascist Italy. The Socialists and the Action Party had reorganised themselves in France and continued their anti-Fascist politics from there. The Liberals and Christian Democrats had no involvement prior to 1943. By 1945 the allied forces had liberated Southern Italy and the Resistance movement, with the support of the allied forces, had liberated Northern Italy.[74]

Post-war Italy provided a fertile ground for cooperative development. Between August 1944 and September 1946 some 9,000 cooperatives were set up.[75] There were a number of factors which contributed to this. The first reason was provision of basic needs. Many cooperatives were set up spontaneously by people in search of employment, housing and food at lower prices. Others were promoted from above. Many cooperatives were set up by the Resistance Brigades, as the historian Onofri stated "there wasn't one Partisan's Brigade which did not attempt to form a cooperative".[76] In areas under the control of the NCL, the partisans promoted cooperatives to build houses, roads, distribute food because they created employment and did not speculate. They were glad to help cooperatives because they had suffered under Fascism and because these assisted the resistance fighters by providing them with food, shelter and ammunitions.[77] Some cooperatives were created by ex-cooperative members who had returned from exile. The local authorities promoted consumer cooperatives in the hope of reducing food prices. By the end of 1947, it was estimated that there were 18,000-20,000 cooperatives operating in Italy with a membership of 4.5 to 5 million people.[78]

One early setback for the cooperative movement was its inability to unite under one organisation. For a while it seemed that the policy of national unity which prevailed at the political level, and which also led to the formation of one trade union confederation, would also lead to the formation of one cooperative organisation. However, this did not eventuate. The same ideological differences which led to divisions prior to the rise of Fascism re-emerged. The Catholics continued to see cooperatives as a way to promote and protect the small property owners (such as the small farmer and middle classes), and as a way to promote social stability rather than class struggle.[79] On the other hand, La Lega wanted cooperatives to play a larger role by engaging in structural reforms in the agricultural, housing and distribution sectors of the economy.[80] Another source of division was the Christian Democrats' view that cooperatives should have a small membership and that in case of dissolution the capital should be divided among the members and non members. On the contrary, La Lega opted for large membership and for the capital to go to a public fund in case of dissolution.[81] The division within the cooperative movement was formally acknowledged with the formation of La Lega on 1 May 1945 and of the Confederazione four days later.

La Lega: Politics, Organisation and Size

One of the consequences of this division is that it reduced the autonomy of the cooperative movement vis-à-vis political parties. This development would become clearer during the Cold War period, but even in these early post-war years political parties wanted to control the cooperative sector to influence its vast membership for electoral and strategic purposes. As already noted, La Lega had always been influenced by political parties but it had always maintained its autonomy. It has also been noted that with the rise of industrialisation and the formation of cooperatives in the then Socialist influenced regions such as Emilia Romagna, Tuscany and Lombardy, the Socialists became the major political faction within La Lega. After the war another change took place within La Lega, with the Communists replacing the Socialists as the major faction.

The Communists' active role within Fascist Italy and in the Resistance movement won it a great deal of legitimacy from the people.[82] Further, it won support of a large section of the working class because of its close relations with the Soviet Union and the prestige of its leader Togliatti. The Communists wanted a united cooperative sector capable of contributing toward structural reforms, especially in the agricultural sector, and of being part of an anti-monopoly alliance in which workers, peasants and the middle classes (small and medium size businesses, employees and professional groups) would contribute in building Socialism in Italy. This became known as the "Italian Road to Socialism".[83]

By 1946, 44 Communist provincial federations made a commitment to cooperatives and persuaded many of its cadres to join or take an interest in cooperative affairs. This organisational effort was rewarded at the 1947 congress of La Lega held in Reggio Emilia where for the first time the Communists became the major faction. At this congress, the Communists won 58% of the votes from cooperatives' representatives, the Socialists 25%, the Republicans 2.5%, and the Social Democrats 6%, the remaining 9.5% of the votes went to Independents. The executive of La Lega was formed by 50 representatives of which 21 were Communists, 14 Socialists, 4 Social Democrats, 8 Republicans and 3 Independents.[84]

At the organisational level La Lega took two important decisions. It moved to institutionalise the existence of political factions within the organisations and it began to develop territorial structures throughout Italy. Factions were institutionalised by distributing important positions to various faction leaders. Thus the president was a Communist and the secretary and the vice president were allocated to a Socialist and a Republican respectively. This was important because it allowed each faction to coexist within the organisation. At the territorial level, La Lega set up provincial federations to provide political and managerial support to cooperatives. By 1947, 70 provincial federations were formed to service the needs of 4,722 cooperatives with over 1.5 million members.[85] In the same year the Catholic Confederation numbered 7,000 cooperatives with over one million members.[86] Considering that there were approximately 20,000 cooperatives in Italy in 1947, close to 8,000 cooperatives did not join either of the two major organisations.

Legal Recognition: "Article 45" and the Basevi Law

The political climate of post-war years proved also to be fertile ground for State support toward cooperatives. Until 1947, Italy was governed by national unity governments formed by the same parties which formed the NCL. Since all parties supported cooperatives, albeit with different ideas, some attention was given to their needs. To further advance its claims, in 1946 the cooperative movement set up a pro-cooperation lobby group comprising of 108 deputies.[87] The two most enduring achievements were the acknowledgment of cooperatives in the Constitution and the Basevi law of 1947.

Article 45 of the constitution recognised cooperative enterprises alongside private and public enterprises and placed the responsibility on the State for its promotion:

> The Republic recognises the social function of cooperation, with its mutually beneficial character, and without aims of

> private speculation. The law favours its increase by the most suitable means and ensures its character and objectives through appropriate controls.[88]

The Ministry of Labour was given the responsibility of taking positive steps to promote and develop cooperatives, spread the cooperative principles and set up training courses for cooperative directors. The State, through adequate control measures and in agreement with the cooperative movement, had been given powers to protect the genuine cooperatives from the spurious ones. This was seen as a major victory because the State had recognised the anti-speculative nature of cooperatives and the importance of cooperative organisations. However, the wording was deliberately vague and it was left to governments of the day to interpret the Constitution and decide the extent of government involvement in cooperative development.[89]

The Basevi Law was passed in 1947 reflecting article 45 of the Constitution and the ICA cooperative principles. It stipulated that cooperatives were to be democratically managed based on the principle of "one person, one vote". It supported an open door policy preventing cooperatives imposing entrance qualification on members. At all times members must number at least 50% of the total work-force. The maximum amount members could invest as shares was restricted to 250,000 lire and interest on capital was limited to a maximum of 5%. Members' shares are not transferable. Surplus was to be distributed in the following manner: a minimum of 20% of profits had to be deposited in a collective reserve fund and could not be recouped by individuals upon leaving the firm, no more than 20% of surplus could be used to supplement wages, while the remainder was to be used either for social activity or to be reinvested back in the enterprise. Professionals were prohibited from setting up cooperatives. White-collar workers were limited to 4% of the total work-force. In the event of dissolution, cooperatives were not allowed to distribute any net assets to their members, instead, they had to be devoted to a public fund.[90]

The law also provided fiscal incentives. Producers' cooperatives were exempt from paying taxes if: the labour costs exceeded 60% of the total costs; entitled to a 50% reduction if the labour costs were between 40% to 60%; and entitled to a 25% reduction if these costs were less than 40%. Agricultural cooperatives were exempt from paying taxes; every other cooperative received a 25% tax reduction.[91] Further benefits included a ten year exemption from stamp duty and public authorities could sign contracts with cooperatives without recourse to competitive tenders for works costing less than 100 million lire.[92]

Two important aspects of the Basevi Law is that it has ensured the re-investments of profits within the enterprise and has made it legally impossible for a cooperative to be sold out to private enterprises for speculative purposes. Firstly, by regulating the distribution of surplus, it virtually guarantees that no more than 20% of profits are used to supplement wages, therefore, the remainder, minus an amount used for cultural or solidarity acts, is reinvested. Secondly, as members' shares are not transferable, and in case of dissolution, the cooperative's assets go to a public fund, the law prevents cooperatives to be transformed into private enterprises through individuals selling their shares to the latter, as was the case with the Plywood cooperatives.[93] This favours the continuity of the enterprise as a cooperative.

However, while fiscal incentives were provided, other financial matters were given little consideration. In this period the only effort was the formation of a cooperative branch within the Banca Nazionale del Lavoro (BNL) with 500 million lire at its disposal. This amount was well short of the 20 to 25 billion needed by the cooperative movement at the time.[94] Considering that between 1945 to 1947 the State had financed private enterprises to the tune of 60 billion lire; the 500 million cooperatives got amounted to only 0.83% of the total funds available. To make matters worse, cooperatives usually received late payments for public works. It is estimated that the State owed them up to 13 billion lire by 1948.[95] In addition, the provisions to limit the interest on capital to 5% acted as a deterrent to personal investments and thus deprived cooperatives of important capital.[96] Furthermore, the representatives of the cooperative movement were not members of the executive of the cooperative branch of the BNL, which meant they could not control or direct funds in accordance with the needs of the cooperative movement.[97]

La Lega had more reasons to feel disappointed. First, the government did not compensate La Lega for the assets seized and the damages caused by the Fascists during their years in power.[98] Secondly, the government did not support La Lega's involvement in major public works, nor did it acknowledge the contribution the consumer movement could have made in preventing speculative activity in the distribution sector, nor the contribution that could have been made by the housing cooperatives. These decisions were basically left to the market. Without money and managerial expertise cooperatives struggled during this period. The only cooperative sector to gain government support was the agricultural sector which benefited from a 1946 law which allowed local councils to allocate uncultivated land to cooperatives for a minimum period of nine years.[99]

The Cold War: Surviving Without Growth 1948-1962

Italian political life changed dramatically after late 1947 with negative consequences for La Lega. This was a period where superpower conflict reached its peak. The period was dubbed "The Cold War" and it heavily influenced the Italian political scene. Political parties and individuals were forced to take sides between a United States-led Western capitalist alliance and a USSR-led Socialist camp. In Italy the Christian Democratic Party (DC) sided with the US. The Communist Party (PCI) and the Socialist Party (PSI) formed the Popular Front and sided with the Socialist forces. This divided the workers' movement. The PSI split and 52 out of 115 deputies formed the Social Democratic Party (PSDI) which sided with the USA. In 1948 an election was called and the DC won convincingly with 48.5% of the popular vote. The Popular Front obtained 31% of the vote, 8.7% less than the combined Communist and Socialist vote of the 1946 election.[100] Two years later, the Social Democrats and the Catholics split from the unitary General Confederation of Italian Labour (CGIL) and formed their own trade unions called Union of Italian Labourers (UIL) and Confederazione Italiana dei Sindacati dei Lavoratori (CISL), further weakening the Popular Front.[101]

The Cold War and La Lega

The politics of La Lega were greatly affected by the Cold War. Prior to the election of 1948 La Lega openly supported the Popular Front, something which the incoming government did not forget. After the election, the Communist Party which until then had supported a unitary cooperative movement, went on the defensive and instructed the Communists within La Lega to ensure that it supported the party's policies and identified itself with the workers' movement. The following statement made by Agostino Ottani, the Vice President of the Provincial Federation of Bologna at the 7th provincial congress held in 1952 clearly illustrates this change:

> The cooperative movement is not simply an economic organisation, but it is an organisation of the Italian workers' movement whose aim is the social emancipation and the solidarity, universal brotherhood and peace between people...[let it be known} that any act against the trade unions, against the partisans, against the democratic forces is an act against the cooperative movement.[102]

> The cooperative movement is a great school of socialism...which teaches workers the art of self management...[It is also important that] workers should become not only the masters of their own labour, but also of the world around them, this is what makes them move forward and prepares them for the road leading to their definitive emancipation.[103]

The emphasis on politics and the need for cooperatives to go beyond their economic goals are clearly expressed. This had a profound impact on La Lega which continued until the late seventies to believe that the growth of cooperatives was directly linked to political change.[104] The politics of La Lega and the influence the Communists were exerting, caused some concern to the Social Democratic and part of the Republican faction. In 1952, these two factions left La Lega and formed their own association called the General Association of Italian Cooperatives (AGCI) which was formally recognised by the State in 1962 after it had managed to associate 1,000 cooperatives.[105]

The Strategy of La Lega

La Lega's strategy during this period was one aimed at surviving this difficult situation. It sought support from the national State and local government and it began to develop a cohesive cooperative movement based on intersectoral trade and support. La Lega placed a number of demands on the State. In 1949, at their 22nd national congress, La Lega asked for 10 billion lire in credit, 20% of public works, and to control a percentage of food imports in order to exert some control over prices.[106] However, these needs were largely ignored. The only decision made by the State in favour of cooperatives was to increase the funds in the cooperative branch of BNL bank from 500 million lire to 2.5 billion lire in 1951, subsequently increased to 7.5 billion in 1962.[107] This was a small amount considering the State had provided private businesses some 714 billion lire in grants or cheap loans in the same period. Nevertheless, these funds were vital especially for the agricultural sector which received 50% of the available finance.[108] The agricultural cooperatives also benefited from a government institution which had the responsibility to support agriculture in the Padana valley of Northern Italy.[109]

The hardline policy of the government toward La Lega was emphasised by the violent methods used by the police forces led by the Ministry of the Interior Mario Scelba. Fearing that La Lega was a source of support for the

Communists, Scelba embarked on a campaign of harassment hoping to weaken the PCI's social base, he:

> Turned his attention to La Lega, instituting a campaign of harassment if not persecution. Individual cooperatives were subject to stringent tax inspections, were put under government appointed commissioners, had their operating license withdrawn, or had to go into liquidation.[110]

According to La Lega's president Cerreti, Scelba wanted to subordinate the cooperative movement to the State by destroying its top 250 cooperatives.[111] La Lega survived but was marginalised throughout this period.

Contrary to the relations that La Lega developed with the national government, the relations with local governments were more fruitful, especially in the "Red Belt" regions of Emilia Romagna, Tuscany and Umbria. The local councils provided land to agricultural cooperatives[112] and housing cooperatives. They granted licences to consumer cooperatives to open stores and they assigned public works contracts to construction cooperatives. It is important to note that the reasons for local councils' support was not simply political. Cooperatives were usually very competitive and were also supported for their social commitment. Local authorities supported cooperatives as a means to protect the local community. This was especially important in Emilia Romagna because it received a small amount of State investments and did not attract private investors because of its left wing traditions.[113]

The Organisational Structure

During this period good progress was made at the organisational level. By 1958 another seven provincial federations of La Lega were formed taking its total to 77. These coordinated cooperatives from all sectors in a particular area, maintained good relations with the trade union movement and promoted a unitary policy.[114] In 1955, the first sectoral associations were formed in the agricultural, consumer and producers' sectors. Another form of association was the consortium. A consortium is an association of various cooperatives from the same sector which pool their resources together enabling them to obtain goods and services at lower prices. The first and most successful was the consumer consortium AICC (Alleanza Italiana delle Cooperative di Consumo - Italian Alliance of Consumer Cooperatives). This consortium acquired raw materials, food and provided storage space for the consumer cooperatives. Costs were reduced by cutting out the costs of the intermediaries.[115] Various consortia of local dimensions were also present in the producers' and construction sector. Through the consortia cooperatives became more competitive without having to increase their actual size.[116]

The provincial federation and the consortia promoted intersectoral trade which also improved cooperatives' chances of survival. Indeed, the housing and the producers'/construction sector worked closely together in these years with the latter building houses for the former. So too did agricultural cooperatives and consumer cooperatives. The latter signed an agreement that by 1964 60% of AICC's sales to consumer cooperatives would come from agricultural cooperatives.[117] What was created during this period was an internal market within the cooperative sector.

In addition to the support from local councils and from the cohesiveness of the cooperative sector, the economic conditions also helped. Indeed, after 1945, the process of reconstruction, urbanisation and population growth all created a demand for retailing, construction, housing and agriculture. However, figures indicate that these were years of stagnation for La Lega's cooperatives: the total turnover increased from 151 billion lire in 1951 to 256 by 1955. Then between 1955 and 1962 it had only increased by 40 billion lire to reach 296 billion by 1962. Thus in seven years since 1955, La Lega witnessed an increase in its turnover of only 15.6%. Considering the inflation rate, this was indeed a period of stagnation.[118] This becomes more obvious when compared with the rest of the economy which grew by an average of 6% per annum during the same period.[119]

Problems Faced by Cooperatives

The economic performance of La Lega's cooperatives indicated that there were problems. One of these was lack of finance. It has been shown that the State provided little financial aid considering the number of cooperatives in operation. However, some problems also originated within cooperatives. For instance, members were not enthusiastic about financing the enterprise, indeed a great number of them had not yet invested the required minimum share of 500 lire.[120] The behaviour of cooperatives also led to financial problems. During this period, cooperatives were more inclined to play a social role on behalf of local communities. Thus construction and manufacturing cooperatives had a policy to employ as many people as possible and to spend money on social activities such as cultural activities and building houses for their members. Consumer cooperatives sold goods on credit, while all cooperatives supported cultural and social activities in one form or another. This meant that the surplus generated was not redirected in making the enterprise more competitive. Furthermore, unlike their Catholic counterparts La Lega had not yet developed a financial structure of its own. During this period La Lega's main concern was to develop cooperatives that would provide employment, housing and food. Finance was still seen as part of the capitalist culture and alien to the Socialist egalitarian culture which permeated the movement throughout the 1950s.[121]

A second major weakness was that the La Lega's cooperatives were small in size and they were mostly locally based. Up until 1962, La Lega was not dominant in any particular sector, and apart from some exceptional large construction cooperatives like CMC of Ravenna and CMB of Carpi which had been working on a national scale, the majority were small firms mainly operating in the local economy. In addition, La Lega had still not yet developed into a national movement. Most of La Lega's cooperatives resided in Lombardy, Tuscany and Emilia Romagna. . Emilia Romagna alone accounted for 30% of all cooperatives and 50% of La Lega's turnover.[122]

A third major problem was lack of specialist managerial skills. As stated, some managerial skills were provided by the consortia and the territorial structures, but it was not enough for a movement which had its sights on expanding nationally. The problem was that most of these managers were generalists with previous work experience in the trade union and political parties. While they proved to be very capable of confronting the repression by Scelba's government, installing a sense of discipline within the work-force, and developing intercooperative relations,[123] they lacked some specialist technical skills normally associated with managers.[124] They also believed that La Lega's growth was linked to the political climate and the relation of power between opposing political forces, thus they tended to concentrate on political rather than economic goals.[125]

A New Strategy: Change, Consolidation and Growth, 1963-1980

The period between 1963 and 1980 were years of change and of growth for La Lega which attracted the attention of all political and economic forces. There were a number of reasons which led to changes being made at the strategic, organisational and cultural level. Firstly, the poor economic results achieved by La Lega and the acknowledgment that a number of problems had to be overcome before any economic improvement could be made, was a major reason why changes were being proposed.

Secondly, the PCI developed a new strategy which had a major influence on La Lega's Communist faction. Known as the "Italian Road to Socialism", the PCI's strategy was first espoused at the 1956 congress and developed in subsequent years. This was a strategy of alliances between the working class, the middle class and small and medium size enterprises as a response to the concentration of power in the hands of monopolies and oligopolies.[126] The Socialist transformation of society was seen as a process which would take place by slowly shifting the balance of class forces. This could take place by initiating structural reforms within the existing Constitution.[127] The cooperative movement was seen by the party as an important institution capable of forging these alliances and of contributing to the development of an anti monopoly alliance capable of realising the structural reforms. In particular, the agricultural and housing sector; the areas of urban and rural planning; and the development of Southern Italy became priority areas. Most importantly, the PCI accepted La Lega as an autonomous organisation.[128] Thus compared to the Cold War policy, the PCI recognised the autonomy of La Lega and linked the cooperative movement with structural economic reforms and not simply political goals.

The third major factor was the changed political climate. While remaining the major party, the DC gradually began to lose votes and was forced to form coalition governments or to enter into power-sharing agreements with left wing parties. In 1963 the Socialists became a member of a centre left government. In the 1963 government, the Socialists and the Republican party initially proposed some form of economic planning, this pleased La Lega which hoped that a better relationship with the government could now be established.[129] In 1976, the Communist vote rose to 34.3% and because the Socialists withdrew support of the previous government, the DC was forced to negotiate with them. This led to the formation of a minority DC government supported in parliament by the Communists. The consequence deriving from the 1963 and the 1976 political outcomes was that left wing parties supportive of La Lega had the opportunity either to be a part of or to influence governments, thus ending the overly discriminatory government behaviour which existed during the cold war years.

The influence of left wing parties on the government also led to a devolution of powers to the regions and the local councils. These were granted greater legislative powers over a number of areas including welfare, housing, commerce, urban planning, tourism, environment and economic development. Considering that 55% of public spending is done at the local level, the role of the local councils and regions became very important for society as a whole.[130]

La Lega's New Strategy

The new strategy of La Lega was first adopted in 1962 and further developed at subsequent congresses held in 1969 and 1973. A plan was developed with the aim to overcome marginalisation and become a major social and economic force in Italian society. Firstly, it wanted to be seen as an autonomous organisation, thus increasing its chances of creating a better dialogue with both private enterprises and the State. Secondly, it proposed to forge alliances with small and medium-sized enterprises and with the urban middle classes. Thirdly, it wanted to play a major role in restructuring certain sectors of the Italian economy such as agriculture, urban planning, the distribution sector, and help to reduce the gap between North and Southern Italy. Fourthly, it portrayed itself as a force capable of reducing inflation by controlling food and housing prices.[131] It was widely acknowledged that for this strategy to be successful La Lega had to become a national movement (therefore increase its presence in Southern Italy); it had to extend its presence in new sectors of the economy; and it had to act as a united group of economically viable and soundly managed firms.[132]

Another major development took place at the 1977 National Conference on Cooperation promoted by the Italian Government. At this conference, La Lega's president Galetti, clearly pointed out (for the first time) that he refuted the idea of creating a "Cooperative Republic" and stated that La Lega was in favour of a mixed economy in which a larger role would be played by cooperatives.[133] This was a major change and was a clear indication that La Lega had chosen to play a larger role within the existing political and economic system. In 1978, the term "Third Sector" of the economy was first used to describe the cooperative movement. This term symbolised the difference between the cooperative enterprise to both private and State enterprises, the democratic nature of cooperatives and their policy of providing goods and services at the lowest possible price.[134]

La Lega's strategic changes were of extreme importance. First of all, by opening up to the middle classes it improved its economic and social base. Important new sectors were formed such as retailing (by organising wholesale and support cooperatives on behalf of privately owned shops), culture, health, tourism, fishing, transport (taxis and truck cooperatives), while others like agriculture were enlarged by organising small farmers. Secondly, by accepting a mixed economy it reduced the hostility from the private business sector and the State bureaucracy, and opened up the possibility of business cooperation with the private and State sector. Thirdly, the new strategy portrayed the cooperative movement as a social and economic actor wanting to contribute to solve major structural problems in collaboration with the State. La Lega was not simply asking for support in the interest of the cooperative movement as it had done in the past, but it presented itself as an interlocutor capable of solving national problems such as housing, inflation, job creation for the young and Southern Italy.

Organisational Structure

This strategy was accompanied by organisational changes such as the creation of territorial regional structures, national sectorial associations and national consortia. In line with changes at the national political level, which, since 1970, began to assign a larger role to democratically elected regional governments, La Lega developed regional territorial structures to lobby regional governments.[135] During this period national sectorial associations were also formed. Their role was to provide cooperatives within a particular sector of the economy with technical expertise and planning skills on a national scale. National consortia were also established. They provided those business requirements that the individual enterprise did not possess such as: managers, technicians, marketing, accounting, economies of scale and business strategy. In particular, the consortia and the national sectoral associations jointly developed a strategy to create large cooperatives through mergers and specialisation. This was seen as necessary for cooperatives in order to outgrow its focus on the local economy.[136]

La Lega developed other supportive structures in the area of finance and trade. In the area of finance, both the financial consortium Fincooper and the insurance company Unipol were formed. Unipol was a private insurance firm bought by cooperatives in 1963. Initially it only sold car insurance and made a number of investments in real estate on behalf of cooperatives. Fincooper was formed in 1969 by 200 cooperatives. Its purpose was to recycle money within the cooperative movement (attracting money from the large cooperatives and lending them to those in need) and to facilitate access to credit from banks by acting as a guarantor.[137]

In the area of trade La Lega had formed an import-export company Intercoop in 1956, but it really brought results from the late sixties onwards. In the seventies, La Lega bought two other trading companies: Restital and Ital-Impex. Together these three companies were present in Eastern Europe, Asia (China, India and Vietnam), Central and South America and Africa. Their role was to trade products produced by cooperatives and to import products needed by them. Part of the trade was also done on behalf of small and medium size enterprises. In the late seventies they also developed into general contractors winning major contracts such as building storage centres, factories, flour mills, pasta factories and tomato processing plants. Overall, their contacts, presence and knowledge of overseas markets provided by these trading companies proved invaluable for small and medium sized cooperatives which individually could not have met the costs of such services.[138]

At the sectoral level cooperatives had undergone a phase of restructuring which paid dividends. The consumer cooperatives closed the small stores and opened up larger ones. They also amalgamated cooperatives from the same province and later, from the same regions in order to achieve economies of scale.[139] In Tuscany, eight cooperatives already controlled 80% of the total cooperative sales from that region.[140] Agricultural cooperatives became larger, and through their own consortia were beginning to process and to market their products.[141] The producers' cooperatives had achieved economies of scale through a process of mergers and acquisitions of other cooperatives and private enterprises. They had also acquired an enterprise culture: money was invested in technology and in re-skilling the work-force; production was diversified; they began to attract high level managers by paying attractive salaries. Some of the larger cooperatives had by now become nationally and internationally known.[142] During this period cooperatives began to form in new sectors such as the services, culture, fishing, tourism and private retailing giving La Lega a wider economic presence.

Cultural Adaptation

The new strategy created some cultural and identity problems within the movement. First, the policy of alliance was not openly received by all cooperatives. The consumer cooperatives and the collectively owned agricultural cooperatives took years to accept that privately owned retailers and small landowners were now their allies.[143] Second, the decision to make cooperatives more competitive meant paying more attention to the economic side of cooperatives, thus more investments had to be directed in buying new machinery, in technology and in training the work-force. Third, the increase in the size of cooperatives and the bigger role played by management, especially in the consumer sector, created concerns among members about the lack of internal democracy within large cooperatives.[144] Steps began to be taken to develop forms of participation for members and to create smaller members' branches to encourage participation. This is a continuing debate.[145]

Continuous Growth

The organisational support structures and the restructuring which took place at the sectoral level improved the competitiveness of La Lega's cooperatives. However, other factors were also responsible for a period of continuous economic growth. Compared to the private sector, cooperatives enjoyed better productivity thanks to better industrial relations[146] and savings on managers' salaries, since cooperative wage differentials did not exceed 3:1.[147] Cooperatives also enjoyed lower levels of debt because workers increased their personal investments in the form of members' shares and members' loans.[148] The success of cooperatives was revealed by a study of the largest 225 cooperatives conducted by La Lega. It revealed that while similar size enterprises from the private sector had reduced their work-force and had incurred losses between 1975 and 1977, La Lega's cooperatives had increased their turnover by 37.7% in 1977 and 32.3% in 1978; their profits by 155% and 96.2% respectively, and employment from 40,518 to 45,958.[149] This trend continued up to 1980. A study by Stefanelli comparing the level of value added as a percentage of the turnover at constant prices between La Lega's cooperatives operating in the construction, manufacturing and service sector with the national average, revealed that between 1976 and 1980, cooperatives increased their value added share of the turnover by 42% while the national average was 18%. A similar study comparing employment levels revealed that La Lega's cooperatives increased their employment levels by 15% compared to a national average of 6%.[150]

Another indicator of its strength is that from 1974 to 1978 it managed to convert into cooperatives 100 enterprises saving 10,000 jobs.[151] The latter shows both a demand for cooperatives and the ability of La Lega to convert private enterprises successfully into cooperatives saving jobs and production, and also providing tax revenue for the State.

All of these factors contributed to a steady growth of La Lega. In 1969 it had 7,735 associated cooperatives with 1,721,000 members and a total turnover of 619 billion lire.[152] By 1976, the number of cooperatives increased to 10,680, with 2.8 million members and a total turnover close to 2,500 billion lire.[153] Between 1969 and 1976 the turnover increased 403% at a time when the Italian economy grew by only 4.3% per annum between 1969 and 1973, and by only 2.8% per annum between 1973-1980.[154] It's not difficult to see why some of La Lega's officials proposed the idea that cooperatives could solve the unemployment crisis in Italian society.[155] Further, this was a period when the other cooperative movements also grew in size. In fact, it was estimated that in 1976 the cooperative sector as a whole controlled 6% of the economy, something which the State began to take into consideration.[156]

The State and Cooperatives

The greater influence at the governmental level exercised by the political parties close to La Lega provided a political climate more responsive to the needs of cooperatives. During this period a number of legislative changes were made which: improved the capacity of cooperatives to raise finance; invested more money into the cooperative branch of the BNL; increased public spending on public works; produced job creation projects benefiting some sectors of the cooperative movement.

In 1971, for the first time since 1947 the cooperative law was altered. The new laws were dubbed the "Mini Reform of 1971". The changes made did not alter the overall legislative framework, but they were an improvement and contained a number of fiscal incentives. The new law increased the amount each member could invest as shares from a maximum of 500,000 lire to a maximum ranging from 2 to 4 million lire.[157] Consortia were excluded from paying company tax. On the administrative side the following changes were made: the minimum number of members required by a cooperative wishing to bid for public contracts was raised to 25; the number of white collar workers as a percentage of the total work-force was also increased from 4% to 8% for agricultural cooperatives and to 12% for the other cooperatives.[158] The latter change responded to the personnel changes that were taking place in some of the large cooperatives where the white-collar employees were increasing in numbers.

Two more legislative changes were made to expand the availability of finance. In 1973 members' loans were introduced. In this scheme members were allowed to lend money to their cooperatives. To encourage this form of self financing, members had tax concession which entailed paying only a 10% flat tax rate on interests received, which compared favourably with bank depositors who paid twice this amount.[159] Finally as of the mid-1970s, profits rolled directly into the collective reserve fund have not been taxable. This has generated a savings of nearly 30% of overall profits.[160]

To further improve the financial viability of cooperatives, in 1971 the State increased the holdings of the cooperative credit branch of the BNL from 30 billion to 100 billion lire. While this was a dramatic increase in the funds available, it was not sufficient to meet their needs. In fact, this sum of money was small considering that the State had 32,000 billion lire available in public funds for investment purposes. In the same year, the Ministry of Labour also decided to give the three main cooperative associations a seat on the board of directors of the cooperative credit branch of the BNL.[161]

Cooperatives also benefited from increased public spending during this period. In response to the problems caused by urbanisation and the baby boom of the 1950s, left-wing parties forced the government to increase public spending for social projects such as transport, schools and housing.[162] These were all areas where cooperatives figured prominently and won many contracts. In the housing sector alone, in 1979 the cooperative movement as a whole built 20% of the total housing market. La Lega controlled 7% of the national housing market and managed to build houses at a cost which was 30% to 40% below the market rate.[163] Funds were also provided for youth employment projects. To counter the effects of youth unemployment, in 1977 the State developed a scheme which provided financial support and public works contracts to young people forming cooperatives or conventional businesses. It is estimated between 1977-1979 that 1,248 cooperatives were formed in this way creating 16,000 jobs.[164]

Cooperatives also benefited from the policies of regional and local governments, especially those like Emilia Romagna which had a long Socialist/Communist tradition. First, like other enterprises, they have benefited from: reduced costs due to infrastructures, social services, financial support, and the enterprise services provided by the regional government's agency Ervet and its subsidiaries.[165]

Secondly, cooperatives have had access to regional and local council resources. Agricultural cooperatives received some land from local councils and finance and services from the regional government. It is estimated that over 20% of the regional agricultural budget is spent on cooperatives.[166] The construction cooperatives received public works contracts such as roads, schools, hospital, maintenance of city sewerage, restoration of historic buildings and water purification.[167] In the area of health and social services cooperatives have been prominent in providing social services for the aged, homes for the aged, rehabilitation for drug addicts, caring for abandoned children and psychiatric help for ex-detainees.[168] Other cooperatives from the service sector have won contracts to supply the regional and local governments with office equipment,[169] environmental control services,[170] management of the publicity on council property,[171] management of local theatres,[172] food catering for the aged and students.[173] This is an indication that although both local and regional governments depended on the central State for finance and had limited free choice on how to spend that money, they had a degree of freedom in spending benefiting the local cooperatives.

In a couple of areas a combination of access to resources and market regulations helped the cooperative movement. If we take housing as an example, the relationship between public spending - devolution of power to sub-national governments - political power at the local level and cooperative development can be explored. At the national level the 1971 housing reform handed down powers and transferred funds to local authorities, powers were also granted to expropriate land paying average agricultural prices.[174] In addition, local authorities had already been given powers in 1962 to set aside land for housing to accommodate low income families. This was usually reserved for public housing and for cooperatives. Under this law the Bologna council set aside land for up to one third of its inhabitants.[175] The regional government also played its part by subsidising loans and by ensuring that cooperatives and small and medium sized enterprises would build the dwellings.[176] As stated earlier, La Lega came to control 7% of the national market, but a greater proportion came from Emilia Romagna. Similar policies were applied in the retail sector benefiting consumer cooperatives.[177]

Managing Change: the World Economy and Political Crisis 1981-1991

The 1970s produced an unparalleled expansion for the La Lega's cooperatives. The developmental model adopted to date was based on cooperatives competing mainly in: local economies (although as pointed out some did compete in the national and international market); trading in a cohesive cooperative market; relying on the market created by public spending on infrastructures and on socially useful objectives such as public housing, schools etc. However, the globalisation of the Italian economy and the fiscal and managerial crisis faced by the Italian State in the 1980s put an end to this model.

The 1980s symbolised an acceleration of the globalisation of the economy. National economies were ever more integrated and local markets had been penetrated by goods from all over the world.[178] Italy was faced with competition from the industrialised countries which competed on high-technology, high-value-added products, and the emerging newly industrialising countries which competed on low-technology, low-value-added goods by taking advantage of their low wages[179] and low level of trade unionism.[180] Competition was further heightened by the declining rate of GATT tariff barriers which had been reduced to 5% by 1991, against the average rate of 40% in 1947.[181] In addition, the EEC was accelerating its economic integration and hoped to abolish all trade barriers among member nations by 1993, with the aim of creating a market in which goods, capital and labour would be free to travel within Europe.[182]

The Italian State faced a fiscal and managerial crisis. The financial problems were caused by inefficient use of public resources, increasing pension payments amounting to 14% of GDP [183] and tax evasion which has been estimated to amount to 25% of the GDP.[184] These factors created a burgeoning public debt which grew to 104% of the GDP by 1991.[185] The consequences have been lower levels of public spending and privatisation of public companies.[186]

The managerial crisis refers to the inability of the Italian State to identify and solve economic and social problems. One example which links the fiscal and the managerial crisis is the construction industry. The State now expects construction enterprises to plan, execute and manage entire projects, whereas before it used to plan and manage projects and subcontract the execution side to private and cooperative enterprises. A car park built in Bologna is a clear example of this new approach. It was planned, financed and build by a cooperative and later managed on its behalf by Wilson Car Parking, an Australian company. The local government provided the land and set the fees. The cooperative makes a return by selling a portion of the car parking space and by getting a commission fee from Wilson Car Parking.[187]

Both the globalisation of the economy and the fiscal and managerial crisis of the State has placed a lot of strain on the previous cooperative growth model. The globalisation of the economy has led cooperatives to face more competition from foreign companies in all sectors of the economy. In order to compete successfully, cooperatives must grow larger, achieve greater economies of scale and expand into the national and international markets. The fiscal crisis of the State will mean that sectors such as the housing and construction can no longer rely on continuous expansion of the public sector for growth. Consequently, the cooperative sector will need to look increasingly to the private sector for work opportunities. Construction companies in particular, must either plan, manage and finance their own projects or try to penetrate more into the private market. Once again, this means that cooperatives must have managerial skills and finance in order to adapt to these changes in the market place.

The Strategy, Organisational Structure and Culture of La Lega

La Lega responded to this period by delineating a strategy strengthening the cooperative sector within a mixed economy. The plan consisted on widening the policy of alliances; on exploiting the opportunities offered by a State in crisis and embarking on a process of selectivity by strengthening the competitiveness of large cooperatives. Firstly a strategy of alliance with small and medium sized enterprises was pursued, concurrently with more openness towards the State and the progressive large businesses.[188] Alliances were also developed with cooperative movements in Europe. By 1992 the insurance, consumer and the construction sector had formed European consortia.[189] Secondly, La Lega realised that the fiscal and managerial crisis of the State opened opportunities for cooperatives especially in areas such as health, transport, environment and construction. Because of the cooperatives' non-speculative nature and its ability to link cooperatives from various sectors, La Lega was in an advantageous position to win public works contracts in these areas.[190] The third aspect of this strategy occurred at the enterprise level. La Lega continued to support the formation of large enterprises through mergers and to encourage efficiency and productivity. Since the 1980s, it also embarked on a process of selectivity, preferring to create fewer but more robust cooperatives.[191]

The organisational structures of La Lega were improved to meet these new challenges. The regional territorial structures were becoming increasingly the pillar of the organisation. They had the responsibility to lobby and influence the regional government's policy direction and to coordinate the activity of cooperatives.[192] However, most of the improvements were made in the areas of finance and management. The financial structures showed signs of progress. In 1990, 2,000 cooperatives had become members of the financial consortium Fincooper, which along with Unipol Finance formed the centre of La Lega's financial structure. The financial companies of La Lega had by 1990 increased to include not only Unipol Insurance, which had become the sixth largest insurance company in Italy, but also: Banec (Bank of the Cooperative Economy) established in 1987; Finec, a merchant bank, also formed in 1987; Sofimer, a finance company to promote development in Southern Italy; factoring and leasing companies and a host of local and regional financial institutions.[193]

In the area of management rapid progress was made throughout the 1980s. Today there are 30 companies affiliated to La Lega scattered throughout Italy, the most important being Inforcoop, Sinnea, Smaer, Promosviluppo and Icie. Inforcoop coordinates the activities of all 30 companies, plus it has the responsibility to lobby regional, national and European institutions to finance training and managerial courses given by specialist companies associated to La Lega.[194] Sinnea has the task to train managers how to manage change in turbulent times. Some of the courses offered include language training for business, business communication, general management, marketing and sales, finance and monitoring, and human resources.[195] Smaer provides consultancy expertise at the organisational level. A major concern is to develop forms of participation and conflict resolution skills between management and the work-force. This is particularly useful for cooperatives which have grown large in size and want to maintain a democratic form of management.[196] Icie was established to provide cooperatives with technological expertise and to encourage R&D projects.[197] Finally, Promosviluppo mainly concentrates on promoting new enterprises, on worker takeovers of private enterprises and on feasibility studies of geographic areas which offer opportunities for cooperative development. In 1991, it was working on 109 projects worth 209 billion lire.[198]

Communication was another area which was becoming important. Two major companies operate in this area, Comunicazione Italia formed in 1985 and Editrice Cooperativa. Comunicazione Italia acts as an advertising agency on behalf of cooperatives and as a company promoting the image of La Lega. The latter involves selling the history and identity of the cooperative movement as well as its products. Some of the activities that have been organised by Comunicazione Italia include sponsorship of various sporting events, public showings of a visual history of La Lega and the inclusion of cooperative information in major newspapers.[199] Editrice Cooperativa is La Lega's publishing house. It publishes books on the history, conference proceedings, cooperative laws and government programmes. It also publishes the magazine La Cooperazione Italiana which was first published in 1886.[200]

The culture of the movement also underwent major changes. The working-class culture of egalitarianism which emphasised secure employment, low wage differentials and hostility to private business gave way to one which emphasised the need to compete in the market. This led to the development of an enterprise culture in which cooperatives also valued economic efficiency, innovation and workers' incentives as well as social goals. Members were being transformed from workers to worker-entrepreneurs and were being encouraged to invest money in shares and loans and be rewarded for it. Managers were now being sought from outside of the movement and were rewarded accordingly, thus increasing the wage differentials between workers and managers.[201]

Restructuring and Growth

La Lega's cooperatives adapted to this new economic and political environment by continuing, and at times accelerating, the policy of mergers and concentration that was initiated in the 1960s. This can be most clearly seen by analysing the traditional sectors of La Lega: consumer, producers and agricultural cooperatives. The consumer sector is the sector where the changes are most visible. Between 1956 and 1990 the number of consumer cooperatives fell from 3,300 to 431. At the same time the number of retail outlets fell from 7,000 to 1,281.[202] This process created cooperatives controlling many retail outlets and servicing a wider area through very large retail stores. The results of the mergers led to a high level of concentration. In 1990, 21 cooperatives which amount to 4.9% of all cooperatives, managed 43% of the total retail outlets, 75.4% of the total retailing area, 78% of its total employment and 85% of the total sales.[203] It is estimated that by 1990, 88.4% of the total retail area under the ownership of La Lega's consumer sector, was managed by the large cooperatives through supermarkets, megastores and commercial centres. The remainder (11.6%) was made up of outlets less than 400 square metres, an area smaller than a supermarket.[204] As Table 4.1 indicates, this strategy had positive ramifications on the retail sales, employment and the membership level.

Table 4.1 National Statistics of La Lega's Consumer Sector

	1980	1985	1990
Cooperatives	620	503	431
Retail Outlets	1502	1361	1281
Retail Area	330,000 Sq/M	419,000 Sq/M	585,000 Sq/M
Sales	1,261 Billion Lire	3,960 Billion Lire	7,431 Billion Lire
Employees	13,500	20,000	27,634
Members	930,000	1,649,000	2,271,900

Source: Moreno D'Angelo, "Annibale ha Varcato Le Alpi", in *Consumi e Societá,* Anno V, Numero 3, Maggio Giugno 1991, p.15.

The producers' sector showed a contraction in the number of construction cooperatives and an increase in manufacturing cooperatives. The number of construction cooperatives were reduced from 957 in 1980 to 630 in 1989. The number of employed were also reduced from 57,300 to 50,684, mostly taking place in the early 1980s when the country was experiencing negative growth. However, the turnover increased from 1,530 billion lire to 4,440 billion lire and the average size of cooperatives increased from 60 to 81 persons per cooperative. The industrial sector increased the number of cooperatives from 403 in 1980 to 660 in 1989, most of which were cooperatives formed out of private enterprises in crisis.[205] In total, the turnover increased by 667 billion lire to 2,997 billion lire and the average size stayed constant at 40 employees per cooperative.[206] It is important to note that in both the manufacturing and constructions sector there are many cooperatives which employ between 500 to 3,000 persons.[207] Furthermore, by 1989 there were 120 cooperatives of architects, engineers, urban planners, and professionals providing feasibility studies and micro and macro economic analysis, all providing valuable support to the construction and manufacturing cooperatives.[208]

The third traditional sector is that of agriculture. The process of restructuring and mergers has led to a reduction in the number of cooperatives from 2,849 in 1982 to 2,058 by 1989. The individual producer-members declined from 459,000 to 385,456. The total turnover increased from 5,500 billion lire in 1987 to 7,000 billion lire in 1989. The turnover per enterprise increased from 1.15 billion lire in 1982 to 3.4 billion lire in 1989. These figures indicate the larger dimensions of cooperatives and a higher turnover per member-producer.[209]

The newer sectors which were formed in the early 1960s had by 1989 also grown. The private retailers had formed 108 cooperatives selling food, domestic appliances and Hi-Fi, textiles and apparel. They represent 12,560 shopkeepers who employ 3,220 persons. The food sector is the largest sector and accounts for 63% of the turnover made by these cooperatives. Another sector started in the 1960s, the service sector has grown to become the largest growing sector of La Lega. In all there are 2,062 cooperatives operating in the areas of road haulage, transport of people, cleaning and maintenance, catering and welfare with a total membership of 88,702, employing 74,200 persons. In the area of tourism, La Lega associates 475 cooperatives with 7,400 members, providing employment to 4,600 persons. The fishing sector organised 16,670 fishermen in 207 cooperatives which employed 2,000 persons. The cultural sector consisted of 15,000 members organised in 638 cooperatives providing employment for 2,500 persons in activities such as theatre, film making, audiovisual equipment, libraries, music, televisions and radio.[210]

Overall, in spite of continuous mergers and takeovers the number of cooperatives affiliated to La Lega increased from 10,680 in 1976 to 12,889 in 1989 (see Table 4.2). Membership increased from 2.8 to 4.18 million members. The turnover rose from 2.5 trillion lire to 32.3 trillion lire. A closer analysis of La Lega comparing its economic power at a national, regional and sectoral level reveals the presence of a nationally important economic group of enterprises. La Lega produced 2.73% of the national GDP. Statistics for Emilia Romagna for 1988 show that La Lega's cooperatives controlled 12.75% of the Regional GDP, making them a crucial component for the region's economy.[211] Further proof of their importance is their ability to export, something which is extremely important for a country which imports raw materials. In the mid-1980s after Fiat, Montedison and Olivetti, the cooperatives associated to La Lega were Italy's next highest export earners.[212] While these figures do not include the turnover created by La Lega's financial sector and the companies owned by cooperatives, they do signify that La Lega is an important part of the national economy.

Table 4.2 Statistics of La Lega for 1989

Sectors	Cooperatives	Members	Employed	Turnover (Billions/Lire)
Agriculture	2058	385,465	36,000	7,000
Producers/ Labour	1410	71,310	78,580	7,630
Consumers	431	2,271,900	27,634	7,431
Retailers	108	12,560	3,220	3,440
Services	2,062	88,702	74,200	3,270
Tourism	475	7,400	4,600	605
Housing	4,000	492,000	2,000	2,109
Fishing	207	16,670	2,000	516
Culture	638	15,000	2,500	380
Mutual Aid	1,500	825,000	n/a	n/a
TOTAL	12,889	4,186,207	230,734	32,381

Source: The figures for the mutual aid societies refer to 1985, see Onelio Prandini, *La Cooperazione Italiana: Organizzazione, Storia e Futuri Sviluppi del Movimento Cooperativo*, Roma, 1986, p.85. The rest of the figures refer to 1989, see La Lega Nazionale delle Cooperative e Mutue, *Principali Indicatori del Movimento Cooperativo Lega*, Roma, 1991, pp.41-42.

The economic significance of La Lega can be further analysed by looking at its presence in particular sectors in the economy. The fishing sector controls 21% of the national market.[213] In the construction industry cooperatives hold 17.27% of the national share and most of that share is held by cooperatives associated to La Lega.[214] In the food retailing sector consumer cooperatives (5.5%) and the retailing cooperatives (5.2%) together hold 10.7% of the national market.[215] The wine consortia control 10% of the national market.[216] The private electrical appliances stores associated to ECO Italia, La Lega's consortium, have 8% of the national market.[217] In the food catering business, they hold 7% of the national market.[218] The agricultural sector overall has a 6% share of the national market.[219]

At the enterprise level many cooperatives are leaders in their field. The construction cooperative CMC of Ravenna is the seventh largest in Italy, employing 3,792 people with a turnover amounting to 496.2 billion lire, of which 112.7 billion lire (22%) were earned abroad.[220] Sacmi is the world's leader in the production of machineries and plants (turn key installations) for ceramic tiles and of closure bottles (crowns, aluminium and plastic caps).[221] In 1991, consolidated net sales reached US $334.5 million of which exports accounted for 84% of its sales.[222] La Ceramica of Imola, is the fifth largest producer of wall tiles in Italy and the 15th largest in the world. In 1988 it employed 649 people, reached a turnover of 94 billion lire and it exported 72% of its production.[223] Evergomma is a cooperative that produces all rubber products for automobiles except tyres. It is the third largest Italian enterprise in this vital sector of the economy employing 287 people.[224] In the dairy industry a recent merger between two large cooperatives Giglio of Reggio Emilia and Cerpl Granarolo of Bologna has produced a cooperative which holds a national market share of 9.3% of butter, 34.7% of pasteurised cream, 15.4% of the commercialisation of Parmisan Cheese,[225] 8.6% of fresh milk and 10.7% of long life milk.[226] Camst is the third largest Italian enterprise in the food catering sector, catering within factories, schools, hospitals and self service restaurants. In 1989 its turnover was 144 billion lire and it employed up to 2,350 people.[227] Coop Service is a cooperative which is active in the security sector, installing and measuring the security needs of factories, offices, banks and museums. It was started by 12 people twenty years ago, and by 1992 it employed 1,600 persons with a turnover close to 75 billion lire.[228] The Consortia Gruppo Italiano Vini (GIV) is the largest Italian wine maker. Each year GIV bottles 60 million bottles of wine of which 50% are exported.[229] These are only a few examples of the competitiveness of the large cooperatives.

These large cooperatives form the backbone of La Lega. This is confirmed by La Lega's own statistics which revealed that 394 cooperatives of medium to large dimensions produce 54% of La Lega's total turnover emphasising the crucial economic role they play within the organisation.[230]

One final consideration is the geographic distribution of La Lega. It has already been pointed that La Lega is an organisation mostly present in Northern Italy. Since the 1970s some efforts have been made to start cooperatives in Southern Italy and results show that the percentage of cooperatives located in the South has increased. In 1976 53.5% of cooperatives were situated in Northern Italy, 21.9% in Central Italy and 24.6% in Southern Italy. Ten years later, the South had increased its share to 30.3% (+5.7%), the Centre to 25.8% (+3.9%) and the North had its share reduced to 43.9% (-9.6%). However, this change has come about partly due to a genuine rise in cooperative formation in Southern Italy and partly due to the policy of mergers pursued by Northern cooperatives, especially those from Emilia Romagna. An analysis of the territorial distribution of turnover seems to confirm this. In fact, in 1986 the Northern area produced 72.4% of the total turnover, the Central area produced 21.3% and the South only 6.3%.[231]

The Response by the State to Cooperatives' Needs

During the 1980s the State gave a further indication that it was taking the cooperative sector seriously. The State's response partly reflected the problems faced by the Italian economy and partly reflected the demands of the cooperative movement. The actions from the State can be divided into three areas: legislative changes, job creation programmes and access to State resources.

The major legislative changes were enacted in 1983 and 1992, but some minor ones appeared earlier. The primary goal was to improve the self-financing capabilities of the cooperative enterprises by encouraging members to invest more. Indeed, before 1980 members rarely invested more than 830,000 lire in their cooperatives.[232] The 1983 Visentini law sought to overcome this problem by providing members with a number of incentives. The interest paid on members' shares was increased from the original 5% limit to 2.5% more than the interests paid on government bonds. In 1983 interest paid on members' shares equalled 18.5% p.a., much higher than the previous limit of 5%.[233] In addition, the enterprise was allowed to use profits to increase members' shares without being taxed so long as it did not exceed 10% of the existing amount.[234] The maximum sum that a member could invest in shares, was raised from 2 to 4 million lire to 20 and 30 million lire, the higher amount was allowed for producers and agricultural cooperatives.

Changes were also made regarding members' loans. The interest rate paid on members' loans was the same as members' shares. The withholding tax was increased from 10% to 12.5%, yet it was still half that paid by bank depositors. The maximum amount allowed to be lent as members' loans, initially set at 17 million lire for producer cooperatives and 10 million lire for others,[235] was increased to 20 and 40 million lire respectively in 1987. These changes increased the self financing capacity of cooperatives. In 1987, the 1,750 cooperatives from Emilia Romagna had received 1,749 billion lire in members' loans and 197.8 billion lire as members' shares.[236]

The 1983 legislation also allowed cooperatives to hold shares in limited companies. This allowed cooperatives to issue bonds and to set up various companies, especially in the field of finance.[237] The only other amendment in cooperative legislation, not related to finance, was an increase of the quota of white-collar employees from 8-12% (depending on the type of cooperative) to 20% in 1985. The following year, the quota was abolished for cooperatives formed under a "Youth Job Creation Scheme" aimed at creating employment in Southern Italy.[238]

Further, major legislative changes were enacted in January 1992. This legislation once again increased the maximum amount of money members could invest in their cooperatives as shares to 120 million lire for agricultural and producer cooperatives and to 80 million lire for the others, and as loans to 80 million lire per person for agricultural and producer cooperatives and 40 million lire for other cooperatives. Most importantly this legislation will be remembered for establishing a cooperative solidarity fund and for allowing external shareholders to invest in cooperatives. The solidarity fund is to be funded from 3% of the profits from every registered cooperative. This fund is to be managed by the major central associations of cooperatives and utilised in support of existing and new cooperatives.[239]

The major innovation was the introduction of external shareholders with voting and non-voting rights. External shareholders with voting rights must never exceed 30% of the total vote in the general assembly, thus allowing the work-force to control the majority of votes. Non-voting shares should not exceed the cooperative's net assets or the amount held in indivisible reserves and 50% of them should be offered to members and employees. Remuneration of non voting shares should be 2% higher than the remuneration of members' shares. Finally, certified annual reports have been made compulsory for medium to large cooperatives, to ensure that they comply with the cooperative law.[240]

In response to high unemployment levels of the 1980s and the de-industrialisation of the Italian economy, the State initiated two job creation programmes in 1985 and 1986.[241] The first was called the "Marcora" programme which was approved by parliament in 1985 and came into operation in 1987. This programme established two separate funds with total assets amounting to 250 billion lire.[242] One fund, called Foncooper, provided low interest loans to cooperatives for the purpose of: increasing productivity through the introduction of technology and organisational innovation; maintaining employment by restructuring or reconverting their plant. The loans granted ranged from 200 million lire to 2 billion lire and were repayable within 8 to 10 years. The maximum amount is made available for restructuring and reconversions. The interest paid on the loans varies between 25% and 50% of the market rate.[243] Between 1987 and 1991, 273 cooperatives received loans under this scheme.[244]

The second fund established by the Marcora law, named the "Special Fund", is designed for Worker Take Overs (WTO) of private enterprises. Under this scheme workers have to invest at least 4 million lire, of which half is paid up front and the rest within two years, (usually taken from their redundancy payments). In support, the State provides grants not exceeding the equivalent of three years of wages normally paid under the special unemployment scheme for temporary laid-off workers (Cassa Integrazione Guadagni) which pays up to 80% of a person's income.[245] In return, the workers taking part in this scheme had to agree to a clause which forbade them from seeking unemployment benefits for three years. One major innovation introduced by the Marcora Law was that it allowed companies formed by cooperatives to invest in WTO's as long as their investments did not exceed 25% of the total members' shares. These companies have to be at least 80% owned by cooperatives and were eligible for State grants provided they matched the amount invested by the State. Under this scheme, between 1987 and 1991, 86 cooperatives were created of which 81 were in the areas of manufacturing (furniture, clothing textile and footwear, printing etc) and five cooperatives operated in the service industries. These cooperatives employed 3,254 people, an average of 38 people per cooperative.[246] The average amount invested by each member was 9 million lire, far exceeding the 4 million minimum requirement.[247] In all, the two schemes (Foncooper and Special fund) supported 354 cooperatives of which 208 or 57% of the total were members of La Lega.[248]

Another job creation scheme was initiated in 1986 and targeted youth unemployment in Southern Italy. This law, known as the "De Vito" law, was open to cooperatives and private enterprises as long as the majority of members were people between the age of 19-29. This scheme funded up to 60% of the initial start up capital for plants and equipment, including feasibility studies and market analysis. It provided loans for up to 30% of start up capital at low interest rates (30% of the market rate) payable over 10 years. It made available grants covering 75% of the administration costs in the first year, 50% in the second and 25% in the third.[249] One major innovation in this scheme was that each new cooperative or private enterprise was assigned under the tutelage of another established enterprise whose task was to help them survive and grow by providing managerial and technical expertise. From the cooperative movement 11 cooperatives took part in this scheme.[250] By 1991 the State invested 2,315 billion lire in 440 enterprises creating 16,360 jobs.[251] Over one quarter of these projects were approved to cooperative enterprises, indicating a high level of demand for them.[252]

These programmes have had their problems. The Marcora Law in particular has been heavily criticised. The first criticism is lack of adequate funds to meet the needs of the cooperative sector.[253] Secondly, the fund seemed more concerned with short term solutions, solving problems of enterprises in crisis rather than long term growth of the cooperative sector. Indeed, cooperative associations would have preferred to manage and invest funds according to the needs of the cooperative sector. Some observers are critical of this law, Silvia Gherardi says: "The main features of the Marcora law seem to lie in the belief that what is required is financial relief, rather than those structures that will meet the needs of the third sector of the economy".[254] Thirdly, there are long delays of up to 18 to 20 months before the enterprises receive any money.[255] Fourthly, La Lega feels that funds should also be used for any firm whose workers are in a position to take over, including small businesses without an heir and public firms which are being privatised.[256]

While all of these criticisms are true, the Marcora law is regarded as a good law that needs to be improved. Evidence suggests that after the first five years of operation the Marcora and the De Vito job creation programmes have been very successful. It is claimed that all of the cooperatives formed under the Marcora legislation were still active three years after their formation.[257] This compares favourably with the 30% to 60% failure rate of small to medium size private enterprises in Italy during the first three years of operation.[258] The Marcora programme has also turned out to be a low cost job creation programme. Estimates indicate that each job created through the Marcora programme cost only 22 million lire. It is also estimated that in return for 77 billion lire invested, the State got 120 billion in return through personal income tax, social security contributions and indirect taxes.[259] It is also estimated that after three years, 70% of the enterprises formed under the De Vito legislation can be regarded as viable, efficient enterprises, while the failure rate stands at only 6%.[260]

The State has also given cooperatives access to public resources through the use of a number of government measures enacted in the 1970s, but operational in the 1980s, with the twin intention of reducing the impact of the economic crisis and of promoting enterprise restructuring. In 1976, the State provided grants for small and medium sized enterprises for the purpose of acquiring land, machinery and other equipment. In 1977, the "Industrial Reconversion" law was approved by Parliament allowing firms to obtain 10 year loans for amounts up to 500 million lire at low interest rate.[261] The Ministry of Agriculture provided cooperatives a total of 1,063 billion lire between 1986-1990, of which 10.91% went to cooperatives associated to La Lega.[262] The EEC also made available a number of grants either for the purpose of modernising the enterprise's plant and equipment or for the maintenance of employment.[263]

There is no doubt that the State has supported cooperatives. Yet, even in the 1980s, there is evidence to suggest that the potential of the cooperative movement is not fully appreciated. Italico Santoro, representing La Lega at a conference held in Bologna in 1985, stated that La Lega had been excluded from the Industrial Reconversion Law.[264] Another way of measuring the impact of the various laws is to measure how funds are distributed. In 1989, 96% of the funds allocated to encourage technological innovation went to large private enterprises.[265] Fiat alone received 3,100 billion lire in 1991 to build a factory in Southern Italy and this alone was more than the entire amount spent on the two job creation funds.[266] Another indicator of State support is provided by the Ministry of Finance. Research from this department has revealed that each year Treasury forgoes up to 80,000 billion lire through various types of exemptions and grants offered by the Italian government to businesses and non businesses entities. Out of this sum, only 1,400 billion lire equivalent to 1.75% of the total is attributable to the cooperative movement.[267]

Conclusion

The purpose of this chapter was to introduce La Lega and the political, economic and social environment in which it operated and to set the scene for the elaboration of the main themes of this thesis such as the inter-relationship between the cooperatives, La Lega and the State and how cooperatives have overcome the problems they face when competing in a market economy. In doing so this chapter has provided enough information to make some preliminary remarks regarding the character of the Italian cooperative movement and of La Lega. It has also provided some details which help explain how La Lega's cooperatives have overcome some of the problems normally associated with cooperative development.

The research has shown that the Italian cooperative movement has a number of characteristic features. It is a cooperative movement which although it has witnessed periods of high growth and stagnation has always continued to exist in large numbers. Therefore when favourable conditions have prevailed, it has flourished since the structures, people and knowledge were there to provide support.

Another feature is that the movement has always been divided along political lines as parties saw in its large membership and economic potential either a form of political support or a mechanism with which changes could be brought about in the economic as well as the political sphere. Political division has led to the formation of three Central Associations of various political leanings grouping cooperatives from all sectors of the economy.

What also stands out is the highly regulatory and supportive role played by the State since the 1880s. Indeed, the State's cooperative law regulates the level of membership, how the surplus should be distributed and that assets should be collectively owned. State support has come in the form of tax concessions, loans, grants, public works and land.

This chapter has also provided some insights into La Lega. Since its formation in 1886, La Lega has evolved from an organisation representing 246 cooperatives to one representing over 12,000. This analysis has recognised a number of characteristics of La Lega as an organisation. First, La Lega has developed into an organisation which can be described as a modern network of enterprises. The main characteristics of La Lega as a modern organisation are: it is an intersectoral organisation having as members cooperatives from many sectors of the economy; it has formed a number of support structures providing economic support through the consortia network and the various companies which deal in management, finance and trade; it comprises of many large cooperatives which produce the bulk of the total turnover; while it is an organisation present throughout the national territory, those from Northern Italy are still more numerous and produce most of the turnover; it has developed good relations with the local economy through its locally based cooperatives, intercooperative cooperation, cultural activities and support from the local councils; it has shown an ability to manage change and develop appropriate structures suitable for the needs of the cooperatives.

The second main feature of La Lega as an organisation is the role played by political parties. The research has shown that three main parties, the Communists, the Socialists and the Republicans are organised in factions within La Lega. They have influenced the overall strategy of La Lega, they have provided personnel, discipline, ideas and most importantly they have provided invaluable political support when dealing with the State.

The third major aspect of La Lega is its relationship with the State. Unlike the early cooperators in the UK and those of Canada, La Lega has always identified the State as an institution which could support cooperative development capable of providing public works, tax concessions and finance for the cooperative sector. Consequently, it has always sought to influence the State from within and from without. La Lega has successfully influenced the State from within by promoting a parliamentary lobby group, by electing its own deputies, by having representatives in a number of parliamentary commissions and since 1971 in the executive of the cooperative branch of the BNL. Activity external to the State institutions has included supporting various left wing political parties, lobbying ministers and bureaucrats through its own national, regional and provincial sectoral structures and influencing public opinion through newspapers, conferences and public demonstrations.

The historical analysis made in this chapter, has also provided information on how Italian cooperatives have overcome some problems they have faced when competing in a market economy. It has shown that cooperatives have been promoted by individuals supporting cooperatives, by the Resistance movement, by the trade unions, by La Lega and by the State through job creation policies. This provides answers to the question on how cooperatives have overcome the entrepreneurial problem. The role of the State and of La Lega's financial structures also give an indication of how the financial problems were overcome. The vast number of La Lega's companies and consortia dealing with management, trade and technology have provided much needed managerial support to cooperatives. All of these factors have contributed in making cooperatives more competitive in the market.

The purpose of this chapter was to introduce the Italian cooperative movement and to set the scene for future investigation. It is the task of the next chapters to provide further analysis and a full explanation of how the individual cooperatives, La Lega and the State have contributed in overcoming the problems cooperatives face when competing in the economy.

Notes

1 Renato Zangheri, "Nascita e Primi Sviluppi", in Renato Zangheri, Giuseppe Galasso and Valerio Castronovo, Storia del Movimento Cooperativo in Italia, Giulio Einaudi Editore, Torino, 1987, p.11.
2 Di Romarin, "Dal Nostro Inviato Speciale", *La Cooperazione Italiana*, Ottobre 1986, p.133.
3 Nicola Zotti, *La Cooperazione Italiana di Consumatori*, Editrice Cooperativa, Roma, 1983, p.10.
4 J Carroll Moody and Gilbert C Fyte, *The Credit Union Movement: Origins and Development 1850-1970*, University of Nebraska Press: Lincoln, 1971, p.13.
5 Ugo Bellocchi, "Mille Banche per il Popolo", *Storia Illustrata*, Luglio 1986, pp.118-125.
6 Zangheri, *op.cit*, pp.55-62.
7 Giuliano Procacci, *Storia Degli Italiani*, Editori Laterza, 1984, pp.411-419.
8 Martin Clark, *Modern Italy,1871-1982,* Longman, London, 1982, p.130.
9 Maurizio Degl'Innocenti, "Geografia e Struttura della Cooperazione in Italia", in Giulio Sapelli, *Il Movimento Cooperativo in Italia: Storia e Problemi*, Giulio Einaudi Editore, Torino 1981, pp.23-24.
10 Bellochi, *op.cit.*, p.126.
11 Degl'Innocenti, *op.cit*, pp.17-18.
12 Giuseppe Mazzini, "Lavoro e Capitali nelle Stesse Mani", in Walter Briganti (ed), *Il Movimento Cooperativo in Italia 1854-1925*, Editrice Cooperativa, Roma, 1978, pp.26-29.
13 Zangheri, op.cit., pp.40-48.
14 Zeffiro Ciuffoletti, "Dirigenti e Ideologie del Movimento Cooperativo", in Giulio Sapelli, *Il Movimento Cooperativo in Italia: Storia e Problemi*, Giulio Einaudi Editore, Torino 1981, pp.121-127.
15 Marco Pelliconi, "Uomini e Strutture della Cooperazione Imolese", in Angelo Varni (ed), *Emilia-Romagna Terra di Cooperazione*, Eta/Analisi, Bologna, 1990, pp.121-122.
16 Franco Bojardi, "Cooperazione Reggiana e Tradizione Riformista", in Angelo Vardi (ed), *Emilia-Romagna Terra di Cooperazione*, Eta/Analisi, Bologna, 1990, p.162.
17 Zangheri, op.cit., p.158.
18 Onelio Prandini, *La Cooperazione Italiana: Organizzazione, Storia e Sviluppi del Movimento Cooperativo*, Editori Riuniti, Roma, Seconda Edizione, 1986, pp.100-101.
19 Nicola Lisanti, *Il Movimento Operaio in Italia:1860-1980*, Editori Riuniti, Roma, 1986, pp.40-42. Gianni Baget-Bozzo, "Il Pensiero Sociale Cristiano", in Norberto Bobbio et.al., *Dizionario di Politica,* TEA/UTET, Torino, 1990, pp.779-783.
20 The majority of cooperatives were consumer (139), producers (42) and mutual aid societies (32), the rest were made up of credit and construction cooperatives. See Zangheri, *op.cit.*, p.76.
21 Maurizio Degl'Innocenti, *Storia della Cooperazione in Italia*, Editori Riuniti, 1977, pp. 96-99.
22 Orazio Pugliese, *Il Sistema Cooperativo*, Marsilio Editori, Venezia, 1987, pp.34-35.
23 Robert Oakeshott, *The Case for Workers' Cooperatives*, Routledge and Kegan Paul, London, 1978, p.150; Degl' Innocenti, op.cit., *Storia della Cooperazione in Italia*, p.105.
24 Degl' Innocenti, *ibid.*, pp.106-107.
25 Lisanti, *op.cit.*, pp.46-47.
26 Degl' Innocenti, op.cit., *Storia della Cooperazione in Italia,* pp.126-128.

27 Zangheri, *op.cit.*, p.187.
28 Procacci *op.cit*, p.417. John Earle, *The Italian Cooperative Movement*, Allen and Unwin, London, 1986, p.16.
29 Procacci, *ibid.*, p.451.
30 Valerio Castronovo, *L'Industria Italiana Dall'Ottocento a Oggi*, Mondadori Editore, Milano, 1990, Table 9. Roberto Romano, *Nascita dell'Industria in Italia*, Editori Riuniti, Roma, 1984, p.81.
31 Guido Gerosa, "I Notabili al Parlamento", *Storia Illustrata*, Luglio 1987, p.86. Aurelio Lepre, "La Rivoluzione del Voto", *Storia Illustrata*, Luglio 1987, p.90.
32 Pier Paolo D'Attorre, "Solidarietà, Innovazione, Impresa: La Cooperazione Ravennate", in Angelo Varni, *Emilia Romagna Terra di Cooperazione*, Eta/Analisi, Bologna 1990, p.138.
33 Procacci, *op.cit.*, pp.450-468.
34 Giuseppe Galasso, "Gli Anni della Grande Espansione e La Crisi del Sistema", in Renato Zangheri (ed), *Storia del Movimento Cooperativo in Italia*, Giulio Einaudi Editore, Torino, 1987 p.248.
35 Degl' Innocenti, *op.cit.*, *Storia della Cooperazione in Italia*, pp.196-202.
36 Alberto Basevi, "L'Istituto di Credito alla Cooperazione", in Walter Briganti (ed), *Il Movimento Cooperativo in Italia 1854-1925*, Editrice Cooperativa, Roma, 1982, pp.229-230.
37 Degl' Innocenti, *op.cit.*, *Storia della Cooperazione in Italia*, p.212.
38 Maurizio Degl'Innocenti, "Le Origini della Cooperazione in Emilia Romagna", in Angelo Varni (ed), *Emilia Romagna Terra di Cooperazione*, Eta/Analisi, Bologna 1990, p. 27.
39 Between 1989 and 1907 cooperatives received 56.4 million lire worth of public contracts out of a total of one billion going to private enterprises. Galasso, *op.cit.*, p.299.
40 Degl' Innocenti, *op.cit.*, *Storia della Cooperazione in Italia,* p. 327.
41 Degl' Innocenti, *op.cit.*, "Geografia e Struttura della Cooperazione in Italia", pp.39-45.
42 La Lega, "Statistica della Cooperazione 1902", in Walter Briganti (ed), *Il Movimento Cooperativo in Italia 1854-1925: Scritti e Documenti*, Editrice Cooperativa, Roma, 1982, pp.193-200. Roberto Tremelloni, "Per Una Statistica Della Cooperazione 1915-1921", in Walter Briganti (ed), *Il Movimento Cooperativo in Italia 1854-1925: Scritti e Documenti*, Editrice Cooperativa, Roma, 1982, pp.278-287. Galasso, *op.cit.*, pp.285ff.
43 Of these 8,000, 3840 had paid their membership fee directly to the central organisation, the remainder either had not paid their fees or were associated with the local federations. Galasso, *op.cit*, p.285.
44 *Ibid.*, pp.282-285.
45 *Ibid.*, p.426.
46 Paolo Spriano, *The Occupation of the Factories*, Pluto Press, London, 1975.
47 Lepre, *op.cit.*, p.91.
48 Pier Paolo D'Attorre, "La Politica", in Renato Zangheri (ed), *Bologna*, Editori Laterza, Bari, 1986, p.138.
49 Degl' Innocenti, *op.cit.*, *Storia della Cooperazione in Italia*, p.378.
50 Procacci, *op.cit.*, p.501. D'Attorre, *op.cit.*, p.145.
51 D'Attorre, *ibid.*, p.139.
52 Procacci, *op.cit.*, pp.502-505.
53 Dino Alfieri, "Il Fascismo e la Cooperazione" *La Cooperazione nell'Italia Fascista*, Milano 1929, in Walter Briganti (ed), *Il Movimento Cooperativo in Italia 1926-1962: Scritti e Documenti*, Editrice Cooperativa, Roma, 1978, pp.40-43.

54 Angelo Tasca, "Gli Attacchi del Fascismo alla Cooperazione", *Nascita e Avvento del Fascismo*, Quarta Edizione, Bari 1972, in Walter Briganti (ed), *Il Movimento Cooperativo in Italia 1854-1925: Scritti e Documenti*, Editrice Cooperativa, Roma, 1982, pp.249-253.
55 Galasso, *op.cit.*, p. 423.
56 Earle *op.cit.*, p.25.
57 Vera Zamagni, "L'Economia", in Renato Zangheri (ed), *Bologna*, Editori Laterza, Bari, 1986, p.288.
58 Zotti, *op.cit.*, p.24.
59 Mariella Nejrotti, "La Lunga Notte dell'Era Fascista", *La Cooperazione Italiana*, Ottobre 1986, p.184.
60 Galasso, *op.cit.*, p.286.
61 *Ibid.*, p.459.
62 Guido Bonfante, "La Legislazione Cooperativistica", in Giulio Sapelli (ed), *Il Movimento Cooperativo in Italia: Storia e Problemi*, Einaudi Editore, Torino, 1981, p.215.
63 Luciana Ricci Garotti, "La Cooperazione in Emilia Romagna nel Periodo Fascista", in Angelo Varni (ed), *Emilia Romagna Terra di Cooperazione,* Eta/Analisi, Bologna, 1990, p.41. Galasso, *op.cit.*, p.484.
64 The elections were a foregone conclusion because members knew that there was little they could do since they risked not getting any public works.
65 Nuova Muratori was formed in 1910 after ideological differences with the Socialists prompted the Republican members to form their own cooperative. Pierpaolo Vichi, *La Cooperativa Muratori Cementisti di Ravenna 1916-1926*, Grafiche Galeati Imola, 1981, pp.17-31.
66 Vichi, *Ibid.*, pp.125-163; see also Giovanni Montanari, *la Cooperativa Muratori e Cementisti di Ravenna Durante il Fascismo 1926-1945,* Feltrinelli, Milano, 1986, pp.21-63.
67 Nejrotti, *op.cit.*, pp.186-187.
68 Degl' Innocenti, *op.cit.*, "Geografia e Strutture della Cooperazione in Italia", p.60.
69 Garotti, *op.cit.*, p.43.
70 Nejrotti, *op.cit.*, p.182.
71 For a general discussion on Fascism see Edda Saccomani, "Fascismo", in Norberto Bobbio, et al., *Dizionario di Politica*, Tea/Utet, Torino 1990, pp.365-374.
72 Nejrotti, *op.cit.*, p.188.
73 D'Attorre, *op.cit.*, "Solidarietà, Innovazione, Impresa: La Cooperazione Ravennate", p.98.
74 Paul Ginsborg, *A History of Contemporary Italy; Society and Politics 1943-1988*, Penguin Books, London, 1988, pp.8-71.
75 Giuliana Ricci Garotti, "Il Movimento Cooperativo Bolognese e la Federazione Cooperative e Mutue dal Secondo Dopoguerra agli Anni 50", in *L'Unione dei Mille*, Editrice Emilia Romagna, Bologna, 1991, p.185.
76 Nazario Sauro Onofri, "1945: Rinasce la Cooperazione Bolognese", *L'Unione dei Mille*, Editrice Emilia Romagna, Bologna, 1991, p.106.
77 Some famous partisans include Giulio Cerreti who became president of La Lega after 1947, Cinzio Zambelli who is regarded as the father of Unipol, Silvio Miana was president of La Lega in the 1960s, Gustavo Trombetti (Gramsci's cell friend) founded the cooperative Camst, Vilmo Piccioni was a major figure for the fishing cooperatives.
78 Valerio Castronovo, "Dal Dopoguerra ad Oggi", in Renato Zangheri (ed), *Storia del Movimento Cooperativo in Italia*, Giulio Einaudi Editore, Torino, 1987, pp.500-507. It is

important to note that these figures are only an approximation. For an explanation of how the Ministry of Labour calculates the number of Cooperatives operating in Italy and the margin of error in such calculations see Appendix B.

79 Stefania Conti, "La Ricostituzione della Lega: 1943-1948", in Fabio Fabbri (ed), *Il Movimento Cooperativo Nella Storia D'Italia 1854-1975*, Feltrinelli Editore, Milano, 1979, p.323.

80 Walter Briganti, "Introduzione", in Walter Briganti (ed), *Il Movimento Cooperativo in Italia:1926-1962*, Editrice Cooperativa, Roma, 1978, p.10.

81 Onofri, *op.cit.*, p.118.

82 Giorgio Galli notes that between 2/3 and 3/4 of the leaders of the Italian Resistance were Communists. see Giorgio Galli, *Storia dei Partiti Politici Europei*, Rizzoli, Milano, 1990, p. 248.

83 Eric Hobsbawn, *The Italian Road to Socialism: an Interview with Giorgio Napolitano*, Translated by John Cammet and Victoria De Grazia, Lawrence Hill and Company, Westport, Connecticut, 1977.

84 Castronovo, *op.cit.*, "Dal Dopoguerra ad Oggi", p.556.

85 *Ibid.*, pp.509 and 559.

86 R Forte, "Il Secondo Congresso della Confederazione Cooperativa Italiana", *La Rivista della Cooperazione*, Roma, Ottobre-Dicembre 1947, in Walter Briganti (ed), *Il Movimento Cooperativo in Italia 1926-1962*, Edizione Cooperativa, Roma, 1978, p.190.

87 Earle, *op.cit.*, p.30.

88 Walter Briganti (ed), "l'Articolo 45. La Relazione e La Discussione", in *Il Movimento Cooperativo In Italia, 1926-1962,* Editrice Cooperative, Roma, 1978, p.188.

89 Walter Briganti, op.cit., "Introduzione", p.22.

90 See, Filippo Strati, "Gli Strumenti di Politica Attiva del Lavoro Aventi per Soggetto L'Autogestione", in *I Nuovi Scenari della Cooperazione in Italia: Problemi di Efficienza, Efficacia e Legittimazione Sociale*, A Cura di A Carbonaro and S Gherardi, Franco Angeli Editore, Milano, 1988, pp.327-328. Riccardo Azzolini and Patrizia Di Monte, "L'Impresa Cooperativa: Regolamentazione Legislativa e Problemi Economici", in *Pubblico e Privato: Secondo Rapporto Cer-Censis sull'Economia Italiana*, Edizione Del Sole 24 Ore, Milano, 1987, pp.110-114.

91 Michele Balboni, "L'Impresa Cooperativa: Aspetti Legislativi e Fiscali", in Francesco Carella (ed), *Il Movimento, Il Sistema, La Rete: Un Decennio di Cambiamenti nelle Imprese Cooperative*, Editrice Emilia Romagna, 1991, Bologna, pp.56-58.

92 Oakeshott, *op.cit.*, pp.153-154.

93 See section on the Plywood cooperatives in Chapter 2, pp. 33-34.

94 Castronovo, *op.cit.*, "Dal Dopoguerra ad Oggi", p.595.

95 *Ibid.*, pp.546 and 548.

96 Bonfante, *op.cit.*, p.230.

97 Briganti, *op.cit.*,"Introduzione", p.18.

98 Roberto Vighi, "La Resistenza e il Maltolto", in Walter Briganti (ed), *Il Movimento Cooperativo Italiano, 1926-1962*, Editrice Cooperativa, Roma, 1978, pp.115-121.

99 Castronovo, *op.cit.*, "Dal Dopoguerra ad Oggi", p.559.

100 Ginsborg, *op.cit.*, pp.115-118.

101 Donald Sassoon, *Contemporary Italy: Politics, Economy and Society Since 1945*, Longman, New York, 1987, p.125.

102 Agostino Ottani, "Introductory Speech Given at the VII Provincial Congress of Bologna June 1952", in La Lega Provinciale di Bologna, *Atti del VII Congresso Provinciale, 7-8 Giugno 1952*, Bologna., p.3.
103 *Ibid.*, p.26.
104 Roberto Calari, *Autonomia e Collateralismo del Movimento Cooperativo nella Provincia di Bologna del 1945-1962. La Lega Provinciale delle Cooperative tra Economia e Politica nel Secondo Dopoguerra*, Tesi di Laurea, Facolta di Scienze Politiche, Università degli Studi di Bologna, 1988-89, p.222.
105 AGCI, *AGCI Dopo Trenta Anni*, Ravenna, 1990, p.3.
106 La Lega, "Delibere del XXII Congresso Nazionale della LNCM", in Walter Briganti (ed), *Il Movimento Cooperativo in Italia: 1963-1980*, Editrice Cooperativa, Roma, 1982, pp. 256-259.
107 Walter Briganti, "Introduzione", in *Il Movimento Cooperativo in Italia: 1963-1980*, Editrice Cooperativa, Roma, 1982, p.13.
108 Castronovo, *op.cit.*, *L'Industria Italiana Dall'Ottocento a Oggi*, p.278.
109 In all between 1951 to 1975 the Ente Delta Padano promoted and supported a total of 100 agricultural cooperatives investing a total of 42 billion lire. Not all cooperatives were affiliated to La Lega. See Ente Delta Padano, *Venticinque Anni di Cooperazione*, Bologna, 1976, p.35.
110 Earle, *op.cit.*, pp.31-32.
111 Castronovo, *op.cit.*, "Dal Dopoguerra ad Oggi", p.665.
112 Onofri, *op.cit.*, p.142.
113 Emilia Romagna received only 0.75% from the Marshall Aid funds compared to the 25% received by Piedmont and 28% by Lombardy. In addition, State owned factories which had employed 12,000 persons before the war employed 700 in 1952. see Vittorio Capecchi, "A History of Flexible Specialisation and Industrial Districts in Emilia Romagna", in F. Pyke (ed), *Industrial Districts and Inter-Firm Co-operation in Italy*, International Institute for Labour Studies, Geneva, 1990, p.27.
114 Castronovo, *op.cit.*, "Dal Dopoguerra ad Oggi", p.578.
115 *Ibid.*, p.646.
116 For a concise overview of the role of consortia see Giancarlo Pasquini, "La Cooperazione fra Imprese Cooperative: La Formazione del Sistema Consortile", *Rivista della Cooperazione*, Ottobre-Dicembre 1981, pp.43-50.
117 Castronovo, *op.cit.*, "Dal Dopoguerra ad Oggi", p.726.
118 *Ibid.*, pp. 623 and 686.
119 Overall the economy grew by 5.3% between 1951-1958 and by 6.6% between 1958-1963. See Donald Sassoon, *op.cit*, p.31.
120 Castronovo, *op.cit.*, "Dal Dopoguerra ad Oggi", p.596.
121 Alessandro Skuk, research interview.
122 Castronovo, *op.cit.*, "Dal Dopoguerra ad Oggi", p.712.
123 Alessandro Skuk and Emilio Severi research interviews.
124 Castronovo, *op.cit.*, "Dal Dopoguerra ad Oggi", p.716.
125 The view that economic success was directly linked to political realignement lasted until 1975, see Calari, *op.cit*, p. 222.
126 Between 1966 and 1967 29 private firms owned directly or indirectly 34% of all shares while the top 100 firms (out of 60,000 in the manufacturing industry) controlled 40% of all exports. See Castronovo, op.cit., "Dal Dopoguerra ad Oggi", p.723.

127 For a detailed description of the political economic programme of the PCI see the introductory speech given by the then secretary Palmiro Togliatti at the eighth party congress and the political economic programme approved at the same congress. In *Il PCI e La Svolta del 1956*, Rinascita Supplement, Editrice L'Unità, 1986, Roma, pp.49-141.
128 Moruzzi, *op.cit.*, pp.195-198.
129 Castronovo, *op.cit.*, "Dal Dopoguerra ad Oggi", p.684.
130 Garzanti Editore, *Enciclopedia del Diritto e dell' Economia Garzanti*, Milano, 1985, p.1091. More information on this topic will be provided in Chapter 8 where the nature of the Italian State is discussed and analysed.
131 See La Lega, "Per Una Politica di Piano", Dalla Dichiarazione Programmatica della LNCM, Roma, 1962, in Walter Briganti (ed), *Il Movimento Cooperativo in Italia 1926-1962, Editrice Cooperativa*, Roma, 1978, pp.372-376. La Lega, "La Linea della Lega al 28mo Congresso", in Walter Briganti (ed), *Il Movimento Cooperativo in Italia 1963-1980*, Editrice Cooperativa, Roma, 1982, pp.134-151. Silvio Miana, "Proposte Programmatiche del Movimento Cooperativo", Relazione Introduttiva al 29mo Congresso della Lega (1973), in Walter Briganti (ed), *Il Movimento Cooperativo in Italia 1963-1980,* Editrice Cooperativa, Roma, 1982, pp.208-218.
132 Silvio Miana, *op.cit.*, pp.211-214.
133 Vincenzo Galetti, Intervento, *Atti della 1a Conferenza Nazionale della Cooperazione*, Primo Volume, Roma, 1977, p.92.
134 Briganti, op.cit., *Il Movimento Cooperativo in Italia 1963-1980,* p.43.
135 Castronovo, *op.cit.*, "Dal Dopoguerra ad Oggi", p.773.
136 Giuseppe Vitale, "L'Integrazione nei Consorzi", in *L'Autogestione in Italia: Realtá e Funzione della Cooperazione*, De Donato, Bari, 1975, pp.80-81; and Cavina Mauro,"I Problemi Organizzativi e Gestionali nell'Impresa Cooperativa", in *La Lega della Cooperative di Fronte alle Trasformazioni, le Modificazioni Strutturali dell"Economia: il Nuovo Rapporto Produzione-Ambiente*, La Lega-Convegno Dei Dirigenti e dei Quadri, Bologna, 3 Luglio 1985, p.119.
137 Giorgio Bettini, "Un'Impresa del Nostro Tempo", in *La Cooperazione Italiana*, Ottobre 1986, pp.265-267; and Giorgio Bettini, "Un'Unica Rete fra Credito e Coop", in *La Cooperazione Italiana*, Ottobre 1986, pp.288-291.
138 Intercoop, *Intercoop Information Booklet,* Roma, 1987. Vittorio Marzocchi, "Un Patrimonio da Valorizzare", *La Cooperazione Italiana*, Ottobre 1986, pp.296-297. Vittorio Marzocchi, "Di Qua e di la Dell'Atlantico", *La Cooperazione Italiana*, Ottobre 1986, pp.298-300. Pier Luigi Orvieto, "Trent'Anni sulle Vie del Mondo", *La Cooperazione Italiana*, Ottobre 1986, pp.292-295.
139 Ivano Barberini, "Quando i Consumatori Fanno Impresa Insieme", *La Cooperazione Italiana*, Ottobre 1986, p.233.
140 Castronovo, *op.cit.*,"Dal Dopoguerra ad Oggi", p.756.
141 *Ibid.*, p.741.
142 *Ibid.*, pp.743-746. See also Earle, *op.cit.*, pp.105-106.
143 Castronovo, *ibid.*, pp. 699 and 757.
144 *Ibid.*, pp.716 and 769.
145 More information will be provided in Chapter Eight when dealing with the cooperative case studies.
146 Indeed, since 1962 Italy had a very high strike record which reduced the competitiveness of private enterprises, Giuseppe de Rita, *La Cultura del Sociale nell'Impresa Cooperativa*, Club 87, Febbraio 1989, Bologna, p.14.

147 Mark Holmstrom, *Industrial Democracy in Italy*, Avebury, Aldershot, 1989, p.139.
148 See Glossary for an explanation of how members' loans operate.
149 Briganti, *op.cit.*,"Introduzione", in *Il Movimento Cooperativo in Italia 1963-1980,* pp. 34-35.
150 M D'Ambrosio and R Stefanelli, *La Cooperazione nell'Industria*, Editrice Cooperativa, Roma, 1983, p.75.
151 Oakeshott, *op.cit.*, p.152.
152 Castronovo, *op.cit.*, "Dal Dopoguerra ad Oggi", p.738.
153 Galetti, *op.cit.*, *La Cooperazione in Italia*, Editori Riuniti, Roma, 1976, p.51.
154 Garzanti Editore, op.cit., p.1263.
155 I am referring to a book written by Vincenzo Galetti, president of La Lega titled *Cooperazione:Forza Anticrisi* which literally translates as *Cooperation: an Anti-Crisis Force*. see Vincenzo Galetti, *Cooperazione Forza Anticrisi*, Feltrinelli Editore, Milano, 1975.
156 Galetti, *op.cit.*, *La Cooperazione in Italia*, p.51.
157 The higher amount of 4 million lire was allowed only in producers and agricultural cooperatives. Strati, op.cit., p.328.
158 Aldo Ricci, "I Problemi Lasciati Aperti dalla Piccola Riforma", in Walter Briganti (ed), *Il Movimento Cooperativo in Italia 1963-1980*, Editrice Cooperativa, Roma, 1982, p.188.
159 Renato Midoro, *Gli Strumenti per il Finanziamento delle Cooperative*, Editrice Cooperativa, Roma, 1984, p.30.
160 Alberto Zevi, "The Financing of Cooperatives in Italy", in *Annals of Public and Cooperative Economy*, Volume 61, Number 3-3, April-September 1990, p.356.
161 Briganti, *op.cit.*, "Introduzione", in *Il Movimento Cooperativo in Italia 1963-1980*, pp.13-16.
162 In 1978, the national government drew up a ten year housing plan allocating to it 4,000 billion lire. Under this plan 125,000 apartments were built by 1984. Ginsborg, *op.cit.*, p.391.
163 Max Jaggi et al, *Red Bologna*, Writers and Readers, London, 1977, p.58.
164 Not all of these cooperatives were associated to La Lega. See Jenny Thornley, "Workers' Cooperative and Trade Unions: The Italian Experience", in *Economic and Industrial Democracy*, Volume 4, 1983, pp.326-331.
165 For an overview see Claudio Tolomelli, "Policies to Support Innovation in Emilia Romagna: Experiences and Prospects and Theoretical Prospects", in Enrico Ciciotti et al., *Technological Change in a Spatial Context,* Springer-Verlag, Berlin, 1989, pp.356-378.
166 Brusco, *op.cit.*, p.180.
167 Most construction cooperatives have access to public works. In Bologna the largest is Edilter which in 1991 was refurbishing Piazza Maggiore, the largest and most famous piazza in the city.
168 See the case study on the cooperative Spepcoop in Chapter Eight.
169 I am referring to the cooperative Altercoop from Bologna which provides recycled paper to the local council of Bologna.
170 The cooperative Alveo receives work from the regional councils to control the pollution levels in enterprises.
171 The cooperatives Altercoop and Saragozza perform this task in Bologna.
172 The cooperative "Nuova Scena" manages a couple of theatres on behalf of the local council of Bologna.

173 The cooperative CAMST of Bologna manages one of the student refectory of the University of Bologna.
174 Rochat, *op.cit.*, p.27.
175 Giuseppe Campos Venuti, "Bilancio della Legge 167", in Giorgio Rochat (ed), *La Casa in Italia 1945-1980: Alle Radici del Potere Democristiano*, Zanichelli Editore, Bologna, 1980, p.187.
176 See Regione Emilia Romagna, *Bilancio 1976: Come Agisce la Regione*, Bologna, 1975, p.78; Regione Emilia Romagna, *I Provvedimenti D'Emergenza della Regione*, Bologna, 1977, pp.38-39.
177 These policies will be explained in the case study on the consumer cooperative Coop Emilia Veneto in Chapter Eight.
178 Levitt argues that markets have been homogenised therefore local poducts will come under more fierce competition. See Theodore Levitt, "The Globalisation of Market", *Harvard Business Review*, May-June 1983, Number 3, p.93.
179 In 1988, the average monthly wage stood at US $643 in Taiwan, $558 in Hong Kong, $401 in Singapore, $610 in Korea, $132 in Thailand, $129 in Malaysia, and $209 in Indonesia. See Walden Bello and Stephanie Rosenfeld, *Dragons in Distress: Asia's Miracle Economies in Crisis*, Penguin Books, London 1990.
180 The degree of unonism is very low: for instance only 14% of the workforce are union members in Hong Kong, In Thailand (1.01%), Indonesia (4.08%), South Korea (7%), Malaysia (8.07%), Singapore (16%), Taiwan (17.03%). See Abe David and Ted Wheelwright, *The Third Wave: Australia and Asian Capitalism*, Left Book Club, Sutherland, 1989, pp.216-228.
181 *The Australian*, "Why GATT Matters", Monday December 6, 1993, p.9.
182 This was ratified by the Maastricht treaty which was signed in 1991 and has been ratified by all European countries by 1993.
183 Robert Grahams, "Italians Lose Golden Pensions", *Financial Times*, 11 July 1991, p.2.
184 Maurizio Tortorella, "Tutto Castello e Bottega", *Panorama*, 4 Ottobre 1992, p.53.
185 *The Economist*, "A Survey of Italy: Until the Fat Lady Sings", June 26 1993, p.20.
186 Between 1983-1985 IRI the largest Italian public corporation sold 20 companies and acquired only one. OECD Economic Surveys, *Italy*, Paris, 1989, p.52.
187 Stefano Stanghellini, "L'Impresa di Costruzione Soggetto Innovativo nel Processo Produttivo delle Opere Complesse", in Ecosfera (ed), *Le Imprese di Costruzione nel Mercato Europeo*, Il Sole 24 Ore, Milano, 1990, p.201.
188 The idea here was to cooperate with businesses which practised good industrial relations and paid their taxes and not to deal with those businesses which operated in the hidden economy or those which practiced dubious industrial relations policy. La Lega, *Congresso Nazionale della Lega delle Cooperative e Mutue: Documento Politico*, Roma, 1990, p.12.
189 In the insurance sector the company Euresa was formed in 1990 by four European cooperative insurance companies: Unipol (Italy), Macif (France), Prevoyance Sociale (Belgium) and Folksam (Sweden). Walter Dondi, "Unipol Assicura L'Europa: Obbiettivo i Paesi dell'Est", *L'Unità,* 15 Dicembre 1989, in Unipol Press, 16 Gennaio 1990, p.12. The construction and manufacturing cooperatives have formed a European organisation Cecop. Walter Dondi, "Cecop c Euroc", in *Lega Senza Frontiere*, L'Unità, 16 Giugno 1989, p.30. The small retailers are organised in Ugal, see Chiara Poletti, "Salve le Differenze", in *Lega Senza Frontiere*, L'Unità, 16 Giugno 1989, p.42. The consumer cooperatives have formed Intercoop a consortia which bulk buys goods on behalf of cooperatives and which helps forge

economic links between cooperatives from all European countries. Paola Bergonzoni, "Una Scelta Europea per Crescere Ancora", in *La Cooperazione Italiana,* Giugno-Luglio 1991, p.38.

190 La Lega could help modernise the State railway system by co-ordinating the activities of a variety of cooperatives which can: build and service railway tracks, manage the transportation of goods, provide expertise in building maintenance, cleaning and catering services, operate the passengers' luggage compartments, build and manage the car parking facilities, manage the taxi service, even do the ticketing. See Mauro Gori, "Per un Nuovo Rapporto tra Pubblico e Privato", *La Cooperazione Italiana,* Maggio 1991, p.9. See also Nino Lucantoni and Filippo Vita, "Un'Alleanza per L'Ambiente", *La Cooperazione Italiana,* Maggio 1991, pp. 13-53; and Viviana D'Isa, "Una Mano allo Stato", *La Cooperazione Italiana*, Aprile 1989, pp.38-45.

191 For the overall strategy during the eighties see: La Lega, *Atti del 32o Congresso: Società, Economia, Impresa: La Proposta Cooperativa, Roma, 1987,* pp.17-46; La Lega, *Congresso Nazionale della Lega delle Cooperative e Mutue: Documento Politico*, Roma, 1990.

192 Luigi Rosafio, "Relazione Introduttiva", in *La Lega: Conferenza Nazionale D'Organizzazione-Montecatini 1986*, Editrice Cooperativa, Roma, 1986, p.31.

193 More detail of La Lega's financial structure will be provided in Chapter Seven.

194 Federico Boccaletti, "Una Fase Nuova per la Formazione", *La Cooperazione Italiana,* Aprile 1993, pp.72-73.

195 Angelo Varni (ed), "Sinnea, Formazione Manageriale: Una Decisione Strategica per il Cambiamento Aziendale", in *Emilia Romagna Terra di Cooperazione*, Eta/Analisi, Bologna, 1990, pp.412-413.

196 *La Cooperazione Italiana*, "Un Sensore che Segnala come Cambiano le Coop", Ottobre 1991, pp.46-47.

197 More information on ICIE will be provided by the case study in Chapter Six.

198 Giuseppe Fabbri, "La Scommessa della Promozione", *La Cooperazione Italiana,* Ottobre 1986, pp.321-322. *Spazio Impresa*, "Costruire una Rete di Servizi per l'Azienda del Sud", 2 Aprile 1991, p.21.

199 Viviana D'Isa, "L'Universo Cooperativo Attraverso L'Immaggine", *La Cooperazione Italiana*, Ottobre 1986, pp.305-307.

200 Marzocchi, *op.cit.*, p.33.

201 About 20% of managers had once worked in the private sector, see Holmstrom, *op.cit.*, p.146.

202 For the 1956 statistics see, Ivano Barberini, *op.cit.*, p.233. For the 1990 figures see, *op.cit*, La Lega Nazionale delle Cooperative e Mutue, *Principali Indicatori del Movimento Cooperativo*, Roma, 1991, p.5.

203 Tommasini Nazzareno, "Crescere Cambiando", In *Consumi e Società,* Anno V, Numero 3, Maggio-Giugno 1991, p.21.

204 Associazione Nazionale Cooperative di Consumatori, *La Cooperazione di Consumatori*, Roma, 1990, Appendix 9.

205 Between 1981 and 1987, 94 cooperatives were formed from converting private enterprises. Roberto Malucelli, "Relazione Introduttiva", *Ottavo Congresso Nazionale delle Cooperative di Produzione e Lavoro*, La Lega, Milano, 1988.

206 For the 1980 results see M D'Ambrosio and R. Stefanelli, *op.cit.*, p.74. For the 1989 results see La Lega Nazionale delle Cooperative e Mutue, *op.cit.*, *Principali Indicatori del Movimento Cooperativo*, Roma, 1991.
207 In 1988 at least 20 cooperatives employed more than 500 persons, with the construction cooperative CMC employing 2,427. See La Lega Nazionale delle Cooperative e Mutue, *1988: Cento Profili di Imprese Cooperative,* Roma, 1988.
208 *Ibid.*
209 Le Certificate, "Produttività e Dimensione Aziendale in Aumento", *La Cooperazione Italiana,* Novembre/Dicembre, 1988, p.97.
210 For more informationn on sectoral activities see Orazio Pugliese (ed), *Il Sistema Cooperativo*, Marsilio Editori, Venezia, 1987.
211 For an explanation of how these percentages were calculated see Chapter 1 notes 10 and 13.
212 Castronovo, *op.cit*, "Dal Dopoguerra ad Oggi", p.833.
213 In 1988 the turnover of La Lega's fishing sector was 500 billion lire, 21.7% of the national total of 2,307 billion lire. See Ettore Iami, "Dove Compriamo Pesce? Anche dalla Montagnosa Svizzera", *L'Unità* 21 Luglio 1989, p.18; and Mario Bello, "I Progetti ci Sarebbero ma, Ovviamente, Mancano i Soldi", *L'Unità* 21 Luglio 1989.
214 There are ten cooperatives associated to La Lega in the top 45 construction firms in Italy. See Costruire, *Le Classifiche 1990*, Milano, Novembre 1990, pp.36 and 64.
215 For consumer cooperatives see Daniele Martini, "Sono Compagni che Sbagliano", *Panorama*, 13 Giugno 1993, p.200. For retail cooperatives see Placido Putzolu, "Offerta Diversificata e Unione delle Forze", *La Cooperazione Italiana*, Giugno-Luglio 1991, p.31.
216 Gabriella Ammassari, "Obiettivi Possibili per un Mercato Difficile", *La Cooperazione Italiana*, Dicembre 1992, p.34.
217 *La Cooperazione Italiana*, "Nuova Struttura Europea a Favore del Dettaglio", Novembre 1991, p.26.
218 Viviana D'Isa, "Servizi Integrati per Stare in Europa", *La Cooperazione Italiana*, Aprile 1989, p.45.
219 *La Cooperazione Italiana*, "Le Certificate-Produttività e Dimensione Aziendale in Aumento", p.97.
220 CMC, *Bilancio Consuntivo 1990*, Ravenna, 1991, p.16.
221 It is estimated that half of the world's production of bottle caps are produced by machinery manufactured by Sacmi. See La Lega, "Sacmi", *Cento Profili di Imprese Cooperative:1988*, Roma, 1988, p.153.
222 Sacmi Group, *Consolidated Balance Sheet 1991*, Imola, 1991, p.11.
223 Robert Oakeshott, *Workers as Entrepreneurs: Two Striking Success Stories from Italy*, Partnership Research Limited, London, 1990, pp.21-22.
224 Frediano Baldi, "Evergomma", in AROC (ed), *Organizzare L'Autogestione,* I Quaderni di Quarantacinque, Bologna, 1987, p.99.
225 Giancarlo Martelli, "Come Unire le Forze Senza Perdere Identità", *La Cooperazone Italiana*, Febbraio-Marzo 1throughout th
1Maria Silvia Sacchi, "Latte Concentrato", *Panorama*, 7 Giugno 1992, p.191.
227 Angelo Varni (ed), "Camst: Una Grande Associazione di Idèe per la Ristorazione Italiana", in *Emilia Romagna Terra di Cooperazione*, ETA/Analisi, Bologna, 1990, p.324.
228 Pietro Gentilucci, "Cooperservice il Segreto di un Successo", *La Cooperazione Italiana*, Maggio, 1992, p.30.
229 Ammassari, *op.cit.*, p.36.

230 Rino Petralia, *Movimento Cooperativo: Prospettive e Problemi*, Lega Nazionale Cooperative e Mutue, Roma, 1988, p.6.
231 Pugliese, *op.cit.*, pp.208-212.
232 The highest level of investment was made by members of producer cooperatives from Northern Italy whose average investment amounted to 830,000 lire per person in 1980. Midoro, *op.cit.*, p.17.
233 Ettore Dazzara, "La Questione Finanziaria e lo Sviluppo dell'Impresa Cooperativa", in *La Lega: la Questione Finanziaria e lo Sviluppo dell'Impresa Cooperativa,* Editrice Cooperativa, Roma, 1984, p.17.
234 Midoro, *op. cit.*, p.16.
235 *Ibid.*, p.30.
236 Zevi, *op.cit.*, "The financing of Italian Cooperatives", pp.354-355.
237 Azzolini and Di Monte, *op.cit.*, p.114.
238 Strati, *op.cit.*, p.328.
239 Gazzetta Ufficiale della Repubblica Italiana, *Nuove Norme in Materia di Società Cooperative*, Roma, 31 Gennaio 1992. See Also Sandro Bonella, "Finalmente Cittadine del Mercato", *La Cooperazione Italiana*, Gennaio 1992, pp. 4-9.
240 *Ibid.*
241 These programmes were made available to all cooperatives.
242 Zevi, *op.cit.*, "The Financing of Italian Cooperatives", p.358.
243 See the full text on the Marcora Law in Onelio Prandini, *op.cit.*, pp.141-154.
244 Renato De Bertoli, "Foncooper: Adeguare la Normativa e le Risorse ai Reali Bisogni", in *La Cooperazione Italiana*, Gennaio-Febbraio 1993, (Supplement: Legge 49/85 "Marcora" Stato di Attuazione e Nuove Proposte), p. 7.
245 *La Cooperazione Italiana,* "I Meccanismi della Legge", 4 Aprile 1989, p. 23.
246 Marco Marini e Chiara Cavallaro, "Miliardi Ben Spesi", *La Cooperazione Italiana*, 4 Aprile 1989, p.19. See also De Bertoli, *op.cit.*, p.5.
247 Alberto Zevi, "Uno Strumento Valido da Sfruttare Meglio", *La Cooperazione Italiana*, Ottobre 1991, p.40.
248 De Bertoli, *op.cit.*, p.7.
249 See the full text of the De Vito Law in Onelio Prandini, op.cit., pp.155-162.
250 Gianfranco Franci, "Il Vantaggio delle Coop Non Partire Favorite", *La Cooperazione Italiana*, Settembre 1990, p.11.
251 Viviana D'Isa, "Per Farle Crescere Ci Vuole il Tutor", *La Cooperazione Italiana*, Ottobre 1992, p.59.
252 Franci, *op.cit.*, "Il Vantaggio Delle Coop Non Partire Favorite", p.8.
253 In 1993 there were 481 applications waiting to be processed. Renato de Bortoli, *op.cit.*, p.5.
254 Silvia Gherardi, "Worker Takeovers: The Italian Experience", *Analysis of the Experiences and Problems Encountered by Worker Takeovers of Companies in Difficulty or Bankrupt,* Main Report, Commission of the European Communities, Luxembourg, 1987, p.171.
255 Massimo Tognoni argues that each application has to go backwards and forwards between a number of departments on 18 occasions. See Massimo Tognoni, "Marcora: Da Aziende in Crisi a Cooperative efficienti", in *Quarantacinque*, Anno XI, Luglio-Agosto 1989, p.37; Edoardo Marinelli, "Una Legge dai Buoni Esiti che va Potenziata e Sviluppata",

in *La Cooperazione Italiana*, Gennaio-Febbraio 1993, (Supplement: Legge 49/85 "Marcora" Stato di Attuazione e Nuove Proposte), p. 3.

256 Alberto Zevi, "Una piu Ampia Partecipazione dei Lavoratori anche in Imprese non in Crisi", in *La Cooperazione Italiana*, Gennaio-Febbraio 1993, (Supplement: Legge 49/85 "Marcora" Stato di Attuazione e Nuove Proposte), p.18.

257 Walter Dondi, "È Appena Iniziato il Viaggio di Cipputi", *La Cooperazione Italiana*, April 1989, p.35.

258 *La Cooperazione Italiana*, "Il Business Plan è la Prima Cosa", Ottobre 1992, p.57.

259 This estimate refers to the 95 cooperatives which have a Cooperative Financial Company as a shareholder. Carla Straini, "Una Nuova Legge 'Marcora' per Snellire le Procedure e Allargare le Aree di Intervento", in *La Cooperazione Italiana*, Gennaio-Febbraio 1993, (Supplement:Legge 49/85 "Marcora" Stato di Attuazione e Nuove Proposte), p.16.

260 D'Isa, *op.cit.*, "Per farle Crescere Ci Vuole il Tutor", p.59.

261 Midoro, op.cit., pp.147-148.

262 Michele Menichella, "Goria Sblocca i Fondi all'Agricoltura e il Cipe Distribuirà 2,700 Miliardi", *Il Sole 24 0RE*, 20 Luglio 1991, p.3.

263 Midoro, *op.cit.*, p.148.

264 Earle, *op.cit.*, p.208.

265 Virginia Lori, "Europa Sociale", in *Lega Senza Frontiere*, Editrice L'Unità, 16 Giugno 1989, p.20.

266 Mangiaterra, op.cit., p.135. Texas instruments received half of its 1,700 billion lire invested in Southern Italy from the Italian government either as grants or as cheap loans. See Enrico Marro, "Nasce il Silico in Abruzzo", *Corriere della Sera*, 9 Maggio 1992, p.29.

267 Virgilio Chelli, "Se lo Stato Si Mette In Cooperativa", *La Cooperazione Italiana*, Maggio 1991, p.7.

5 La Lega: The Central Association

The previous chapter has explained the genesis and the evolution of La Lega. The discussion has also identified La Lega to be a complex organisation made up of four components, these are: the cooperative enterprise; the consortia; a number of conventional companies wholly or partly owned by cooperatives; and a Central Association which affiliates all cooperatives at a territorial and a sectoral level. From the previous chapter we can arrive at a tentative definition of La Lega: a complex organisation which through a number of support structures promotes the growth of the cooperative sector by representing their interests when dealing with the State, ensuring that it does not discriminate against the cooperative sector. It also provides a number of services aimed at improving the economic competitiveness of individual cooperatives.

The purpose of the next three chapters is to further analyse the complexity of La Lega by examining the Central Association, the consortia network and the financial structures in more detail. This will provide a better understanding of La Lega. In addition, an analysis of the relation that exists between the various support structures and the individual cooperatives will be made. This will give the necessary evidence to evaluate the role played by the organisational structure in the economic success of the individual cooperatives. Further, the relationship between the organisational support structures and the State will also be evaluated to assess whether the latter has hindered or supported the growth of cooperatives. Finally, an analysis of the way the problems identified in chapter two have been overcome will be made.

This chapter will analyse the components and the functions performed by the Central Association.

The Central Association

The Central Association usually referred to as La Lega is the central organisation to which all cooperatives are affiliated. This organisation performs a number of non-economic and non-commercial activities on behalf of cooperatives through the territorial structures and sectoral associations.

The territorial structures perform various functions on behalf of all cooperatives from a given area or territory. The sectoral associations represent cooperatives from a particular sector of the economy over a given area or territory (see Figure 5.1).[1]

Territorial Structures - System of Governance

There are three main territorial structures. The main body is a central organisation which operates from Rome. This is supported by twenty regional councils and eight provincial federations. The provincial federations are present only in Emilia Romagna. The provincial federations have continued to operate in this region partly because they are very strong and do not want to relinquish power; but also because they can better represent the interest of cooperatives at the local level.

The internal structure of these bodies consists of a general council, a board of directors, an executive and a president. To elect the national body the electoral process is a lengthy one. Each individual cooperative holds its own congress and elects its representatives to regional congresses. Each regional congress then elects delegates to the national congress. The regions with the highest cooperative density are allocated more delegates and voting power. The delegates can be members of cooperatives or directors and employees of the organisational support structures. However, at all times, at least 50% of the delegates must come directly from the cooperatives. In addition, the consortia can elect their own representatives directly to the national congress. In 1991, the total number of delegates to the national congress amounted to 805, of which 85 were elected by the consortia (see Table 5.1). The congresses are held every four years.

The national congress then elects the various bodies which will govern the national territorial structures of La Lega for four years. These include: the general council, the board of directors, the executive, the president and two vice-presidents. It is the task of the general council to administer La Lega between congresses and to set up a date and an agenda for the next congress. It also has the responsibility to elect a board of directors, the executive council, the president and vice-president. In 1982 the general council comprised of 301 members who were required to meet at least four times a year. The board of directors was made up of 60 members who are required to meet once a month. The tasks of the board of directors are many: they have the responsibility to implement the decisions made by the general council, to lay down the conditions of employment for headquarters'

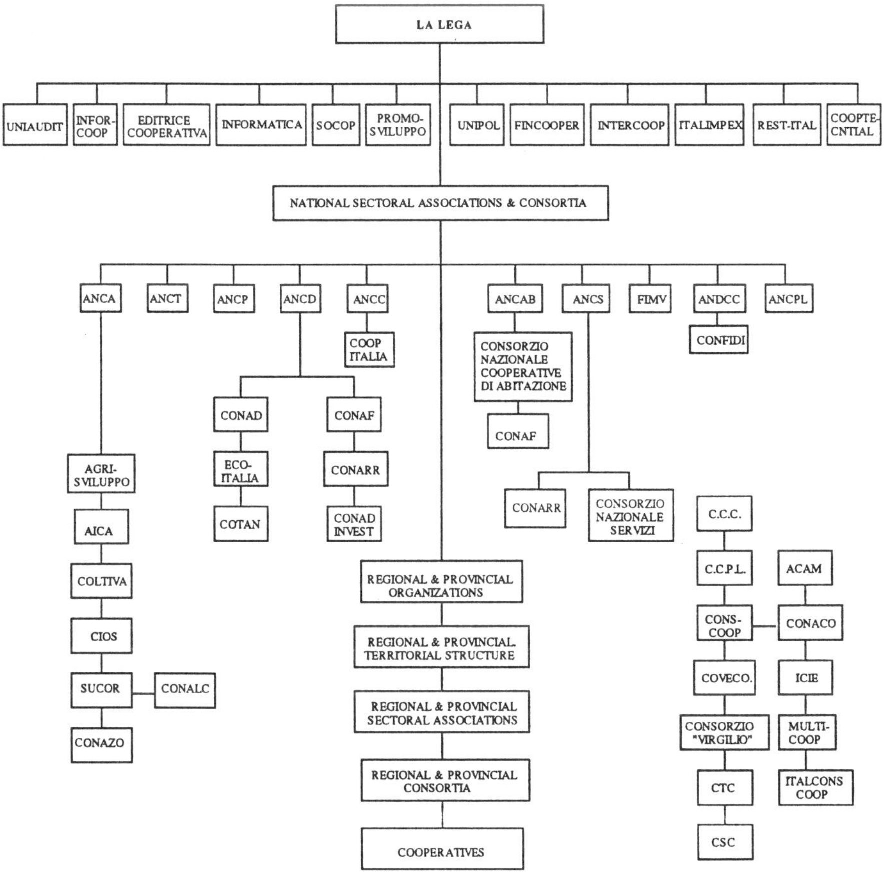

Figure 5.1 The Organisational Structure of La Lega

staff and appoints La Lega's representatives in public bodies. The day-to-day running of La Lega is left to the president, vice-president and the executive council.[2]

Table 5.1 Regional Delegates and Congressional Votes [3]

Region	Number of Delegates	Number of Votes
Valle D'Aosta	2	190
Piemonte	34	168,388
Liguria	39	244,788
Lombardia	69	440,248
Veneto	26	86,705
Trento/Bolzano	6	6,903
Friuli	16	122,900
Emilia/Romagna	262	761,483
Toscana	107	692,606
Marche	25	43,993
Umbria	26	90,975
Lazio	52	129,865
Molise	4	4,066
Abruzzo	6	16,099
Campania	22	91,091
Puglia	22	73,949
Basilicata	8	16,101
Calabria	9	26,778
Sicilia	31	99,917
Sardegna	14	56,852
Mutual Aid Societies	25	765,000
TOTAL	805	3,938,897

Source: La Lega Nazionale delle Cooperative e Mutue, *Documento Politico: 33mo Congresso Nazionale Roma 1991*, Roma, 1990, pp.41-42.

As it has been outlined in chapter three, La Lega enjoys a close relationship with political parties. This relationship is institutionalised through organised internal party factions that play a significant role in policy making and job allocations within La Lega. The executive positions in the various territorial structures are divided between the factions, these in turn nominate their candidates.[4] The distribution of power that takes place is not allocated by a numerical count through an electoral process, but it is negotiated for at the national congress. To ensure that the composition of the national congress reflects the wishes of the political factions, the bargaining process begins at the enterprise level and continues through the provincial and regional assemblies.[5] The factions use a number of arguments to increase their power. Some of the arguments are: level of support from members, electoral support of political parties,[6] positions of parties in government,[7] the contribution made by their faction to the history of cooperation,[8] the importance of portraying an image of a pluralist organisation, and, finally, the level of skills of available personnel. At the last congress held in 1991, the 371 members of the national assembly were members of the following factions: Democratic Party of the Left (ex PCI, 49.07%), Socialist Party (36.21%), Republican Party (10.8%), New Left and Greens (2.41%), Liberal Party (1.33%), Communist Renewal (1%).[9] The job allocation within La Lega's territorial structures also reflects the factional composition of the national assembly.

Functions of the Territorial Structures

The territorial support structures perform the following functions on behalf of cooperatives: representation of interests, supervision, provision of a number of services, promotion of cooperatives and coordination and direction for the whole movement.

Representation of Interests. The territorial structures represent the interests of cooperatives towards the external environment. The primary aim is to obtain from this environment a recognition of the importance that cooperatives play in the economic and the social sphere. To fulfil this task the territorial structures lobby the relevant political parties, unions and State ministries. In addition, they organise conferences which provide a forum where cooperative ideals and their economic potential are debated and discussed.

Most of its lobbying is directed toward the State to ensure that public policies take into account the needs of cooperatives and to remind it of its obligations under article 45 of the constitution clearly placing the responsibility on the State to promote cooperatives. The territorial structures influence the State in a number of ways. First, it has its own sponsored representatives in parliament. It has been a practice of the political parties close to la Lega to nominate the factional leaders, usually the presidents, vice presidents and other notable leaders as members of parliament. This is also practiced by the other cooperative organisations. Thus the members of parliament sponsored by the respective cooperative organisations along with other sympathetic parliamentarians, especially those from areas where the cooperative movement is strong, form a powerful lobby within parliament. Proof of the parliamentary support for cooperatives is the fact that the 1992 legislation was presented in Parliament by over 80 Members of Parliament representing the ex-Communists, the Socialists, Republicans and Christian Democrats.[10]

At the national level representatives from La Lega lobby the relevant ministries. Particular attention is devoted to the Ministries of Agriculture, Industry and Commerce, Labour and Public Works to ensure that their economic policies also consider the importance of cooperatives. In the past, the Ministry of Labour has been targeted the most because it has the responsibility over the cooperative legislation and various forms of general funding. The Ministry of Labour is also in control of the Banca Nazionale del Lavoro (BNL) which has a cooperative branch providing credit to cooperatives. Since the 1970s the influence of the cooperative sector has increased. In 1971, members from the three major cooperative associations began to sit on the board of directors of the cooperative branch of the BNL.[11] In 1977 the government organised a national conference on cooperatives highlighting the important role they played in society. In 1991, the State has given the cooperative movement the highest possible status as a policy maker by holding talks with the three largest cooperative centrals on the state of the economy. This has practically given the cooperative movement equal status to business and trade union organisations.[12]

At the regional level, La Lega influences the various ministries in a similar fashion as is done at the national level. However, since the region of Emilia Romagna has always been administered by left wing governments, La Lega has had easier access to regional ministers and decision makers. This is confirmed by representatives of La Lega sitting on the board of directors of various regional institutions such as Ervet (Institute for the Promotion of the Regional Economy) and Ersa (Institute for the Development of Agriculture). La Lega is also represented in other regional institutions which provide services to all businesses such as Quasco (Construction Industry), Aster (Technological Development) and Svex (Export Promotion).[13] By participating in these regional institutions, La Lega is able to exert pressure and to influence the policy decisions made by the regional government.

This continuous relationship that La Lega has been able to establish with bureaucrats and ministers from national ministries and regional economic institutions, has contributed to overcome the lack of knowledge that normally these institutions have with respect to cooperatives. It is also important to note that La Lega has structured its organisation to maximise its capacity to lobby the institutions of the State. In particular, it created regional structures as soon as the State decentralised many of its functions since 1970.

Supervision. The function of supervision is carried out by La Lega on its associated member cooperatives on behalf of the State and in the interest of the cooperative movement. The purpose of this is to ensure that cooperatives comply with the legal requirements stipulated by the Italian legislation and by the normative requirements outlined by the ICA's general principles on cooperation. This is done by checking the annual reports and bookkeeping. Other forms of control are carried out to ensure that cooperatives respect the norms and statutes of La Lega, such as the agreements signed with the trade unions.[14] Recently control measures have been tightened. The 1992 legislation stipulates that cooperatives over a certain size must produce certified annual reports each year. In addition, at their 1991 congress, the Provincial Federation of Bologna passed a resolution that cooperatives should produce a social annual report as well as an economic one.

Funding for this activity is derived from several sources. The Ministry of Labour allocates funds to all recognised cooperative organisations. In 1986, La Lega received 700 million lire to perform its supervisory duties, although part of it was also to be used for other duties such as vocational training. However, most of La Lega's funds come from cooperative membership fees which range from 0.4% and 0.8% of their turnover.[15]

Services. The territorial structures also provide a number of services to cooperatives. These include: legal and fiscal assistance, preparation of pay slips, accountancy and industrial relations. These services are vital for cooperatives especially in the start up phase. In the 1950s and 1960s the territorial structures also provided other services such as signing up agreements with banks to facilitate the provision of credit, consultancy at the enterprise level and personnel training. Today these activities are being carried out by the consortia network.

The territorial structures are now concentrating on providing qualitative information to cooperatives. One such initiative entails monitoring the economic performance of the major cooperatives in order to detect any positive or negative trends.[16] Another service provided is an annual report comparing the economic performance of cooperatives with private enterprises of similar size. The report analyses the profit levels, productivity levels, forms of credits, the level of value added, cash flow and labour costs as a percentage of total costs. Using these statistics cooperatives can better plan their future business strategies.[17] Another service, mainly directed at small to medium size cooperatives, provides a list of people within the cooperative movement who are regarded as experts on various aspects of financial and legislative matters. This service facilitates access to such information which at times is difficult to obtain and time consuming for the individual cooperative.[18]

In 1988 the central office in Rome established a permanent branch in Brussels to closely monitor the activities of the European Economic Community. From this office La Lega produces a bulletin four times a week informing cooperatives of new legislation, EEC economic programmes, opportunities for joint ventures, availability of funds for specific programmes and public works opportunities. The individual cooperatives receive this information through the regional territorial structures and various consortia. In addition to this, the branch comes into contact with potential economic partners from all over the world. When potential economic opportunities arise these entrepreneurs are put in touch with cooperatives in Italy. Through this service cooperatives increase their economic opportunities and have access to vital information which is used to develop successful business strategies.[19]

The central organisation at the national and the regional level also stipulates industrial relation agreements with the trade union confederations. These may include wages and general working conditions, health and safety measures, re-training schemes, as well as undertakings to give employment to disadvantaged labourers such as the handicapped, immigrant workers, disabled people and provisions to protect the environment.[20] Cooperative Managers too have sought union representation to work out pay scales and conditions. The agreement signed in 1992 stipulates pay increases, higher pension contributions and protection of pay and conditions should a manager be transferred to another cooperative.[21] To most cooperatives, especially the smaller ones, this service reduces conflicts, and it saves time and money for not having to employ an industrial relations officer.

Promotion of Cooperatives. Promotion of cooperatives involves those activities that promote the ideals of cooperation, the growth of existing cooperatives and help establish new cooperative enterprises.

The territorial structures promote the ideals of cooperatives by organising conferences, films, by participating in public debates, by publishing books on the history and ideals of the cooperative movement. This has the twin function of creating the right public image and attracting new members.

One way of promoting existing cooperatives is by lobbying the State to have access to public works. In recent times, because of the State's financial and managerial problems, the territorial structures at the national and regional level have been organising forums and making proposals outlining ways that cooperatives can solve some of the State's problems in areas such as the public railway system, environmental degradation or the public health system. Once the proposals are accepted by the relevant government departments then the territorial structures allocate the works to cooperatives or various consortia. The territorial structures are the most appropriate for these type of negotiations because they can group cooperatives from various sectors which then as a group can plan and execute particular projects, thus facilitating negotiations with the State. Since these relations with the State are usually coordinated by the main central cooperative associations, the territorial structures are the best available means through which liaison between the centrals takes place.[22]

La Lega also promotes economic activity through agreements with other nation States. In 1991 La Lega was part of a delegation of business leaders led by the Italian Foreign Trade Ministry in Kuwait. On this occasion La Lega managed to win a number of contracts in the construction sector. In particular, La Lega will be responsible for rebuilding the supermarket chains which were devastated during the Iraqi occupation.[23]

The national structure has also managed to promote cooperatives through agreements with cooperative movements from other countries. An example of this is the agreement signed between La Lega and Centrosoyuz, the organisation representing the consumer movement of the Soviet Union in 1989. This agreement has laid the foundation of the collaboration between cooperatives from Italy and the Soviet Union in sectors in the areas of agribusiness, leather goods, manufacturing, tourism, and management. It was estimated the value of this economic activity was going to be worth 2,000 billion lire within a few years.[24]

Another aspect of promotion is the development of new cooperative enterprises. The Bologna Federation is said to have started the insurance sector by employing a few persons to sell insurance policies. It later led to the formation of Unipol group of finance which will be described in chapter six. The Bologna Federation also established the first cultural cooperative which began by managing a theatre in Bologna. This experience led many other cultural cooperatives to be established.

The territorial structures have also helped newly formed cooperatives by establishing commercial links with other cooperatives. This was the case with the cooperative Altercoop which sells paper and other office equipment. When it started, the territorial structure of Emilia Romagna advised other cooperatives of Altercoop's economic activity and encouraged them to support it. According to the director of Altercoop, Mr Giolitti, cooperatives supported Altercoop from the start, and whilst today's share of the total sales sold to cooperatives has declined it still comprises 20% of its total turnover.

The territorial structures have also encouraged the formation of cooperatives from ailing private enterprises. It is estimated that between 1974 and 1978 La Lega created 100 enterprises in this way saving a total of 10,000 jobs.[25] In 1981 it was estimated that 50% of all manufacturing cooperatives were formed this way.[26] In these situations usually the trade unions would approach the territorial structures to canvass the possibility of a takeover by the work-force. The territorial structures (with the support of the particular sectoral association) allocates its officers to prepare feasibility studies and to prepare the work-force to change to a cooperative form of enterprise. This form of ad hoc response to worker takeovers changed in the early 1980s when La Lega delegated this function to Industrial Promotion Societies like Promosviluppo, the company CFI, as well as other structures.[27]

It is important to note that while Industrial Promotion Societies have been formed, the territorial structures still receive a demand for providing assistance to new cooperatives. The problem is that at the moment they are not well equipped to create and monitor the progress of newly formed enterprises. La Lega in Emilia Romagna, which has most of the resources, does not have a specific department which provides this service. Promotion usually takes place in an ad hoc fashion. What usually happens in the province of Bologna is that cooperatives approach the provincial territorial support structure, then they are sent to the relevant sectoral association which is best suited to provide information about the market of the relevant industry.

The sectoral association are not well equipped to deal with this and usually the quality of service and support depends on the good will of the person with whom they come into contact. This has prompted some prominent members within the Provincial Federation of Bologna to call for the creation of a job creation department to accommodate this demand.

Coordination and Direction. The terms coordination and direction refer to all those activities which aim to unite the individual cooperatives and get them to act as a group in their relation with the external environment. The territorial structures coordinate cooperatives in a number of ways. First, they provide information coming from a variety of sources such as the government, institutions, political parties, which may be of interest to cooperatives. Secondly, it performs a mediating role when conflicts arise between cooperatives.[28] Thirdly, it provides a forum where the directors of cooperatives can get to know one another. One benefit from this is that it facilitates commercial activity between cooperatives. Furthermore, it promotes cooperatives to support one another to solve common problems.

The second function, that of providing direction and planning, has been vital for the success of the movement. As noted in the previous chapter, the territorial structures, working together with the sectoral associations, delineated the major strategic changes such as: the formation of alliances between cooperatives and small private enterprises and the middle classes; the promotion of cooperatives in new sectors of the economy; the promotion of cooperatives of large dimension through mergers and buyouts.

Sectoral Association

The second element of La Lega's organisational support system are the sectoral associations. They represent cooperatives from a particular sector of the economy. In all there are ten sectoral associations affiliated to La Lega: housing, agriculture, culture, consumer, retailing, social insurance and welfare, fishing, production and labour, services and tourism. These sectoral associations are divided into national and regional associations. The former mainly concentrates on matters of national importance such as legislation, national public works etc, while the latter's role is directed at similar matters but which have a regional dimension.

System of Governance. The governance of these associations is similar to that of the territorial structures. It consists of a general council, a board of directors and an executive committee. All the cooperatives have a representative in the general council. The members of the general council elect the directive committee. They in turn elect a council of presidency from which a president is chosen. The congress is held every four years. The structure is financed by the member cooperatives. These associations are autonomous, but it is generally agreed that they should abide by the overall guidelines set out by the national congress of La Lega.[29]

Functions of the Sectoral Associations. The sectoral associations perform four important functions on behalf of cooperatives. These are: representation of interests, control, direction and mediation of conflicts. The sectoral associations represent the specific interests of cooperatives from particular sectors by lobbying the central and regional governments to ensure that legislation and political and economic policies do not harm the cooperative economy. Mr Drei, of the Regional Producer Cooperative Association of Emilia Romagna, ARCPL, (Associazione Regionale Cooperative Produzione e Lavoro), stated that the role of the association is to ensure that regional policy in areas such as construction, urban planning, industry policy, environmental control, housing, etc, does not harm the economic position of cooperative enterprises present in the region.

The second function is that of control covering three main areas: the enterprise, the whole sector and the ideals of the movement. At the enterprise level the association collects and analyses data from various economic indicators and from cooperatives' annual reports and suggests ways of how the performance can be improved. This information is then collated so that the organisation can gauge how the whole sector is performing. At the sectoral level the association encourages cooperation between cooperatives and the development of large viable cooperative enterprises. These twin objectives have been achieved by promoting a policy of mergers, of specialisation and of expansion throughout the national territory and the international market.[30] Lastly, control is also exercised to ensure that cooperatives maintain their ideals. The ARCPL of Emilia Romagna in 1991 was carrying out a survey over safety standards in cooperative workplaces. It is assumed this is not done to save costs, but as an important part of the cooperative mission.

The third function is to provide guidance and direction to the whole sector. One such important policy was developed in the 1970s. The Association encouraged mergers and a policy of growth in order to withstand Italian and European competition in the construction industry.[31] This role performed by the sectoral association will become more important in view of the European Economic Community's attempt to reduce national discrimination against foreign companies.

Finally, the association mediates conflicts which may occur between cooperatives. One form of mediation is to arrange that cooperatives do not compete against one another. This is done by allocating areas to specific cooperatives. For instance, in the consumer sector cooperatives are allocated a province or a region or even two regions depending on the density of cooperation in the area. The same takes place with the construction sector. In the construction sector some conflicts have taken place over the amount of work distributed by the consortia network. Conflicts may arise between large and small cooperatives over which cooperative should get most work. This especially surfaces in times of economic recession. As it will be shown later, the consortia has a formula which it adheres to when distributing work, but if conflicts continue then the sectoral association intervenes.

Conclusion

The Central Association through its territorial and sectoral structures provides general guidance and cohesiveness to the cooperative movement. This is achieved in a variety of ways. One major contribution is that they unite cooperatives into one movement by promoting shared values, a non competitive culture and by mediating conflicts that arise between cooperatives. In additions, these structures provide a forum where personal relations are forged, ideas are exchanged and commercial relations are established. The ability to unite the whole movement is of extreme importance because it has laid the foundations for the establishment of other support structures, all of which improve the competitiveness of cooperatives in the market.

Secondly, La Lega has managed to represent the interests of the individual cooperatives versus the State. Being able to organise over 12,000 cooperatives gives La Lega a lot of economic and political power. Usually pressure group organisations organise themselves outside of the State institutions and then attempt to influence its bureaucrats and politicians through direct lobbying. In addition to this, La Lega has also been able to influence the State from within by placing its members in Parliament, in the Ministry of Labour, and various regional institutions. This form of representation organised externally to the State and from within, has given La Lega the power to influence the content of public policy.

It is also important to note that La Lega has developed territorial structures to resemble the three tiers of the Italian State (national, regional and local) and that the rapport established with the State and its institutions is a continuous one. Through this multiple form of relations and contact with the State and its representatives, La Lega has been able to overcome the obstacles outlined by Laylock and Cornforth. It could be stated that forms of discrimination caused by the ministers' and bureaucrats' lack of knowledge on cooperatives has been overcome. As a consequence, the laws and government policies have taken into account the interests and the particular character of cooperatives.

Third, the organisational structures have provided many services which help to overcome managerial problems faced by cooperatives. Cornforth stated that cooperatives lacked managerial skills because the low wages offered failed to attract managers and because of their anti-managerial culture. In this case, the problem has been overcome by having an external source, the Central Association, providing a number of skills needed by the enterprise. Some of these managerial skills include: the long term planning strategies such as the formation of interclass alliances and the policy of concentration through mergers and buyouts; services such as the provision of data comparing cooperatives with their competitors and information regarding State programmes; administrative skills in the area of accounting, preparation of pay slips, industrial relations have all been vital for cooperatives in their initial phase of development.

Fourth, La Lega's promotional functions have helped overcome the entrepreneurial problems. The problem caused by cooperatives' low rate of formation has been alleviated by promoting cooperatives from worker takeovers of private enterprises. Until the early 1980s the organisational support structures co-ordinated the takeovers through its own personnel. Since then, they have promoted legislation to facilitate this process, but the work has been carried out by specialist cooperative societies. Another way that the territorial structures have overcome this problem is by promoting cooperatives in new sectors such as finance, private retail, tourism, health and culture. This has led to an expansion and a diversity which has enhanced the role cooperatives play in Italian society.

Notes

1 Source: Onelio Prandini, La Cooperazione: Organizzazione Storia e Futuri Sviluppi del Movimento Cooperativo, Editori Riuniti, Roma, 1986, Seconda Edizione, pp.82-83.
2 Nicola Zotti, *Lega Nazionale delle Cooperative: la sua Storia, la sua Immaggine, la sua Politica,* Editrice Cooperativa, Roma, 1983, pp.28-30. See also John Earle, *The Italian Cooperative Movement*, Allen and Unwin, London, 1986, p.35.
3 Note that the number of delegates do not correspond to the number of cooperative members present in each region because the ratio member-delegate was lower in some sectors. For example the producers sector elected 1 delegate for every 391 members, whereas the consumer sector one for every 12,621. Secondly, please note that the total number of members amounting to 3,938,989 was from the year 1988.
4 Stefano Zan, "The Management of Entrepreneur Associations: the Case of La Lega Nazionale delle Cooperative e Mutue", Paper Presented at the Joint Session of the European Consortium for Political Research for the Workshop on Markets, Politics and Associations: the Case of Welfare in Public, Private and Cooperative Sectors, Rimini, April 1988, p.9.
5 Stefano Zan, *La Cooperazione in Italia: Strutture, Strategie e Sviluppo della Lega Nazionale Cooperative e Mutue*, De Donato, Bari, 1982, pp.332-333.
6 A change in electoral support may prompt a faction to claim more positions.
7 Members of the Socialist and Republican factions whose parties have been in governmental majorities for over 30 years claim to have a greater influence over government decisions therefore want more of a say within La Lega.
8 The Republicans as followers of Mazzini and the Socialists as followers of Italian reformism claim to be the true heirs of co-operation. The Communists claim their role in the resistance as been a major contribution to establishing democracy in Italy.
9 *L'Unità,* "Sul Nome di Turci La Lega Ritrova la sua Unanimità", 12 April 1991.
10 Roberto Seghetti, "Leggina Continua", *Panorama*, 16 Febbraio 1992, p.155.
11 Aldo Ricci, "I Problemi Lasciati Aperti dalla Piccola Riforma", in Walter Briganti, *Il Movimento Cooperativo in Italia; 1963-1980,* Editrice Cooperativa, Roma 1982, p. 188.
12 Virgilio Chelli, "Se lo Stato si Mette in Cooperativa", *La Cooperazione Italiana*, Maggio 1991, pp.4-7.
13 Ervet, *Attività e Composizione del Sistema Ervet,* Bologna, 1990.
14 Zan, *op.cit.*, *La Cooperazione in Italia: Strutture, Strategie e Sviluppo della Lega Nazionale Cooperative e Mutue,* pp.299-300.
15 There seems to be no fixed percentage, some cooperatives have stated 0.4% while others have stated 0.8%.
16 See Emanuel Danieli (ed), *Le Imprese Cooperative: Trend 1982-1989*, Editrice Emilia Romagna, Bologna, 1991.
17 *La Cooperazione Italiana,* "Rapporto sulla Imprenditoria Cooperativa a Confronto con le Imprese Private", Luglio-Agosto 1990, pp.17-40.
18 Lega Emilia Romagna, *Rete di Servizi Finanziari*, a Cura del Dipartimento Finanziario, Bologna, 1991.
19 Ida Ossi, "Euro Sportello Targato Lega", *La Cooperazione Italiana*, Giugno 1990, pp.37-41.
20 *La Cooperazione Italiana*, "Il Testo Integrale Dell'Accordo Coop Sindacato", Maggio 1990, pp. 10-12.

21 Alberto Sisto, "Manager Più Mobili col Nuovo Contratto", *La Cooperazione Italiana*, Febbraio-Marzo 1993, pp.70-71.
22 For the agreement signed between cooperatives and the State railway system see *La Cooperazione Italiana*, "Tra Coop e Ferrovie un Rapporto Speciale", Dicembre 1991, p.9.
23 *Spazio Impresa*, "Golfo: La Lega Interverrà in Kuwait", 7 Maggio 1991, p.17.
24 *La Cooperazione Italiana*, "Turci; non Cerchiamo Solo il Business", Dicembre 1989, pp.6-7.
25 Robert Oakeshott, *The Case for Workers' Co-ops*, Routledge and Kegan Paul, London, 1978, 152.
26 Jenny Thornley, "*Workers Cooperatives and the Trade Unions: The Italian Experience*", Economic and Industrial Democracy, Vol. 4, 1983, p.330.
27 See previous chapter for more information on Promosviluppo, CFI and other supporting companies.
28 Zan, *op.cit.*, *La Cooperazione in Italia: Strutture, Strategie e Sviluppo della Lega Nazionale Cooperative e Mutue*, p.301.
29 Zotti, *op.cit.*, pp.30-31.
30 Fabio Carpanelli, president of the Consorzio Cooperative Costruzioni (Consortium of the Construction Cooperatives), notes that specialisation within construction cooperatives had to be promoted after a shift in demand from residential construction to public works. The demand shifted from an 80:20 ratio in favour of housing construction to a ratio of 50:50. This led to the creation of cooperatives which specialised in freeway construction, railways and restoration of public monuments. See Le Certificate Supplement, interview with Fabio Carpanelli, *La Cooperazione Italiana*, Dicembre 1988, p.53.
31 This policy has been successful. In 1990 10 of the fifty largest construction enterprises in Italy were members of La Lega. Costruire, *Le Classifiche 1990*, Novembre 1990, Milano, pp.64-65 and 79.

6 The Consortia Network

The purpose of this chapter is to analyse the various forms of economic integration that take place between cooperatives and evaluate how these have helped them to compete in the market. The focus will be on La Lega's consortia which have the responsibility of developing the technical and practical means to put in place the overall strategy delineated by the Central Association.

This chapter will begin with a brief introduction explaining some characteristics of the consortia. Secondly, a typology of consortia will be constructed. Third, five case studies of consortia from various sectors of the economy will be analysed. These include: the agricultural consortium Giglio, the manufacturing and construction consortium ACAM, the construction consortium CCC, the consortium for the consumer sector Coop Italia, and finally, the consortium for research and development ICIE. These have been chosen because they operate in different sectors of the economy providing a better understanding of La Lega's consortia network. Each case study will explore the relationship that exists between the consortia and the individual cooperatives, La Lega's Central Association and the State. The final part will summarise the findings and discuss the ways in which the consortia network has managed to overcome some of the problems normally faced by cooperatives when competing in the market.

What is a Consortium?

A consortium is an association formed by cooperatives that performs a number of functions for the purpose of increasing market competitiveness of the associated members. As stated in chapter three, consortia were first established in the agricultural sector in the 1850s. In the construction sector they were first formed in 1909 after the State passed a law which enabled cooperatives to organise themselves in consortia when bidding for public works.[1] After 1945, consortia were set up in greater numbers to support the large number of small cooperatives that had been formed soon after the collapse of Fascism.

The governance of the consortium resembles the other structures of La Lega. The internal structure of a consortium is formed by a general council where each associate cooperative member has weighted representation which allows the large cooperatives a maximum of five votes.[2] The general council then elects a board of directors which is then responsible for electing an executive and the president.

The costs of administering the consortium are covered through members' shares and by charging a commission fee. The commission fee may differ between the consortia. For instance, CONCOOP (an industrial consortium) charges 2% of the value of the work subcontracted to individual cooperatives.[3] In similar fashion, CONAD, (retailing consortium), derives its income by charging members a commission fee equivalent to 1.5% of their total turnover. In 1987, CONAD received the total sum of 2.5 billion lire in this way.[4] Out of the commission fee a small surplus is made which is reinvested in the consortium.

A Consortia Typology

The first distinction that can be made between consortia is that between those which provide only services and those which process and sell cooperative products. The service consortia centralise a number of functions on behalf of the member cooperatives. Some of these are: acquisition of raw and semifinished materials, negotiating contractual arrangement with suppliers, provision of storage space, and access to technical expertise. These are all services provided in support of cooperative enterprises which ultimately maintain a relation with the market.

The consortia which process and sell cooperative goods are called enterprise consortia. They are called enterprise consortia because they buy the factors of production and maintain relations with the market. In essence, they perform a manufacturing and commercial function on behalf of their member cooperatives. An example of this type of consortia are the agricultural consortia which process raw materials (raw milk or wheat) into finished products (yogurt, cheese, pasta) and sell them directly to the market.[5]

The difference between service and enterprise consortia is not the only distinction that can be made within the various types of consortia attached to La Lega. Since the 1960s the role of the consortia within the cooperative movement has changed to meet the needs of the cooperatives and the strategic needs of La Lega.[6] Three other types of consortia have been identified which differ in both size and the role they perform within La Lega.

The earliest type of consortia were those of local dimensions. These usually covered a provincial area, and at times expanded into consortia of regional dimension. These consortia catered for the needs of their associated members from a particular sector either by providing a service or by processing or marketing their products.[7]

The second type of consortia are the national ones which cater for the needs of cooperatives from the same sector on a national scale. These were first suggested at a congress organised by La Lega in 1968. These new consortia had the task of achieving greater economies of scale by organising a larger number of cooperatives operating within the same sector. Their task also included encouraging intersectoral trading between cooperatives and providing services to newly established cooperatives in every part of Italy. This last objective had strategic importance. Previously consortia were formed by existing enterprises. Through the establishment of national consortia, La Lega reversed this trend. This was beneficial to all newly formed cooperatives, especially those which operated in areas with few cooperatives. In fact, the changes allowed the latter to have access to services through the national consortia without having to wait for the formation of other local cooperatives as was practiced in the past.[8]

In the late-1970s, a number of changes were made to the operations of the national consortia. One change led the national consortia to specialise in particular markets within particular sectors of the economy. In the agricultural sector for instance, specialised consortia processed and marketed olive oil or wine. Today, the construction cooperatives have formed one major consortia which specialises in bidding only for national public contracts. Another change led these consortia to provide cooperatives with support to help them restructure. Furthermore, the national sectoral associations also expected these consortia to contribute to the planning of cooperative growth in Southern Italy and in other areas where cooperatives had a low presence.[9]

The third type are called national intersectoral consortia. Their purpose is to provide services to cooperatives from various sectors of the economy. These consortia are mainly concentrated in the tertiary sector. Some examples of national intersectoral consortia are the financial consortium Fincooper, the Cooperative Institute for the Transfer of Technology and Innovations (ICIE), and the management consortium Sinnea.

Case Studies

To understand further the role played by the consortia and to support the general assumptions made above, five case studies will be analysed. While greater emphasis will be placed on how the consortia operated in the 1980s, the study will also take into account their overall history. This will provide sufficient evidence to analyse the evolution of the various consortia and the dynamic relationship that exists between the consortia, the enterprises, La Lega and the State.

Case Study 1: Giglio - Local Enterprise Consortium

Giglio is a dairy consortium from Reggio Emilia founded in 1934. The consortium's role is to process the raw milk into finished products such as processed milk, yogurt and cream and to market them. This arrangement between Giglio and the cooperatives is quite simple: Giglio buys all of the cooperative's produce at the average market price. This arrangement also guarantees producers a fair price for their products by supplanting the intermediaries. Prior to the establishment of dairy cooperatives and consortium, intermediaries created competition between producers to reduce the price of raw milk. Since producers had to sell the raw milk within 24 hours, they accepted lower prices. Producers responded by setting up cooperatives to bargain collectively with the intermediaries. Later, they went one step further by setting up the consortium Giglio which bought, processed and sold their products.[10] Any profits made are usually distributed to shareholders or reinvested in the enterprise, usually the latter prevails. Currently Giglio has a membership of 160 cooperatives which in turn have 8,000 producers as members.

Giglio's Strategy in the 1980s

The way the consortium meets the needs of its cooperative members can be best understood through its business strategy. Business strategy is comprised of three areas: product and process, market share and organisation, all of which are complementary to one another. The product strategy is one of diversification. Products are produced in modern highly mechanised plants[11] which are supported by a high level of quality controls.[12] Production flexibility has also been achieved by getting other firms in Italy or in Germany to produce new products with a limited market. This type of collaboration with other firms has allowed Giglio to enter a new market quicker and to reduce risks in case the new product failed to win an adequate market share. Giglio also has an agreement with a dairy firm owned by the Milan local council to produce high quality milk.[13]

The market share has been gradually increased. This has been achieved partly by processing good quality products at Giglio's own plants, and partly through a series of acquisitions of private firms and cooperatives. Thanks to the 1983 legislation which allowed cooperatives to form financial companies,

Giglio formed the financial company, Giglio Finanziaria e di Partecipazione, through which it bought shares in private companies. Between 1987 and 1990 alone, Giglio bought the private firms Corradini, Spondilat, Fanticini, Rocca, Latteria Sociale del Massenzatico, and the cooperative Co-e-zoo. Since these firms were present in other regions and produced different products, Giglio was able to have access to new products and new markets; for example, Spondilat is a dairy firm operating in Lombardy. Rocca and Fanticini are producers of "Grana Padana" (a cheese product) which was exported to a number of countries.[14]

It is important to note that other than the cooperative Co-e-zoo, which was incorporated into Giglio, these firms were not transformed into cooperatives, but managed as conventional firms. This was due to a number of reasons. Companies that Giglio did not fully own could not have been converted into cooperatives. However, the main reason was Giglio's policy to expand whilst attracting external finance; consequently the legal status of these firms was not changed because Giglio wanted to have the flexibility to sell part of the shares if needed, as long as it kept at least 51%. This strategy also included the finance company fully owned by Giglio which in the future could sell part of its shares.[15]

Organisational Structure

To accommodate this new strategy Giglio slowly developed a new organisational structure which came to resemble that of a holding company (see Figure 6.1). This consisted of two financial companies Giglio Finanziaria e di Partecipazione which was the major shareholder in private companies and Cremeria Emiliana SPA whose primary role was to attract investments from individuals. In addition to the already cited dairy firms, these two financial companies also controlled two real estate companies which manage properties owned by Giglio and two trading companies. The two trading companies are Giglio Grana Trading specialising in marketing Grana Padana cheese and Giglio Trading which sells the rest of the products produced by Giglio. All of these companies are controlled and run by personnel from Giglio.[16]

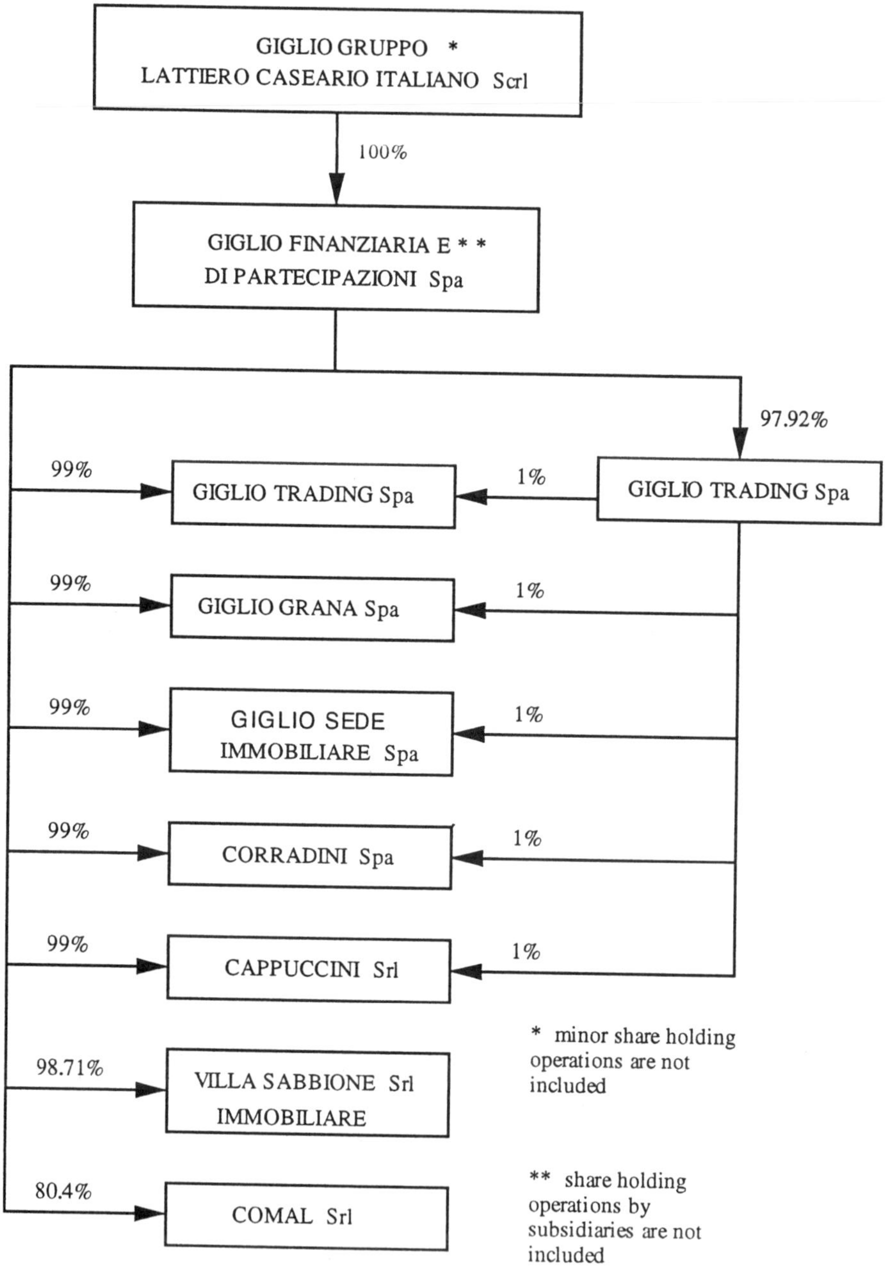

Figure 6.1 Giglio's Group of Companies

This type of structure gives Giglio many advantages over its previous structure. The first main advantage derives from specialisation. Different skills and knowledge are needed to market the various products, thus the creation of the two trading companies was seen as a way to increase efficiency. This type of division also allows Giglio to monitor the costs by breaking them into separate firms and trading companies. Finally, with each company having its own management a faster decision-making process has been developed.

Another reason behind the development of this new structure is the need to attract capital. As stated, Giglio has formed the financial company Cremeria Emiliana Finanziaria to attract individual investors. This decision aimed at overcoming the existing legislation which allows only cooperatives to invest in a consortium. In fact, this negates the consortium the opportunity to seek capital from individuals or private companies. The 1983 legislation allowed consortia and cooperatives to set up finance companies as long as the profits were invested in the cooperative's reserve funds. The main thrust behind Cremeria is to attract investments by supplanting the intermediation of the bank. Giancarlo Chiusa explained that if a bank pays 8% interest to its depositors and charges 13% interest to borrowers, then Giglio's finance company will pay 10% interest to depositors instead of 8% and charge the cooperative 11% instead of 13% interest. The end result is that through the consortium's own Finance company the individual will get an extra 2% on his deposit, the cooperative will save 2% on loans and the finance company will make 1% profit.

Recent Developments

In 1992, the organisational development gained further momentum. The catalyst to this has been the moves toward the formation of a single European market and the aggressive takeovers and market strategies of foreign multinational companies in Italy.[17] Giglio has made two moves aimed at attracting finance and at achieving economies of scale. First it has formed an alliance with the Parmalat dairy company which is one of Italy's largest. As of March 1992, Parmalat became a shareholder in Giglio's financial company Finanziaria e di Partecipazioni by buying 30% of its shares. In addition, Giglio has formed a holding company, Societa Generale Alimentare (SGE), with the other major consortium from Emilia Romagna CERPL (Consorzio Emiliano Romagnolo Produttori Latte-Consortium for the Milk Producers of Emilia Romagna).[18] The role of SGE is to coordinate the financial and commercial operations of the two consortia. Even in this new venture, alliances have been constructed with State and private institutions. Indeed, the ownership of SGE belongs to Giglio (35%), CERPL (35%), the national bank Banca Nazionale del Lavoro 15%, and the local bank Credito Emiliano 15%.[19]

Is this a Form of Degeneration?

One question that needs to be answered is whether these changes that have taken place at Giglio can be regarded a form of cooperative degeneration. What has taken place is that while Giglio has externalised some aspects of its business, namely the commercialisation of its products through conventional enterprises of which it is a major shareholder, the goals and the original organisation have remained unaltered. As noted, in the introduction to this case study, the role of Giglio was to buy all the produce from its member cooperatives, to process it and sell it. This role has not changed. Even in this new scenario Giglio buys all of the produce from its members. Further, the original organisational structure has remained the same. The cooperative members still elect their representatives within Giglio. These then implement forms of control over the consortium's professional management and give guidelines to those who represent Giglio in the board of directors of the conventionally managed enterprises. Thus the internal organisation can still be regarded as democratically managed through forms of direct and representational democracy.

Nevertheless, it is quite clear that by investing in private firms Giglio is getting a return on capital invested and jointly managing conventional firms. This can be classified as a form of degeneration; however, a couple of qualifications need to be made. First, Giglio own work-force and that of private firms are employees and are paid award wages, thus Giglio's work-force does not benefit from such arrangements. Secondly, Giglio's profits have been minimal over the years. For instance, in 1987 it made 23 million lire in net profits, in 1988, 69 million lire, in 1989 1 billion lire. In 1990 net profits rose to 24.6 billion lire only because it sold to its jointly owned trading companies the exclusive rights to sell Giglio's products for 15 years. It would seem that the strategy has been one of market share rather than maximising profits.

Giglio, La Lega and the State

The relationship between Giglio and La Lega has taken many forms. Giglio has come to the rescue of cooperatives by taking them over thus ensuring that their members did not lose their jobs.[20] Secondly, Giglio participates as a shareholder to the movement's major institutions such as Fincooper, Unipol (insurance) and Banec (bank), and makes use of their services. It is also a shareholder of the television station Rete Sette which is mostly owned by the consumer cooperative Coop Emilia Veneto.

Thirdly, it has been estimated that between 30% to 40% of Giglio's products are sold through La Lega's consumer and retailing cooperatives. Selling the produce through the outlets of the consumer cooperatives was very important for the consortium to become established. In fact, Giglio also produced products sold under the consumer cooperatives' own brand name. However, in order to expand it has had to move into the wider market. Nevertheless, the latter point is a clear indication of the level of intersectoral trade that takes place between cooperatives and it is a point which will be further analysed in later case studies.

The case study has also indicated that Giglio has developed a sound relationship with the State. Giglio has received some support from various tiers of government by applying for grants under the several schemes administered by the EEC, the Italian government and the regional governments. The agricultural sector in Europe is heavily subsidised and supported in various ways. It is therefore vital for an enterprise which operates in this sector to be aware of the legislation and the various opportunities offered by the various schemes. The skills involved are not simply information gathering but also political lobbying to ensure that some grants are obtained. Giglio has recently managed to obtain from the regional government partial funding to build a regional warehouse to store Parmiggiano Reggiano cheese.[21] It has also received funds from the Italian government for projects which introduced new technology and energy saving measures. In 1990, it received from Ministry of Agriculture and Forests 10.5 billion lire to subsidise cheese producers whose income fell dramatically during the year as a result of overproduction.[22]

Further collaboration with the State has taken place with the State owned companies. As already noted, BNL has invested risk capital in the new agricultural holding company SGE. In addition, Giglio has signed an agreement with Italimpianti, a subsidiary of the State corporation IRI, to manufacture and provide technology for agricultural plants for the overseas market.[23]

Concluding Remarks

Over the last five years Giglio's total sales revenue has increased from 272 billion lire in 1985 to 480 billion lire in 1990, of which 40.65% is made up from partially or fully owned companies. The market share of Giglio and CERPL is quite high. It is estimated that these two consortia control 9.3% of the national butter production, 34.7% of cream, 15.4% in parmesan cheese,[24] 8.6% of fresh milk, and 10.7% of long life milk.[25] Its success can be partly attributed to its ability to delineate a successful business strategy supported by organisational changes to meet the demands of efficiency and finance. In addition, Giglio has had the financial support from the State and advantages of being part of the cooperative movement. The latter has provided a market for its products and an opportunity to form the holding company (SGE) which will further increase its chances of competing in the market.

Case Study 2: ACAM - A National Service Consortium

ACAM (Consorzio Nazionale Approvviggionamenti - National Consortium for Purchases and Supplies) is a national consortium which provides a number of services to manufacturing and construction cooperatives. It was founded in 1960 by 24 cooperatives, 19 of which were in the construction sector, to provide services to cooperatives from Bologna. The initial role accredited to ACAM was to lower costs for its members through the collective acquisition of materials, to develop common commercial policies and to improve relations with private and public bodies. In practice it also performed other functions such as providing experts for negotiations of finance and contracts, as well as marketing cooperative made products. By 1970 its membership increased to 73 and it began to open branches in other parts of Italy.[26] By the late 1970s ACAM ceased to provide services such as finance and marketing because by that time other consortia providing those services had been established. In addition, some of the cooperatives had become large enough enterprises to have their own marketing department. Accordingly, ACAM adapted to this new situation by specialising in providing fewer services.

ACAM in the 1980s

The main function of ACAM since the 1980s has been to lower costs by negotiating contracts with suppliers on behalf of its members. It does not actually buy or sell products. The cooperatives deal directly with the suppliers and pay according to the agreement signed between ACAM and the suppliers. The consortium establishes a fair relationship with the suppliers. While it does not guarantee the solvency of its members, it only represents cooperatives which are in a good financial position. ACAM's contractual power comes from the group purchasing power and in the stability and prestige of the large cooperatives which are among the oldest and largest in the country. Indeed, as a group ACAM's cooperatives are the country's largest buyers of ceramics' material, concrete, reinforced concrete, insulators, equipment and fixtures for the housing industry and related activities. [27]

In addition to the collective purchasing power of the group, ACAM increases its bargaining power in a number of ways. One argument used when bargaining is to claim that it saves suppliers a lot of time and money by channelling negotiations through a single agency. The consortium can further bargain with suppliers by organising cooperatives to pay before the agreed 60 day limit if the supplier needs liquidity. Prices are also renegotiated if the supplier is a short distance from the construction site. A further reduction of the original price may be obtained by selling advertising space in a prestigious site. For instance, ACAM may allow the suppliers to place an advertisement at the construction site in return for slightly lower prices.

The other major service provided by ACAM is the provision of up to date information on the costs of all materials close to the building location. This enables cooperatives to present quick and the correct costing when making a bid for a public works contract. In 1991, ACAM was in the process of developing a fully computerised information system so that cooperatives can have access to the available data immediately through a computer network.

Organisation

ACAM services its member cooperatives through a central administration office situated in Bologna and thirteen decentralised branches scattered throughout Italy. The local branches keep in contact with local cooperatives and collate information of cooperatives' business strategies in order to plan for their future needs. They also negotiate contracts with local suppliers. The central office coordinates the activity of the decentralised branches and negotiates contracts on major materials such as steel, ceramics etc.

These structures are financed through a membership fee of at least one million lire per cooperative which can be increased if needed. By 1990 ACAM had accumulated a total of 600 million lire in membership fees. The other form of self financing adopted by the consortium is to charge a commission fee of approximately 0.5% of the total purchases made by cooperatives through making use of ACAM's contractual arrangements and information services.

ACAM has been very successful. In 1990 cooperatives bought 1,183 billion lire worth of goods and services through ACAM, with savings averaging 4,9%. It has truly become a national consortium with a membership of 311 cooperatives of which 79% are in the construction industry, 11.1% in the industrial sector and 9.9% in the service sector.[28] ACAM's success is mainly due to the role played by large cooperatives. It is the large cooperatives which have the market power and it is they which have the financial credibility which enables ACAM to clinch good deals for all its members. ACAM's own statistics reveal that 76 of its 311 members were responsible for 79% of its total acquisitions.[29]

Relation with La Lega

ACAM is strategically important to La Lega. It provides a service to all cooperatives aimed at improving their competitiveness by lowering costs and by providing vital information.[30] Secondly, it is a shareholder in major companies of the cooperative movement like Fincooper, ICIE and Unipol. By being a shareholder ACAM is not only helping the movement to establish other consortia and companies, but it is also contributing to creating forms of unity between the various consortia.

Thirdly, it encourages intercooperative trading. In 1990, 172 billion lire amounting to 14.5% of the total acquisitions made through ACAM by cooperatives were supplied by other cooperatives associated with La Lega.[31] This intercooperative trade takes place mainly between the industrial and the construction cooperatives. However, it is important to point out that while the consortium encourages intercooperative trading, generally transactions between cooperatives are made only if the products are competitive in both price and quality.

Finally, ACAM also supports the development of cooperatives as enterprises.[32] This has meant that a lot of the large cooperatives have their own purchasing units. Furthermore, once a cooperative becomes large, the suppliers go directly to the cooperative offering attractive deals. It seems that suppliers searching for a larger market share offer the large cooperatives better deals than those agreed to with ACAM. The result is that the largest 76 cooperatives associated to ACAM buy only 35.19% of their total acquisitions through the consortium.[33] ACAM then is faced with a dilemma: it is much more indispensable to small and medium size cooperatives, but it relies on the large cooperatives for its bargaining power. ACAM has been trying to overcome the problem by negotiating with suppliers to give a further price reduction to large cooperatives. This is thought to increase the acquisitions of goods made by the large cooperatives through ACAM. If this succeeds, then ACAM can increase its bargaining power, otherwise its role could be undermined. This would mostly hurt the smaller cooperatives who rely more heavily on the consortium's ability to deliver lower prices.

Concluding Remarks

ACAM has been very successful. Its success can be measured by the way it has managed to reduce costs for its members and for having provided vital data on prices, quality of goods and the location of suppliers. Of particular importance is also the role it has played in encouraging trade among cooperatives which has improved the cooperatives' chances of survival and growth. Unlike Giglio, ACAM has no contact with State institutions.

Case Study 3: CCC - A National Specialised Consortium

The Consorzio Cooperative Costruzioni, CCC, (Consortium for the Construction Cooperatives) was formed in Bologna 1912. Initially CCC represented the cooperatives from the province of Bologna. In the 1960s it became an inter-provincial consortium representing 56 cooperatives from Bologna, Ferrara and Modena, including 15 from three other regions of Italy.[34] Following the decision by Central Association to create specialised consortium of national dimensions, in 1990 CCC developed into a national consortium representing some two hundred cooperatives based all over Italy.[35]

The nature of the services provided by the consortium have changed over time. In the 1960s and 1970s the consortium bid for public contracts at the local level and maintained close relations with the housing cooperatives. In addition, because cooperatives were small and mostly locally based, CCC also provided a range of valuable services to them. These included: technical and financial assistance, skills for developing long term enterprise planning and expertise in management and accounting. The consortium was also instrumental in promoting technologically advanced construction methods and in providing the venue where many managers, who later went on to work for individual cooperatives, developed their skills.

CCC in the 1980s

In the 1980s the consortium adopted a different strategy in response to a number of factors. First, as stated in the previous case study, La Lega developed a number of consortia in the areas of finance, management and technology, therefore CCC was no longer required to provide these services. Secondly, many of the cooperatives had by the late-1980s become large enough to have their own accounting and management branches. Thirdly, the

State was facing financial and managerial problems. It had difficulty in programming and financing public works, at a time when many public works such as infrastructures, public car parks, efficient public railways and subways were becoming very important for improving the urban quality of life, for generating employment and for reducing transportation costs for commuters and businesses. CCC responded in a number of ways.

The first response by CCC was to concentrate primarily on winning public contracts and subcontract the work to cooperatives. The consortium bids for public contracts either on its own or through the formation of *ad hoc* consortia formed by CCC with private and/or State enterprises. Working with private and State enterprises is a major part of CCC's business strategy. The benefits derived from these alliances is to have access to knowhow and finance. This improves the chances of winning major public works which may otherwise have been difficult to obtain.[36]

The second major strategy is in response to the problems faced by the State. CCC has formed a holding company (Sinapsi) for the purpose of developing specialised companies which are wholly controlled, or in partnership with private and public partners, which have the ability to plan, finance, build and manage particular projects. These companies can be very useful in the areas of public car parking, health assistance, distribution of gas and electricity, urban and industrial wastes etc. Complementary to this strategy, CCC, with the support of other cooperatives, has created the company STS (Specialised Companies in the Tertiary Sector) to operate on its own, or in partnership with private and public enterprises, in the areas of health, the environment, urban development and urban transport. Both Sinapsi and STS are to operate in partnership with the State to solve some of the problems associated with these areas.[37] The costs may either be recovered from the State or by charging fees to consumers over a long period of time; for instance, fees could be charged in the areas of public car parking, gas distribution and urban waste recycling.

This strategy is showing signs of success. In December 1990, STS in partnership with Fiat Engineering and Ispedil has won a three year contract from the Ministry of Health to build 54 hospital wings capable of housing 2,303 hospital beds catering especially for Aids sufferers. The cost for the project was 623 billion lire. STS has the responsibility to build 35% of the total amount equalling to 22 wings and 807 hospital beds. In 1991, it had plans to build 18 health care centres for the aged and the disabled.[38] The major outcome to derive from this strategy is the possibility of entering into medium to long term agreements with the State. This will help cooperatives overcome the cyclical fluctuations of public sector work. In reality, through this strategy CCC is attempting to create both the demand and the supply for particular sectors hoping this will lead to a constant flow of public contracts.[39]

Results and Organisation

In 1989 CCC managed to win 2,223 billion lire worth of public contracts open to tendering which amounts to 12% of the national market.[40] In 1990, the amount rose by 6% to 2,359 billion lire.[41] The members are serviced through twenty six offices spread throughout Italy of which the largest four can bid for public contracts. The largest office is in Bologna which has the responsibility to coordinate the activities of the other offices. The main office also centralises a number of functions in the area of finance, marketing, planning, commerce and administration. The consortium finances itself by charging cooperatives 1.85% of the work contracted out.

CCC, La Lega and the State

The consortium performs two vital roles for La Lega. First, it has improved the competitiveness of the construction cooperatives by organising their collective bargaining power when bidding for public works. This has enabled cooperatives to achieve economies of scale and improve their competitiveness against larger private firms. The importance of CCC to cooperatives is further highlighted by the high percentage of work it provides to individual cooperatives. Figures for the year 1976 reveal that the percentage of work obtained through the consortia ranged from 33% for small cooperatives to 56% for larger ones.[42] Today the large cooperatives get approximately 50% of their total acquisitions through CCC while the smaller ones get up to 70%. Figures for 1976 also reveal a high level of intersectoral trading between the construction and the housing sectors. In that year, 48.71% of all of CCC's work was conducted on behalf of housing cooperatives.[43]

The second major role of the consortium is to regulate the relationship between the member cooperatives. This is achieved through a carefully defined method of distributing work and by mediating (or avoiding) possible conflicts. Work is distributed using the following criteria: need, size, geographic area (public works are given to local cooperatives), and to support the strategy to help the development of small cooperatives. This at times leads to conflicts and competition. The consortium has been successful in avoiding competition by encouraging specialisation and mergers between cooperatives. This strategy has successfully lead many cooperatives to merge and others to specialise in areas such as freeways, restoration of public works and railways.[44] If conflicts do arise the consortium attempts to deal with them, if it does not succeed then it is the role of the regional or national sectoral association to intervene.

The relationship between the State and CCC is developed between CCC and Ministry of Public Works and between CCC and State owned enterprises with which CCC forms *ad hoc* consortia to win public contracts. The fact that CCC won 12% of the total national public works contracts allocated by the State is a clear indication of the non discriminatory behaviour of the Italian State toward construction cooperatives.

Concluding Remarks

Some major conclusions can be drawn from this case study. First, like ACAM the bargaining power of CCC is constituted by the large cooperatives. It is they which have the prestige, the knowhow and finance (or ability to obtain finance) which permits the consortium to bid for important public works which are redistributed by CCC to all members.

The second point to be emphasised is the proven ability of CCC to manage change. The strategic changes made by the consortium in the late 1980s were a response to the changes that had been taking place within cooperatives, within La Lega and within the State. The change from a consortium which provided a number of services to one which concentrated on bidding for public works on a national scale are an indication of the dynamic relationship that exists between the consortium, the enterprises, La Lega's other structures and the State. Thus the ability to adapt is important for an institution to survive, otherwise it could become redundant.

Thirdly, this case study also revealed the ability of CCC to influence the planning strategies of cooperatives by encouraging them to merge or specialise in particular areas within the construction sector. In addition, in response to the fiscal and managerial crisis of the State, CCC has created Sinapsi and STS to improve its ability to win public works contracts.[45] This indicates that the consortium is also an integral part of La Lega's policy-making process. The policies to create large cooperatives through mergers and specialisation was made in conjunction with the national sectoral association. However, the decision to create Sinapsi and STS were taken independently of the national sectoral association. This is an indication that CCC has a certain degree of autonomy from the national sectoral association.

Case Study 4: Coop Italia - National Service Consortium

Coop Italia is a national consortium which was formed in Bologna in 1946 to cater for the needs of the consumer cooperatives. In 1968 it became a national consortium whose major role was to coordinate the very fragmented consumer sector. This fragmentation slowed the modernisation programmes and reduced the movement's bargaining power. The role of Coop Italia was to improve the competitiveness and the modernisation of the sector through: collective bulk buying of goods, direct ownership and management of warehouses, and improve the range and quality of products sold by cooperatives.[46] In addition, the profits made from the transactions with cooperatives were used to provide them with managerial expertise and finance.

The above policy lasted until 1975 when inflation and a decline in consumer spending created financial difficulties for many cooperatives. Because these were all buying products from Coop Italia, there was a risk that the non performing cooperatives could bring down the whole system. Subsequently, a number of changes were made. First, Coop Italia no longer bought and sold products. Instead, it negotiated contractual arrangements with producers leaving it to the individual cooperatives to do the buying directly. Second, Coop Italia returned the wholesale warehouses to the individual cooperatives which were asked to manage them on their own or as members of a consortium. Both of these two measures were meant to make the individual cooperatives more responsible for their actions.[47] Thirdly, the national sectoral association supported a strategy of mergers and concentration which involved closing down many unprofitable small retail outlets and initiated a process of modernisation by promoting more supermarkets.[48]

Coop Italia in the 1980s

Today Coop Italia provides cooperatives with four main services: the collective acquisition of products, the promotion and control of cooperatives' own brand products, marketing and related information. As was decided in 1975, its main task is to organise the collective acquisition of products in order to reduce administrative costs and prices. This is still arranged through contractual arrangements with producers and suppliers. Usually the contractual arrangements are binding on all cooperatives, but the larger ones are in a position to negotiate a better deal if the producers or suppliers agree. In addition, since cooperatives now own very large supermarkets and megastores and sell a wide range of non food products, the contractual arrangement for non food items is done through a specialist branch in Florence.[49]

The second service is one which promotes and controls the quality of consumer cooperatives' own brand name products and those under the label "Prodotti con Amore". The latter literally translates "Products With Love" and are premium products which have to meet very stringent criteria demanded by Coop Italia from suppliers. Before a product is accepted Coop Italia's own technicians visit the suppliers' plants to make sure that they meet the Cooperative's requirements regarding raw materials used, type of technology, ingredients and food quality controls.[50] Then Coop Italia regularly tests the products to ensure that the quality is consistent. The consortium conducts close to 40% of the overall testing in its own laboratories. The remainder of the tests are carried out by other specialised laboratories in Italy from either the public or private sector.[51] In 1990, 335 products carried the consumer cooperative logo and 100 more were going to be introduced in the following year.[52] Some of the products are very successful, these include: pasta which has a 45% market share of the total pasta sold by Coop Italia, butter (30%), peeled tomatoes (34%), milk (50%), olive oil (40%) and vegetable oil (40%).[53]

Coop Italia also applies stringent controls to products sold under the label "Prodotti con Amore". For meat products sold under this label, Coop Italia requires breeders to use livestock which have not received antibiotics nor oestrogens. It requires animal husbandry to be extensive and that animals be fed certain type of food. In addition, the arrangements also stipulate the type of transport to be used and the way animals should be killed. This process is less painful for animals and as a consequence it reduces the level of stress and improves the quality of the meat.[54] The costs incurred to control the products "Prodotti con Amore" are paid by producers who in turn benefit for having access to a large market. It is estimated that in 1990, these arrangements saved consumer cooperatives 3 billion lire. In all, products sold under the consumer cooperatives own label and "Prodotti con Amore" amount to 15% of total sales. They contribute to improve the image of the cooperative because they are of high quality and environmentally "friendly".

Marketing is the third function of Coop Italia. The national advertising strategy for the consumer cooperatives is coordinated by Coop Italia and the national sectoral association. It is their responsibility to sell the image of the consumer movement highlighting aspects such as democratic management, low price policy and their proven social responsibility toward the consumers and the environment. However, advertising at the local level for periodic specials is conducted by the individual cooperatives. In addition, some of the marketing costs incurred by Coop Italia is paid by producers. In 1991 alone, Coop Italia managed to raise 12 billion lire from producers to help market their products and the Coop supermarkets.[55]

Fourth, Coop Italia also provides the single cooperatives important data on the retail sector and consumer behaviour. Data is provided to analyse the retail sector in Europe and the strategies adopted by Italy's major competitors. An important study on consumer behaviour revealed that over 60% of consumers are mostly attracted to a store by its appearance, rather than by low prices. The availability of data and information on consumer behaviour has been vital for the business strategy of the individual enterprises.

Results

The success of Coop Italia is unquestioned as 90% of all acquisitions made by consumer cooperatives are made through contractual arrangements promoted by Coop Italia. In 1990 the total amount of acquisitions made through these arrangements amounted to 4,811 billion lire. To cover its services Coop Italia charges a commission fee based on 0.3% of the total acquisition made by each cooperative, thus in 1990 it received 16.5 billion lire for the services provided. In the same year Coop Italia registered a profit of 314 million lire.[56]

Coop Italia, La Lega and the State

The consortium plays a strategic role for La Lega by providing services on a national scale and by promoting a unitary promotional and commercial policy. It also promotes intersectoral trading between agricultural, industrial and consumer cooperatives. Statistics show that 45% of products sold with the cooperatives' own brand name are produced by industrial and agricultural cooperatives,[57] and 28 out of the 37 enterprises which produce "Prodotti con Amore" are also cooperatives.[58] In 1990 consumer cooperatives' acquisition of cooperative products through Coop Italia amounted to 600 billion lire which is the equivalent of 12.5% of Coop Italia's total sales.[59]

The relations between Coop Italia with the State is minimal. Coop Italia makes use of the local health authorities to help monitor the quality of some products and it has signed contractual arrangements with state enterprises operating in the agricultural sector.[60]

Concluding Remarks

A number of important points emerge from this case study. The fact that 90% of total purchases are obtained through Coop Italia makes this La Lega's most integrated sector. Secondly, it is also important to point out that it is the large cooperatives which are the backbone of this sector. In 1990, 21 cooperatives which represent only 4.9% of the total number of consumer cooperatives, controlled 43% of the retail outlets, 75.4% of the total sales area, employed 78% of the work-force and sold 85% of the total sales.[61]

Third, Coop Italia has also promoted intersectoral trading between the agricultural, manufacturing and the consumer sectors. The actual percentage of intercooperative trading between the agricultural sector and the consumer sector may be only 12.5% overall purchases by consumer cooperatives, but its significance to individual cooperatives should not be underestimated. For instance the consortium Giglio sells approximately 25% through the consumer sector (a further 5% to 15% through the retailing cooperatives) and this influences 160 other cooperative members and 8,000 producers. Another example is provided by Corticella, a consortium which produces pasta, flour and bread. It sells 50% of its total pasta production through the consumer cooperatives (another 20% through the retailing cooperatives). Considering that pasta production alone makes up 57% of its turnover, it is fair to conclude that most of Corticella's production is sold through the cooperative sector.[62] Once again Corticella employs over 400 persons and represents hundreds of small to medium size producers and cooperatives. Thus Coop Italia plays an important role not only for the consumer sector, but also for the agricultural and manufacturing sector by providing them a market for their products.

Case Study 5: ICIE - A National Intersectoral Consortium

The consortium Istituto Cooperativo per L'Innovazione, ICIE, (Cooperative Institute for Innovation Transfer), is a research institute which conducts research and monitors the changes that take place in the field of technology and innovation and then transfers that knowledge to cooperatives. When it was formed in 1972 it was mainly a research centre for the building industry. In 1984, it was restructured into an intersectoral research centre capable of conducting research in the area of energy, environment, construction, agriculture and various aspects of urban development.

ICIE operates from three main centres based in Rome, in Bologna and in Genoa. Originally its membership only consisted of other consortia, but after

1980 individual cooperatives also began to join. The centre is partly funded by its members, but most of the research is funded by grants made available by the Italian State through its ministries and various State institutions, by the regional governments and by the European Economic Community.

The Role of ICIE Today

ICIE provides a number of services to Cooperatives. First of all it provides information in the area of research and technology. This may be basic information on new technological developments which may be of interest to cooperatives. It makes cooperatives aware of new patents made available by the Italian government.[63] It informs cooperatives on the various grants available in Italy and in the EEC for the development of research and technology in the areas of product and production innovation, energy saving, building improvements: all economic areas where cooperatives are active. This is an important service especially for those small and medium sized cooperatives which are not well informed.

The second service provided by ICIE is to transfer this information to cooperatives. This is done in a number of ways. ICIE passes on information through its own quarterly journal and through the various cooperative publications. For more specific information, conferences, seminars and educational courses are organised where managers and technicians from interested cooperatives are invited to attend.

The third function performed by ICIE is to promote and to organise the actual research project. Usually, ICIE receives information from La Lega's own office in Brussels regarding grants available through the EEC and from the various Italian ministries about grants available in Italy. The next step is to contact the cooperatives and various institutions. Once a working party is formed, which can include researchers from ICIE, cooperatives, private and public institutions, then an application is lodged with the relevant agency. One such example is the *ad hoc* consortium CORIRE which conducts research on building maintenance and restoration. This is a consortium where the private sector, the cooperative movement through the National Association of Producers Cooperatives (ANCPL), and the State holding company IRI are all equal shareholders. This consortium has received 10 billion lire from the Italian government. Once an application is successful, like the CORIRE project, experimentation proceeds and the results are conveyed to cooperatives. The importance of getting cooperatives to participate from the beginning of the project is to ensure that the new technology developed can then be applied by the same cooperative.

ICIE has been involved in many projects covering a wide area. In the building industry it has developed better quality glass, ceiling fixtures for heating and air-conditioning, and bricks with a high insulation capability. Other projects include: building energy efficient housing complexes, setting up 11 centres to promote technological centres in Southern Italy, developing ways to solve the pollution problems associated with the Po' river and the Adriatic sea, and developing techniques to preserve heritage listed buildings and artistic monuments. These are all areas where cooperatives operate, thus having access to knowhow and technology will improve their competitiveness.[64] An agreement has also been signed with the State owned ENEA (National Institute for Atomic and Alternative Energy) allowing ICIE to transfer new technology and innovative techniques in the areas of laser energy, product recycling, and energy saving projects for the housing sector.[65]

ICIE, La Lega and the State

ICIE plays an important role in La Lega's overall strategy. It is a research centre which provides cooperatives with access to information and research facilities in the area of technology. ICIE's importance is supported by evidence provided by a recent study conducted on 87 cooperatives from five different sectors which have undertaken Research and Development (R&D) programmes. This study revealed that cooperatives which have introduced new products, or new productive processes, experienced a reduction in costs and an an improvement in efficiency, in the quality of the products and in the image of the enterprise, which are vital for the enterprise's competitiveness.[66]

The second major contribution made by ICIE is in the area of culture. ICIE is concentrating in bringing about change in the cooperative's view toward technology. In 1988, research conducted by ICIE on producers' cooperatives found that they invest 0.3% of their turnover on R&D whilst similar private enterprises invest an average of 2%.[67] A more recent survey revealed that of those producer cooperatives which did undertake research, only 27% of them applied to receive State grants.[68] Considering that the State finances up to 50% of each research project these cooperatives are missing out on an important source of finance, as well as access to new technology.[69] Part of the problem is cooperatives' lack of information or awareness of the available grants. The members' fear of losing their job if technology is introduced is another problem.[70] However, a major reason for this is caused by State inefficiencies and this brings us to ICIE's third major contribution which is lobbying the State.

There are many problems associated with government funding which may explain the reason why some cooperatives (but not only cooperatives) may be deterred from applying for State grants. First, the procedures are costly and complicated. The costs can only be recovered when large grants in the sum of five to ten billion lire are obtained. This deters both cooperatives and small businesses from applying. Secondly, the duration of the procedures are lengthy and the outcome uncertain. By the time any funds are received the project may have lost its significance. Thirdly, information about these grants is mainly concentrated in the hands of State personnel and institutions and is not readily available.[71] ICIE has been lobbying the State to ensure that these problems are overcome. This is extremely important for cooperatives and small and medium size industries which together have only received 4% of the total funds made available by the State.[72] Considering State expenditure on research accounts for 50% of the total money invested on R&D in Italy, there is a clear shift of resources to large enterprises.[73]

Finally, while ICIE is the national consortium in the area of technological research and transfer for La Lega, it does not conduct all of the cooperative's research in this area. For instance the construction consortium CCC conducts its own research. The construction cooperatives CMC of Ravenna and CMB of Carpi have their own research centre for the environment (SECIT).[74] In addition, the already cited research on 87 cooperatives, revealed that 36% of the agricultural cooperatives and 60% of the others had developed their own R&D units within the enterprise. It was also noted how these also cooperated with local universities and research centres as well as ICIE to conduct research.[75] This is a clear indication that research and development takes place in many centres. While ICIE is the largest, it is not large enough to cater for the need of all the cooperatives. It also implies, especially in the case of the consortium CCC having its own research centre, that the consortium have some degree of autonomy from the national organisational support structures, otherwise CCC would have conducted its own research through ICIE.

The relationship between ICIE and the State takes a number of forms. The capacity of ICIE to lobby the State to improve access to funds for cooperatives of small and medium size has already been mentioned. Second, ICIE relies on the State for funds. The State provides 50% of the total expenditure on R&D in Italy distributed through: the various ministries (11.2%), the national research institutes such as the National Centre for Research (CNR), the National Institute for the Development of Natural and Alternative Energy, ENEL, (15.9%), the universities (18.4%), and other public bodies (4.5%). In addition, the State also invests a further 19.3% through State owned enterprises.[76] ICIE has been successful in obtaining grants through ministries as was the case with CORIRE whose project was funded by the Ministry of Transport and Urban Development. It has also managed to win grants from the national research centres. In 1987, it received from ENEL grants totalling 1.48 billion lire to fund energy saving projects.[77] The third form of collaboration is entering into joint projects with State funded institutions like research centres and universities.

ICIE is of strategic importance to cooperatives. It operates in an area which in the future will be very vital for cooperatives' economic success. The range of research undertaken by ICIE and the improved competitiveness of cooperatives indicates that ICIE has been successful. The evidence from this case study also emphasised ICIE willingness to engage in research projects with private and public research centres improving access to finance and the sharing of knowledge. Finally, the work methods which have cooperatives as joint partners of a project ensures that the results will be applied at the enterprise level making this a very productive way of operating.

Conclusion

The purpose of this chapter was to analyse the ways the consortia network helps individual cooperatives compete in the market. In the process the relationship between the consortia and La Lega, and the consortia and the State was also to be evaluated. This conclusion will summarise some of the main characteristics of the consortia. This is followed by an evaluation of the relationship the consortia have developed with La Lega and with the State. Finally, the ways the consortia have helped cooperatives overcome the problems they face in the economy will be discussed.

Main Findings

The first major finding is the ability of the consortia Coop Italia and ACAM to develop trade links between cooperatives from different sectors. The level of trade between cooperatives through ACAM amounted to 172 billion lire and through Coop Italia to 600 billion lire for a total of 772 billion lire. This has led to the developing of networks between the manufacturing and the construction sectors and between the consumer and the agricultural and manufacturing sectors. This means that the construction and the consumer sectors provide a demand also for other cooperative sectors improving the latter's chances of survival and growth in a market economy.

The second finding is the level of cooperation between the consortia and private and State enterprises. This has taken many forms. ICIE has had access to information from State research centres. It has also formed *ad hoc* consortia which included State and private enterprises to conduct research on particular areas of common interests. The construction consortium CCC has bid for public contracts in partnership with private and State enterprises. Coop Italia has had 60% of its products tested by either private or State institutions. Further, it has commissioned private firms to produce a number of its brand name products. Giglio has attracted risk capital from the multinational dairy firm Parmalat and from the State owned BNL bank. It has also commissioned private firms to produce new products. Giglio is also a shareholder in conventional firms. The construction of alliances with the private and State sector is proof that the cooperative sector in Italy is well integrated with the rest of the economy. The advantages differ for each venture but they provide cooperatives access to knowledge (ICIE), to public works (CCC), good products for consumers (Coop Italia), and finance and managerial expertise in the case of Giglio. All of these improve the competitiveness of cooperatives.

The third finding to come out of these case studies is the important role played by the large cooperatives within the consortia. The 76 largest cooperatives buy 79% of the total acquisitions made through ACAM's contractual arrangements with buyers. In the consumer sector the largest 21 cooperatives sell 85% of that sector's total sales. In the construction industry, it is the large cooperatives which ultimately provide CCC with vital experience and knowledge to execute the work. This provides CCC with a lot of contractual power necessary for it to win public contracts. These large cooperatives play an important role because by being members of a consortium, not only do they help themselves by reducing costs and having access to markets, but also help the small and medium size cooperatives which also benefit from these arrangements.

The fourth finding is the consortia's ability to manage change. ACAM, Coop Italia, Giglio and CCC all managed to change during their lifespan. They have shown an ability to understand the changes that were taking place in cooperatives, in La Lega's other structures, in the market and in the State's public policies, and have changed accordingly to meet the economic needs of cooperatives. If they had not done so they would have become redundant and would not have helped the cooperatives succeed in the 1980s and 1990s.

Relations with La Lega

The case studies have identified the consortia to play a number of important roles for La Lega. First, they provide economic support for individual cooperatives helping them achieve economies of scales and economic success. Second, through economic integration the consortia have become a source of unity for La Lega's cooperatives. Third, the consortia CCC and Coop Italia have developed a close relationship with the national sectoral association and have contributed to the planning strategies of their respective sectors. Fourth, CCC has also provided evidence that they also play a role in managing conflicts between cooperatives. This was achieved by dividing work fairly between cooperatives and for providing a forum where disputes can be solved.

The ICIE case study also revealed that La Lega has developed a fragmented rather than unitary approach when it comes to R&D. ICIE was established to provide cooperatives from various sectors' R&D facilities and technology information. While ICIE has been successful, it has not prevented other cooperatives and consortia from developing their own centres or from cooperating with public and private centres of research. A number of reasons have been identified. The cooperatives CCC and CMB have bought the Eco-business company SECIT because they were the first to identify the importance that environmental policies would have on the construction business. In addition, they had the financial resources to buy the company. CCC on the other hand set up its own R&D centre when ICIE was having difficulties and undergoing changes. The reason for CCC setting up the research centre was to improve the competitiveness of CCC. It too had the financial resources to set up a research centre. Another reason for not cooperating with ICIE could be market driven. The agricultural cooperatives have at times chosen local research centres in Parma and Lodi to conduct research on their behalf, (instead of ICIE's) because these centres have achieved a high level of quality.[78]

In summary, these case studies have identified a number of factors which have influenced cooperatives and the consortia to develop their own R&D, these are: the level of managerial expertise, financial resources, enterprise strategy and the market. This does not necessarily mean that they do not cooperate with ICIE. Indeed, the construction cooperatives CMB and CMC and the consortia CCC are still members of ICIE showing still a willingness to join a particular project if it is in their interest.

The case study on the consortium CCC has added more information in the relationship between the national sectoral association and the consortium.

It was stated in the last chapter that the strategy to develop large cooperatives through mergers and concentration largely developed within the national sectoral association. The decision to create large national consortia was also developed by the same. However, CCC's decision to form the companies Sinapsi and STS was developed within the consortium. This indicates that the managerial capacity of the consortium exceed those of the national sectoral association hence the reason why the consortium developed these new business ventures first. Further, it also indicates a degree of autonomy by the consortium from the sectoral association. This is another indication that decisions are not made in a hierarchical way from the national territorial and sectoral structures down to the consortium.

Relations with the State

The case studies have provided sufficient evidence to indicate that a non discriminatory relationship has developed between La Lega's consortia and the State. The consortia have had access to a number of State resources which have improved their capacity to serve the economic needs of individual enterprises. CCC has had access to 12% of the total amount of the national public works market. It has also formed consortia jointly with State enterprises. ICIE has had access to resources such as patents and knowhow from State research centres. The consortia have also received finance from the State. ICIE has received grants for a number of projects. Giglio too has received funds from the regional and national governments. The latter also received finance in the form of risk capital from the BNL bank. Finally, Coop Italia collaborates with Local Health Authorities to conduct testing on consumer products.

Cooperative problems

The consortia network has highlighted how some of the cooperative problems could be overcome. There is evidence which proves how consortia have contributed to overcome the problems of finance, management, place of cooperatives in the economy, constraints on takeovers and discrimination. Each of these will now be discussed.

Finance. Finance is probably the hardest barrier to overcome. Cornforth argued that cooperatives lacked finance because they were unable to issue shares and because members had low incomes and little money to invest in the enterprise. This led them to rely on external borrowing facing the risk of high gearing. The consortia studied here do not specialise in providing finance, although CCC and Coop Italia did provide some finance prior to the formation of the financial consortium Fincooper. However, they have reduced the financial burden of their members in a number of ways. ICIE has provided cooperatives access to finance for projects in research and development. Coop Italia has reduced the financial burden of cooperatives for marketing and for the costs involved in controlling the products sold under the cooperative labels by getting the suppliers or producers to contribute to the costs. Indeed, Coop Italia raised 16 billion lire in 1990 on behalf of cooperatives. Giglio raised finance through its own finance company and by attracting external shareholders to invest in its finance and marketing companies which were set up as conventional firms.

Management Skills. The second major barrier is lack of managerial skills. Generally cooperatives have been found to lack a number of managerial skills such as knowledge of the market, inability to introduce technological changes, marketing, long term planning. This problem is made worse by cooperatives' inability to pay high wages to attract outside managers. To some extent all of these skills were provided by the consortia. The consortia studied have knowledge of the market which is passed on to individual cooperatives. CCC and ICIE have improved the capacity of cooperative managers: CCC by providing experience on the job to potential cooperative managers and ICIE for providing training courses in the area of technology. Giglio, Coop Italia and CCC have all contributed in planning their respective sectors. CCC for instance helped cooperatives to specialise in particular segments of the market. Coop Italia helped consumer cooperatives to set up large supermarkets. Giglio, CCC and Coop Italia have also been influential in marketing the cooperative products for their respective sectors. In the area of technological innovation ICIE is the consortium which has more than any contributed to change the cooperative culture toward technological change by engaging cooperatives in a wide variety of projects.

Place of Cooperatives in the Economy. Another problem faced by cooperatives is their inability to compete in sectors dominated by large firms and to move out of low wage/low income sectors of the economy. The case studies have clearly shown that La Lega's consortia network has improved cooperatives' competitiveness. The consortia have basically provided small and medium size cooperatives the opportunity to achieve economies of scale and to have access to a variety of services which they would not have been able to obtain on their own. In doing so, the consortia have provided the groundwork for cooperatives of small dimensions to survive and grow in size and expertise, and for those of larger dimension to become leaders in their field. Basically costs were reduced, access to the market was improved and other enterprise functions were provided. The consortia ACAM and Coop Italia have reduced the costs of raw materials and food respectively for the manufacturing, construction and the consumer cooperatives. CCC and Giglio have provided cooperatives from the agricultural and construction sector access to a market. These consortia also provide a number of services: ACAM provides data on costs of materials, Coop Italia does the marketing and food controls on behalf of its members, ICIE provides information and organises research projects.

In addition, the economic competitiveness of cooperatives was further promoted by organising intersectoral trading and by managing the growth of certain sectors. As already stated, the consortia ACAM and Coop Italia organised intersectoral trading. This provides cooperatives with the advantage of having access to a market, which is particularly important for new and small cooperatives. Having access to a market allows small and new cooperatives to acquire experience, knowledge and consolidate before embarking on a strategy of growth.[79] Indeed, the most difficult years are the first three after which the chances for survival are much higher.[80]

Another factor which has improved the place of cooperatives in the economy is the ability of consortia to manage growth. One such example is provided by CCC. In accordance with the overall policy of La Lega's national sectoral association, the consortia CCC has distributed work to all cooperatives and has also contributed in getting them to merge and to specialise in particular niche markets within the construction industry. This has led to the survival and then the growth of cooperatives into large enterprises employing over 1,000 persons. Further, those specialising in road constructions, public parking, or soccer stadiums have become leaders in their field.[81]

Constraints on Takeovers. Another factor which diminished the ability of cooperatives to compete in the market is their inability to take over other firms. This is caused by legal restraints and by the difficulty of integrating workers with no prior experience of working in a cooperative. The way cooperatives have overcome this problem will be dealt with in a future chapter. In this chapter the consortium Giglio has given evidence of taking over other enterprises. This was made easier because Giglio is a consortium and the industrial relations within it are of a conventional nature. In other words the workers are not members, they are employees just like in a conventional enterprise.

However, the relationship between cooperatives and private enterprises need not always be adversarial. Giglio has shown that a consortium's chances of survival can also be improved by becoming partners with conventional firms. Giglio is a shareholder in a number of conventional enterprises and has allowed one of its competitors Parmalat, to become a shareholder in its financial company. This strategy has provided Giglio with access to finance and managerial expertise further improving its chances of survival. CCC and ICIE have also collaborated with private and State firms through the formation of *ad hoc* consortia. The point made here is that survival need not necessarily mean taking over private enterprises, forms of collaboration with the private sector may also improve their chances of survival.

Discrimination. The final problem which will be discussed here is the proposition that cooperatives are discriminated against by corporations, businesses and unions which feel threatened by them, and by the State's taxation and the financial system which are geared toward the needs of large private companies. The relationship between the State and the consortia has already been discussed and it has been found not to behave discriminatory. The main concern here is to show that through the consortia, the cooperative sector has become well integrated with the private economy. The evidence suggests that 85.5% of products bought through ACAM and 87.5% of products bought through Coop Italia are produced by the private and State enterprises. Since both of these two consortia are the largest of their kind in Italy, it is really the cooperatives who are in a position of strength when dealing with the private sector. The other consortia, ICIE, Giglio and CCC all have established collaborative relations with private and State enterprises. In particular Giglio sells over 60% of its produce in private stores. The reasons for this development are that all three sectors are economically integrated and indispensable to one another. Indeed, in the case of ACAM and Coop Italia, it is the cooperative sector which is providing a market for private enterprises. Secondly, since all sectors accept the legitimacy of the other, while the differences between cooperatives and private enterprises remain, relations between them are based more on economic need rather than ideological confrontation.

Notes

1 Guido Bonfante, "La Legislazione Cooperativistica in Italia dall'Unità ad Oggi", in Guido Sapelli (ed), Il Movimento Cooperativo in Italia: Storia e Problemi, Piccola Biblioteca Einaudi, Torino, 1981, p.205.
2 Michele Balboni, "L'Impresa Cooperativa: Aspetti Legislativi e Fiscali", in Francesco Garella (ed), *Il Movimento, Il Sistema, La Rete: Un Decennio di Cambiamenti nelle Imprese Cooperative*, Editrice Emilia Romagna, Bologna, 1991, p.49.
3 Le Certificate, Intervista con Dante Fantini, *La Cooperazione Italiana*, Novembre-Dicembre, 1988, p.69.
4 Le Certificate, Intervista con Enrico Gualandi, *La Cooperazione Italiana*, Novembre-Dicembre, 1988, p.117.
5 Stefano Zan, *La Cooperazione in Italia: Strutture, Strategie e Sviluppo della Lega Nazionale Cooperative e Mutue*, De Donaato, Bari, 1982, pp.309-310.
6 An excellent account of the evolution of the consortia network can be found in Giancarlo Pasquino, "La Cooperazione fra Imprese Cooperative: La Formazione del Sistema Consortile", in *Rivista della Cooperazione*, Ottobre-Dicembre 1981, pp.43-50.
7 Zan, *op.cit.*, p.313.
8 Giuseppe Vitale, "L'Integrazione nei Consorzi", in *L'Autogestione in Italia: Realtà e Funzione della Cooperazione,* De Donato, Bari, 1975, pp.80-81.
9 Pasquini, *op.cit.*, pp. 44-45.
10 Angelo Varni (ed), "Giglio Leader Mondiale nel Commercio del Parmiggiano Reggiano", in *Emilia Romagna Terra di Cooperazione,* Eta/Analisi, Bologna, 1990, p.399.
11 Giglio has directed a high level of investments on research and development: its latest processing plant alone costs 20.6 billion lire. Giglio, *Relazione del Consiglio di Amministrazione al Bilancio 1990*, Reggio Emilia, p.20.
12 For instance milk is controlled 1,384 times per day. *L'Unità,* "Giglio", 1 May 1991, p.15.
13 Giglio, *op.cit*, *Relazione del Consiglio di Amministrazione al Bilancio1990,* p.10.
14 Giglio, *Relazione del Consiglio di Amministrazione al Bilancio 1988,* Reggio Emilia, pp.10-13.
15 Giglio, *op.cit.*, *Relazione del Consiglio di Amministrazione al Bilancio 1990,* p.3.
16 Giglio, *op.cit.*, *Relazione del Consiglio di Amministrazione Bilancio,1990,* p.9.
17 Tullio Fazzalari, "Assalto al Piatto", *l'Espresso*, 22 Gennaio 1989, pp.158-162.
18 CERPL is a consortium formed in 1972 by cooperatives from La Lega and the Confederazione. In 1989 it had a turnover of 600 billion lire, 13,000 producer members, 7 cooperative members, and employed 1,300 persons. See Angelo Varni (ed), "Granarolo Felsinea CERPL un Ruolo di Primo Piano in un Settore Strategico Nazionale", *Emilia Romagna Terra di Cooperazione*, Eta/Analisi, Bologna, 1990, p.401.
19 *Corriere della Sera*, "Parmalat, un Giglio delle Coop nell'Occhiello di Tanzi", 26 Marzo 1992, p.27. See also, Giancarlo Martelli, "Come Unire le Forze Senza Perdere Identità", *La Cooperazione Italiana*, Febbraio-Marzo 1992, p.65.
20 The Cooperative Co-E-Zoo was incorporated in 1988 and Giglio is in the process of incorporating another cooperative (Cooperativa Agricola Ovina Cusna). See Giglio, *op.cit.*, *Relazione del Consiglio di Amministrazione al Bilancio 1988,* p.11.
21 Giglio, *op.cit.*, *Relazione del Consiglio di Amministrazione al Bilancio 1989,* p.14.
22 Giglio, *op.cit.*, *Relazione del Consiglio di Amministrazione al Bilancio 1990,* p.6.

23 Giglio, *Relazione del Consiglio di Amministrazione al Bilancio 1985,* Reggio Emilia, p.10.
24 Martelli, *op.cit.*, p.65.
25 Maria Silvia Sacchi, "Latte Concentrato", *Panorama,* 7 Giugno 1992, p.191.
26 Jenny Thornley, *Workers' Cooperatives: Jobs and Dreams*, Heinemann Educational Books, London, 1981, pp.160-161.
27 Angelo Varni (ed), "ACAM, un Consorzio Nazionale per L'Approvvigionamento, da Trent'Anni al Servizio delle Imprese Associate", *Emilia Romagna Terra di Cooperazione,* ETA/Analisi, Bologna, 1990, p.318.
28 ACAM, *Assemblea di Bilancio: Elementi Statistici,* a Cura del Servizio Informatico Aziendale, Bologna, 28 Giugno 1991, p.10.
29 ACAM, *op.cit.*, pp.6 and 14.
30 ACAM, *Assemblea di Bilancio: Relazione della Presidenza*, Bologna, 28 Giugno 1991, p.8.
31 Cooperatives supplied items such as timber, metal fixtures, concrete, tiles, bricks, petroleum products, electrical equipment, furniture, hi-tech plant installations, provided transport vehicles. see ACAM, *op.cit.*, *Assemblea di Bilancio: Elementi Statistici,* pp.15 and 17.
32 ACAM, *op.cit.*, *Assemblea di Bilancio: Relazione della Presidenza,* p.7.
33 ACAM, *op.cit.*, *Assemblea di Bilancio: Elementi Statistici,* p.6.
34 *Consorzio Provinciale delle Cooperative di Produzione e Lavoro,* Notiziario Numero 1, Bologna, 31 Gennaio 1977, p.3.
35 *L'Unità,* "Una Rete per il Mercato", 8 Giugno 1991, p.22.
36 Le Certificate, *op.cit.*, "interview with Fabio Carpanelli", p.53.
37 *L'Unità, op.cit.*,"Una rete per il Mercato", p.22.
38 Eugenio Arbizzani, "Verso Una Nuova Gestione degli Interventi Complessi", *La Cooperazione Italiana*, Ottobre 1991, p.78.
39 *L'Unità, op.cit.*, "Una Rete per il Mercato", p.22.
40 Tognoni Massimo, "La Ricetta è una Sola: Integrazione tra Pubblico e Privato", in *Spazio Impresa*, Editrice l'Unità, 2 Aprile 1991, p.19.
41 *L'Unità, op.cit.*, "Una Rete per il Mercato", p.22.
42 *Consorzio Provinciale delle Cooperative di Produzione e Lavoro, op.cit.*, Allegato Numero 3.
43 *Consorzio Provinciale delle Cooperative di Produzione e Lavoro, op.cit.*, p.26.
44 Le Certificate, *op.cit.*, Interview with Fabio Carpanelli, p.53.
45 *Ibid.*
46 Angelo Varni (ed), "Il Coop Italia", *Emilia Romagna Terra di Cooperazione,* Eta/Analisi, Bologna, 1990, p.365.
47 *Ibid.*
48 Ivano Barberini, "Quando i Consumatori Fanno Impresa Insieme", *La Cooperazione Italiana,* Ottobre 1986, p.233.
49 Associazione Nazionale Cooperative dei Consumatori, *La Cooperazione di Consumatori,* Roma, 1990, p.28.
50 Nadia Tarantini, "Come si Costruisce la Qualità Totale", in *La Cooperazione Italiana,* Giugno 1990, p.30.
51 Nadia Tarantini, "Il Prodotto è Svestito", in *La Cooperazione Italiana,* Giugno 1990, p.29.

52 Tassinari Vincenzo, *45a Assemblea Generale Ordinaria: Relazione del Presidente del Consiglio di Amministrazione,* 20 Giugno 1991, Coop Italia, Bologna, p.12.
53 Associazione Nazionale Cooperative dei Consumatori, *La Cooperazione dei Consumatori,* Roma, 1990, p.24.
54 Nadia Tarantini, "Bue Stressato fa Cattiva Bistecca", in *La Cooperazione Italiana,* Maggio 1991, p.31.
55 Tassinari, op.cit., p.25.
56 *Ibid.,* pp.25 and 26.
57 Associazione Nazionale Cooperative dei Consumatori, *op.cit.*, p.24.
58 Tassinari, *op.cit.*, p.13.
59 *Ibid.*, p.28.
60 The Italian State through its company SME owns businesses which produce a variety of food products such as: olive oil, milk, tomatoe cans, vinigar, pasta etc.
61 Tomassini Nazareno, "Crescere Cambiando", *Consumi e Società*, Anno V, Numero 3, Maggio-Giugno, 1991, p.21.
62 Corticella, *Corticella Information Booklet,* Bologna, 1990.
63 The State National Research Centre (CNR) had made available to all enterprises 80 patents. See Alberto Sisto, "Un Tabù che si Chiama Ricerca", *La Cooperazione Italiana,* Dicembre 1989, p.55.
64 *La Cooperazione Italiana,* Intervista con Alessandro Brusca, "Primo Cambiare la Testa dei Managers", Dicembre 1989, p.63.
65 *La Cooperazione Italiana,* "Energia: Un Ponte tra Ricerca e Aziende", Dicembre 1989, pp.74-75.
66 Alessandro Brusca, *Qualità, Ricerca, Innovazione: Nuove Sfide per le Imprese Cooperative,* Lega Nazionale delle Cooperative e Mutue, Maggio 1991, p.36.
67 Sisto, *op.cit.*, p.55.
68 Icie, *Innovazioni nelle Imprese Cooperative,* Lega Nazionale delle Cooperative e Mutue, Maggio 1991, Roma, p.21.
69 Sisto, *op.cit.*, p.57.
70 *Ibid.*, p.59.
71 Brusca, *op.cit.*, *Qualità, Ricerca, Innovazione: Nuove Sfide per le Imprese Cooperative,* p.32.
72 Virginia Lori, "Europa Sociale", in *Lega Senza Frontiere*, Editrice l'Unità, Roma, Giugno 1991, p.20.
73 This is not withstanding the fact that companies wholly or partly owned by the State have invested a further 19.3%. See *La Cooperazione Italiana*, "La Parte del Leone la fa il Pubblico", Dicembre 1989, p.71.
74 CMC and CMB and a consortium from Empoli have bought the Eco Business Company in 1974, eight years before ICIE began to conduct research on the environment. See Franco Buzzi, "Il Caso CMC", in Anna Avitabile (et al)., *Cooperare e Competere*, Feltrinelli Editore, Milano, 1986, p.41. See also Luca Torrealta, "I Mattoni di Carpi", *Il Manifesto*, 11 Dicembre 1990, p.2.
75 ICIE, *Innovazioni nelle Imprese Cooperative, op.cit.*, pp.9-24.
76 *La Cooperazione Italiana, op.cit.*, "La Parte del Leone la fa il Pubblico", p.71.
77 *La Cooperazione Italiana, op.cit.*, "Energia: Un Ponte tra Ricerca e Aziende", p.75.
78 Icie, *op.cit.*, *Innovazioni nelle Imprese Cooperative,* p.10.

79 A clear example of this is provided by the transport cooperative CTA. Formed in 1972, initially it transported goods on behalf of the consumers, retailers and wine cooperatives only. In 1985 it began to transport goods on behalf of the multinational company Unilever. Later it expanded to work all over Italy and in Eastern Europe as well. *La Cooperazione Italiana*, "Servizi Integrati Contro la Concorrenza", Aprile 1992, p.60.
80 *La Cooperazione Italiana*, "Il Business Plan è la Prima Cosa", Ottobre 1992, p.57.
81 For instance the cooperative Coopsette of Reggio Emilia specialises in building car parks, Edilter of Bologna builds and refurbishes soccer stadiums.

7 La Lega's Financial Institutions

The financial institutions of La Lega help cooperatives compete in the market by providing them with finance and a number of financial services. This is a major contribution since lack of finance has always been one of the major hurdles faced by cooperatives. Chapter three has already identified how the State, through the cooperative branch of the BNL bank, the various job creation schemes and favourable tax concessions, has helped cooperatives tackle their financial problems. This chapter will analyse and evaluate how La Lega's financial institutions have helped cooperatives overcome their financial problems.

The financial institutions, just like the consortia analysed in the previous chapter, implement the general policies outlined by the La Lega's Central Association. To discover the ways in which the financial institutions have fulfilled their task, this chapter has been divided into four parts. The first part will analyse the national financial consortium Fincooper which is the hub of the system. The second part concentrates on the role played by the Unipol Group of Companies which includes Unipol Finance, Unipol Insurance and their subsidiaries. The third part provides an explanation of the role played by the cooperative bank Banec and the merchant bank Finec. All of these financial institutions are regarded to be of national importance because they cater for the needs of the whole of the cooperative sector associated to La Lega. The fourth part will analyse what are regarded as local financial institutions which include: territorial financial companies, sectoral financial companies and local savings banks. The conclusion will highlight the main findings and provide an analysis of the role these companies perform within La Lega, the relations they have developed with the State and how the financial institutions have helped cooperatives overcome the problems they face in the economy.

Fincooper: The Centre of the Financial System

Fincooper is an intersectoral consortium which provides a number of financial services. It was formed in 1969 by 200 cooperatives and it has grown steadily since. In 1990, it had a membership of 2,011, members' shares amounting to 24 billion lire and net assets valued at 74 billion lire.[1] Fincooper finances itself by making each cooperative pay a minimum of 2 million lire in shares, although there are some that have invested up to 100 million lire. The second form of finance is obtained by attracting deposits from cooperatives which are then invested in secure capital markets. From these transactions, Fincooper retains a margin of approximately 2% (being the difference between interest received less interest paid) which covers administrative costs and in part produces a profit.[2] It is important to note that while all cooperatives deposit funds with Fincooper, the consumer cooperatives are its major investors accounting for 59% of the total deposits.[3]

Being a consortium, Fincooper has been supported by a number of legislative measures which have contributed to its success. Such legislation has helped Fincooper become competitive in the financial market in three ways. First, because it is a consortium, Fincooper is exempt from depositing a percentage of its deposits with the central bank of Italy. This is an advantage because the central bank usually pays a very low interest rate on deposits. Second, depositors with Fincooper pay a flat 12.5% tax on their interest while bank depositors pay a flat rate of 25%. The advantage here is evident, since even if the consortium offers the same return on deposits as that offered by banks, the after tax return will be greater. Third, the interest paid on members' shares is tax exempt as long as it does not exceed a set level, namely the interest rate payable on interest bearing postal bonds plus 2.5% (14.5% in 1990).[4] In 1989 Fincooper paid a 5% dividend on members' shares.[5]

Function of Fincooper

Fincooper provides its members with services from a central office in Bologna supported by ten decentralised offices throughout Italy. The consortium's activity can be divided into three areas. First, Fincooper acts as a financial company on behalf of all cooperatives associated to La Lega. Second, it acts as an instrument which provides cooperatives with a range of financial services. Third, it acts as an instrument of control for La Lega by being a major shareholder in companies of strategic importance to the cooperative movement.

The first function of Fincooper is that of distributor and guarantor of invested funds within the cooperative movement. Fincooper attracts deposits from cooperatives which, along with members' shares, provides the liquidity needed to meet the loan requests from other cooperatives. In this instance, Fincooper will act as a guarantor to those cooperatives which provide funds. Fincooper usually manages to pay depositors a highly competitive rate of interest and charges between 1% to 1.5% below the prime rate.[6] In 1986, about 500 cooperatives deposited money with Fincooper and in turn 440 cooperatives had received loans.[7] In 1991, Fincooper had a total lending capacity of 550 billion lire, and in addition it held 250 billion lire in reserve in order to meet withdrawals from cooperatives.

Since Fincooper does not possess sufficient funds to meet the demands of all the cooperatives associated with La Lega, it has entered into a number of arrangements with major national and regional banks. These arrangements have given cooperatives access to loans from these institutions at a level of interest slightly lower than the prevailing commercial rate. Further, these agreements are valid throughout Italy and have been especially beneficial to cooperatives from Southern Italy which usually had to pay higher relatively interest rates which incorporated a higher risk premium because of the higher insolvency rate of businesses in that area. Fincooper's arrangements with these national banks has also facilitated cooperatives' access to loans from State and regional banks.[8] It was estimated that in 1986 cooperatives had access to loans totalling 90 billion lire through such agreements.[9] In addition, Fincooper also provides bridging finance to cooperatives awaiting a bank loan or funds from State institutions.[10]

The second activity is the provision of financial services. A major strength of Fincooper is its ability to provide a wide range of such services from one location at competitive prices.[11] Its services include financial consultancy, acting as manager and treasurer of cooperatives' liquid assets, providing information and assistance in obtaining credit from various State schemes, raising loans on the national and international market, providing bill-paying facilities, investing money on behalf of cooperatives and assisting cooperatives in foreign transactions. Most recently, Fincooper is developing a communication system, in collaboration with cooperatives and banks, which provides up to date information on the financial state of cooperatives.[12]

Fincooper's third major area of activity is a vital one for the cooperative movement in that it participates as a shareholder in strategic and instrumental companies for the development of the cooperative sector. The strategic operations are those financial investments in companies considered vital for the success of the strategy of La Lega as a whole. These include involvement in the Unipol Group of Companies (financial/insurance company) where Fincooper holds 32.68% of the shares, the merchant bank Finec (62%%), and the bank of the cooperative movement Banec (27%) (see Figure 7.1).[13]

The instrumental operations are directed toward those companies which allow Fincooper to be involved in areas which can provide new services to cooperatives. For this purpose it became a shareholder in private credit institutions which provide loans to cooperatives. Investments were also made in leasing and factoring companies and in businesses which are involved in research, technology, the service sector and management. At the end of June 1989, Fincooper had invested 164 billion lire in shareholding operations, an increase of 38% compared to the previous year. By January 1990, it held shares in 41 companies, all of which were of importance to the cooperative movement.[14]

Unipol Group of Companies

The most important company controlled by Fincooper and La Lega's cooperatives is the Unipol Group of Companies. This is comprised of Unipol Finance, Unipol Insurance and a number of other companies operating in the areas of financial services, real estate, communication and tourism. As already stated, Unipol Insurance was originally bought by cooperatives in 1963. Initially Unipol was an insurance company selling car insurance mainly in Emilia-Romagna and Tuscany. Since 1973, Unipol has embarked on a growth programme which included both territorial expansion and product diversification. In order to finance this programme, it began to sell shares to a variety of companies with close ties to the cooperative sector. The first alliance occurred in 1973 when the insurance group Volksfursorge, owned by the West German trade union movement, became a major shareholder buying almost 30% of the shares in Unipol. In that same year two Italian trade union confederations (CGIL and UIL), and the National Artisans Association (CNA) also purchased shares. By 1978 the Catholic Trade Union Confederation (CISL), the Small Farmers' Association (Confcoltivatori), and the Small Retailers' Association (Confesercenti) also became shareholders. This allowed Unipol to finance its operations and to increase its support base to include the trade unions and artisans as well as the cooperative movement. By the early 1980s it had become one of the biggest insurance companies in Italy.[15] Product diversifications also occurred since the 1970s. This was in response to the emerging needs of cooperatives and consumers. Cooperatives were becoming larger and needed

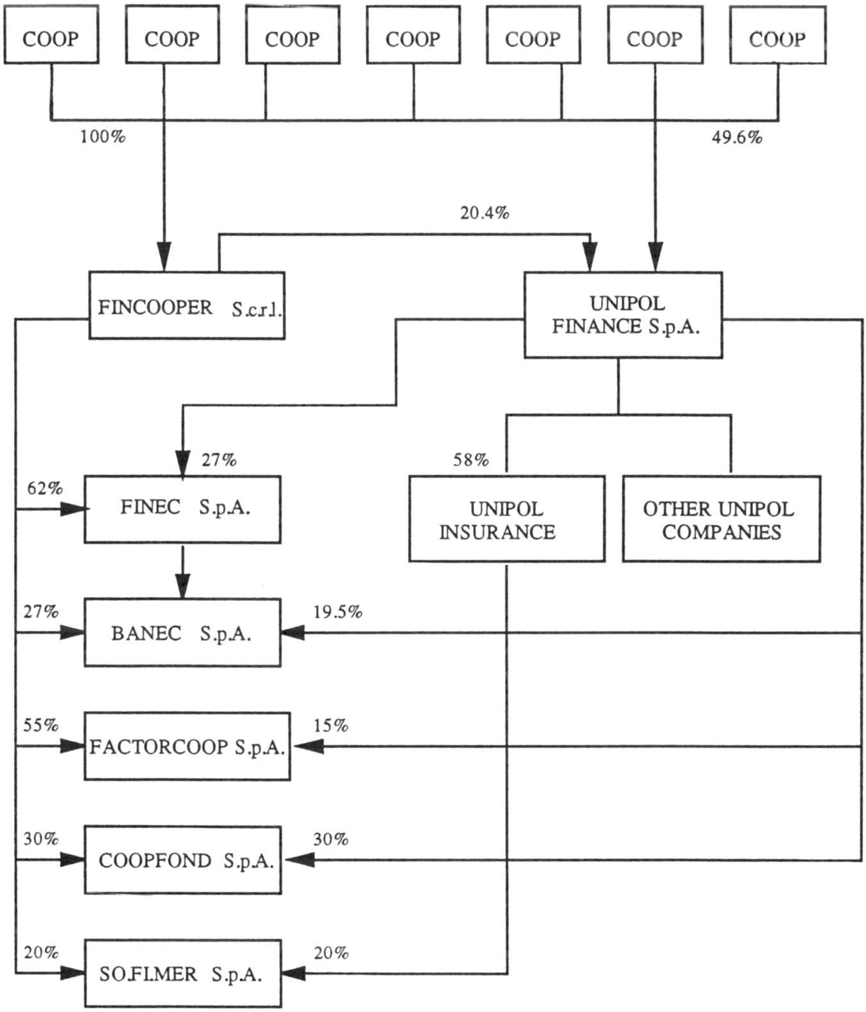

Figure 7.1 La Lega's Financial System

to have access to expanded financial services such as loans, factoring and leasing services. Consumers too sought different products such as life and health insurance. In addition, rising standards of living and a higher level of savings among working people created a demand for a number of financial services.[16] In response to this, Unipol expanded into life insurance, health insurance, real estate, financial services, communications and tourism.

This expansion once again led Unipol to seek external capital. This time it chose to attract capital via the stock exchange. Initially, in 1986 it issued preferential shares. Three years later in December 1989, Unipol embarked on what was a most significant move for a cooperative controlled company, issuing ordinary shares on the stock exchange. Equally extraordinary was the fact that they were fully subscribed within three hours, with demand 55 times greater than supply.[17]

The level of product diversification and, especially, Unipol's listing on the stock exchange prompted La Lega to restructure the Unipol group of companies. In 1990, it created a holding finance company, Unipol Finance, whose major role was to ensure that Unipol Insurance remained under the control of the cooperative sector. In addition, many of the companies previously controlled by Unipol Insurance were divided between the newly formed Unipol Finance and Unipol Insurance (see Figure 7.2).[18] What follows is a description of the group after the 1990 restructuring.

Unipol Finance

When it was first formed in 1990, Unipol Finance was owned by 98 cooperatives, six of which owned 24.8% of the shares.[19] In 1992, 30% of the shares were sold to other insurance companies. Unipol Finance is now 70% owned by the cooperative movement with Fincooper controlling 20.4%, the consumer cooperatives 22.5%, manufacturing and construction cooperatives 22.9%, and other cooperatives 4.2%. The rest of the shares are owned by a number of Italian and foreign companies. These include: two French cooperative societies (Maif (3.5%) and Macif (7%)); one cooperative society from Belgium (Prevoyance Sociale 3%); another 2% is owned by Eptaconcors which is a merchant bank owned by Italian Local Savings Banks and 1.8% is owned by Istituto Mobiliare Italiano (IMI) a State-owned special credit institution. Minor shareholders own the remaining 12.7%. The major reasons for selling 30% of the shares of Unipol Finance is part of a strategy of alliances with European cooperative movements and Italian local banks. A major benefit of this strategy is the access to capital which facilitates growth.

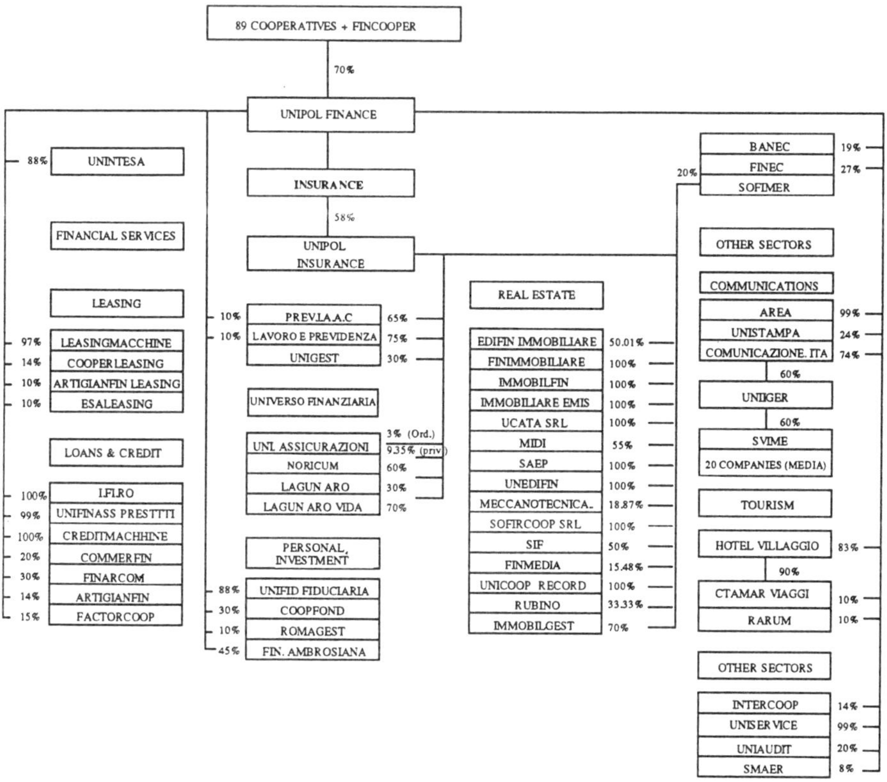

Figure 7.2 Unipol Group of Companies

Another important factor is that through the alliance with Italian local banks, agreements have been made which allows the local banks to sell financial products offered by some of Unipol Finance's subsidiaries, especially insurance.[20]

Unipol Finance is crucial to La Lega because of its holding of shares in companies of great importance for the cooperative movement such as the savings bank Banec (19%) and Finec (27%), Unipol Insurance (58%) and the insurance agency Unintesa (88%). In addition to these, Unipol Finance is a shareholder in four leasing companies, seven companies which provide loans and credit to small and medium sized businesses (including cooperatives), four companies which provide services for personal investments, over twenty companies in the area of communications, three hotels, one trading company and three companies which provide managerial services. Furthermore it is a minor shareholder in two health insurance companies, Previaac and Lavoro e Previdenza.[21] The most important of these companies are undoubtedly Unipol Insurance and Unintesa.

Unipol Insurance

Since the 1990 restructuring of the group, Unipol Insurance has been concentrating on two major sectors of the financial market, insurance and real estate. In addition, it also holds 20% of the shares in SOFIMER, a finance company operating in Southern Italy. In the insurance sector, Unipol has signed many agreements with the three trade union confederations, CNA, Confesercenti, the Association of Small Businesses, and many others which have led to the development of policies suited for their respective members. Two examples of this are the insurance companies Previaac Assicurazioni and Previdenza Assicurazioni whose purpose is to develop policies of life and health insurance for workers and small retailers respectively. In both of these companies Unipol insurance is the major shareholder with 65% ownership of Previaac and 75% ownership of Lavoro e Previdenza. Unipol Finance owns 10% of both and the trade unions and Confesercenti own the rest.[22]

Since the late 1980s Unipol has also been concentrating on expanding into Europe. It is a member of the International Association of Cooperative Insurance Companies, which operates under the auspices of the ICA. The role of the international organisation is to help develop cooperatives in other countries and to develop forms of cooperation between its members. Unipol has initiated various forms of cooperation with many cooperatives in Europe. An investment has been made with the Insurance company of the Mondragon group, Lagun Aro, which is 30% owned by Unipol. In addition, Unipol

(70%) and Lagun Aro (30%) own the insurance company Lagun Aro Vida which specialises in life insurance. In March 1990, Unipol and three other European cooperative insurance companies: Macif from France, Prevoyance Sociale from Belgium and Folksam from Sweden formed Euresa.[23] The aim of Euresa is to improve the competitiveness of the cooperative insurance sector in Western Europe, and assist its development in Eastern Europe especially in Hungary, Czechoslovakia and Poland. The overall strategy is to create a group of cooperative companies capable of procuring 20% of the European market.[24] Unipol's future European plans have targeted other cooperative societies such as Atlantis which operates in the Basque region of Spain, Triglav from Slovenia which is already a shareholder of Noricum, a company controlled by Unipol, a Greek, a Portuguese and a British mutual aid society. An office has also been established in Russia to explore possible collaboration with the Russian cooperative movement.[25]

The other major area of involvement is in the real estate market. Unipol fully owns eight real estate companies, it is a major shareholder in another four and is a minor shareholder in three others. Through this activity, Unipol Insurance has been very supportive of the cooperative sector. Some of its investments in commercial real estate provide cooperatives with office space and plants in strategically located areas. In particular, Unipol played a vital role in modernising La Lega's consumer sector. This was achieved by Unipol buying land and building supermarkets on their behalf and then leasing the site. Through this type of development Unipol attracts savings and redirects them toward the same sectors of the economy from which they originated.[26]

Unipol Insurance has become a diversified and successful company. In 1991, it managed to sell policies worth 2,725 billion lire, registering a profit of 33 billion lire. It employs a total of 1,300 persons at its central office and it is estimated that another 1,800 are employed through its 595 agencies spread throughout Italy.[27] By 1986, it had become the seventh largest insurance company in Italy in a very competitive sector where 220 companies are present. In that year it commanded 3.2% of the national market and 10% of the market in Emilia Romagna.[28] By 1990 it had become the sixth largest insurance company in Italy with a national market of 3.6%.[29]

There are a number of reasons which help explain Unipol's success. First, the insurance group has a reputation for having lower prices and has also generated substantial customer goodwill and consumer confidence. Indeed, a survey placed Unipol as the second most trustworthy insurance company in Italy.[30] Second, Unipol benefited from the experience that its partner Volksfursorge was able to pass on, especially in the area of life insurance. Third, Unipol has become more aware of and responsive to market changes and consumer needs through the feedback it receives from its own regional branches. These are comprised of shareholders, cooperatives, employees and insurance salespersons. Their role is to discuss the policies of Unipol and to evaluate whether they satisfy consumer needs. When a problem is identified, possible solutions are discussed and referred to Unipol.[31] Finally, the policy of alliance in Italy and abroad, culminating in the formation of joint ventures, has increased Unipol's support base and it has enhanced its chances of reaching particular groups of people and economic sectors.

Unintesa

The other company which plays a major role within the Unipol Group of Companies is Unintesa. Through its 300 agents Unintesa's role is to sell the various financial products offered by the subsidiaries of Unipol Finance. These include the following: personal loans, leasing, factoring and a financial investment advisory service. The major companies are Factorcoop, Coopfond and two leasing companies (Cooperleasing and Leasemacchine).

Factorcoop is a factoring company. It was formed in 1983 and is jointly owned by La Lega (70%) and the BNL Bank (30%). La Lega's shares are owned by Fincooper (55%) and Unipol Finance (15%). The remainder of the shares are owned by BNL (20%) and by BNL's factoring company, Ifitalia (10%).[32] BNL is the leading bank in the area of factoring and it has provided valuable managerial expertise to Factorcoop. The role of Factorcoop is to facilitate commercial relations between cooperatives and private enterprises. It does this by purchasing from cooperatives the accounts receivable from a creditor. Thus, a cooperative which is owed money from another company can sell the accounts receivable to a factor (Factorcoop) at a discount rate. The factor then proceeds to collect the full value of the debt and makes a profit: the difference between the full rate and the discounted rate.[33] For the cooperative this arrangement provides a number of advantages. First, it will receive money early thus ameliorating the cash flow. Secondly, the factor assumes all the risks when collecting the debt. Third, money is also saved by reducing the administrative costs and loss of time in collecting the debt. These advantages reduce costs and improve a cooperative's ability to plan for the future.[34]

Coopfond is a company which was formed in 1988 for the purpose of providing financial expertise to small investors. It is 90% owned by La Lega through Fincooper (30%), Unipol Finance (30%), various consumer cooperatives (25%), agricultural cooperatives (5%). The remainder of 10% is owned by Fincomit, a subsidiary of the State owned Banca Commerciale Italiana.[35] Coopfond provides small investors, such as individual cooperative members, professionals, small retailers and artisans, with a number of investment options. These include investment in ordinary and preference shares in Italy and abroad, national savings securities, government bonds. As stated, Coopfond sells its polices through Unintesa, but it also has its own office and has signed agreements to sell its products also through its shareholder the Banca Commerciale Italiana, two cooperative banks (Banec and Cooperbanca) and two local banks (Banca del Monte di Bologna e di Ravenna and Cassa Rurale e Artigiana di Azzano Emilia).[36] Coopfond will play two major important roles in the future. The first is to provide consumers with investment advice. This is a major reason why the consumer sector has become a major investor. Secondly, for those who wish to invest their money in shares, Coopfond can direct these persons to cooperatives, which since 1992, have been allowed to attract external shareholders.[37]

The third major financial sector that Unintesa is involved in is Leasing. The two major companies in this area are: Leasecoop, which is 97% owned by Unipol Finance, and Cooperleasing, which is jointly owned by the three major cooperative associations (La Lega, La Confederazione and L'Associazione) and the BNL Bank. In Cooperleasing, La Lega's shares are held by Unipol Finance 14% and Fincooper 5.4%.[38]

The major function performed by leasing companies is that they allow cooperatives to have access to machinery and other plant and equipment without having to outlay any capital. Through the leasing company, cooperatives can have access to plant and equipment in return for monthly payments for a specified period of time. At the end of the contract, cooperatives have the option of buying the equipment at a set price. This arrangement provides cooperatives with many advantages. First, it facilitates modernisation and the maintenance of a high level of technological content in the enterprise. Second, since machineries are rented only for a specified period it reduces fixed costs making it easier for the cooperative to adapt to changes in the market. Third, since no capital outlay is required, the cooperative has greater working capital at its disposal which it can use to finance other business needs and manage its cash flow requirements. Fourth, all the rental and maintenance costs are tax deductable.[39]

Finec and Banec

Finec

The third major financial company of La Lega is Finec (the National Finance Company for the Cooperative Movement), a merchant bank set up as a joint stock company in March 1987. Finec is a company jointly controlled by La Lega and IMI, the largest State owned Italian credit institution. La Lega holds 70% of its shares divided between Fincooper 32.7%,[40] Unipol Finance 27%,[41]the consumer cooperative Coop Lombardia and the consortia CONAD and ACAM own the remaining 10.3%. IMI owns 30%. It has a working capital of 50 billion lire.[42]

The role of Finec is to provide investment and financial services to the cooperative sector. It performs three basic functions. First, it provides short term venture capital. This is used to invest in companies which are vital for the cooperative sector and in purchasing private firms. In both of these cases, Finec invests money with the intent of eventually selling these firms to individual cooperatives within three to five years from the date of purchase. The second function is the provision of long term investment. This type of investment is made in companies which are vital for the long term interests of the cooperative movement. For instance, Finec holds 9% of the shares of the cooperative bank Banec and it also owns shares in import and export companies. The third function is to provide financial services to cooperatives. including economic evaluation, advice on restructuring and market analysis.[43]

Finec provides an important contribution to the growth of cooperatives. It provides an avenue to buy private enterprises, reducing the risk incurred by the eventual cooperative buyers because this risk is shared by its shareholders. Finec also provides cooperatives with the opportunity to enter new sectors of the economy. The merchant bank has also the ability to respond quickly to market changes because of its greater financial liquidity. Finally, Finec provides a series of financial services which have become very important to cooperatives, especially since the 1980s when they had to restructure and diversify their operations.

Banec

The last company of national importance is Banec (Bank of the Cooperative Movement). Banec is a joint stock company formed in 1987 which operates as a retail bank and trading bank. The bulk of its shares are held by cooperatives, consortia and conventional companies owned by cooperatives associated to La Lega. Its major shareholders are: Unipol Finance (19%), Finec (19%), Fincooper (14.5%) and 32 other cooperatives owning approximately another 36.5%. The remainder of the shares are owned by the trade union CGIL (a small amount not in excess of 2%); three State owned banks, BNL Bank (2%), Istituto Bancario San Paolo di Torino (2%) and Monte dei Paschi di Siena (2%). Minor shareholders own the remaining 3%. In 1987 it had a working capital of 40 billion lire.[44] In 1992, this increased to 80 billion lire.[45]

The objectives of the bank are to provide credit and banking services to individuals, families and small and medium sized (SME) firms from the cooperative and private sector. The bank has entered into a number of agreements with representative associations of artisans and SME businesses to facilitate the provision of credit for their members. It offers all depositors the "prime rate" interest rate. If Banec cannot provide credit to its business clients, it arranges for them to obtain credit from one of its three shareholding banks. Moreover, Banec arranges for leasing and factoring services to be provided by subsidiaries of Unipol Finance and Fincooper. The bank also provides clients with a free bill paying service and does not charge bank fees on "At Call" accounts with a minimum balance of two million lire.[46]

It is important to note that the bank operates under strict guidelines set by the Bank of Italy. The bank is not allowed to offer any type of privileges to its members. Second, the bank is not allowed to accept guarantees outside of the banking norm. Third, the bank is also obliged to charge a rate of interest set by the market. Fourth, the bank management has the responsibility to operate according to the criteria set by the board of directors.[47] It is clear from these requirements that the bank operates like other private banks with rates set by the market, unlike the Mondragon bank which can provide loans at favourable interest rates.

The relationship that Banec has established with the cooperative movement, the trade unions and private small and medium size enterprises provides the basis for future growth. In 1991, it operated from one branch in Bologna, but others are soon to be opened in Milan, Florence and Rome.[48] La Lega is well aware that a bank of this size will have difficulty competing with larger European banks once the European Financial System is fully deregulated.[49] To increase its size, Banec has plans to grow through acquisitions, mergers and the incorporation of other banks. One proposal could involve the merger with the Local Cooperative Bank of Reggio Emilia, "Cooperbanca". Another avenue for growth is to create further links with the consumer sector. This has great potential since the consumer cooperatives could provide the bank with investment funds, depositors and the opportunity of opening up bank branches in commercial centres.[50]

Local Cooperative Financial Institutions

While the four major national companies form the backbone of La Lega's financial network, there are three smaller types of financial institutions which are fully, or partly owned, by the cooperative movement and which provide important services. The first two can be classified as local and sectoral finance companies. The third are local banks. These financial institutions allow La Lega's financial system to decentralise its services and to create a better relationship between the local banks and the cooperatives in specific areas.[51]

Local Finance Companies

Locally based finance companies are formed as public companies and are either fully or partly owned by cooperatives. Their role is to provide financial services to cooperatives of a given territory ranging from a province to an entire region. In 1988, there were ten such institutions, five of which provided services to the provinces of Bologna (Fibo Srl), Ravenna (Federcoop Ravenna), Forli (Financoop), Reggio Emilia (Consorzio Cooperative Ferrovie Reggiane), Rome (Finidea). The following five were of regional dimension: Sofimer (Southern Italy), Sofincoop (region of Liguria), Fincoop Piemonte (the region of Piemonte), Sofimar (the region of Marche)[52] and Finpuglia (region of Puglia).[53]

Both sorts of territorial institutions provide direct finance, and assistance in obtaining finance from the State and private credit institutions, to locally based small to medium size cooperatives. This is because the large national institutions of La Lega do not have enough resources for all cooperatives and, as a consequence, they tend to cater for the large cooperatives.[54]

Sectoral Financial Companies

Sectoral finance companies cater for the needs of cooperatives from a specific economic sector. Some of these are: Finabit (housing), Confidi (fishing), Consorzio Confidi Culturale Nazionale (culture), Fincomma, Conad Invest and Conaf (retail), Agrisviluppo, Fingel and Finaica (agribusiness). These sectoral finance companies provide different services for large and small cooperatives. They provide loans directly to small cooperatives. They facilitate access to loans from private and public banks. They make available bridging finance, especially to those cooperatives awaiting public grants or loans. They act as a guarantor. They make available factoring services and provide investment vital for the whole sector. In addition, for the small cooperatives these financial companies also provide consultancy services, feasibility studies, sectoral research and investment analysis.[55]

The support provided for large cooperatives is less than that provided to smaller cooperatives. As already stated, this is partly because large cooperatives have access to services provided by the larger national institutions. Secondly, large cooperatives have sound managerial structures and personnel. Thirdly, being large and profitable, they can get credit directly from private and public institutions. Fourthly, many large cooperatives have their own financial structures. As a consequence, the sectoral financial structures offer large cooperatives support in the form of feasibility studies for specific projects, support for takeovers of private enterprises and finance for strategic investments.[56]

Having established the role played by the territorial and local financial companies, clear differences have emerged between the two. The national financial companies are more orientated toward large cooperatives and the traditional cooperative sectors such as construction, consumer and manufacturing. In addition, they operate in areas which are strategically important to the whole of the cooperative movement such as banking, insurance and financial services. The local institutions are more concerned with smaller cooperatives, they are locally based and function in newer sectors of the cooperative movement such as culture, private retailing and fishing. In addition, where the cooperative movement is strong, such as Ravenna, Bologna and Reggio Emilia, local institutions have also been formed to finance newly formed cooperatives.

Another important consideration is the financial support provided to the local institutions from Fincooper and Unipol Insurance. Fincooper, for instance, owns shares in many such institutions such as Sofimer (20%), Sofincoop (5%), Sofinmar (27.5%), Finpuglia (0.15%).[57] Unipol Insurance owns 20% of Sofimer. The latter has also attracted investors for 40% of its issued shares from external sources: 20% from the State owned Banco di Napoli and 20% from ISVEIMER, the Institute for the Economic Development of Southern Italy.[58]

Local Banks

The third group are the local rural and artisan banks and local popular banks affiliated to La Lega. The rural and artisan banks are small autonomous institutions operating mainly in areas where the cooperative movement is strong. Usually cooperatives are shareholders and they, along with their members, are also clients. In all, 30 rural and artisan banks are affiliated to La Lega. Their existing size is small for a variety of reasons which include: limited access to deposits because they usually operate at one branch, individual shares cannot exceed 2 million lire and that at least 80% of members must be either small farmers or artisans.[59]

The local popular banks are much larger than rural and artisan banks as they do not have the restrictions imposed on the latter. The largest local bank affiliated to La Lega is Cooperbanca (Cooperative Bank of Emilia Romagna). This bank was originally a local bank servicing the city of Reggio Emilia. It has always had a good relationship with the cooperative movement. In 1990, it had 6,271 members who owned 1,172,492 shares. Cooperatives associated to La Lega own the majority of shares, the rest are owned by workers, employees, artisans, farmers, professionals, retailers and businesses. The bank caters for the needs of individuals, cooperatives, artisans and small private businesses. It now has 18 branches spread throughout Emilia Romagna.[60] In 1991, its deposits amounted to 2,000 billion lire and it earned a profit of 6 billion lire.[61]

In addition to Cooperbanca, cooperatives are shareholders in many local banks and have established a good working relationship with them.[62] A 1990 study conducted by the finance department of La Lega on 147 cooperatives from Emilia Romagna (except the province of Modena) highlights the importance of local banks to the cooperative sector. This research sought to discover the sources from which cooperatives obtained their loans other than those obtained from Fincooper. The research revealed that 63.64% of cooperatives' total loans were obtained from local banks, of which 7.14% was advanced by Cooperbanca. Various State owned banks provided the remainder, of which the cooperative branch of the BNL provided 10.45%.[63]

Conclusion

This chapter has identified a number of specific characteristics of La Lega's financial network. One important characteristic is the way the financial network is co-ordinated. It was found that the consortium Fincooper co-ordinated the surplus funds of 2,011 cooperatives by channelling them into important companies of strategic importance to the cooperative sector. It was also found that the large cooperatives provided most of the funds, especially those operating in the consumer sector.

The second important finding was that the financial structure is highly decentralised. There are basically three tiers in this structure. One tier is formed by the national structures comprising Fincooper, Unipol Group of Companies, Banec and Finec catering for the needs of all cooperatives, but in particular the large cooperatives from traditional sectors. The second tier consists of local sectoral and territorial structures and cooperative controlled local banks which mainly cater for the needs of small cooperatives from newer sectors. The final tier is constituted by all those institutions external to La Lega comprising of local banks and State owned banks which have entered into agreements with Fincooper.

The third important characteristic is the level of intersectoral co-operation. This experience further highlights the importance for cooperative movements to develop links between cooperatives from different sectors. Indeed, a principle reason for their success of La Lega's financial structures was their ability to attract funds from cooperatives from all sectors. For example, Fincooper attracted shares and loans from 2,011 cooperatives from various sectors. Unipol Finance is partly owned by 91 different cooperatives (49.6%) and by Fincooper (20.4%). Without this wide ranging support from cooperatives from all sectors, La Lega would not have been able to develop the financial structures that it did. Thus, it is vital for cooperative movements to co-ordinate their financial activity if they are to succeed.

Relations with La Lega

The financial structures play a very important role within La Lega. Fincooper co-ordinates the excess liquidity of cooperatives in the interest of the whole movement. In doing so, Fincooper acts as a source of unity for La Lega's cooperatives. Another contribution made by the financial structures is the provision of loans, risk capital and various financial services. These create operational interdependencies between the cooperatives and the financial structures which further mould the cooperatives into a cohesive movement. Finally, the financial structures have implemented a policy of alliance formation with small and medium size businesses, the trade unions, State owned banks and local banks. This has allowed them to attract external capital to its companies, as well as gaining access to vital managerial expertise in areas such as leasing and factoring.

Relations with the State

The previous chapter on the consortia network has already shown the constructive relations that the various consortia have established with the State. In the area of finance, the State has given further support to cooperatives. This support has been provided in a number of ways. First, the State has enacted legislation favourable to Fincooper enabling it to offer attractive rates of return to its members. Through its State controlled banks, it has entered into agreements with Fincooper to provide loans to cooperatives at favourable rates. Third, it has provided risk capital to a number of companies set up by the movement such as Factorcoop, Sofimer, Finec, Banec, Coopfond. Fourth, the State owned banks and their subsidiaries have also provided managerial expertise especially in the areas of leasing, factoring and merchant banking. Once again this is a further indication that the State in Italy has been supportive of cooperatives.

Overcoming the Problems

Finance. The financial structures have overcome the financial problems faced by cooperatives in a number of ways. The financial structures facilitated cooperatives' access to credit by making available loans from Fincooper, Unipol Finance and the various local banks associated to La Lega and by facilitating access to loans by making arrangements with and providing guarantees to public and private banks. These support structures have overcome the problem cooperatives had in obtaining loans because of a lack of collateral or security. Another problem overcome is that of high gearing. This was overcome by providing financial services in the area of leasing and factoring which in turn reduced the level of borrowing. Unipol has also reduced cooperatives' borrowing by investing in commercial real estate on their behalf. This may be new offices, new plants, and, as in the case of consumer cooperatives, new commercial centres. The financial structures through Finec have also provided risk capital for the cooperative enterprises formed from private enterprises.

Management. The financial structures have provided managerial expertise in a number of related areas. Fincooper provides financial consultancy services, information on how to obtain financial assistance from State schemes, raises loans on the national and international markets and assists in foreign transactions. The local and sectoral financial institutions provide managerial expertise in relation to feasibility studies, sectoral research and investment analysis. The merchant bank Finec provides market analysis, economic evaluation and advice on restructuring.

Discrimination. The chapter has provided sufficient evidence to support the view that cooperatives have been able to develop working relationships with the State, the trade union movement and the associations of artisans and other small businesses in areas of mutual interest. This supports the view that the interests of cooperatives and that of small businesses and the State need not be incompatible.

Position in the Economy. The provision of funds and services provided by the financial support structures to cooperatives have contributed to cooperatives overcoming the difficulties they face in growing out of fragmented economies and in competing against large conventional enterprises. It has been acknowledged that Unipol contributed to the success of consumer cooperatives by buying land and building supermarkets on their behalf, thus accelerating their growth and increasing their ability to withstand competition from large supermarket chains. Factoring companies have facilitated trade and reduced administrative costs for cooperatives. Leasing companies have reduced fixed costs, increased flexibility and provided access to the latest machinery and technology thereby improving the competitiveness of cooperatives. These services have improved cooperatives' position in the economy and are important factors contributing to their overall success.

Notes

1 La Lega, *Il Sistema Finanziario della Lega delle Cooperative*, Bologna, 1990, p.2.
2 In 1989 the rate of interest paid to depositors was 10.53% and the rate of interest received from borrowers was 12.55%. See Fincooper, *Bilancio Consuntivo 1 Luglio 1988-30 Giugno 1989*, Bologna, 1989, p.12.
3 John Earle, *The Italian Cooperative Movement*, Allen and Unwin, London, 1986, p.73.
4 Alberto Zevi, "The Financing of Cooperatives in Italy", *Annals of Public and Cooperative Economies*, Volume 61, Number 2-3, April-September 1990, p.364.
5 Fincooper, *op.cit.*, p.13.
6 Earle, *op.cit.*, p.72.
7 Bettini Giorgio, "Una Rete fra Credito e Coop", *La Cooperazione Italiana*, Ottobre 1986, p.290.
8 Stefano Sacconi, "Da Quel Sogno del Vecchio Cassina", *La Cooperazione Italiana*, Ottobre, 1986, p.276.
9 Lega Nazionale delle Cooperative e Mutue, *Lega*, Roma, 1987, p.3.

10 Renato Midoro, *Gli Strumenti per il Finanziamento delle Cooperative*, Editrice Cooperativa, Roma, 1984, pp.38-39.
11 *La Cooperazione Italiana,* "La Cassaforte Coop", Ottobre 1990, p.81.
12 *Sintesi del Sistema*, "Fincooper: Strumento Finanziario della Lega", 17 Marzo 1989, p. 3.
13 The information in Figure 7.1 is derived from the following sources: La Lega Nazionale delle Cooperative e Mutue, *Il Sistema Finanziario della Lega delle Cooperative*, Bologna, 1990. Walter Dondi, "Fincooper Punta alla Leadership in Banec", *La Cooperazione Italiana*, Febbraio-Marzo 1992, p.55. Walter Dondi, "Unipol Finanziaria ha Messo Ordine", *La Cooperazione Italiana*, Febbraio-Marzo 1992, pp.58-59.
14 La Lega, *op.cit.*, *Il Sistema Finanziario della Lega delle Cooperative,* p.6.
15 Giorgio Bettini, "Un'Impresa del Nostro Tempo", *La Cooperazione Italiana*, Ottobre 1986, p.266.
16 Sacconi, *op.cit.*, p.277.
17 Massimo Mucchetti, "I Retroscena del Grande Boom", *L'Espresso*, 24 Dicembre 1989, in *Unipol Press,* 16 Gennaio 1990, pp.5-6.
18 The information in Figure 7.2 is derived from the following sources: Unipol, *Unipol Insurance Information Booklet*, Bologna, 1990. Dondi, *op.cit.*, "Unipol Finanziaria ha Messo Ordine", pp.58-59.
19 The six were Sacmi (manufacturing) 4.88%, Edilter (construction) 3.23%, and four from the consumer sector: La Proletaria 5.92%, Coop Emilia Veneto 4.75%, Unicoop 3.02%, Coop Estense 3%. See Massimo Mucchetti, *op.cit.*, p.6.
20 Walter Dondi, *op.cit.*, "Unipol Finanziaria ha Messo Ordine", p.58.
21 See Figure 7.2.
22 La Lega, *op.cit.*, *Il Sistema Finanziario della Lega delle Cooperative*, p.6.
23 Walter Dondi, "L'Unipol Assicura L'Europa. Obbiettivo: I Paesi dell'Est", *LUnità,* 15 Dicembre 1989, in *Unipol Press*, 16 Gennaio 1990, p.12.
24 Massimo Degli Esposti, "Le Coop D'Europa Fondano Holding delle Assicurazioni", *Il Sole 24 Ore*, 18 Novembre 1989.
25 *La Cooperazione Italiana*, "Compagnie alla Sfida della Professionalità", Febbraio-Marzo 1992, p.57.
26 Sacconi, *op.cit.*, p. 278.
27 Angelo Varni (ed), "Unipol: La Compagnia d'Assicurazioni del Mondo del Lavoro", in *Emilia Romagna Terra di Cooperazione*, Eta/Analisi, Bologna, 1990, p.425.
28 Giorgio Bettini, "Una Strategia per Stare sul Mercato", *La Cooperazione Italiana,* Ottobre 1986, p.284.
29 Degli Esposti, *op.cit.*
30 Gilberto Polloni, "L'Utopia a Portata di Polizza", *La Cooperazione Italiana,* Ottobre 1986, p.270.
31 *La Cooperazione Italiana*, Intervista con Giancarlo Brunello, "Una Crescita nella Democrazia", Ottobre 1986, pp.282-283.
32 La Lega, *op.cit.*, *Il Sistema Finanziario della Lega delle Cooperative*, p.10.
33 For a brief description of what a factoring company does see *The Penguin Macquarie Dictionary of Economics and Finance*, Penguin Australia, 1988, pp.108-109.
34 *La Cooperazione Italiana*, "Mercato Dinamico Aperto alle Coop", Settembre 1990, pp.53-54.
35 *Sintesi del Sistema*, "Factorcoop, Coopfond e i Nuovi Strumenti: La Rete di Vendita dei Fondi Comuni", Bologna, Numero 1-2, Anno 2, 1990, pp.7-8.
36 *La Cooperazione Italiana*, "Fondi su Misura per i Soci Coop", Giugno 1990, pp.54-55.

37 Walter Dondi, "Debutta Coopfond, Venderà ai Piccoli Risparmiatori", *L'Unità*, 31 Marzo 1990, p.15.
38 See Figure 7.1; and *Sintesi del Sistema*, "Le Partecipazioni in Forte Crescita", Gennaio-Febbraio 1990, p.6.
39 Renato Midoro, *Gli Strumenti per il Finanziamento delle Cooperative*, Editrice Cooperativa, Roma, 1984, pp.116-117.
40 *Sintesi del Sistema*, *op.cit.*, "Le Partecipazioni in Forte Crescita", p.6.
41 See Figure 7.2.
42 Piero Collina, "Finec", in Lega Nazionale delle Cooperative e Mutue, *Il Sistema Finanziario di Fronte all'Innovazione Finanziaria*, Roma, 1988, p.72.
43 *Ibid.*, pp.73-74. See also La Lega, *op.cit.*, *Il Sistema Finanziario della Lega delle Cooperative*, p.7.
44 *Il Giornale della Banca*, "Voglia di Mercato", September 1989, in *Unipol Press*, 16 Gennaio 1990, pp.16-17.
45 Walter Dondi, *op.cit.*,"Fincooper Punta alla Leadership in Banec", p.55.
46 La Lega, *op.cit.*, *Il Sistema Finanziario della Lega delle Cooperative*, p.7. See also Le Certificate, "Intervista con Pietro Verzelletti", in *La Cooperazione Italiana*, Dicembre 1988, p.37.
47 *Il Giornale della Banca*, *op.cit.*, pp.16-17.
48 La Lega, *op.cit.*, *Il Sistema Finanziario della Lega delle Cooperative*, p.7.
49 Pietro Verzelletti, "Il Ruolo della Lega delle Cooperative nel Nuovo Scenario Economico", in La Lega Nazionale delle Cooperative e Mutue, *Il Sistema Lega di Fronte All'Innovazione Finanziaria,* Roma, 1988, pp.19-30.
50 Walter Dondi, *op.cit.*, "Fincooper Punta alla Leadership in Banec", p.55.
51 Alberto Zevi, "La Strumentazione Finanziaria per le Imprese Cooperative", in *La Questione Finanziaria e lo Sviluppo dell'Imprese Cooperative,* Editrice Cooperativa, Roma, 1984, p.42.
52 Lega Nazionale delle Cooperative e Mutue, *Il Sistema Lega di Fronte all'Innovazione Finanziaria,* Firenze, 1988, p.8.
53 *Sintesi del Sistema*, *op.cit.*, "Le Partecipazioni in Forte Crescita", p.6.
54 Raffaele Cuccurullo and Dora Jacobelli, "Finanza Locale e Settoriale", in Lega Nazionale delle Cooperative e Mutue, *Il Sistema Lega di Fronte all'Innovazione Finanziaria,* Firenze, 1988, p.230.
55 *Ibid.*, pp.230-233.
56 *Ibid.*, p.233.
57 *Sintesi del Sistema*, *op.cit.*, "Le Partecipazioni in Forte Crescita", p.6.
58 La Lega, *op.cit.*, *Il Sistema Finanziario della Lega delle Cooperative*, p.10.
59 Illio Zani,"Le Casse Rurali: Problemi Legislativi e di Prospettiva", in La Lega Nazionale delle Cooperative e Mutue, *Il Sistema Lega di Fronte all'Innovazione Finanziaria*, Roma, 1988, pp.173-177.
60 Angelo Varni (ed), "La Banca Cooperativa dell' Emilia Romagna: Importante Realtà Presto su Scala Regionale", in *Emilia Romagna Terra di Cooperazione*, Eta/Analisi, Bologna, 1990, p.427.
61 Bocconi, *op.cit.*, p.29.
62 For instance the construction cooperative CMC of Ravenna is a shareholder of the Banca del Monte di Bologna e Ravenna, Banca Popolare di Faenza and the Banca Popolare di Ravenna. See CMC, *Bilancio Consuntivo 1990*, Ravenna, 1991, p.71.

63 Michele Balboni, "Indagine Annuale sul Credito e Sulla Gestione Finanziaria nelle Cooperative Lega", in Francesco Garella (ed), *Il Movimento, il Sistema, La Rete: Un Decennio di Cambiamenti nelle Imprese Cooperative*, Editrice Emilia Romagna, Bologna, 1991, pp.239-241.

8 Managing Change: Cooperatives and the Market

The last four chapters have investigated how the State and La Lega's principle structures (the Central Association, the consortia and the financial network) have helped cooperatives overcome some of the problems they encounter when competing in a market economy. They also explored the relationship that has developed between cooperatives, La Lega and the State.

The purpose of this chapter is to continue this research from a different angle. In this chapter the relationship between cooperatives, La Lega and the State and the way the problems have been overcome will be evaluated by analysing the manner in which four cooperatives, from different sectors of the economy, have managed to compete in the market since 1945. Such an analysis will provide empirical evidence to support the information provided in the previous four chapters. It is also important to discover how the cooperatives themselves make business decisions, otherwise it would appear that the provision of support from La Lega's structures and favourable State policies produces automatic success for cooperatives. Further, because the four case studies examine cooperatives from different sectors, they disclose the various types of relationships that have developed between the cooperatives and La Lega and cooperatives and the State.

This chapter is divided into six parts. Part one will explain the methodology used to analyse the case studies. The next four parts will examine individual case studies of the following cooperatives: the construction cooperative Cooperativa Muratori e Braccianti (Cooperative of Bricklayers and Labourers) of Carpi,[1] the consumer cooperative Coop Emilia Veneto, mainly centred in Bologna, the manufacturing cooperative SACMI, of Imola[2] and the cooperative Spepcoop, also from Bologna, which operates in the health services sector. Part six summarises the major findings of the case studies and assesses what they reveal about the relationship between the individual cooperatives, La Lega and the State. In addition, a discussion of the manner in which cooperatives solve problems they encounter will also be provided.

Methodology

The methodology used below to analyse the cooperative enterprise is a longitudinal analysis of the strategy, structure and culture of the enterprise. This approach will enable us to understand the specific characteristics of the cooperatives and how these have influenced their decisions.[3] A good definition of "strategy" is given by Alfred Chandler Junior in his pioneering study of American industrial enterprises:

> "A strategy can be defined as the determination of the basic long term goals and objectives of an enterprise, and the adoption of a course of action and the allocation of resources necessary for carrying out these goals." [4]

For a particular strategy to be successful it has to be supported by an adequate organisational structure. An organisational structure includes the decision-making process and the enterprise subunits which together constitute all the material and human resources needed to implement the long term strategy.[5] These resources may include technology, research and development, distribution network, finance etc, all of which are vital for the implementation of a strategy.

The third element of this methodology is the cultural characteristics of an organisation. In this instance, "culture" refers to the way individuals perceive their role in a cooperative and the way the cooperative enterprise perceives its role in a capitalist economy. Some of the elements of a cooperative culture are: human relations, industrial relations, democratic management, egalitarian pay structure, solidarity toward other cooperatives and the local community. In addition, Giulio Sapelli notes that the level of accumulated knowledge such as technological, organisational and economic knowledge are also part of an organisation's culture.[6]

Chandler argues that changes in an enterprise's strategy precede changes in its structure. The aim of this chapter is neither to prove nor to disprove this claim. What is important is that for a strategy to be successfully implemented, an adequate structure and culture must co-exist. If a cooperative cannot produce a synthesised understanding of its strategy, structure and culture, then their full potential will not be realised.

Case Study 1: CMB, Construction Cooperative

The Cooperativa Muratori e Braccianti (CMB) was formed in 1977 as a result of the merger between two cooperatives: the Società Cooperativa di

Lavoro fra i Braccianti del Comune di Carpi and Villa Limidi (Cooperative of Labourers from the Communes of Carpi and Villa Limidi founded in 1904) and Società Anonima Cooperativa Lavoratori Muratori di Carpi (Bricklayers Cooperative from the Commune of Carpi originally formed in 1908). CMB is one of the oldest and best known construction cooperatives associated to La Lega. In 1991, it was ranked the 20th largest construction enterprise in Italy. This case study will examine its performance by using the above methodology and analyse its strategy, structure and culture since 1977.

Strategy

To get an understanding of the decisions which have led CMB to evolve from a small construction firm to a general contractor capable of winning international contracts, three major strategic decisions will be analysed. These are: the policy to merge the two cooperatives in 1977; the willingness to become a general contractor in 1983; and the policy of alliances which led CMB to work alongside not only other cooperatives, but also private and State enterprises.

The Merger of 1977. There were four main reasons advanced for the merger of the two cooperatives in 1977. The first of these was the need to engage in complex public works (commercial centres, subways, high speed railway lines and road tunnels), which was an emergent market within the construction industry in the 1970s. These were more demanding than the traditional public works such as road construction and housing. By the mid-1970s, the Cooperative Muratori, through one of La Lega's consortia, had managed to win some of these major contracts which required both greater financial resources and greater technical expertise. Some of these contracts included building a high speed railway between Rome and Florence, a dam in Mozambique and a contract to clean the polluted waters of the Gulf of Naples. In light of these market changes, both cooperatives thought that by merging and by achieving economies of scale they would be in a better position to compete in the market.[7]

The second reason was the need to attract technicians. Before the merger, both cooperatives had been losing young technicians to private enterprises because they paid higher wages. The decision to merge and create a large enterprise engaging in complex works was also part of a strategy to attract young technicians back to the enterprise by providing larger and more stimulating work. In addition, attracting younger personnel would also reduce the average age of the work-force.[8]

The third reason was the need to diversify their productive capacity to overcome a sectoral crisis. A diversification of products (adding complex works to the traditional products and services) improved the cooperative's capacity to provide employment to its work-force. In other words, as the amount of work in housing and road construction declined, the cooperative would be able to work on complex works, thus improving its chances of survival. In addition, CMB became well placed to diversify into complex works since the two original cooperatives had already established permanent branches in other parts of Italy. The Cooperative Muratori had a branch in Rome since 1949 and another in Milan since 1953. The Cooperative Braccianti had worked in Latina, near Rome, on several land reclamation projects.[9]

Finally, the policy of mergers was in accordance with La Lega's overall political policy. As already stated in Chapter three, since the mid-1970s, La Lega expressed its willingness to contribute to solve some of the country's structural economic and social problems in the area of agriculture, housing, urban planning, retailing, and most importantly help to develop Southern Italy. For this policy to be credible, La Lega needed strong, viable, modern cooperatives. To this end, the directors of the Central Associations and the consortia began to persuade cooperatives to merge: CMB is also a result of this process.[10]

1983: Towards a General Contractor. The idea of developing into a general contractor took place in 1983. This was in response to both changes in the direction of public spending and to increased competition faced in the housing sector. The major cause of this was the State's credit squeeze of 1982 which reduced spending in public works by approximately 25%. In addition, the State's new policy on public works redirected funds from housing and prefabricated construction towards more complex public works programmes[11] and, later, environmental projects. The cooperative also faced a stagnant and extremely competitive housing market. Within this context, CMB had to choose whether to compete in the housing and traditional public works market, where it faced fierce competition from extremely competitive small firms,[12] or to concentrate on the complex public works projects, which were mainly the domain of large private enterprises, State holding groups such as IRI's Italstat and private holding companies such as Fiat Impresit.[13] CMB chose to concentrate on the latter because it suited its policy of attracting young technicians, it accorded with the policy of La Lega and it was an expanding market at the local and international level.

In 1983, CMB's business strategy encouraged product diversification and geographic expansion of its operations. Product diversification was encouraged by concentrating on new complex public works market as well as continuing in the more traditional construction market. The area of operation was further expanded and, to this end, another branch was opened in Matera, a small city of Southern Italy. In addition, CMB planned to expand its operations overseas, thus adding an international dimension to its activities.[14]

CMB was by now becoming a "general contractor". This required CMB to be in control of the whole of the productive process from the planning phase to the building phase. Romanelli points out that for CMB to be competitive it required a capacity to plan projects, to have adequate financial and organisational means (managerial expertise) and to hold contractual power.[15] By contractual power is meant the ability of a firm to win public contracts through a mixture of expertise, reliability, importance for the national economy and political support. Since CMB could not meet these requirements on its own, a "policy of alliances" was developed which led the cooperative to create a network of relationships with enterprises both within and outside of the cooperative movement.

The Policy of Alliances. The policy of alliances sought to establish joint ventures with private, cooperative and public companies as a strategy to overcome some of the enterprise's deficiencies and to satisfy some of its needs. These alliances have served mainly to win public works contracts, to diversify into other areas of the industry and to gain access to vital services.

The first major advantage of this strategy is that it improved CMB's chances of winning public contracts which, but for such alliances, it would not have been able to win on its own for various reasons such as a lack of finance, lack of expertise or contractual power. The major alliance is that formed with La Lega's national consortium CCC, whose role is to bid for major public works on behalf of cooperatives.[16] The role played by CCC in the success of CMB cannot be underestimated. In fact it provided 50% of CMB's work contracts.

The second type of alliance is formed with individual cooperative enterprises or State and private enterprises. This has been achieved by the creation of a number of consortia set up for particular projects. Examples of these are: CORACO, formed with the cooperative CMC of Ravenna; COBOCO, a consortium formed with cooperatives, private and State enterprises to build a major dam in Mozambique; and VASCO, formed by similar alliances which built part of the subway in Milan.[17] In these consortia, all enterprises are shareholders and once a contract is won the work is divided among the shareholders according to their expertise.

The third type of alliance aims to provide services to cooperatives. These are usually made within the cooperative movement either with individual enterprises or with La Lega's consortia network. For instance, CMB is a shareholder of the company SECIT, a major enterprise dealing in eco-business, along with two other cooperative enterprises, CMC of Ravenna and the Consortium Etruria of Empoli. CMB has formed other alliances with other cooperatives by being a member of La Lega's own consortia which provide various services to its members. Some of these are: ICIE in technological development, Fincooper in financial services, Smaer and Sinnea in the area of consultancy, training, and management.

The fourth form of alliance has led to the formation of property development companies. These companies are either wholly owned by CMB or are formed in partnership with private and cooperative enterprises. They are engaged in various types of work such as building commercial centres, leisure centres (golf clubs), public car parking facilities and urban housing developments. The last mentioned two are in response to fiscal problems faced by the State which has decreased spending on public works and reduced its incentives for housing. In the housing sector, CMB has entered into many arrangements with housing cooperatives which, being unable to finance the construction of houses for their members because of the high building costs and high interest rates, are now trying to provide home ownership to its members at the lowest possible price by bargaining with CMB and its partners. In effect, the housing cooperatives provide the clients as long as CMB will build good quality housing at a lower price than that offered by private enterprises. This relationship with housing cooperatives is enabling CMB to overcome sectoral crisis because it facilitates its ability to supply housing to potential clients. Another advantage gained from establishing property development companies is the acquisition of knowhow from other partners. This is especially vital for the leisure industry and the commercial centres, both of which are new types of projects for CMB. The diversification into property development has become very important to CMB. In 1983, it participated in 10 such companies. By 1987, the number had increased to 20.[18] In 1990, the revenue generated from them amounted to 41.763 billion lire, equivalent to 12.6% of its total turnover.[19]

Organisational Structure

Organisational changes needed to be made in support of the above mentioned strategy. Basically, CMB needed risk capital, managerial expertise and a more sophisticated organisational structure capable of coordinating the cooperative branches which it operated in other parts of Italy.

Finance. CMB's financial needs are satisfied in a number of ways. The most common method is to re-invest surplus generated by the enterprise. The ability of cooperatives to re-invest their surpluses in the firm is well documented.[20] CMB is no exception. It has always followed a policy of re-investing all of its profits back into its operations in the enterprise. In fact, bonus payments, although allowed by law, were only paid once in 1983 on the occasion of its 75th anniversary.[21] Recently, a policy of bonus payments based on productivity gains has been implemented which is payable to all workers.[22] The 1990 budget shows that CMB re-invested 90.8% of its surplus in the enterprise's indivisible reserve fund.[23] The remainder was used to pay interests on members' shares credited to their individual accounts. Thus 100% of the surplus was re-invested in the enterprise either as indivisible reserves or as members' shares.

Since 1983, more emphasis has been placed in attracting finance from individual members in the form of shares and loans. The new enterprise strategy needed more finance and attracting it from members would reduced the need to obtain it from banks. Secondly, the 1983 "Visentini Law" increased the amount of money each member could lend to construction cooperatives as "members' loans" from 4 to 30 million lire and it exempted from tax the surplus paid into a members' shares account so long as it did not exceed 10% of the nominal sum invested at that time.[24]

The policy of attracting investment from members had some success. Between 1983 and 1990, the total amount invested as members' shares increased from 1.432 billion lire to 4.571 billion lire, an increase of 319% and equivalent to 9.087 million lire per person. The 1990 annual general meeting further emphasised the importance of this strategy by resolving that all members pay between 40 thousand and 150 thousand lire per month into their shares accounts, depending on their income.[25] In the same year, the annual general meeting decided to remunerate members' shares by 14.5%, which was the highest limit allowed by legislation for that particular year.

Aided by favourable tax law and high interest rates, members' loans also increased during this period.[26] Between 1984 and 1990, the amount members invested as members' loans increased from 6.841 billion lire to 14.681 billion lire. This amounts to an average investment of 17.175 million lire per person.[27]

Another form of generating finance is by diversifying investments and investing the enterprise's liquid assets in profitable areas not related to the construction industry. One such area in which CMB has been investing is the textile industry. With its own financial company, Finanziaria Immobiliare, CMB has formed a holding company in partnership with a private company, Gruppo Mit, which has invested money in various textile companies. The aim of the group is to provide firms in the area around Carpi[28] with financial capital and the necessary services in the area of finance, marketing and retail outlets to help them compete in the world markets. This policy has two major aims: first, is to make a return on capital invested and, secondly, to establish good relations with the local community by investing in local businesses. This is also likely to improve the cooperative's chances to win public contracts, as local authorities look favourably towards locally owned businesses who invest in the local economy. In the first year of operation, this venture accounted for 7.5% of CMB's turnover amounting to 25 billion lire.[29]

Managerial Skills. Another major requirement of this new strategy was the need to have good managerial skills. The policy of alliances provided access to some skills, especially through the eco-business company, Secit, the consortia, CCC and Acam, and private enterprises in areas such as property development and the leisure industry. However, CMB also needed to develop its own management skills if it was serious in becoming a general contractor. Attracting good managers had not been easy. In fact it has been hampered by the low wage policy practised by the cooperative. This was altered in 1983 and since then the wage differentials between the lowest and highest paid members have increased from a ratio of 1.5:1 applied up to 1983, to 4:1 in 1989. This increased managers' salaries but was still below the going rate in private enterprises by 20% to 40%.[30] Nevertheless, the policy succeeded in attracting good managers. By 1987, the percentage of employees with a diploma or a degree amounted to 25% of the total number of employees, compared to a low 7% in 1977.[31]

Administrative and Productive Process. The other major change at the structural level dealt with the administrative and the productive processes. The objective was to achieve efficiency at the administrative level and flexibility at the productive level. The major change to take place in the organisational structure was a decentralisation process through the introduction of five semi-autonomous branches. These branches included one in Carpi, one in Lombardy, one in Lazio, one concentrating on complex public works in Italy and one specialising in public works abroad. The main reason behind this decision was that a central structure was no longer capable of managing such diverse operations because specialist skills and local knowledge were required for each branch. This led to a division of labour between a head office operating from Carpi and the semi-autonomous branches. The central administrative body operating in Carpi provided basic needs such as planning, finance, marketing and technical and commercial services to the whole organisation (see Figure 8.1).[32] The operational branches were given the responsibility over their own budgets, the freedom to do their own planning, feasibility studies, buy equipment and bid for and manage entire projects. These changes ensured better budgetary controls, relations with the local economies and it also encouraged democratic management at the branch level.[33]

The productive process was made more flexible by reducing fixed costs through the externalisation of some of its functions. The basic problem faced by CMB, and the cooperative movement in general, in the early 1980s was an oversupply of labour. This was made worse because the traditional replacement of workers between cooperative enterprises could not take place because other cooperatives were experiencing the same problems.[34] This was further exacerbated because CMB's strategy created a demand for white collar instead of blue collar workers. CMB had responded in a number of ways. First, in 1981, it placed a freeze on the employment of blue collar workers. Secondly, CMB had recourse to Cassa Integrazione Guadagni, (CIG), an unemployment relief fund for workers temporarily laid off and pays up to 80% of their wages.[35] In 1982, CIG was used for an average of 11.98 hours per person. In 1983 the hours increased to 53.17 and in 1984 to 94.84 hours per person. As a consequence, the total number of its work-force was reduced gradually from 1,121 in 1977 to 733 in 1986.[36]

The size of the labour force has remained steady since then, even though the CMB's turnover has increased from 186 billion lire in 1986 to 331 billion lire in 1990. The reason for this is that the problems of oversupply of labour encountered in the early 1980s led the cooperative to adopt a more flexible approach to work. One such solution was to employ workers from local areas on a fixed contract. On some occasions this is unavoidable, for instance when working overseas. In 1990, these workers amounted to 300 out of a total work-force of 1,033, equivalent to 29% of the total work-force.[37] In addition, in order to reduce fixed costs, cooperatives from the construction

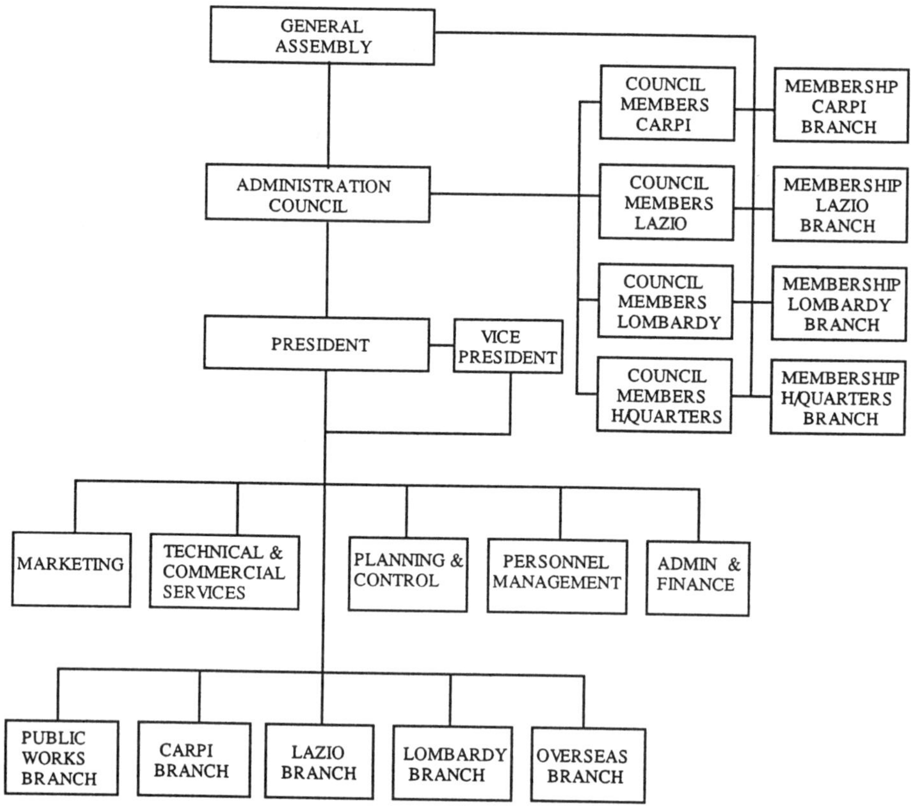

Figure 8.1 CMB Organisational Structure

industry started to subcontract part of the work such as carpentry, plumbing, electrical and tiling to artisans or to firms with a good reputation in industrial relations. A recent survey conducted by La Lega on the largest cooperatives from the construction industry revealed that up to 50% of their work is subcontracted to other firms.[38] This has not only reduced overall employment but it also led to a change in the composition of the work-force. The net result has been a reduction of labourers from 1039 to 478 and an increase in white collar employees from 107 to 255 between 1978 and 1990.[39]

The manner in which CMB managed to change in the 1980s has brought some benefits. It has reduced fixed labour costs and achieved greater flexibility, both of which are vital for the enterprise's capacity to adapt to a changing environment. The externalisation of some of the manual work allowed CMB to specialise in other areas such as planning, finance, management and marketing, all of which are important for the success of the new strategy. These changes also allowed the cooperative to maintain employment stability. It is important to note that while the decision to subcontract work was motivated by a desire to reduce costs and improve flexibility, it also contributed to the forging of political alliances with artisans and small businesses.

Culture

In order to conform to the new enterprise strategy the culture of the enterprise underwent some changes. The first change was an alteration to its egalitarian principles. The two cooperatives which formed CMB had a strong working class culture whose objectives were to create employment, share work and pay equal wages. The decision to attract and retain managers meant the cooperative's egalitarian culture had to be modified to allow greater wage differentials from 1.5:1 to 4.5:1. This also implied that the cooperative began to acknowledge that skills had to be rewarded and, in part, it also began to accept the market as a factor in determining managers' wages.

The other major change involved changing the members' culture from a wage earner culture to a that of a worker-entrepreneur culture. The former saw workers as providing labour in exchange for a salary and secure employment. The latter asked them not only to work, but also to invest their savings in the enterprise. In response to this, the cooperative began to pay higher interest to members' shares and members' loans. The decision to attract and remunerate members' investments was the first step in acknowledging that capital invested had a right to adequate remuneration. It was also the start of a rethink on the role that capital could play in a cooperative enterprise, a debate which led to the passing of the 1992 law which allows limited external ownership.

However, other changes made by the cooperative reinforced, rather than changed, the culture of the enterprise. The decision to decentralise the productive process by creating semi-autonomous branches reinforced the practice of democratic management. Through decentralisation, each branch practised a form of direct democracy by being accountable for their own budgets, and a form of representational democracy by electing representatives for the general assembly which in turn represented all branches. In addition, that each branch has a local membership and the investments made in the local textile industry, have both reinforced the relationship between CMB and the local community: a long held characteristic of the cooperative identity.

Economic Evaluation of the Business Strategy

An analysis of Table 8.1 further illustrates the success of CMB's business strategy. The first factor to support this is the increase in turnover. This increased from the amount of 83.491 billion lire of 1981 to 247.568 billion lire in 1990, an increase of 296.5% in ten years.

Another indicator is the percentage of turnover generated by CMB through alliances. In 1990, the total turnover generated by CMB in this category was 83.835 billion lire, which is the equivalent to 25.35% of total revenue.[40] The success of CMB's business strategy can be further demonstrated by examining the percentage of turnover generated by the new products (complex works in Italy and abroad, property development and textile, see (b-h) in Table 8.1 that CMB has added to its traditional activities of housing and infrastructure). The 1990 figures show that these categories generated 178.273 billion lire being 53.8% of the total turnover and thus playing an important part in the enterprise's success.

A final examination of the success of the strategy is to see the geographical distribution of work contracts. In 1990, the area of Carpi managed to win 51.6 billion lire worth of contracts (21% of then total), Milan 55.1 billion (22.4%), Rome 64.2 billion (26.1%), complex works in Italy 69.1 billion (28.2%) and complex works abroad 5.5 billion lire (2.3%). This clearly shows the importance of moving out of the local economy and establishing branches in other areas. However, there is a problem in respect of some contracts obtained abroad which is that the traditional areas where CMB had been working (Mozambique, Angola, Ethiopia, Algiers) have undergone political crisis making them financially risky places to invest and to enter into agreements with governments. As a consequence, overseas works as a percentage of total turnover has declined from the 18.2% in 1987 to 4.3% in 1990.

Table 8.1 Turnover by CMB (in Billions of Lire) 1988-1990

	1988	1989	1990
Production by CMB Only			
(a) Construction	86.630	108.124	153.162
(b) Property Development Companies	15.476	27.610	7.737
(c) Complex Public Works	36.740	50.330	78.128
(d) Overseas Works	4.340	16.111	8.541
Total Production by CMB	143.186	202.175	247.568
Production through Alliances			
(e) Property Development Companies	25.031	2.398	34.026
(f) Public Works Italy	6.109	11.362	9.652
(g) Overseas Works	12.215	8.328	5.752
(h) Other Activities (textile & environment)	n/a	4.132	34.437
Total Production through Alliances	43.355	26.220	83.867
Total Production by the CMB Group	186.541	228.395	331.435

Source: CMB, *Bilancio Consuntivo 1990: Relazione al Consiglio di Amministrazione, Carpi, 1990, p.14.*

CMB, La Lega and the State

CMB is well integrated with La Lega's support structures. The Central Association developed the strategy of encouraging cooperatives to merge and to create alliances, both of which improved the competitiveness of CMB. At the economic level, CMB obtains 50% of its total contracts from the consortium CCC. It has also formed consortia with other construction cooperatives and has cooperated with housing cooperatives. This integration is further enhanced through economic relations established with other consortia such as Acam, Icie, Sinnea and Fincooper, all of which provide CMB with a number of services.[41]

A qualification needs to be made regarding the relationship between CMB and La Lega's structures. While the contribution made by the Central Association and the consortia network is considerable, there is evidence from this case study which indicates that it is not sufficient to meet all CMB's needs. For instance, CMB, together with other cooperatives, bought the private firm SECIT in order to have access to managerial expertise environmental matter. In addition, while the policies to merge and to create alliances were esposued by La Lega, the decisions to diversify into other areas such as the leisure industry, commercial centres and the textile industry were made by CMB. This indicates that the consortia system responded too slowly to the cooperative's needs. Indeed, CMB is concerned that CCC is looking after its own interests by bidding for contracts on its own so it can then charge a commission, instead of getting cooperatives to participate in the decision-making process and its overall business strategy.[42] As a consequence, the enterprise is building its own network of alliances to compete in the market place.

This analysis also highlights the interrelationship between cooperatives and the State. The State has given CMB access to public works, which amount to half of the work it carried out. The tax incentives of the 1980s have contributed to increasing the amount of members' loans and members' shares, both of which have improved the ability of CMB to self-finance its operations. CMB has also received 450 million lire from the State at low interest rates to buy Italian machine tools under the scheme known as the "Sabatini Law".[43] Another contribution by the State was provided through the unemployment relief fund CIG which facilitated the restructuring process. Finally, the State's policy of redirecting funds from housing to complex public works influenced CMB's strategy to diversify its operations by moving into the complex public works and the property development market.

Summary

This case study has examined the interrelationship that exists between CMB, La Lega and the State. La Lega provided the initial business strategy which led to the merger of two enterprises and also economic support through the consortia system. The State has provided the cooperative with access to public works, it has facilitated its drive to raise internal finance through a series of tax measures and, through the State's unemployment relief fund, it has helped CMB to restructure its operations. The relationship with La Lega, in particular, is a clear indication that the enterprise competed in the market as a member of an integrated group of enterprises.

However, part of CMB's success is also due to its ability to manage change in difficult circumstances. The complexities of formulating and implementing a successful strategy supported by an adequate organisational structure and culture are the product of the enterprise itself. In particular, the decision to expand into the textile and environment sectors and property development activities with private partners were made at the enterprise level. This indicates that while La Lega and the State are important factors in CMB's success, the whole picture becomes apparent only when the enterprise's own contribution to this success is also included.

Case Study 2: Coop Emilia Veneto, A Consumer Cooperative

The consumer cooperative sector is the oldest and most developed form of cooperation in both Italy and Europe. In Italy, since the first consumer cooperative was formed in Turin in 1854, the major reason for forming consumer cooperatives has been to provide food to consumers at the lowest possible price. Today, La Lega's consumer sector comprises 431 cooperatives which manage 1,281 retail outlets whose retail sales are in excess of 7,431 billion lire. Most importantly they have a membership of over 2.2 million persons.[44] This has made La Lega's consumer movement the largest retail chain in Italy, controlling over 5.5% of the national market.[45] To understand the reasons for this success the strategy, structure and culture of Coop Emilia Veneto will be analysed from 1945 to this present day.

Strategy

From Coop Bologna to Coop Emilia Veneto. Coop Emilia Veneto is a consumer cooperative formed in 1975 which operates in the province of Bologna and the region of Veneto. However, to understand its history one needs to go back to 1945. After 1945, 45 small cooperatives were established in the city of Bologna, each managing one or two retail outlets. Following the policy of La Lega, the cooperatives of Bologna began to merge and by 1975 they were all grouped under one cooperative, named Coop Bologna, which managed all the retail outlets. In 1975, Coop Bologna merged with the cooperatives from the region of Veneto and was given the name Coop Emilia Veneto. This last move was also made in order to stimulate growth of cooperatives in the region of Veneto, where the cooperatives from La Lega had a low presence.[46]

Alongside the policy of mergers, larger retail stores were also being promoted. This was a response to the trend set by large retail chains which had been promoting supermarkets since the 1950s. The aim was to close the smaller conventional stores and open up small supermarkets. Fearing, from the late 1980s, competition from European retail groups, Coop Emilia Veneto began to build and manage commercial centres and megastores. So far, two have been built, one in Imola and one in Bologna. This policy has reduced the number of retail outlets from 65 in 1975 to 39 in 1990. A consequence of the construction of commercial centres and megastores has been to increase the amount of retailing space from the 15,000 square meters in 1975 to 35,498 square meters in 1990. In addition, the type of retail outlet changed with supermarkets now using 92.5% of the total space, compared to 34% in 1975.[47]

The third element of its strategy has been "market growth through alliances". One example of this strategy occurred in 1987. In that year, Coop Emilia Veneto, in partnership with Coop Estense,[48] bought a private supermarket chain, "FULL", which operated in the region of Veneto.[49] This type of activity enabled the two cooperatives to increase their market share in another region. Another form of growth through alliances has been the formation of the company "Coop Adriatica" with three other consumer cooperatives.[50] The aim of "Coop Adriatica" is to build commercial centres along the Adriatic coast all the way to the region of Puglia. This new strategy is in response to both recent market developments in Italy and to European integration. Statistics for the Italian retailing sector indicate that in 1990 modern supermarket chains, including those of cooperatives, controlled 40% of the food market compared to only 12% in 1982.[51] In Europe at large, the concentration is even higher.[52] Fearing the expansion into Italy of European multinationals, plans are already under way for the merger of the four cooperatives which form Coop Adriatica.[53]

The final part of the strategy was to cater for all consumers and not just members. This meant that in addition to the traditional role of providing food at the lowest possible price, Coop Emilia Veneto began to concentrate on consumer protection and information. For instance, consumer cooperatives were the first retail stores to remove PVC plastics, detergents with phosphate and drinks with artificial colouring from their shelves. The food packaging is very informative regarding nutritional content such as vitamin, calories and food content. Since the mid-1980s it has promoted environmentally friendly products under the label "Products with Love", which are grown without the use of chemicals.[54]

In recent years, the cooperative has placed a lot of emphasis on providing services. Greater emphasis has been placed in providing consumers with car parking space, stores have been made more spacious, a cooperative credit card has been introduced and the variety of food and the number of items offered for sale has been increased. Coop Emilia Veneto also owns a number of travel agencies which provide lower travel fares to consumers.

Organisational Structure

Coop Emilia Veneto has become a large and complex organisation. It now manages different types of retail outlets: small supermarkets, large supermarkets, megastores and commercial centres. Each has different managerial needs and requires different managerial techniques. Some of these retail outlets are managed directly by the central administration of Coop Emilia Veneto. Others are managed by separate companies controlled by Coop Emilia Veneto or managed jointly with cooperative partners. For instance, the commercial centre in Bologna is managed by the company Ca' Nova, which is 100% owned by Coop Emilia Veneto. The commercial centre in Imola is owned by the company Centro Leonardo, 99% owned by the cooperative. As already mentioned, Coop Emilia Veneto owns 25% of the shares in Adriatica SRL and is a 50% owner of Stargill, the company which owns the "FULL" supermarkets.

Coop Emilia Veneto also owns a variety of companies which perform various tasks complementary to retailing. These include the following: Demetra (travel agencies), Rete Sette (television station), Delco (invests the cooperative's cash reserves), SEP (cooperative credit card). Furthermore, it is a shareholder in several financial institutions. Its investment in Unipol Finance is 20.678 billion lire. It has invested 700 million lire in the cooperative bank, Banec and 101 million lire in the local bank, Banca del Monte di Bologna and Ravenna. Investments amounting to 1.185 billion lire have also been made with other cooperative associations.[55]

The organisational structure of Coop Emilia Veneto has been developed in response to the increase in size and complexity of its operations. What was needed was an efficient administration, a capable management and the financial means to support the cooperative strategy.

Administration. At the administrative level, Coop Emilia Veneto has developed into a cooperative managing a "group of enterprises". The activities of the group are co-ordinated through the board of directors which provides policy guidelines to which the other subunits (companies) must adhere. While these subunits retain managerial autonomy in respect of their operations, Coop Emilia Veneto maintains overall control through a process of "interlocking directorships".[56] This is achieved by carefully placing members of the board of directors of Coop Emilia Veneto on the boards of directors of the various retail outlets and companies which Coop Emilia Veneto wholly or partially owns. Usually the president of these companies is also appointed by Coop Emilia Veneto. It is through this process of interlocking directorships that control is maintained, that the values of Coop Emilia Veneto are transmitted into the new companies and that policy implementation is co-ordinated.[57]

The advantages derived from these organisational changes are many. The operational division between the different types of retail outlets provide each retail outlet with specialised management who possesses the most appropriate expertise. The managerial autonomy of each sub unit also speeds up the decision-making process within each different form of enterprise.

The other advantage, is obtained from the creation of separate public companies. These companies facilitate the attracting of external capital. The choice of creating many separate companies was also made to reduce the burden of taxation. Apparently more taxes would have to be paid if all the companies were grouped together.[58] Another reason is that the conventional form of enterprise is more appropriate than the consortium. For instance, if Adriatica SRL builds four commercial centres and the four partners no longer wish to remain in one company, then the company can be liquidated and each cooperative take possession of one commercial centre. In a consortium this could not occur because the assets would have belonged to the consortium, the cooperatives would only own the nominal sum invested.

Management. For the organisational structure to implement successfully Coop Emilia Veneto's strategy, appropriate managerial skills had to be employed in the following areas: ability to manage large retail stores, introduction of technology, purchasing expertise and power, marketing, quality control and administrative and human relations skills. Being a highly integrated sector, many of these managerial skills have been provided by the consortia network. Most of the support comes from the national consortium Coop Italia. The consortium provides support in purchasing, marketing and quality control. Coop Emilia Veneto purchases 90% of its goods through contractual arrangements entered into by Coop Italia.[59] Marketing at the national level is organised by Coop Italia and La Lega's National Sectoral Association for Consumers. This mainly involves the marketing of consumer cooperatives and in particular their environmental concerns, democratic management, social responsibility, quality of products and consumer protection policy. The quality of products sold and consumer protection is also guaranteed by Coop Italia either through its own laboratories or through collaboration with private and public laboratories.[60] Through these arrangements the individual cooperative reduces costs and has access to managerial expertise which would have been difficult to obtain on its own.

Since the mid-1980s other consortia have been formed. Coop Italia opened a branch in Florence specialising in non-food items which had by then become the major selling items in large supermarkets and commercial centres. In 1986, the consortium SCICO was formed with the task of providing technical, managerial and marketing information for the management of commercial centres and megastores. INRES, another consortium, has the task of providing cooperatives with information on future market trends, new technology, and equipment to cooperatives which manage stores of medium to large dimensions.[61]

Coop Emilia Veneto also performs a number of important management functions. It purchases 10% of its products directly from producers without the intermediation of Coop Italia. It organises marketing at the local level by advertising periodic specials.[62] It is capable of providing most of the internal training facilities for its members, although support is sought from the consultancy consortium, Sinnea. Most importantly, the local consumer cooperative is best equipped to respond to specific and local customer needs such as level of service, amount of space in the store, opening hours, car parking facilities all of which have to be satisfied to maintain member loyalty to the cooperative.

Finance. The other major element of a successful organisational structure and a vital part of any business strategy is the procurement of finance. Considering the expansive and diversification strategy is one which aims to build and manage commercial centres, the financial issues became crucial for the modernisation process that occurred. Coop Emilia Veneto has overcome this problem by raising finance from within the enterprise, its members, La Lega's structures and the State.

At the enterprise level, finance was generated in a number of ways. One source was the annual surpluses, which in 1990, amounted to 32.7 billion lire. Another form of finance is a return on the various investments. Coop Emilia Veneto has also managed to increase the effective working capital pursuant to agreements made with wholesalers and producers allowing three months credit before payment is required. The formation of joint ventures and public companies is another way to reduce the financial burden. Through joint ventures, Coop Emilia Veneto shares cost and risk with other cooperatives.

Finally, through Coop Italia, cooperatives have also managed to raise 12 billion lire from producers for marketing their products.[63]

Members are another source of finance. They provide finance to the cooperative through their subscription for shares and members' loans. The overall amount invested as members' shares has risen throughout the 1980s due to an increase both in membership fees and in the number of members. The minimum amount required from members has increased from 5,000 lire prior to 1980 to 25,000 lire in 1990. However, the average investment from each member equalled 42,000 lire in 1990.[64] Membership also increased from 80,000 in 1979 to 189,225 in 1990. The result of this has been an increase in the value of members' shares from 396 million lire in 1979 to 7.9 billion lire in 1990.[65]

Members' loans have also been another way of attracting finance from members. Members have usually preferred this scheme because of the competitive interest rates paid and because they pay lower taxes on earnings in comparison to those on bank deposits. The cooperative invests the members' deposits under strict conditions,[66] yet, because it invests a large amount of money, it manages to obtain a high return. This enables the cooperative to pay the same or a higher interest rate than the banks, making an attractive investment proposition considering that members pay only half the taxes paid on bank deposits. The cooperative on the other hand makes between 2 to 2.5% of profits out of these transactions. This scheme has been very successful. In 1990, 46,860 members lent the cooperative an average of 8 million lire each amounting to 377.8 billion lire.[67] This means that at an average of 2.5% profit, the cooperative can make up to 9.4 billion lire per annum from this scheme.

The financial structures of La Lega have been another source of finance. They have provided Coop Emilia Veneto primarily with loans to finance its activities. The 1990 annual report states that Coop Emilia Veneto owes 23.745 billion lire to the financial structures of La Lega. They are very important in that their loans amount to 59.2% of Coop Emilia Veneto's total loan repayments. The remainder are owed to private regional banks.[68] A different form of financial support is provided by Unipol. Unipol has played a vital part in the modernisation of consumer cooperatives by building supermarkets and commercial centres on their behalf in return for rent. This arrangement saved Coop Emilia Veneto having to fund or outlay capital on land and building costs and allows it to implement its strategy at a faster rate.

The last source of finance comes from the State. In 1975, the government enacted a law which made available funds for up to 2 billion lire, later increased to four, at low interest rates for both the private and the cooperative sector for the purpose of modernising existing retail stores.[69] The 1990 budget of Coop Emilia Veneto shows that it owes 2.7 billion lire to this fund.[70] The regional government of Emilia Romagna also made available funds totalling 3 billion lire between 1973 to 1983 to both cooperatives and private enterprises for modernising retail outlets and storage facilities.[71] Considering that it costs up to 80 billion lire to build a commercial centre[72] and that the profits made by Coop Emilia Veneto in 1990 amounted to over 32 billion lire, these sums of money are a limited source of finance in comparison to the others discussed above.

Culture

There have been two major changes in the culture of consumer cooperatives. The first change occurred in the late 1950s when it was decided to enlist the middle class to increase its membership. The second change took place a few years later when it developed a strategy to compete against large supermarkets instead of the small shopkeepers. Members had two major fears about this new strategy. The first was the concern that a cooperative with a large membership could not be democratically managed.[73] The second was the feeling that, by competing against the large supermarkets, a new managerial culture geared to profit making would develop and, which in turn, would lead to a degeneration of the cooperative. The available information seems to indicate that the members' fears were groundless.

Democratic Management. By 1990 Coop Emilia Veneto had a membership of 189,225 (34,000 of whom are in the region of Veneto). This has meant a change in the form of democracy practised by the cooperative from direct to representational democracy. To deal with this influx of members and to encourage participation, 30 different branches have been created. Each member has one vote and each branch elects its own representatives to the general assembly. In all 428 committee members are elected to the general assembly, who then elect a board of directors.[74] Zan notes that although the actual decisions are made by the board of directors, on more than one occasion they had to be changed or modified because of opposition voiced by the branches.[75]

To overcome the problem of apathy, members' participation has been encouraged in a number of ways. The cooperative's management team conducts courses explaining the cooperative's strategy, structure and identity to members, providing them with vital information needed for them to participate in the decision-making process.[76] Secondly, it publishes and distributes free a monthly magazine which informs members about the policies and products sold by the cooperative. In 1990, the cooperative distributed just over two million copies to consumers at a cost of 717 million lire.[77] Thirdly, through its own television station live coverage of the annual general meetings is provided. A telephone link up is also made available for 14 branches, through which members can ask questions regarding matters of concern. It is estimated that in Bologna alone between 35,000 and 40,000 persons watched this telecast.[78] Lastly, members are also given the option to vote for their representatives either by attending the meetings or by casting their ballot by mail.

Another indication of the close relationship that exists between the cooperative and its members is in the various forms of participation. For instance, investing money whether by way of shares or loans is a form of participation in the life of the enterprise. Other forms of participation have also occurred, including: 22,271 members voted for their board representatives in 1990; 27,051 voted for their favoured products which are offered at a special discounted rate to members each year,[79] and 100,000 members have kept their (shopping) receipts and were eligible to receive a 1% dividend refund at the end of the year.[80]

Cooperative Identity. The second concern for members given the change in strategy was whether the cooperative would lose its identity in its quest for profits. One indicator of cooperative identity is food prices. For 1990, Coop Emilia Veneto's food prices were generally 1.25% below the national average and 2% lower in the city of Bologna.[81] These were savings available to all consumers. Members, however, have access to further savings. They are eligible to a number of specials throughout the year, which in 1990, amounted to a further average saving of 51,776 lire per member.[82] Furthermore, members receive a dividend set at 1% of their yearly expenditure. In 1990 this amounted to an average payout to each member of 38,805 lire.[83]

Further savings can also be made by members by making use of the cooperative's travel tour offers and by investing money by way of loans. The travel tours have been highly successful. Between April and September 1987, 2,124 members joined tours promoted by Coop Emilia Veneto.[84] The cooperative's 1990 budget estimates that this service saved members 152.6 million lire (71,845 lire each).[85] Likewise, through members' loans, members can make further savings because they pay half the taxes that they would have payed if they had invested their savings in a bank.

Another element of the cooperative identity is their level of consumer protection. The cooperative has always invested funds and time in educating the community about its products and their relation to health and the environment. This information is provided through its monthly magazine, its television station and through courses organised for members and school children. In 1990, 27,354 persons attended such courses.[86] The cooperative also protects the consumer by placing strict control measures on their products. Cooperatives have been at the forefront of the campaign to remove harmful chemicals from products, avoid products using PVC plastic and detergents with phosphate. They have refused to sell drinks with artificial colourings and are also renowned for their reliable packaging information.[87]

Another indicator of their identity is their level of social responsibility towards society. In 1990 the cooperative supported 130 environmental, cultural and recreational activities which attracted the participation of 61,847 persons.[88] It has implemented an employment policy which supports the re-employment of women over 30, immigrants, the handicapped, young persons in search of first employment and persons receiving unemployment benefits.[89] An example of the cooperative's humanitarian approach has been the guarantee of employment to workers previously employed in a factory which was replaced by a commercial centre.[90] Acts of solidarity toward developing nations, the poor and the elderly are also common.[91]

This evidence suggests that an increase in size and a culture geared to generating a surplus has not led to degeneration, but rather to adaptation within the new circumstances. This included a change from direct to indirect democracy and an identity which catered for the needs of members and consumers in general. It should be noted that a successful policy toward the consumers and the local community is also an economically sound policy as it will attract more consumers and more members.

Coop Emilia Veneto, La Lega and the State

The consumer sector is the most highly integrated sector of La Lega. The Central Association and the consortia network have given Coop Emilia Veneto access to managerial expertise, greater purchasing power and storage facilities. Secondly, La Lega's financial structure supplied finance in the form of loans and investment. A third form of integration is with other cooperative sectors. It could be argued that because Coop Emilia Veneto and the consumer sector are the largest investors in La Lega's financial structures, they indirectly support the whole movement which, in turn, benefits from the loans and the financial services provided to them. Coop Emilia Veneto is also a shareholder in companies owned by cooperatives such as the pasta factory,

Corticella, and the consultancy firm, Smaer. It also provides retail space products produced by other cooperatives.

As already noted, the State, at the national and regional level, has made available a small amount for loans to help develop the consumer sector. However, where the State has made an impact has been through legislation affecting the commercial sector. One such piece of national legislation, which favoured cooperatives and small and medium size enterprises, was passed in 1971. This law allowed any small retail outlet to increase its selling space by up to 200 square metres without having to seek council approval. It also made allowances for a number of retail outlets to merge and open a single outlet of up to 400 square metres, later increased to 600 square metres. This law favoured the growth of cooperatives which, until then had small outlets, and prevented the large supermarket chains from getting larger. Through this law, and their successful business strategy, cooperatives were able to catch up with their competitors.

The law regulating shopping hours also improved the competitiveness of cooperatives. In 1982 trading hours were increased from 44 to 66 hours per week.[92] This provided more flexible hours for consumers who, according to a survey conducted by Coop Emilia Veneto, have been convenienced by this change.[93] Longer trading hours also gave cooperatives an advantage over family run retail stores, which usually closed in the afternoons.

The regional and local governments of Emilia Romagna also supported the expansion of consumer cooperatives. In accordance with their overall policy to create a locally owned economy based on small and medium sized enterprises, they used their power over building licences to limit the expansion of the large supermarket chains. Another great advantage of operating in Emilia Romagna is the political stability of the region and its long tradition of urban planning. This makes investment a lot safer because the cooperative plan and then build a supermarket knowing that it will be surrounded by housing estates and that co-ordinated public infrastructures will be provided. It was only in the mid-1980s, fearing greater European competition after 1993, that licences to build commercial centres were granted. By that time, the consumer cooperative movement and Coop Emilia Veneto had become the largest in Italy. In 1990, La Lega managed 27.9% of the total retailing space occupied by supermarkets for the region of Emilia Romagna.[94] Coop Emilia Veneto controls 15% of the market in Emilia and 9% of the market in the Veneto, making it the second largest consumer cooperative in Italy.[95]

This case study also sought to discover the importance of an enterprise's business strategy and, in doing so, further evaluate its relationship both with La Lega and with the State. In this instance, it is clear that the enterprise heavily relied on the various support structures to achieve its economic success. The contribution at the enterprise level was important, but it relied heavily on the managerial expertise provided by the consortia network. The State contributed as a legislator, but, unlike the previous case study, it did not provide much resources to the consumer sector. Overall, as the following Table 8.2 indicates, the strategy to develop large retail outlets, to cater for the middle class and to foster an entrepreneurial culture among the work-force has been highly successful.

Table 8.2 Coop Emilia Veneto Performance for 1979 and 1990

	1979	1990
Members	80,000	189,225
Social Capital	396 million Lire	7.974 billion Lire
Social Loans	26 billion Lire	377.8 billion Lire
No of Retail Outlets	57	39
Retail Area	22,000 Sq Metres	35,498 Sq Metres
Retail Sales	100 billion Lire	700 billion Lire
Employees	909	2,361

Source: For the 1979 statistics see Stefano Zan, *La Cooperazione In Italia: Strutture, Strategie e Sviluppo della Lega Nazionale Cooperative e Mutue*, De Donato, Bari, 1982, p.122. For the 1990 statistics see Coop Emilia Veneto, *Bilancio di Responsabilità Sociale 1990*, Bologna, 1991.

Case Study 3: SACMI, an Industrial Cooperative

Sacmi is a worker cooperative which operates in the manufacturing sector. It was established in 1919 by nine unemployed persons for the purpose of performing mechanical repairs to and the maintenance of agricultural machinery. A loan provided by the local cooperative bank and an empty gymnasium provided by the Socialist run local council helped to set up Sacmi. After the Fascists gained power in 1922, Sacmi was evicted from the gymnasium, but it managed to survive because of the support it received from a local cooperative which first rented and then sold them one of its buildings. By 1933, Sacmi was already building its own machinery for the food and chemical industry. During the Fascist period, the cooperative managed to survive, but achieved little growth. In 1947 it employed a total work-force of

26 members and 42 wage earners.[96] A longitudinal study from 1945 to 1991 follows.

Strategy: Competition on a Global Scale

Since 1945, Sacmi's strategy has evolved in two directions. The first is product diversification, the second is market diversification.

In respect of product diversification, by the time World War Two ended, Sacmi was designing and manufacturing machine presses for the ceramics industry. This enabled the cooperative to prosper during the period of post war reconstruction because the demand for this equipment increased. In addition, in 1949 it began to diversify its operations by producing machinery for making metal caps for bottles for a businessman from Bologna.[97] In the 1980s, Sacmi further diversified its operations by manufacturing packaging machines covering both aseptic and non-aseptic food and drinks. However, the ceramic sectors is by far its most important sector representing 80% of Sacmi's total production.[98]

The next phase of Sacmi's strategy was its expansion into the international market. In the 1960s, the cooperative realised that it had a number of products which could be exported. In the early stages, it sold machines, spare parts, and machinery necessary for the production of ceramic products. By the early 1970s, Sacmi developed into an enterprise capable of providing the whole plant (turn-key installations), plus the technical training for its operators and after sales service.[99] Today, Sacmi produces machinery and whole plants for ceramic tiles; machinery and plants for the production of closures for bottles (crowns, aluminium and plastic caps); machinery for the production of refractory materials; machinery and whole plants for the production of ceramic sanitary and tableware; and machinery for packaging. In the first two fields, Sacmi is recognised as a world leader. The strategy today is to remain competitive in these niche markets on a global scale. This is vital for Sacmi's survival, especially since figures for 1991 indicate that its products were exported to over 110 countries, with export earnings amounting to 84% of its total sales.[100]

Organisational Structure

To support this strategy, Sacmi had to develop from being a small artisan firm to a modern enterprise with a commercial and production structure capable of meeting the requirements of a global strategy. This in turn had to be supported by suitable managerial and financial resources.

Sacmi's commercial structure began to change in 1965. In that year, Sacmi opened up its first trading company, Sacmi Impianti Milano, in Milan, in partnership with private shareholders. The purpose of this trading company is to: sell its products, develop knowledge of international markets, maintain contact with clients, provide after sales technical assistance and sell spare parts and machinery. In the 1980s, other trading companies were set up in Germany, Spain, Portugal, Singapore, Hong Kong, Mexico, Argentina and Brazil. One feature of these trading companies are that they operate as conventional enterprises, with Sacmi being a major shareholder ranging from controlling 99% of the shares in Sacmi Impianti (Milan) down to 40% in Sacmi Impianti (Argentina).[101] There are many advantages derived from this commercial structure. Basically, these companies enable Sacmi to control the whole process including production, distribution and after sales service. The legal structure of the public companies has facilitated access to external capital. In addition, forming subsidiary trading companies in partnership with local entrepreneurs, provided Sacmi with access to managerial expertise and local knowledge and contacts. The latter are vital for establishing long lasting relations with clients.

The second major organisational change was the development of a decentralised production structure with its headquarters at Imola. As with the trading companies, Sacmi is a major shareholder in six conventional companies, in each of which it holds not less than 60% of the shares. Four of these companies are part of the ceramic division: Sacmi-Sassuolo, Sacmi-Forni and Poppi manufacture kilns, driers, moulds and equipment. A fourth company, SMI, has the task to develop the activity of assembling and installing machinery and plants and to provide technical assistance world wide. Two other companies, Impak and Benco Pack, manufacture food and drink packaging machines.[102] The result is that only 35% of Sacmi's total production occurs at its headquarters of Imola, with the other six companies, all from Emilia Romagna, producing the rest. The decentralisation of production has promoted greater specialisation and a quicker decision-making process. Another benefit derived from the formation of conventional enterprises is that they have given Sacmi access to external finance and to managerial expertise in new areas.

Further decentralisation has occurred through subcontracting work and by purchasing some parts and machinery from private firms. This gives Sacmi a more flexible structure and a reduction in overall fixed costs. Estimates suggest that Sacmi indirectly creates a further 250 jobs in the local economy by subcontracting part of its production to local artisans.[103]

The changes that have been implemented in the commercial and productive sphere have made Sacmi into a group of companies which are controlled from its headquarters in Imola. Sacmi has developed from an enterprise which controlled the whole of the productive process from one location, into a holding company controlling fifteen subsidiaries, eight of which are in Italy (see Table 8.3). While still producing 35% of the total production from Imola, the headquarters mainly plays a coordinating role for the group's activities by concentrating on general management, research and development,[104] marketing, sales, planning and finance.

Table 8.3 Sacmi Group of Companies

Subsidiary Trading Companies	Sacmi Shares
Sacmi Impianti-Milan	99%
Sacmi Deutchland	60%
Sacmi Iberica	99%
Sacmi Portuguesa	45%
Sacmi Singapore	99%
Sacmi Hong Kong	99%
Sacmi Mexico	80%
Sacmi Brasil	99.9%
Sacmi Argentina	70%
Subsidiary Manufacturing Companies	
Sacmi Forni	70%
Sacmi Sassuolo	98%
In-Pak SPA	99.48%
Poppi SPA	76%
Benco Pack	70%
SMI	60%

Source: Sacmi, Sacmi, un Nome su cui Contare: 1919-1989, Bologna, 1989, pp. 72-99.

Management. As with the previous two case studies, modern enterprises and expansionary strategies need suitable managerial expertise and adequate finance. In the area of management the cooperative replaced the generalist "do all" managers with specialist managers. These specialist managers, who now constitute one third of the work-force, occupy positions in research and development, marketing, administration and finance.[105] A minority of these managers came from private enterprises but the majority were successfully trained on the job by Sacmi. The recruited managers can only become members after a probationary period of up to five years. This cautious recruiting process has facilitated the creation of an homogeneous enterprise culture reducing conflicts between workers and managers.[106] In addition to attracting managers, the policy of joint ventures has also facilitated excess to knowledge, information, and specialist skills vital for the success of the Sacmi group of enterprises.

Finance. Sacmi has managed to attract most of the finance it needed from its members and from its own profits. Profits have been made every year, ranging from a low 2.9 billion lire in 1978 to a high of 40.8 billion lire in 1991. Most of these are re-invested in the firm. In 1984, 94.7% of the profits were re-invested in the firm as indivisible reserves.[107] Sacmi has also attracted a high level of investment from members through loans scheme and shares. The amount invested as loans has increased from 3 billion lire in 1983[108] to 7.4 billion lire by 1992 which indicates that each member has invested an average of 31.224 million lire.

The amount of money invested as members' shares has also risen since 1983. In that year, the general assembly decided to increase the amount each member had to invest from 4 million lire to 19 million lire. To achieve this target members were being asked to contribute 500,000 lire per year which were to be deducted out of their pay. New members were asked to pay four million lire within the first two years and 500,000 lire per year thereafter. In 1992, members' shares invested amounted to 5.4 billion lire, equal to 22.785 million lire per person. This level of internal financing and the economic success of Sacmi has also meant that whenever the cooperative seeks an outside loan it usually gets favourable rates. In addition to all of these, Sacmi has also used the formation of conventional enterprises as a means of attracting external finance and thereby reduce financial burdens.

However, despite the fact that Sacmi is essentially self funding, it still faces some financial problems or constraints. In Sacmi's case, it would be beneficial to its commercial operations if it could organise finance for its customers. Sacmi sees this to be a way to increase its competitiveness in the market. Unfortunately, La Lega does not have the resources to finance such operations. To overcome this problem, Sacmi has organised a conference in which fifteen international banks participated for the purpose of convincing them to finance customers purchasing its equipment and services. This would further enhance trade with other countries.[109]

Culture

The changes that took place in the strategy and structure of the cooperative were accompanied by changes in the enterprise culture. One of these changes was the increasing wage differentials between workers and management. By the mid-1980s managers' wages exceeded those of the workers by 3:1, but, were still 40% less than those received by their counterparts in the private sector.[110] A recent study found that the managers at Sacmi are now paid almost as much as their private enterprise counterparts.[111] Similarly to CMB, managers' salaries are based not only on the amount of work done, but also on both qualifications and market signals.[112]

Just as the need to increase managers' pay was in response to the enterprise's strategy, so too was the development of an entrepreneurial culture among the work-force. Since 1983 investments in the cooperative of members' shares and members' loans increased dramatically to the point that each member has now invested a total of 54 million lire with the cooperative. To encourage further investment, the cooperative pays the highest possible remuneration allowable by law. It is important to note that by allowing members to pay by instalments, the cooperative has maintained the availability of membership open to all.

In addition to the open door principle, Sacmi has remained true to its original culture by maintaining a strong bond with the local community. For instance, all of the six manufacturing companies controlled by Sacmi are located in the region of Emilia Romagna employing another 214 persons.[113] This is in addition to another 250 jobs created through subcontracting part of their production to local artisans.

There is also sufficient available evidence on hand to suggest that, in spite of growing to a relatively large size with a total work-force of 651 persons, democratic management still operates. Oakeshott's recent study concluded that although Sacmi is "management managed...they are not management led" because the ultimate power resides with the board of directors elected by the members and in the general council. The latter approves the budget and future strategies and has the right to appoint and dismiss managers.[114] The democratic nature of the organisation is also reinforced because most managers are internally trained while those who come from the private sector are properly screened to ensure that they meet the cultural requirements for working in a cooperative.[115] This is a major reason why at Sacmi they are adamant that it is the members who finally decide. This is summed up by a former president of Sacmi, Mr Benati, who said:

> "Members feel, and really are the owners of their business. Nobody over the last twenty years has succeeded in imposing any business choice against the members' will. Nobody has succeeded in imposing the appointment of any board of directors or chairperson undesirable to members."[116]

There are two further questions that require further debate. The first question regards Sacmi's strategy to own and manage conventional enterprises. Is this a contradiction of cooperative principles? In part it is, because profits are made from an investment in another firm. However, the profits made are not distributed to members but are allocated to the cooperative's indivisible reserve fund, thus maintaining the principle of limited return on capital. Yet there is no doubt that a dual structure is operating: the original cooperative is still managed along cooperative principles while the subsidiaries are conventional firms.

The second question relates to the low level of membership among the work-force. In 1988, only 242 out of 537 employees were members (45%), and the percentage seems to have decreased to 36.4% by 1991 when approximately 237 out of 651 employees were members. Is this a denial of the "open door policy?", are the members exploiting the non-members? It is not clear whether Sacmi is overlooking the open door principle by not admitting members. The low number of members is caused by cooperative rules which allows membership to be granted only after a five year probationary period. Secondly, the cooperative has also imposed an age limit on membership. Another reason for the low membership is the restrictive State legislation which limits white collar work-force to 20% of the total membership. Since over a third of the work-force are now part of management or the technostructure this limits the number of eligible members. Taking these into consideration, the total eligible members are 344 and of these 237 or 68.9% are members. Oakeshott has also suggested that a reason for the low membership is that fewer members means higher bonus payments for the remaining members.[117] This is difficult to ascertain, however bonus payments are limited by law to a maximum of 20% of a person's wage. In addition, more members also means a higher level of investments, thus it would be in the enterprise's financial interests to attract new members. On the basis of this evidence, it is clear that Sacmi is very cautious when granting membership. It will be interesting to see what happens in the future, since the 1992 legislation removed the 20% membership restrictions placed on white collar employees who may become members. In addition, since 1986, 202 new employees have been employed, most of whom should also be eligible for membership by 1992.

Sacmi, La Lega and the State

Compared to Coop Emilia Veneto and CMB of Carpi, Sacmi is not economically integrated with the movement.[118] Instead it is an enterprise which has managed to develop its own strategy, supported by capable managers and sufficient finance. This is not surprising considering that, because products produced by Sacmi are not produced by other cooperatives, it is not possible to create synergies between firms or sectors like those in the construction and consumer sectors. Politically, however, Sacmi is still associated to La Lega: it invests in La Lega's financial structures, it duly pays its membership fees, but sees La Lega more as a lobby group representing the interests of cooperatives to the government, rather than an association capable of giving economic direction to enterprises.

Sacmi has received little support from the State. Like all cooperatives, it has benefited from favourable tax laws. In addition, the State has provided Sacmi with a modest amount of funding for research and development. This limited reliance on the State can also be explained by the fact that most of its production is sold to the private sector in Italy and abroad and that most of its investments are made from its own operating profits.

Summary

Sacmi has developed into an enterprise which competes on a global scale. There are three important characteristics to note about Sacmi. First, it has become a holding company, wholly or partially controlling, fifteen subsidiaries. Secondly, it controls both the productive and the distribution process of its production and services. Thirdly, it is competitive in three niche markets on a world scale. The coherence of the enterprise's strategy, structure and culture has produced positive results (see Table 8.4). The enterprise's turnover has increased from 25.4 billion lire in 1978 to 315 billion in 1990, and to 339.5 billion lire the following year. It is this sort of economic performance which has led to statements that the enterprise is financially self-sufficient. Indeed, in 1988 the amount of funds available for investment amounted to 173.5 billion lire.[119] The company is highly profitable. In 1991, it made 39.1 billion lire in net profits and had invested 21.8 billion lire.[120] An increase in turnover has also led to an increase in employment. At its Imola headquarters employment has increased steadily from 349 employees in 1979 to 651 employees in 1991, while the whole group employs a total of 931 persons.[121]

Table 8.4 Sacmi Economic Indicators 1978-1991

Year	Turnover (billions lire)	Profits (billions lire)	Exports (% of total sales)	Investments (billions lire)	Number of Employees
1978	25.4	2.977	71%	0.748	352
1982	72.7	12.159	77%	2.775	411
1986	126.0	14.007	85%	6.311	449
1991	339.545	39.134	84%	21.869	651

Source: For years 1978-1986 see Robert Oakeshott, *Workers as Entrepreneurs: Two Striking Success Stories from Italy,* Partnership Research Limited, London, March, 1990, Appendix B; for 1991 see Sacmi Group, *Consolidated Balance Sheet 1991*, Sacmi, Imola, 1991, pp.11-13.

Case Study 4: Spepcoop, A Coop from the Health Sector

Spepcoop is a cooperative which operates in the health sector. It was formed in 1979 by fourteen persons who had previously worked in another cooperative which was unable to provide them with stable employment. Initially, the cooperative managed a couple of children's holiday camps. Although this activity continued until 1987, it was clear from its inception that it would have been very difficult to compete in a market where voluntary work and lowly paid labour flourish. In 1983, the cooperative decided to concentrate on the health sector which until then had been entirely controlled by local health authorities. An account of the changes that occurred in the strategy, structure and culture of the enterprise between 1980 and 1991 follows.

Strategy: Innovation and Diversification

Cooperatives associated with La Lega began to operate in the health sector in the 1970s. This was in response to local health authorities' willingness to subcontract part of their work to the private sector.[122] The first cooperatives practised a strategy which consisted in catering mainly for the local population and in providing labour to the local health authorities.[123] Spepcoop's overall strategy differed greatly from existing practices. First, it wanted to become a cooperative which managed health centres capable of providing services to both the private and the public sector. Second, it wanted to operate on a national scale. Third, it wanted to diversify its operations within the health sector. This third aspect of their strategy was contrary to the political direction of La Lega, which, during 1980-82 period was recommending cooperatives to specialise in particular fields. Specialisation was seen as a way of achieving professionalism, excellence and success. Contrary to this philosophy, Spepcoop thought that through a careful personnel selection process, quality control mechanisms, continuous skill formation and the practice of good accounting procedures it could succeed in many areas.[124]

The first major change occurred in 1980 with the acquisition of a language centre in Bologna for fifteen million lire. The language centre provided the cooperative with two important benefits: low rental accommodation in the heart of Bologna, fixed for five years, and with much needed cash flow.[125] This cash flow became crucial as the cooperative began to work on behalf of the local health authorities which usually delayed payments by three months or, at times, even one year.[126]

In 1990, the language centre accounted for 4% of the cooperative's total turnover, the remainder is obtained from Spepcoop's major area of operation, the health sector. The cooperative has diversified its operations in the health sector and operates in four distinct areas. The first is psychiatric support for the handicapped. In this area, the cooperative manages residential centres, offers support to individuals and teaches craft skills. The second area is rehabilitation, a service provided to patients suffering from mental and physical handicaps. A third is the provision of services for marginalised and alienated youth. Persons in need of such services include drug addicts, ex-prisoners, and those persons with family or other personal problems. The last area is care for the aged. The cooperative manages residential centres, social centres, a home health care service and an emergency unit. [127]

Most of the work in the health sector is obtained pursuant to a range of agreements with local councils and the Local Health Authorities (USL)[128]. One type of agreement is where the cooperative supplies labour to a USL whenever personnel is needed. Another way to obtain work from the local authorities is to tender for a public contract. If successful the cooperative manages a particular project and is paid on a monthly basis by USL. Another form of arrangement occurs in situations where the cooperative manages its own health centres and provides a series of services to both the private and public sectors. In this instance, either private patients or local health authorities pay for services rendered.

Along with product diversification, the cooperative also encouraged geographic diversification. From its base in Bologna, the cooperative has now expanded to other cities. By 1990, it was present in Bologna, Ferrara, Frosinone, Latina, Rome and it has been negotiating to manage health centres in Trento and Chieti.[129] It is important to note that in Bologna and Ferrara, the cooperative took over existing social service centres managed by the local council authorities. In Frosinone and Latina, these services had to be introduced by Spepcoop. This indicates that it is easier for cooperatives to operate in a region like Emilia Romagna, where local authorities are more inclined to support local cooperatives. In all, Spepcoop is now present in four regions of Italy.[130]

Another element of the cooperative's strategy has been a policy of alliances and partnerships. The first venture in partnership occurred in 1982. This venture resulted in the opening of "Villa Guastavillari", a psychiatric centre in Bologna. In 1984, Spepcoop began to manage the centre on its own and it is now the largest in Bologna. The partnership was important because it led to an exchange of ideas and managerial expertise. Other alliances have been formed with cooperatives from Bologna and Ravenna. These alliances too have provided an exchange of skills, but more importantly, they reduce competition and create employment stability. The cooperative is also a minority shareholder in a health laboratory in Rome, and is a major shareholder in an emergency unit in Bologna.[131]

Organisational Structure

There are three basic features of Spepcoop's organisational structure. The first is the relationship that exists between the central office in Bologna and the peripheral health centres in other cities. Spepcoop has developed into an enterprise whereby the central office provides a series of services on a national scale and maintains the responsibility to ensure the quality of its services throughout Italy. The other health centres and the language centre in Bologna have administrative and budgetary autonomy for their operations. This has succeeded both in maintaining good accounting practices and in increasing the participation of members in the affairs of the cooperative.

Spepcoop practices a form of democratic management similar to that of the construction cooperative, CMB. Democratic management is a balance of direct and indirect democracy. Basically, each divisional unit elects its representatives to the general assembly, which then provides the guidelines for the cooperative as a whole. In addition to this, direct democracy is practised by each individual unit. Thus, the relationship between the centre and the periphery has implications for operational and democratic practices.

A second important characteristic of Spepcoop is the role played by the technical group within the cooperative. The technical group is formed by highly qualified personnel and has been in full operation since 1984. Its role is to plan and then monitor the quality and effectiveness of the provision of services provided. In addition, it provides continuous staff training to ensure that all employees possess up to date skills and knowledge.[132] It is estimated that the amount of time spent in training amounts to 6.07% of employees' total working time.[133] The technical group and the training programmes provide a high quality service and the technical knowhow which allows Spepcoop to manage its own health centres. The technical group is most important because it provides staff training and establishes standards which must be met at all levels.

Having acknowledged the importance of the technical group, Spepcoop also obtained some managerial expertise from other sources. In the initial phase, La Lega provided managerial expertise in legal, administrative, fiscal and industrial relations matters, saving the cooperative a lot of time and money. Spepcoop has also had access to managerial expertise by joint management of the "Villa Guastellari" centre in Bologna and other centres in Bologna and Ravenna with other cooperatives, and by being a shareholder in the health laboratory in Rome and the health emergency unit in Bologna.

The availability of finance was the next major organisational requirement. This was a major problem since the cooperative had a start up capital of only 140,000 lire and were in an industry in which the major client, the State, paid late to services rendered. The problem was overcome in a number of ways. For the first two years, members returned 50% of their income to themselves and re-invested the remainder. In 1980, the cooperative bought the language centre which was profitable and thereby enhanced its cash flow position. It then obtained loans from a private local bank. The next step was to increase the amount invested in members' shares from 10,000 lire per person in 1979 to 3 million lire in 1990, paid by monthly instalments equalling 3% of monthly income. This increased the total amount of members' shares to 1.3 billion lire.[134] Finally, involvement in joint ventures and partnerships allowed the cooperative to be involved in productive activity by sharing the financial costs with others.

Enterprise Culture

Spepcoop's enterprise culture has been modelled to support the business strategy and its organisational structure. Since Spepcoop was formed in 1979, contrary to the experience of other cooperatives, it did not have to undergo the cultural changes that others have had to endure. The main challenge faced by the cooperative was to attract managers and, simultaneously, reduce labour turnover. The cooperative succeeded in this by introducing a ten level pay structure. This had the merit of offering good pay packages and a career path within the enterprise. In 1991, the wage differentials did not exceed 3:1, but the cooperative is now in the process of increasing this gap.

Spepcoop has also demonstrated a high level of entrepreneurship. This is manifested in the cooperative's willingness to become an enterprise at a national level, in the degree of computerisation of all administrative and accounting procedures and in the high level of training and skill formation. Indeed, in 1984, the cooperative had a surplus of only two million lire because most of it had been re-invested in the enterprise. In addition, the cooperative has paid the highest possible interest rate permitted by law on members' shares. In 1990 the interest rate paid was 10%.

The third aspect of the cooperative's culture is its innovative capacity and the willingness of its members to make personal sacrifices. The cooperative has shown an ability to predict market trends and provide new services. It went against the then trend which limited cooperatives to either provide labour for the public sector or specialise in one area. This has been supported by a willingness to make sacrifices. Initially, this involved working for the first two years effectively for half wages, and later by providing psychiatric services to the local health authorities without a contractual arrangement for six months. Such commitment and dedication contributed to the success of the cooperative.

Spepcoop, La Lega and the State

Since this is a relatively new sector in which cooperatives are operating the level of integration between Spepcoop and the support structures is not very high. As stated, La Lega provided managerial expertise in the initial phase of the establishment of the cooperative but it has not yet developed the level of synergies evident in the construction or consumer sector. In fact, Spepcoop's business strategy was developed by its own management and the joint ventures established with other cooperatives have been the result of independent initiatives by the cooperatives themselves. Spepcoop would like La Lega to provide information relating to the health sector market, its competitors, about other cooperatives. The last mentioned is important because it can lead to joint ventures and other forms of collaboration.

However, recently the National Association of Cooperatives from the Service Sector (ANCS, Associazione Nazionale Cooperative di Servizi) has made attempts to provide the services needed by cooperatives operating in the health sector. In 1992, the National Consortia for the Service Sector (CNS) and eight cooperatives created a company called "Hospital Day System" with offices in Bologna.[135] In addition, the consultancy consortium SMAER has been commissioned to conduct a study and to make recommendations for future economic strategies for the entire health sector. Further, the national association is creating a body comprised of specialists from each cooperative to formulate plans and strategies for the sector.[136] Considering that there are now 300 cooperatives operating in the health sector who employ a total of 6,000 persons, the potential exists to create synergies and support structures which would improve the competitiveness of these cooperatives.[137]

Over the years, Spepcoop has established good relations with the State. Given that the State is its most significant client, Spepcoop has signed many work agreements with local governments and the USL, through which most of its work is obtained. In addition, on three occasions Spepcoop has received funds from regional employment schemes. These schemes provided between 40% and 70% of the funds for each employment project provided the cooperative met certain employment targets. On each occasion it surpassed the agreed employment quotas. This allowed the cooperative to grow and expand in new areas. It is important to note that the relationship between the cooperative, the local councils and the USL is in the interest of all parties. The cooperative provides employment to its members and a service to the community. The local authorities provide a service to their citizens without having to incur administrative, training and other related costs.

Summary

From humble beginnings, Spepcoop has grown into a very successful cooperative. Since 1980, turnover has increased from 150 million lire to 7.7 billion in 1989. Likewise, employment has increased from the original 14 persons to approximately 800 persons, 650 of whom are employed full time. The amount invested as members' shares increased from 140,000 lire to 1.3 billion lire over the same period and it provided an important source of finance. The reasons for this growth have been the cooperative's capacity to identify a market, its strategy of product and geographic diversification and the establishment of a co-ordinated organisational structure and culture to meet the requirements of the enterprise strategy. In addition, Spepcoop was well supported by La Lega in its formative stages and by the USL, which were willing to subcontract some of the health services.

Conclusion

Each of the four case studies has demonstrated how cooperatives manage change in a market economy. The purpose here is to: compare the strategies, the organisational structures and the culture of these cooperatives; explain the relationships that have developed between cooperatives and La Lega and cooperatives and the State; and discuss how cooperatives have managed to overcome the problems they face when competing in the market.

A Comparative Analysis of the Case Studies

The cooperatives' business strategies all contain a great degree of product and market diversification. This makes it easier to withstand market fluctuations. However, while product diversification is practised by all cooperatives, they concentrate most of their activity in a particular core sector. Sacmi concentrates in the ceramic sector (80%), Spepcoop in the health sector (96%), Coop Emilia Veneto almost 100% in the consumer sector, and CMB in the building sector (87.4%).

Some differences have emerged at the level of market diversification. Spepcoop and Coop Emilia Veneto have developed inter-regional markets. CMB is spread throughout the national territory and has a steady flow of work from abroad. Sacmi mainly exports by providing turn key plant installations and servicing their operation. Another strategy involved the use of joint ventures or partnerships with other cooperatives, and which in the case of Sacmi and CMB, and to a lesser extent Spepcoop, have also been made with private enterprises. What these four cooperatives have in common is that they have all grown beyond the borders of the local economy in which they were formed and have found it necessary to increase their size and market share in order to improve their competitiveness.

The organisational structures of the four enterprises have many similarities and a few differences. Being large enterprises, they all have a professional management team performing specialised tasks. All of them also have the ability to train their own managers. In fact most managers have been promoted from within the enterprise.

However, the two most important aspects are the development both of decentralised structures and of relations between cooperatives and their subsidiaries reminiscent to those between a conventional holding company and its subsidiaries. Sacmi is a typical holding company whereby it controls a number of trading and commercial companies by being their major shareholder. CMB has developed permanent semi-autonomous branches and it also acts as a holding company by controlling shares in companies operating in the textile industry, property development and the environment. Coop Emilia Veneto has also adopted an organisational structure similar to that of CMB. It is formed of a centre which formulates policy and general strategy and provides administrative functions for every retail outlet, but, at the same time, it allows every retail outlet a degree of autonomy and democratic representation. It is also structured like a holding company through its control of a number of conventional companies. Spepcoop is basically structured with semi-autonomous branches but it is also beginning to own shares in other companies.

There are more similarities to be found in the enterprise culture of the four enterprises. They have all developed an entrepreneurial culture geared to economic growth and a greater emphasis on attracting a higher level of personal investment. Secondly, they all practise wider wage differentials than before. This has been in part a response to market forces and an acknowledgment of employee ability and qualification. The third aspect has been the policy of alliance with the middle classes. Sacmi and CMB have established economic relations with artisans and small to medium size enterprises. Coop Emilia Veneto began to cater for consumers in general and not only members, who initially belonged to the working class. The final element of their culture is their support of the local economies in which they operate. This is done through investment in the enterprise, joint ventures or economic relations with local businesses and investments in local banks.

Cooperatives and La Lega

Wider differences have emerged when analysing the relationship between individual cooperatives and La Lega. While all cooperatives are members of La Lega and duly pay their members' fees, invest in La Lega's financial structures and benefit from cooperative laws, differences have emerged in the level of economic integration that exists between each of them and La Lega. The highest level of integration involves by Coop Emilia Veneto. This cooperative is part of a consumer network through which it obtains: 90% of its products, storage space through interregional consortia, marketing skills, managerial skills and the facilities to implement the food control policy on its behalf. The second most integrated cooperative is CMB. CMB gets 50% of its public sector contracts through the consortium CCC, it buys products through arrangements made by ACAM and carries out some research and development through ICIE. The other two cooperatives have formed few economic ties. Spepcoop only recently has become a member of a consortium, otherwise it either worked on its own or with other individual cooperatives. Sacmi does not have any economic ties with La Lega, other than with a few ceramic cooperatives.

It seems that La Lega's consortia network has been best developed in the traditional sectors such as the consumer and the construction. This indicates that economic integration best occurs where there is a cluster of cooperatives operating in a particular sector and when La Lega possess sufficient experience and knowledge enabling it to establish support structures on behalf of these individual cooperatives. In the health sector, little has been done because of a lack of knowledge about and experience in this area, although some progress has recently been made. In Sacmi's case, there is no integration at all because Sacmi is the only cooperative operating in this sector. The only support that Sacmi needs from La Lega is to finance or organise the financing of its clients and La Lega has not been able to do this.

The case studies have also shown that cooperatives are now also creating their own network of relations and are becoming less dependent on the consortia. CMB has entered into joint ventures with private enterprises in property development and the textile industry and is a major shareholder in SECIT with other cooperative enterprises. Coop Emilia Veneto is also a partner in joint ventures with other cooperatives. There are two reasons which explain this development. First, the consortia are not responding quickly enough to the emerging needs of cooperatives. For instance, CMB has had to create alliances with private enterprises to engage in property development to maintain employment at a time when the State reduced spending on public infrastructure and public housing. The second reason is that the legal form of a consortium is not suitable for certain business ventures where cooperatives want to maintain ownership of the assets, such as the case of Adriatica SPA.

Cooperatives and the State

The case studies have also identified a varied relationship between cooperatives and the State. All cooperatives have benefited from legislation which provided tax concessions and the possibility of forming or investing in conventional companies. Two cooperatives, Spepcoop and CMB, were given access to public works from USL and local and national governments respectively. The State also provided loans and grants to all cooperatives. Spepcoop received funds for a number of job creation projects. CMB received low interest loans to buy new machinery. Coop Emilia Veneto has also received small loans. Sacmi received a limited amount of funds for R&D. Finally, Coop Emilia Veneto benefited from the State regulations affecting the commercial sector which gave the opportunity to small and medium size retail outlets, including cooperatives, to catch up and compete with the large companies. It is clear that while the State has provided benefits to all cooperatives, those which benefit most are those that operate in State controlled markets such as the construction or the health sector.

Overcoming Cooperative Problems

The four case studies provided empirical evidence to suggest that a number of options exist for cooperatives to overcome some of the problems identified in Chapter two.

The first of these is the entrepreneurial problem. Since only four cooperatives have been researched here it is difficult to answer adequately questions relating to the rate of formation, individuals' material interests and the level of community awareness of cooperatives. However, a few points can be made. First, Spepcoop was formed by persons who had previously worked in another cooperative. They were already aware of, and were ideologically committed to its establishment to the point of accepting salary cuts for the first couple of years. Second, Coop Emilia Veneto is increasing its membership either by opening up new supermarkets in areas where cooperatives are not present or by taking over private retailers. In this way "consumer-entrepreneurs" are being created from above, reversing the previous trend whereby it was the consumers which set up a cooperative.

The second major problem was that of a lack of finance. This was caused by a lack of initial start-up capital, low investment because of limited return on capital and discrimination by banks. The financial problems were overcome in a number of ways. The cooperatives managed to attract a high level of members' investment in the form of shares and members' loans, especially after 1983, when the law allowed a higher rate of interest to be paid. All of the cooperatives studied have been very profitable and have re-invested most of their profits in the enterprise. This refutes the suggestion that cooperators prefer to distribute profits as wages as suggested by neo-classical economists. Finance has also been raised by investing in commercial activities (CMB and Sacmi) and, in three cases (except Spepcoop), by investing the cash reserves in profitable business activity. Joint ventures between cooperatives and between cooperatives and private enterprises have reduced the financial burden on the individual cooperatives through risk and capital sharing. At least one cooperative, Coop Emilia Veneto, has made extensive use of loans from Fincooper and Unipol Finance. There is also no evidence to suggest that banks have discriminated against cooperatives. In fact, all cooperatives have received loans from banks.

However, the case of Spepcoop, which had to rely on a cut in wages to build up investment from retained earnings, does support the claim that cooperatives have an insufficient capital base during the start-up phase primarily because of the low investment capabilities of their members.

The case studies also demonstrated how managerial problems were overcome. Cooperatives have been known to undervalue the role of managers and have been identified as lacking relevant managerial competencies such as a knowledge of the market and technological innovation. In addition, cooperatives have been unable to attract good managers because of their wages policy. The case studies have demonstrated that managerial skills were obtained from three major sources. First, the consortia network provided planning, marketing and technical skills to Coop Emilia Veneto and CMB. Spepcoop also received support from the Central Association in the area of administration and industrial relations. Second, all cooperatives have become large enough to be able to train their own managers. Finally, cooperatives have also succeeded in attracting managers from the private sector. This has been achieved by offering them comparable salaries and the opportunity to work in modern successful enterprises which are leaders in their sector.

Another problem was that of various forms of discrimination inflicted on cooperatives by government, the taxation system and various power groups such as the trade unions, banks and private corporations. The role of the State and banks have already been discussed and have been found not to discriminate against cooperatives. The taxation laws too have been highly supportive of cooperatives. What the case studies have also revealed is that while cooperatives compete against private and State businesses in the market, commercial relations with them have also been entered into when they have been found to be mutually commercially desirable. These have taken the form of subcontracting work to small and medium size businesses as practised by Sacmi and CMB. Another form of cooperation with private business are the joint ventures entered into by CMB, Sacmi and to a lesser extent, Spepcoop. Further evidence of the commercial relations between cooperatives and private businesses is that 86% of all the products sold by Coop Emilia Veneto are produced by the private sector. Most of Sacmi's products are sold to the private sector. These examples reinforce the proposition that cooperatives and private enterprises can establish commercial relations which are beneficial to both.

It has been argued that various internal characteristics of cooperatives such as members' desire to work in informal, non hierarchical work environments and a commitment to forms of direct democracy have been found to limit their growth. The case studies demonstrated that this scenario does not describe the four cooperatives in question. They have developed a culture with the objective to compete in the market place. This objective was achieved by developing into large cooperatives. They are still democratic enterprises, but are mainly managed through forms of direct democracy (power in the general assembly) and forms of representational democracy, where members elect representatives to the board of directors. Of particular interest has been the development of semi-autonomous local branches. The case study on Coop Emilia Veneto also provided evidence of various ways in which members can participate in the life of the enterprise. It would seem that cooperatives have to face a choice: either to remain small and remain vulnerable to larger enterprises or to become large themselves and develop appropriate, but different forms of democratic management.

Neo-classical economists also suggested that the size of cooperatives would be limited by their tendency to under-employ. All the case studies have shown that cooperatives have aimed at increasing market share and, as a consequence, have increased the size of their work-force.

Another problem identified was the inability of cooperatives to move out of low wage, highly competitive sectors of the economy. The case studies of Coop Emilia Veneto and CMB have shown how cooperatives can move out of a particular niche market to another. Coop Emilia Veneto preferred to build large supermarkets and compete against large supermarket chains because this niche market is more profitable. CMB also decided to compete in the complex public works market for a variety of economic and political reasons. Both of these cooperatives managed to adjust because of the support provided by the consortia network and to very successful business strategies. In the case of CMB, its strategy was also successful because of its decision to enter into joint ventures with private and State companies.

A final reason why cooperatives have been economically impeded has been their inability to take over other enterprises because of financial and legal constraints as well as the difficulty encountered in organising a work-force not accustomed to the principle of democratic management. All cooperatives studied have taken over other enterprises. Sacmi is a majority shareholder in a number of enterprises. Spepcoop took over a language centre. CMB has taken over the private enterprise Secit through joint ventures with other cooperative enterprises and is a shareholder, with other private firms, in companies operating in the textile and construction industry. Coop Emilia Veneto has taken over a travel agency, and through partnership with another consumer cooperative, has taken over a supermarket chain in the Veneto region. Thus, by being profitable, and by means of joint ventures these cooperatives have managed to take over private enterprises.

The problem of absorbing a work-force not accustomed to the principles of democratic management has been overcome in two ways. Coop Emilia Veneto, which is transforming the "FULL" supermarkets into cooperatives, has allocated some of its managers to these new supermarkets and is training the consumers to the ideals of the cooperative and the characteristics of democratic management. However, industrial relations with employees are conventional and proceed through a bargaining process with their trade unions. As Sacmi and CMB do not fully own the companies in which they are shareholders, they cannot be transformed into cooperatives. Once again, the relationship with employees is a conventional one. It should be noted that there are no legal impediments to this type of investment because of a law passed in 1983 which allows cooperatives to make such investments as long as the profits are credited to the indivisible reserve fund.

This chapter has analysed the development of four successful cooperatives. It has then used those experiences to analyse the relationship between cooperatives, La Lega and the State and how these relationship assisted in overcoming the problems cooperatives face when competing in the market. This has proved to be very valuable and has complemented the analysis made previously on La Lega (Chapters five to seven) and on the State (Chapter four). The analysis of these four cooperative case studies has shown that the relationships between cooperatives and the State and cooperatives and La Lega are not homogeneous. It has also shown that some decisions regarding business strategies, organisational structure and organisational culture are made at the enterprise level. This suggests that in order to understand fully the reasons underlining the success of cooperatives, it is important to study how an individual enterprise evolves and manages change over time.

Notes

1 Carpi is a small town in the province of Modena, a major city in the region of Emilia Romagna.
2 Imola is a small town about 50 kilometres from Bologna.
3 Stefano Zan, "Il Quadro Concettuale di Riferimento", in Stefano Zan (ed), *Le Interdipendenze Organizzative in Agricoltura*, Regione Emilia-Romagna, Bologna, 1987, p.22.
4 Alfred Chandler Junior, *Strategy and Structure: Chapters in the History of the American Enterprise*, Anchor Books, New York, (First Published by MIT in 1962), p.16.
5 Stefano Zan, *La Cooperazione in Italia; Strutture, Strategie e Sviluppo della Lega Nazionale Cooperative e Mutue*, De Donato, Bari, 1982, p.350.
6 Giulio Sapelli, "Introduzione", in Carlo Romanelli, *Raccontare Un'Impresa: Cambiare per Restare se Stessi*, Cooperativa Muratori e Braccianti di Carpi, Carpi, 1988, p.23.
7 Carlo Romanelli, *Raccontare Un'Impresa: Cambiare per Restare se Stessi*, Cooperativa Muratori e Braccianti di Carpi, Carpi, 1988, pp.74-76.
8 *Ibid.*
9 Angelo Varni, "CMB: Un'Azienda Leader nel Moderno Mercato delle Costruzioni", in Angelo Varni (ed), *Emilia Romagna Terra di Cooperazione*, Eta/Analisi, Bologna, 1990, p.336.
10 Romanelli, *op.cit.*, pp.74-76.
11 From the late-1970s there has been a tendency to build administrative centres outside of the city centre to reduce traffic decongestion and to preserve the old monuments in the historic centres while at the same time providing office space for the regional and local governments. Examples of this can be found in Bologna and Modena.
12 The Italian construction Industry is saturated with small firms which employ less than 20 employees. They account for 97% of all enterprises, 65.3% of the total labour force and 70% of the industry's total turnover. These enterprises are very competitive and are capable of winning contracts in their own right. See Lorenzo Bellicini, "Mercati, Dinamiche e Strutture del Settore delle Costruzioni Europeo", in Ecosfera (ed), *Le Imprese di Costruzione nel Mercato Europeo*, Il Sole 24 Ore, Milano, 1990, pp.29 and 38.
13 Stefano Stanghellini, "Le Grandi Imprese Nazionali nella Competizione Europea", Ecosfera (ed), *Le Imprese di Costruzione nel Mercato Europeo,* Il Sole 24 Ore, Milano, 1990, pp.135-136.
14 Romanelli, *op.cit.*, p.119.
15 *Ibid.*, p.107.
16 See case study on the consortium CCC in Chapter 6.
17 Romanelli, *op.cit.*, p.108.
18 *Ibid.*, p.111.
19 CMB, *Bilancio Consuntivo 1990: Relazione del Consiglio di Amministrazione*, Carpi, 1990, p.14.
20 A survey of the top 241 cooperatives associated to La Lega revealed that between 1984 to 1988 the total amount of the surplus re-invested in the enterprise increased from 90.55% of the total surplus available to 96.35%. See *La Cooperazione Italiana,* "Rapporto sulla Imprenditoria Cooperativa a Confronto con le Imprese Private", Luglio-Agosto 1990, p.32.
21 Romanelli, *op.cit.*, p.219. However it should be pointed out that the cooperative did spend a total of 185 million lire on recreational and cultural activity for its members. In addition 100 million lire was spent on external study courses. CMB, *op.cit.*, p.36.

22 CMB will pay a bonus to all workers when a target considered to be sufficient to self-finance the enterprise is reached. Patrizia Pirazzoli, in "Retribuzione Variabile nella Cooperazione: Bilancio di un Esperimento in Corso", in *La Cooperazione Italiana*, Maggio 1990, p.58.
23 CMB, *op.cit.*, p.41.
24 Filippo Strati, "Gli Strumenti di Politica Attiva del Lavoro Aventi per Oggetto L'Autogestione", in *I Nuovi Scenari della Cooperazione in Italia: Problemi di Efficacia, Efficienza e Legittimazione Sociale*, A Cura di A Carbonaro e S Gherardi, Franco Angeli Editore, Milano, 1988, p.315.
25 CMB, *op.cit.*, p.35.
26 As stated in Chapter Three interests on members' loans were charged a flat tax rate of 12.5% instead of the flat rate of 25% charged on interest obtained from bank accounts. Interest rates paid could exceed government bonds by 2.5%. This also applied to interest paid on members' shares. See Glossary for further information.
27 CMB, *op.cit.*, p.35.
28 Carpi is one of Italy's major textile centres.
29 CMB, *op.cit.*, pp.14 and 29.
30 Romanelli, *op.cit.*, p.217.
31 *Ibid*, p.191.
32 For information Figure 8.1 see *ibid.*, pp.135-136.
33 Vittorio Casarini, "Cooperative e Gruppi di Società: L'esperienza della CMB", in Roberto Genco (ed), *Cooperative e Gruppi di Società, Le Nuove Dimensioni dell'Organizzazione Mutualistica*, Editrice Emilia Romagna, Bologna, 1990, p.152. See also Romanelli, *op.cit.*, pp.128-133.
34 Between 1982 and 1987, cooperatives from the construction and manufacturing sector in Emilia Romagna reduced their workforce by an average of 4.21% each year. Employment increased again in 1988 and 1989. See Emanuel Danieli (ed), *Le Imprese Cooperative: Trend 1982-1989,* Editrice Emilia Romagna, Bologna, 1990, p.14.
35 Claudio Pellegrini, "Italian Industrial Relations', in Greg J Bamber and Russel D Lansbury (ed), *International and Comparative Industrial Relations*, Allen and Unwin, Sydney, 1987, p.131.
36 Romanelli, *op.cit.*, pp.196-197.
37 CMB, *op.cit.*, p.21.
38 Costanza Fanelli, "Il Pacchetto Coop", *La Cooperazione Italiana*, Settembre, 1990, p.25.
39 For the 1978 figures see Romanelli, *op.cit.*, p.195. For the 1990 figures see CMB, *op.cit.*, p.21.
40 See amounts in e-h (inclusive) in Table 8.1.
41 In all CMB paid a total of 289 million lire in consortia membership fees, indicating a high level of integration. CMB, *op.cit.*, p.63.
42 *Ibid.*, p.26.
43 In this scheme the State provided 5 year loans at a discount rate ranging between 35% to 45% below the market rate. For CMB figures see *ibid.*, p.53. For an explanation of the Sabatini Law see Francesco Pagnetti, *Le Cooperative di Produzione e Lavoro*, Editrice Cooperativa, Roma, 1987, p.150.
44 Lega Nazionale delle Cooperativee Mutue, *Principali Indicatori del Movimento Cooperativo Lega*, Roma, 1991, p.2.

45 Daniele Martini, "Sono Compagni che Sbagliano", *Panorama*, 13 Giugno 1993, p.200. Arnaldo Plateroti, "Da Coop Italia a Coop Europa", *Consumi e Società,* Anno 5, Numero 3, Maggio-Giugno 1991, p.12.
46 Angelo Varni, *op.cit.*, p.369.
47 For figures relating to the years 1975 and 1979 see Stefano Zan, *op.cit.*, *La Cooperazione in Italia*, p.122. For the figures relating to the total retail area see Coop Emilia Veneto, *Bilancio Economico 1990*, Bologna, 1991, p.6. For the figures relating to retail outlets and space occupied by supermarkets greater than 400 square metres see Coop Emilia Veneto, *Bilancio di Responsabilità Sociale 1990*, Bologna 1991, pp. 2-3.
48 Coop Estense is a consumer cooperative associated to La Lega which operates in the province of Ferrara, in the region of Emilia Romagna.
49 Le Certificate, Intervista con Pietro Rossi, *La Cooperazione Italiana*, Novembre-Dicembre 1988, p.139.
50 The three other cooperatives are: Coop Estense, Coop Nord Emilia and Coop Romagna Marche. In total these four cooperatives could count on 700,000 members, 10,000 employees and 600 billion lire of assets. See Walter Dondi, "Nella Hit Parade della Grande Distribuzione Entra il Supercolosso dell'Adriatico", in *L'Unità,* 11 May 1991.
51 Pietro Rossi, "La Strategia della Coop dei Consumatori", in *Sintesi del Sistema,* Maggio 1990, p.13.
52 In France and Britain large retail stores control 50% of overall sales whereas in Italy they only hold 20%. In Germany, there are 500 commercial centres whereas in Italy there are only 160. See D'Angelo, *op.cit.*, p.17.
53 Dondi, *op.cit.*
54 For further information on Coop Italia see the case study in Chapter 6.
55 Coop Emilia Veneto, *op.cit.*, *Bilancio Economico 1990,* p.35.
56 "Interlocking Directorship" is a term used by Stefano Zan to describe the way La Lega coordinates the activities of its sectoral associations and the consortia network. See Stefano Zan, "The Management of Entrepreneur Associations: the Case of La Lega Nazionale delle Cooperative e Mutue", Paper presented at the joint session of the European Consortium for Political Research, Rimini, April, 1988, p.8.
57 Pietro Rossi, lecture delivered at the conference "Organizzazione e Controllo dei Gruppi', Sala dei Convegni della Coop Emilia Veneto, Bologna, 13 Giugno 1991.
58 *Ibid.*
59 See the case study on Coop Italia in Chapter 6.
60 Some of these specialised laboratories are situated in Milan for oils and fats; in Parma for tinned food; and in Imperia at the Local Health Authority (USL) which specialises in hygiene and prophylaxis. See Nadia Tarantini, "Il Prodotto è Svestito", in *La Cooperazione Italiana,* Giugno 1990, p.29.
61 Associazione Nazionale Cooperative di Consumo, *op.cit.*, see section on "La Struttura Consortile".
62 Two examples of marketing at the local level are periodic specials where customers purchase three items for the price of two and specials on ten products chosen by members.
63 For details on Coop Italia please refer to the case study in Chapter 6.
64 Stefano Zan, *op.cit, La Cooperazione in Italia: Strutture, Strategie e Sviluppo della Lega Nazionale Cooperative e Mutue,* p.122. Coop Emilia Veneto, *op.cit.*, *Bilancio di Responsabilità Sociale 1990,* p.13

65 For the 1979 figures see Stefano Zan, *op.cit.*, *La Cooperazione in Italia: Strutture, Strategie e Sviluppo della Lega Nazionale Cooperative e Mutue*, p.122. For the 1990 figures see Coop Emilia Veneto, *op.cit.*, *Bilancio di Responsabilità Sociale*, p.10.
66 The rules indicate which cooperatives can provide this service and how the money may be invested. The requirements for a cooperative are: four years experience, managing retail outlets for at least three years, minimum of one thousand members, net assets totalling two billion lire and adherence to members' loans legislation. The members' loans legislation requires cooperatives to invest not more than 30% in fixed assets, not less than 20% in government bonds, and a liquidity of not less than 20%. Valerio Valeriani, "Il Prestito da Soci nelle Cooperative di Consumo dell'Emilia Romagna", *Lettera E.F.*, a cura del Dipartimento Economico Finanziario-Lega Emilia Romagna, Numero 3, Febbraio 1991, p.5.
67 Coop Emilia Veneto, *op.cit.*, *Bilancio di Responsabilità Sociale 1990*, p.14.
68 Coop Emilia Veneto, *op.cit.*, *Bilancio Economico 1990*, p.35.
69 In all the State outlayed 330 billion lire on a national scale. Giuseppe Codisposti, "Esigenze e Strumentazioni Finanziarie per le Cooperative nel Settore Distributivo", in La Lega (ed), *Il Sistema Lega di Fronte all'Innovazione Finanziaria*, Stampa Nuova Grafica Fiorentina, Firenze, 1988, p.272.
70 Coop Emilia Veneto, *op.cit.*, *Bilancio Economico 1990*, p.3.
71 Onofrio Zappi, Department of Commerce, Regional Government of Emilia Romagna, research interview.
72 *L'Unità*, "Nel 1993 a Bologna .... Un Nuovo Centro Commerciale", 1 Luglio 1991, p.16.
73 Barberini, *op.cit.*, p.232.
74 Coop Emilia Veneto, *op.cit.*, *Bilancio di Responsabilità Sociale 1990*, p.17.
75 Stefano Zan, *The Consumer Entrepreneur: New Synergies Among Needs, Society and Business Strategies*, Report Presented to Coop Emilia Veneto, Sala dei Convegni, Bologna, 1987, p.8.
76 One hundred persons attended the courses in 1990. See Coop Emilia Veneto, *op.cit.*, *Bilancio di Responsabilità Sociale 1990*, p.18.
77 *Ibid.*, p.17.
78 Coop Emilia Veneto, *Assemblea di Bilancio 1991*, Bologna 1992.
79 This information was displayed at "Coop Dagnini", one of Coop Emilia Veneto's retail outlets situated in Bologna.
80 Coop Emilia Veneto, *op.cit.*, *Bilancio di Responsabilità Sociale 1990*, p.15.
81 *Ibid.*, p.2.
82 This figure was obtained by dividing the aggregate value of total savings which is over three billion lire (3,654,744,980 lire) by the number of members (189,225).
83 Coop Emilia Veneto, *op.cit.*, *Bilancio di Responsabilità Sociale*, p.15.
84 Stefano Zan, *op.cit.*, *The Consumer Entrepreneur: New Synergies Among Needs, Society and Business Strategies*, p.13.
85 Coop Emilia Veneto, *op.cit.*, *Bilancio di Responsabilità Sociale 1990*, p.16.
86 *Ibid.*, p.31.
87 For further information see the case study on Coop Italia in Chapter 6.
88 Coop Emilia Veneto, *op.cit.*, *Bilancio di Responsabilità Sociale 1990*, p.31.
89 Providing employment to people receiving unemployment benefits, (Cassa Integrazione Guadagni), which in Italy amounts to up to 80% of one's income, is a way to reduce the State's expenditure.
90 Coop Emilia Veneto, *op.cit.*, *Bilancio di Responsabilità Sociale 1990*, p.32.

91 *Ibid.*, p.33.
92 Nicola Zotti, *op.cit.*, p.96.
93 Coop Emilia Veneto, *op.cit.*, *Bilancio di Responsabilità Sociale 1990*, p.96.
94 Statistics were provided by Onofrio Zappi, research interview.
95 Angelo Varni (ed), "Coop Emilia Veneto: Tanti Soci Consumatori in Grado di Intervenire nella Vita e Nelle Scelte Cooperative", in *Emilia Romagna Terra di Cooperazione*, Eta-Analisi, Bologna, 1991, p.369.
96 John Earle, *The Italian Cooperative Movement: a Portrait of La Lega Nazionale delle Cooperative e Mutue*, Allen and Unwin, London, 1986, pp.84-85.
97 *Ibid.*, pp.85-86.
98 Sacmi Group, *Consolidated Balance Sheet 1991*, Sacmi, Imola, 1991, pp.11, 21.
99 Giorgio Bettini, "La Sacmi di Imola: Servire il Mercato in Modo Completo", *La Cooperazione Italiana*, Marzo 1991, p.103.
100 Sacmi Group, *op.cit.*, p.11.
101 Sacmi, *Sacmi, un Nome su cui Contare: 1919-1989*, Bologna, 1989, pp.76-90.
102 Sacmi Group, *op.cit.*, pp.15-23.
103 It is estimated that its activities indirectly created an estimated 250 jobs in the areas through subcontracting. This is the figure quoted by John Earle *op.cit.*, p.86. A similar figure was quoted by the Sacmi's president Alieri Rodiero during an interview in 1991.
104 In 1990 Sacmi spent 11.7 billion lire on a new research centre. The centre is researching new materials and production processes in the ceramics industry as well as for crown, screw caps and other methods of closure. It also contains 16,000 earth samples so that ceramic tiles plants can be made to suit local raw materials. See John Earle, "Italy's Sacmi", *Worker CO-OP*, Vol 10, Number 1, Summer 1990, p.24.
105 Benito Benati, "Sacmi", in *Organizzare L'Autogestione*, AROC (ed), I Quaderni di Quarantacinque, 2/87, Bologna, 1987, p.82.
106 A survey of La Lega indicated that up to 25% of managers in manufacturing and construction cooperatives came from the private sector. Mark Holmstrom, *op.cit.*, p.146.
107 In that year, profits amounted to 19.9 billion lire, dividends paid as bonus payments amounted to 922 million lire and interest paid on members' shares amounted to 84.6 million. This left a total of 18.593 billion lire re-invested in the enterprise, which equals to 94.7% of profits. See Earle, *op.cit.*, *The Italian Cooperative Movement: A Portrait of La Lega Nazionale delle Cooperative e Mutue,* p.87.
108 *Ibid.*
109 Giorgio Bettini, *op.cit.*, p.103.
110 Earle, *op.cit.*, *The Italian Cooperative Movement: A Portrait of La Lega Nazionale delle Cooperative e Mutue,* p.87.
111 Robert Oakeshott, *Workers as Entrepreneurs: Two Striking Success Stories From Italy,* Partnership Research Limited, London, March 1990, p.146.
112 Holmstrom, *op.cit.*, p.146.
113 Sacmi Group, *op.cit.*, *Consolidated Balance Sheet*, pp.15-23 and p.37.
114 Oakeshott, *op.cit.*, pp.7-8.
115 Benati, *op.cit*, pp.80-86.
116 Earle, *op.cit.*, "Italy's Sacmi", p.25.
117 Oakeshott, *op.cit.*, p.19.
118 Sacmi has built a turn key plant on behalf of La Ceramica, a ceramics cooperative from Imola. In the future it could enter into agreements with cooperatives which need packaging

machinery, but overall, the market for Sacmi's products is mainly constituted by overseas private enterprises.
119 The funds available for finance derived from members' shares, reserve funds and other invested funds (banks, bonds, and shares). See Sacmi, *op.cit.*, *Sacmi, un Nome su cui Contare: 1919-1989*, p.30.
120 The amounts were given in American dollars. I have converted them into lire for the sake of continuity. The sums given in American dollars were US $34 million in profits and US $19 million dollars in investment. The conversion was made at the average 1991 exchange rate of US $1 = 1,151 lire. Sacmi Group, *op.cit.*, *Consolidated Balance Sheet 1991*, p.13.
121 For figures relating to the years 1977 to 1984 see John Earle, *op.cit.*, *The Italian Cooperative Movement: A Portrait of La Lega Nazionale delle Cooperative e Mutue*, pp.86-87. The figures relating to the year 1990 were supplied by Alieri Rodiero during an interview held in 1991. For the figures relating to 1991 see Sacmi Group, *op.cit.*, *Consolidated Balance Sheet 1991*, pp.11-13.
122 Mauro Bianchi et al., "La Cooperazione di Servizio in Emilia Romagna", in A Carbonaro and S Gherardi (ed), *I Nuovi Scenari Della Cooperazione in Italia: Problemi di Efficacia Efficienza e Legittimazione Sociale*, Franco Angeli, Milano, 1987, p.58.
123 As a consequence, the cooperatives would provide psychologists, speech therapists and sociologists to the Local Heath Authorities at a negotiated rate of pay.
124 Nida Peretti, "Quattro Paradossi di Un'Impresa", *Sistema*, Maggio 1990, p.7.
125 Maurizio Cocchi, "Dieci Anni di Spep: Una Cooperativa nel Sistema Sociale e Sanitario", *Sistema*, Maggio 1990, p.7.
126 Cocchi stated that the State departments usually pay months after the service is rendered, but in some areas up to one year.
127 *Sistema*, "I Principali Servizi che Svolge la Spep", Maggio 1990, p.10.
128 USL refers to the original Italian name for Local Health Authorities which is Unità Sanitarie Locali.
129 Spepcoop is present in four regions: Bologna and Ferrara are part of Emilia Romagna, Trento of Trentino Alto Adice, Frosinone, Latina and Rome are in the Lazio region and Chieti is in the region of Abruzzi.
130 Maurizio Cocchi, *op.cit.*, "Dieci Anni di Spep: Una Cooperativa nel Sistema Sociale e Sanitario", p.8.
131 *Ibid.*, p.9.
132 Nida Peretti, *op.cit.*, p.8.
133 *Sistema*, "Spepcoop: Budget 1990, Operatività e Formazione", Maggio 1990, p.9.
134 Nida Peretti, *op.cit.*, p.8.
135 Viviana D'Isa, "Un Sistema di Imprese Verso il Mare Aperto", *La Cooperazione Italiana*, Gennaio 1992, p.27.
136 *La Cooperazione Italiana*, "Dieci Progetti per Cambiare il Volto Delle Imprese", Agosto-Settembre 1992, pp.40-41.
137 Sandro Massarelli, "Radiografia dei Microsettori", *La Cooperazione Italiana*, Gennaio 1992, p.35.

9 The State and the Cooperative Sector

The research so far has analysed the relationship that has developed between cooperatives, La Lega and the State and how individual cooperatives and La Lega's Central Association, the consortia and the financial structures, have managed to overcome some of the problems normally faced by cooperative enterprises when competing in the market. In Chapter four a number of ways in which the State supported cooperatives were identified. In subsequent chapters further information was provided to establish that the State has made a valuable contribution to the success of cooperatives in Italy.

The purpose of this chapter is to find out *why* the State has supported cooperatives and *when* is the State most likely to provide this support. Since the State has been so important in the development of cooperatives in Italy, it is of great importance to know the reasons which have led the State to behave as it did.

To provide these answers this chapter has been divided into two main parts. The first part will explain the main characteristics of the Italian State. The purpose of this is to find out whether there are any nation specific characteristics of the Italian State which have been important for the development of La Lega. The second part seeks to understand the behaviour of the State toward cooperatives in four distinct periods of post-war Italy: 1943-1947, 1948-1962, 1963-1980, and 1980-1992. This relationship will be analysed by exploring the dynamic relationship that has developed between the State, society and the economy. The conclusion will synthesise the findings and analyse the lesson that could be learnt from these experiences.

General Characteristics of the Italian State

Form of the State

The Italian State operates in a capitalist mixed economy, governed and regulated by a liberal democratic political system. There are three basic features that can be identified within the liberal democratic State. The first characteristic is the division of powers that exist at the functional level between the executive, the bureaucracy, the legislative system, and the judiciary; and at the territorial level, between the central, regional and local tiers of governments. The second characteristic is the provision of political choice. This takes place in a social and political environment that guarantees basic human rights such as: free speech, freedom of association, universal suffrage based on the principle of one person-one vote, the right to elect representatives in Parliament, and the principle of majority rule. The third characteristic is the rule of law. This protects the individuals from the executive, thus guaranteeing them their basic liberties and legal rights. In addition, it also limits public powers as a whole by establishing higher laws to which all must abide by.[1]

Function of the State

Although there is no universally accepted definition of what the role or function of the State is, it is generally acknowledged that the State performs four main roles. The first two functions are usually associated with a liberal view of the State also referred to as a minimalist position. This view sees the State performing the function of maintaining law and order at home to ensure that the economic and social system is not overly disrupted. Secondly, the State also has the responsibility to protect the community from external dangers.[2] The State performs this function by engaging in bilateral relations with other States and by being a member of international institutions such as the United Nations or GATT (General Agreement on Trade and Tariffs). Ultimately the State can declare war if its territory and interests are under serious threat from another State.

Two more functions of the State are its economic and welfare roles which are associated with industrialised, liberal democratic societies operating in a mixed economy. Both of these roles are responses made by the State to the excesses and inequalities caused by the market and to the democratisation of societies in which the working people organised themselves in trade unions and political parties to further their economic and political interests. The welfare role emerged as capitalist societies and urbanisation created poverty and unemployment. Initially these problems were tackled by charity organisations and mutual aid societies. However, in the late 19th century the more industrialised countries began to implement a series of social security protection measures. The first large scale measures made in this direction took place in Germany between 1883-1889.[3] Greater

State involvement developed in Britain when old age pensions were introduced in 1908, health insurance act in 1911, and a national health service, unemployment benefits, family allowances and an extensive public housing programme after 1945.[4] While the welfare role of the State, in various degrees, is generally practised in every industrialised country, the best example of what today is sometimes called the "Welfare State" can be found in the Scandinavian countries.

The economic role of the State developed partly to support capitalist development and partly in response to the failure of market forces. The State was instrumental in providing the infrastructure (road and railways) needed for capitalist development to take place. As we shall see later, this role was more accentuated in late capitalist countries like Italy. Since the great depression of the 1930s the State has generally intervened in the market either as a regulator (especially the banking system) and as an economic manager. In the latter role, the State began to use Keynesian methods of economic management, such as fiscal and monetary measures as well as public spending, to manage economic cycles. Another form of State intervention is nationalisation of key industries. Once again the policies practiced by the Labour government in the United Kingdom after 1945 are an example of this. Today's economies in most industrialised countries are termed mixed economies to signify the role of the State in the economic sphere.

By performing these tasks the State gains legitimacy from its citizens. However, the most important of the four main tasks is the management of the economy because without economic growth the State will not have access to the revenue it needs to perform the other roles.

Specific Characteristics of the Italian State

What has been described so far is a general analysis of the State in Western liberal democratic societies. The following section attempts to unravel the characteristics of the Italian State. Four aspects of the Italian State need to be analysed in order to understand its nature. These are: the republican constitution, the high level of economic intervention, the enhanced power of political parties, and, finally, the institutional decentralisation of powers between the central State, the regional and local governments.

The Republican Constitution

For the purpose of this discussion three major points stand out from the Italian republican constitution. The first is that the constitution accepts different forms of property such as private, cooperative and State property.

Second, the constitution places limits on the power of private property. Indeed while private property is legitimate, article 41 states that it "cannot be conducted out against social utility or in a way which damages the security, the liberty and the human dignity of people". Third the constitution places responsibility on the State to implement "the necessary controls and programmes so that the public and private economic activity can be directed and coordinated to achieve social ends" and in article 45, to "promote cooperative enterprises in the most appropriate way".[5]

The importance of the constitution is that it has acknowledged different forms of enterprises and the right of the State to intervene limiting private property, to promote alternative forms of property and to protect its citizens from the excesses of private property and the market. This responsibility assigned to the State by the constitution, was effectively used by cooperatives to pressure the State to fulfil its obligations toward the cooperative sector according to article 45 of the constitution.

Another important aspect of the constitution is that in acknowledging the legitimacy of a plurality of property relations, it cannot be regarded as a capitalist constitution. In fact, the constitution also encourages the State to play an interventionist role limiting the power of capital and promoting other forms of property relations.

Interventionist State

Since the Italian unification of 1861 the State has played a highly interventionist role in the economy. Italy industrialised later than other European countries. In 1861, Italy had 58% of its work-force employed in the agricultural sector, it also had a flourishing textile and cotton industry as well as some parts of the agricultural sector, but it lacked heavy and manufacturing industries. With the economy not being able to stimulate demand, the State intervened to boost local demand with the intention of developing a local manufacturing industry.

The first major intervention was the introduction of the tariffs in 1878, which specifically protected the agricultural sector and the textile industries from foreign competition. In addition, the State developed infrastructures such as roads and railways which stimulated the construction and the steel industry. A further boost was provided by the "war economy" from 1915 to 1918. The war created a heavy demand for the textiles, steel, shipbuilding, armament, automobile industries. To increase business profitability the State also lowered tax rates for the wealthy,[6] it provided liquidity by paying in advance, and allowed businesses to make excessive profits by paying them higher than market prices.[7]

Italy became a Fascist State in 1922. A decade later, the economic depression was the occasion which allowed the Fascists to develop a different form of State intervention. In 1933 the State intervened to save the banks which were on the brink of collapse. These banks had invested heavily in business enterprises and as businesses collapsed, they threatened to bring the whole banking system down. To overcome this, the State provided capital for the banks by buying the majority of their shares and in doing so became a major shareholder in many businesses.[8] In the same year it created IRI (Institute for Industrial Reconstruction) to control these businesses which owned up to 44% of the total capital share market. Through these enterprises, the State controlled 80% of the shipping industry, 77% of the national production of cast iron, 75% of pipes, 50% armament and ammunitions, 45% of steel, 39% engine machineries, 23% of mechanical production, 22% of the aviation industry.[9]

After the Second World War, Italy was still economically precarious: by 1951 it still had a large agricultural sector employing 43% of the total work-force,[10] it was a net importer of raw materials and its manufacturing exports were of low technological content. To overcome these deficiencies, the State protected the national economy through tariffs[11] and boosted exports by constantly devaluing the Lira.[12] It also promoted internal immigration to provide a constant supply of cheap labour to Northern businesses. In addition, the State consistently promoted business development by means of procurement contracts, encouraging innovation and technology, and by providing export subsidies and cheap loans.[13] It has been estimated that in 1990, 3% of the GDP was spent in support of all types of businesses.[14]

The State's involvement in the economy expanded even further after 1945. It is estimated that the State employs a total of 4.5 million people. These are employed in public administration; in trading companies such as post and telecommunications, railways, road construction etc; and in the public corporations. It is estimated that there are some 45,000 agencies that fall under the category of public corporations. These may include the State television service, museums, hospitals, universities, large industrial firms and major banks and credit institutions. The governance of these bodies is legally autonomous from the State, but since they are funded by the State and the directors are appointed by the State they are subject to political influence.[15]

The major part of the public economic sector is formed by the four State holding companies which control 1,000 subsidiaries. The largest is IRI. In the 1980s it had become Europe's largest corporation. In all it owned controlling shares in 600 subsidiaries ranging from Italy's major banks, to iron and steel production, shipbuilding, telecommunication, radio and television, road networks, Alitalia airlincs and many more. The next largest holding company is ENI (National Corporation for Hydrocarbons) with some 300 subsidiaries. The next two are much smaller: EFIM (National Corporation for the Manufacturing Industry) was created to develop new industries and GEPI (Management of Industrial Shareholdings) was given the role of rescuing private firms in crisis. By the 1980s they controlled 80% of the country's banking facilities, 1/3 of its total sales and 1/2 of its fixed investments.[16] In 1991, they employed 677,386 persons.[17] Through these public corporations the State promoted import-substitute industries, directed investment to depressed areas, and promoted strategic industries such as petroleum refineries, chemical and telecommunications.

In all, the totality of these public agencies give the State an enormous amount of power and influence in every sphere of Italian political, social and economic life. Living under a State whose political culture, out of historical necessity, was actively interventionist made it easier for cooperatives to argue for State support, especially since most of it went to private businesses. In addition, the level and variety of State support was an added incentive for cooperatives to organise and influence the political process through political parties. Indeed, the excessive power yielded by political parties in post-war Italy is a major feature of the Italian State which also helps to explain why cooperatives managed to obtain support from the State.

Political Parties and their Control of the State

Political parties are a fundamental part of liberal democratic societies. Individuals, classes and interest groups turn to them to have their interests represented in Parliament and within the State apparatus. What distinguishes the role of the parties in Italy is the amount of power they hold in society and within the State itself. Indeed, the Italian political regime has been called "Partitocrazia", literally meaning party control or power. The sources of this power are many and need to be identified before an evaluation can be made.

A source of party power comes from the legitimacy won from the public because of their anti-Fascist struggles. Throughout the Fascist period the Communists, and to a lesser extent the Socialists, continued to organise anti-Fascist resistance in Italy. After 1943, five political parties including the Catholic Party (the Popular Party), the Action Party (Republicans and Liberal Socialists), and the Liberal Party joined forces with the Communists and Socialists to fight the Germans and Fascists. Although close to 70% of the leaders were Communists[18], these parties fought alongside one another. Estimates suggest that 100,000 were active resistance fighters, some 232,841 had engaged in resistance activities, and 70,000 who had some connection with resistance activity died between 1943 and 1945.[19] However, more participated in the struggle. For instance, the workers who went on strike, the peasants who gave food, people who hid them, including priests, all contributed. The resistance movement liberated Northern Italy and the parties which led it became the backbone of the new republic.[20]

The power of political parties in the new republic was further enhanced by their strategy in becoming mass political parties through which they developed close links with what was then an unorganised civil society. The latter was a legacy of Fascism which, apart from the Fascist and Catholic organisations had forbidden any other form of association.[21] The outcome was a civil society dominated by the Communists, the Christian Democrats and the Socialists. These established associations in every sector of society including trade unions, artisans, peasants, farmers, small businesses, school teachers, youth and women.[22] By 1946 the Italian Communist Party (PCI) had a party membership of 2.1 million, the Christian Democratic Party (DC) had 1.4 million members[23] and the Italian Socialist Party (PSI) numbered 500,000.[24] This linkage with civil society provided them with immense popular support.

After having acquired power in civil society the ascendancy of political parties in Italy culminated in controlling the State, and to use its resources in the interest of the parties. This development is closely linked to the DC which has been in government since 1948. The starting point of this strategy by the DC was the 1953 election. In that election the DC received 40% of the votes, 8% less than they had received in 1948. In response to this, the party's hierarchy decided that it was in its best interest to become more autonomous from both business (who had provided funds) and the church.[25] This was achieved by taking control of the public sector and utilising it for its own ends. Being the dominant party in government, the DC began to staff all departments with loyal personnel. It is claimed that all State departments and State institutions, except for the Bank of Italy, were under its control. In addition, it began to appoint party supporters or loyalists to the various public corporations. In particular, the major holding companies such as IRI and ENI and the welfare agencies were heavily patronised by DC personnel who then used these resources to provide employment, pensions, and economic development in areas where the party was strongest.[26]

This policy which has become known as the "Occupation of the State" was made possible by the political power the DC held within the Parliament and Cabinet. Firstly, the DC completely controlled the Parliamentary agenda and legislative powers. The Parliamentary agenda was usually set by the presidents of the Senate and the Chamber of Deputies who were all DC members until 1968. In addition, Parliamentary Standing Committees controlled by Christian Democrats had the power to pass legislation on behalf of the whole house.[27] Secondly, the Parliament did not have the right to review appointee nominations made by the various ministers and it did not have the power to subpoena officials of the bureaucracy or public agencies to testify before its standing committees.[28] This in fact cleared the way for the DC to make nominees of their choice without any effective controls by Parliament. Thirdly, power was centralised in Rome ignoring the constitutional requirements to set up regional governments.[29]

However, even in this period where the DC had overwhelming power, the opposition was not totally excluded from the decision-making process. Indeed, between 1948-1968 three quarters of the laws passed were supported by the PCI. A number of factors explain this. First, the political culture prevailing among the major parties in Italy is one of accommodation. This takes place partly to ensure that the parties' electorate is catered for, and partly because of necessity since the PCI had little chance of ever forming government in its own right. Second, the PCI, DC and PSI were luring voters from all classes and interest groups in both urban and rural areas, and all felt obliged to support working people, artisans, public servants, small and medium size businesses. Thus, while the party allegiance of these groups varied, all the major parties had an electoral interest in supporting them.[30] Third, during the same period 80% of the laws were passed by the Parliamentary Standing Committees and not the whole house, further facilitating party bargaining and deals being struck during negotiations.[31]

In 1963, with the formation of a centre left government which included the PSI, the DC was forced to share some of its power. This led to what has become known as "Lottizzazione" or allotments of positions between the parties in government. Under this system:

> ...the party loyalists permanently placed in key positions awarded contracts for the construction of highways, buildings and factories. They granted bank loans, pensions and promotions. They allocated franchises, financial subsidies and jobs. The ultimate objective of the whole process was the consolidation and gradual increase of each party and each party's boss's own power, expressed as

> votes at election time and as influence and funds between elections.[32]

After the political stalemate which developed after the 1976 election, where neither the left nor the DC could form a coalition government, an agreement known as the "Historic Compromise" between the PCI and the DC took place. It led to the formation of a DC government supported by the PCI in Parliament. It also led to the PCI sharing the spoils of power. In effect it included the PCI, albeit to a lesser extent, as it had previously done with the PSI, in the DC system of power-sharing arrangements.

The power-sharing arrangements took place in the bureaucracy, in Parliament, in the Cabinet and in the public corporations. Whereas before the DC party controlled the State, now the State was controlled by a number of parties. The patronage over the bureaucracy continued. Cassese estimated that between 1973-1990, 59% of the positions were allocated along patronage lines and not on merit.[33] While the DC had the lion's share of the posts, other parties also shared in the positions.

In 1971 changes were made to ensure that power-sharing arrangements were made when setting up the Parliamentary agenda and in the powers and composition of the Parliamentary Standing Committees. To this end in 1971, a law was passed which gave power to the parties' Parliamentary leaders to set the Parliamentary agenda every three months. They also had the power to decide the composition and terms of reference of these Standing Committees and whether a bill was to be passed by the Standing Committees or be passed by Parliament.[34] Since 1976, the Presidents of the Senate and the Chamber of Deputies have not been Christian Democrats. They have come from the PCI, the PSI and the Republican party.

The power of political parties extended over the cabinet. In Italy it is not the Prime Minister who chooses the cabinet, but the political parties which form the governing coalition and their factions. Furthermore, since 1970 an extra-Parliamentary decision making structure known as "Majority Summits" became the place where decisions were really made. These majority summits comprised the prime minister, some ministers, party secretaries, party experts, and party's Parliamentary group leaders. During the "Historic Compromise" era of 1976-1979, on one occasion the Communists also participated in these summits. These summits had power to make or break governments and to decide on the government's policy agenda. The power of these summits is confirmed by the fact that in 80% of the cases the summit ended with an agreement of the coalition parties. It is also important to note that in 75% of the cases the summits were attended only by party personnel, signifying the power of parties and the limitations of the cabinet in deciding over policy matters without the mediation of political parties.[35]

Another form of power-sharing was over the appointment and control of the public corporations. It is estimated that by the 1980's the DC still controlled 50% of posts in the State enterprises and 75% of the banks. In welfare agencies the DC held 37%, PSI 20%, PCI 20%. In opera houses, theatres and so on the DC held 40%, PSI 26%, PCI 22%.[36] The three State television networks are each managed by one of these three major parties.[37] The rest of the governmental parties, the Liberals, the Republicans and the Social Democrats have all shared in the spoils.

This analysis of the power of political parties in Italy helps to strengthen the case that we are dealing with a nation-specific political system of power centred on political parties, like no other in Western Europe. It is also a system influenced by a political culture geared to political bargaining and political accommodation. Within this context, it is not difficult to understand why the cooperative sector which had links with all major parties managed to influence the State.

The Decentralised State: the Regions and the Local Councils

Another aspect of the pluralistic nature of the Italian State can be identified in analysing the distribution of power between the central State and the regional and local governments in Italy.

When Italy was unified in 1870 a central unitary State was formed, but local councils and provincial governments were also formed to provide basic services to the local populations. During the Fascist period, further decentralisation was out of the political agenda.[38] The Republican constitution of 1947 promoted a more decentralised State by including the regions as another tier of government. However, it was not until 1970 that the regional governments came into being. Since then, the inability of the central government to fulfil the expectations of local populations, pressure from left wing parties, unions and other citizen associations, prompted the reluctant DC-dominated government to give both the local councils and the regions more powers.[39]

In Italy there are 20 regions, 96 provincial governments and 8,010 local councils. The most important institutions are the local councils and the regions. Most of the local councils are small and only 1% of them cater for populations over 60,000 inhabitants.[40] These provide services such as sanitation facilities, fire services, social services, street lights, roads, maintenance of land and buildings and keeping a record of the local population. They have access to their own revenue by collecting a family tax, excise tax and an additional tax. However, the State limited their taxing rights and ensured that their budgets would not be too unbalanced. Revenue was rarely enough and they had to borrow from government agencies in order to meet their capital work programmes.[41]

Since the 1960s the functions of the local councils have been increased. Many State laws regarding urban and school housing, urban planning, transport and environment have given local councils more functions to perform. In addition, the protest movements of the sixties revealed the crisis of the Italian Welfare State. In 1977, a law was passed which gave the local councils the responsibility of solving problems such as day care, school aid, social services for the elderly, housing. By 1980 functions of national importance such as housing and health were decentralised and were now administered by local councils.

Regional devolution commenced with the 1970 regional elections. In 1972, some of the State personnel was transferred to them and later, in 1977, legislative and planning powers over a number of areas were transferred from the central State. There were three basic sectors under the jurisdiction of regions. The first, social services included: human development, health and hospital care, vocational and artisan education, right to study, cultural resources, recreational and cultural activities, information and mass media, voluntarism. Economic development was the second sector and it had jurisdiction over: commerce, tourism and hotel industry, artisan and small industry, agriculture, forestry and mining, co-operation, advanced services to firms and energy, credit. The third sector, territorial and environmental planning, covered areas such as: conservation of agricultural land, national parks and reserves, land use controls, transportation and roads, aqueducts, ports and public works, environmental protection, natural calamity, disaster relief and housing. In all of these three sectors work was done in conjunction with the local councils.[42]

These reforms have the potential of providing local councils and regional governments with a lot of leverage over economic and social policy making. In regions and local councils governed by the left, they could provide the necessary support for economies based on small and medium size businesses, including cooperatives. However, to this day they face many constraints imposed on them by the central government. The first constraint is placed on them by the Prefect (a State appointed commissioner). The Prefect has the power to dissolve local councils, to supervise regional legislation and local government budgets, and to reject legislation on the grounds of legitimacy or merit.[43] There is evidence that in the 1950s and 1960s these powers were used to discriminate against left-wing councils.[44] In addition, statistics also reveal that between 1970 and 1976, 25% of regional laws were delayed or vetoed by the central government.[45] Regional legislation must also respect existing State legislation and must not be found to be against the national interests or against the interests of other regions. Since in most areas of jurisdiction many national laws exist, regional legislation must conform to them. Furthermore, in the agricultural sector, the major decisions are made by the EEC, so both regions and States must conform to EEC legislation.[46]

The most restrictive measure imposed by the State is financial control. As the central State prepared to decentralise some of its powers to regions it also legislated to centralise revenue collecting. This has meant that both regions and local councils are financially dependent. It is estimated that 90% of the regional revenue is transferred by the central State on its own discretion,[47] while on average 73.5% of local councils' revenue is by transfer from the State.[48] In addition, the central State decides how most of the money allocated to regions is to be spent. In 1987, 60% of the region's total spending revenue was spent on the health system which is operating within State legislation.[49] In all 86.5% of the State's transfer funds are spent according to State directives.[50]

However, although the State has retained control through finance and it still directs most of the spending, the actual spending that takes places at the local level as a proportion of total public spending is quite high. In all 13% is carried out by the regions and 25% by the local councils;[51] and if one includes the provinces and all other local public authorities like water, gas, electricity, transport, etc the percentage of public spending spent at the sub-national level amounts to 58%.[52] As stated earlier, the local and regional governments do not have full control over these resources. For instance, if the State says that a certain percentage must be spent for health services then they must go to the health department. But even within these restrictions, local and regional governments have a certain amount of discretion of how money is spent and how policy objectives were to be met. The case study on Spepcoop has clearly indicated that the local authorities solve some of their health problems by subcontracting work to cooperative enterprises. Thus, while the money is still spent on health, the method used is one of privatisation of certain health services provided the subcontractors meet the required health standards set by the local health authorities.

In spite of these difficulties, these sub-national governments are able to support local economic development. Nanetti notes that many sub-national governments, predominantly in Northern and Central Italy, managed to support local businesses by promoting local products abroad, by setting up applied research centres, providing access to credit to needy businesses, developing internal and depressed areas, providing services in the area of vocational training and promoting typical local products.[53]

Of particular interest to this study is the success of the region and local councils of Emilia Romagna. In the areas of the environment, agriculture, public health major improvements have been made. In the area of economic development a lot has been done. The local councils first, and later the regions, have provided infrastructures and industrial parks at low cost land rental to attract and retain businesses. Later they improved public transport, provided low cost housing, child care centres, introduced full time education for the purpose of increasing labour participation, labour mobility and the social wage. Furthermore, the region provided initial finance at low interest rates, and later, through ERVET, (the regional economic planning body), it created a number of research centres in areas where the economy was strong such as ceramics, construction, agriculture, textile etc, to provide businesses in the region with information about market trends, quality control, technological innovation and to develop future strategies to compete in the world economy.[54]

What is important about this process of decentralisation is that in the 1970s and 1980s power shifted away from the national State to the sub-national governments. At the sub-national level the power of political parties prevailed, but a different balance of power between the parties emerged as left-wing parties formed the regional and local governments in many areas. For La Lega this implied that it no longer had to rely solely on the national government for policies supporting cooperatives. Considering that the Communists and other left forces were very strong in the central Italian regions of Emilia Romagna, Tuscany and Umbria and established themselves as the "party of government" in these areas, La Lega could count on friendly governments with much power and resources at their disposal.

Furthermore, three more factors in relation to sub-national governments facilitated the growth of cooperatives. First of all, the fact that sub-national governments had the responsibility to protect and promote local enterprises placed cooperatives in a favourable position because they were locally owned enterprises committed to promote the local economy. Secondly, those regions which were governed by the Communists had developed policies of promoting an economy based on locally owned small and medium size private and cooperative enterprises. Thirdly, cooperatives could count on stable governments which had a culture of economic planning. Indeed, large local councils like Bologna, Reggio Emilia, Modena in Emilia Romagna have since

1945 been governed by Communists. Likewise Communists-led coalitions have always governed the regions of Emilia Romagna, Tuscany and Umbria.

Summary on the Italian State

Between 1948-1962 the Italian State was a centralised State under the predominant control of one party. Since the early 1960s, in response to pressures coming from society, the economy and political parties, and encouraged by the political culture of party leaders geared to accommodation, bargaining and compromises, the State evolved into a pluralist State in which power is shared by political parties and by sub-national institutions. The plurality of the State is further emphasised by the content of the Italian constitution, by the different level of ideas the parties have on economic development and by the diffused level of power in the economy among the public corporations, private enterprises (large and small) and cooperatives.

The purpose of the historical analysis that follows is to find out the extent to which the changes that took place in the Italian economy, society and the State have helped cooperative growth. This will provide enough evidence to answer the question asked at the beginning of this chapter seeking to discover why the State supported cooperatives and when is the State most likely to support cooperatives. The relationship between the State, society and the economy in four distinct periods of Italian history will be analysed.

State - Cooperative Relation: 1945-1992

The Creation of a New State 1945-1947

In the first two years after World War Two a mood of national unity and collaboration prevailed among the parties which supported the resistance movement. Leaders from the Communists, Socialists, Christian Democratic, Liberal and Action Party formed a provisional government soon after the war ended. During the first two years no significant policies were enacted, instead all energy was devoted to the formation of the new democratic State and to the drafting of a new constitution. Important matters such as the role Italy would play in the world economy and the relationship between the State and the economy were dealt with later. In the industrial relations arena, minimum wages and holiday pay were introduced, and disruptions were kept to a minimum. Indeed, by 1947, Italy had the lowest strike rate in Europe.[55]

In 1946 national elections were held for the Constituent Assembly which would then have the responsibility to draft a new constitution. On the same day, the electors were asked to vote in a referendum to choose between a Republic or a Constitutional Monarchy. The election of 1946 revealed a division between a predominant Republican North and a predominantly Conservative Monarchical South. Nationally, 54.2% voted in favour of a Republic. In the South, the highest vote the Republicans got was in the region of Basilicata where 40% of the people voted in favour of a Republic.[56]

The 1946 election demonstrated the balance of power between the Catholics and the left. The parties' vote was fragmented with the DC receiving 35.2%, the PSI 20.7% and the PCI 19%.[57] This balance of power produced a constitution which was a compromise between the Socialist and the Catholic camp. It proposed a proportional representation electoral system and a president elected by Parliament. Article seven recognised Catholicism as the official religion and made it compulsory to be taught at school. The Socialist camp had reasons to be satisfied, especially since articles 41-44 of the constitution posed limits on the power of private property making it legal for the State to expropriate private property in the public interest.[58]

After the end of the war Italy was under the influence of the United States which emerged from the war as the most powerful country in the world. While acknowledging the contribution of the resistance movement, the USA supported a conservative government in Italy. After announcing the Truman Doctrine in March 1947, on May 1 of the same year the US ambassador in Italy formally told the then Christian Democratic Prime Minister De Gasperi to remove the Communists from government in return for continued financial support. The consequences of the Cold War would escalate in the 1948 election, in the meantime the Communists were ousted from government on 31 May 1947.

In the first three years of post-war Italy the cooperative movement managed to achieve two major objectives thanks to the mood of unity that prevailed within the government of "National Unity". The cooperative sector was acknowledged in article 45 of the Constitution and it was also successful in getting the State to draft a cooperative law which would regulate the whole sector. In addition, the cooperative branch of the BNL was opened with a total lending capacity of 500 million lire.[59]

There are a number of factors why the State made these policies. The major reason was that in these early years the antifascist euphoria, especially in Northern Italy, ensured the recognition of all those social forces that had suffered under Fascism, including cooperatives. Second, cooperatives received legitimacy from the State because of the support they received from the anti-fascist political parties who formed the provisional government after World War Two. Third, cooperative sector was becoming a large movement and political parties viewed it as an avenue of electoral support. Indeed, by 1947 it is estimated that there were between 18,000 to 20,000 cooperatives in Italy with about 4.5 to 5 million members.[60] Finally, the cooperative movement, as they had done in the past, organised a Parliamentary lobby group which by 1946 comprised 108 Members of Parliament, about 17.2% of the total deputies, who successfully influenced the government on behalf of the cooperative sector.[61]

The Cold War and a Hostile State: 1948-1962

The hostility that emerged between the USSR and the USA had great ramifications in Italian political and social life. People were being asked to choose between capitalism and communism, between a one party State and a multi party liberal democracy, between God and atheism. While in Italy the Communists practised moderate politics, accepted Catholics as party members, and did not intend to do away with the liberal democratic State, they rallied under a secular party with a strong atheist component, which was anti-capitalist and that sided with the Soviet Union. This was enough to divide the country into two camps.

Divisions soon developed within the left camp as well. In 1947, the PSI split and the pro-USA Italian Socialist Democratic Party (PSDI) was formed. Party conflicts also led to conflicts within the then united trade union movement General Confederation of Italian Labour (CGIL). In 1947, the PSDI formed its own trade union, which in 1950 was named Union of Italian Labourers (UIL). In 1948, the Catholics followed suit by forming a faction within CGIL, which two years later formed their own trade union called Confederation of Italian Workers Union (CISL). Similar divisions appeared in the cooperative movement which in addition to La Lega and the Catholic Confederation, now had a third Central Association, (L'Associazione), formed by Republicans and Social Democrats, who had left La Lega.

The 1948 Election: A Mandate for the Christian Democrats. The April election of 1948 was a bitter campaign. The DC was strongly supported by the United States, most of the business community and the Catholic church. The US provided 176 million dollars in food aid alone between January and March of 1948. The Confederation of Italian Business (Confindustria) gave white-collar workers pay rises just before the election. The church asked voters to vote for Christ or against Christ. The 1948 election was won convincingly by the DC which obtained 48.5% of the popular vote. The Popular Front received only 31% of the votes, 8.7% less than the combined

Communist and Socialist vote of the 1946 election.[62] This gave the DC a clear mandate to implement its policies.

In matters of international relations and security Italy joined a host of international bodies dominated by Western countries. It had already joined the International Monetary Fund and the World Bank in 1947. In 1949 it joined the North Atlantic Treaty Organisation (NATO) which was to provide a defence shield against the Soviet Union. In 1958 it was a founding member of the European Economic Community.

The relationship between Italy and the world economy and the State and the economy was also delineated during this period. It was decided that Italy was to become an integral part of the world economy and the State was to intervene in the national economy in support of business. The economic plan was to favour an export led recovery by exporting to other European countries and the United States. Being at the time a country with limited technology, Italian firms were to compete in world markets by exploiting the cheap labour supply coming from Southern Italy. Indeed, between 1951 and 1967 2.5 million agricultural workers had left the countryside, mainly from Southern Italy, to work in Northern Italian cities and in the industrial sector as a cheap source of labour.[63] With an abundant pool of labour, unemployment hovering at around 7% and a weak and divided trade union movement, wages remained below their European counterparts and industrial conflicts were kept to a minimum. A clear indication of the favourable terms for business is that between 1953 and 1961 while wages increased by 46.9%, productivity increased by 84%.[64]

The role of the State within the national economy was to be one which supported business by providing a number of services. Through its holding company IRI, it provided cheap infrastructures and cheap steel and host of other raw materials.[65] ENI, the second largest holding company, played a major role in providing cheap energy to business by developing natural gas found in Italy and by refining imported oil.[66] In addition, between 1951 and 1962 the State provided grants and cheap loans amounting to 714 billion lire; it constantly devalued the lira; and it protected the national economy by an average of 24% of the GATT protective rate.[67] It is estimated that the State provided a quarter of total investments by 1962.[68]

By the early 1960s it was clear that Italy had industrialised very rapidly. The national economy grew at an average rate of 5.8% per annum throughout the 1950s.[69] This was partly due to a favourable international economic climate and a mixture of public spending increasing domestic demand and business success in the international market. The manufacturing businesses managed to export up to 35% of its production by 1962 and were making enough profits to enable them to re-finance up to 44% of its activity from retained earnings.[70] Other contributors were also the remittances sent back by Italian migrants living abroad and the tourism industry.

The policy of developing an export-led recovery did not benefit cooperative development. During this period La Lega made a number of demands on the State which were not met. In 1949, at their 22nd national congress, La Lega asked for 10 billion lire in credit, 20% of public works, and the management of a percentage of food imports in order to exert some control over prices. For this to happen the Italian State would have had to develop some form of economic planning machinery. Instead, it was basically left to the market to make these decisions. A major reason for this was the fact that only private businesses with the support of the State could have modernised the Italian economy in such a short time and export enough products to pay for the imports needed by the Italian economy. In fact, in 1951 La Lega's cooperatives employed only 0.4% of the manufacturing industry, 7.3% in construction and 2.6% in retailing.[71] These firms, with few exceptions were small and traded mainly in local economies. In addition, 30% of its members and 50% of its turnover was based in Emilia Romagna.[72] It is clear that a locally based cooperative sector, with limited support structures, with financial and managerial difficulties, could not create the economic growth and employment needed by Italy. Thus the State, in order to fulfil its obligation to manage the economy and have access to enough revenue to satisfy its material needs, supported business and State enterprises over cooperatives.

Party Self Interest and Ideology. A second reason why the State did not support cooperatives from La Lega can be found in the ideology and the electoral interest of the Christian Democratic Party. The housing and rural reforms enacted by the government are two such examples. The DC policy toward the housing sector was that it had to provide workers and middle class with their own homes and turn them into a property owning class. Property was seen as a way to support the family and freedom. The DC government supported the housing sector by providing cheap 35 year loans at 4% rate of interest covering up to 75% of the costs. The State did not develop a coherent urban plan, it did not have an efficient State public sector, nor did it control the quality of dwellings leaving it open for abuse by speculators. Without any planning and control, between 1948 and 1963 the private sector built 85% of the dwellings, with the remainder built by State housing authorities[73] and by the cooperative sector.[74] However, most houses built by cooperatives were for private ownership, only in certain areas especially in Milan, Emilia Romagna and Tuscany cooperatives built and managed collectively owned housing. Thus, the DC objective had been achieved by creating a property owning class and winning also the support of the builders and real estate investors. The anti-speculative role that cooperatives could have played was dismissed. Cooperatives could have built housing at lower costs and, being non-profit making, could have contained rental costs for lower income families, but this too was overlooked.

The premise for the rural reforms of 1950 was similar to that of the housing policy. Once again the aim was to win consent from the peasants who had been seeking land reforms and at the same time, by creating property owners the proletarianisation of the countryside could have been avoided, thus reducing the influence of the Communists. In all 700,000 hectares were distributed to some 109,425 families.[75] In addition, by 1965 a further 1.1 million hectares were transformed into small holdings thanks to cheap loans provided by the State to individual proprietors.[76] The cooperatives which had been formed prior to the 1950 reforms were disbanded.[77] In both the housing and the agrarian reform La Lega was supporting collectively owned farms and housing, but on both occasions the State discriminated against collectively owned properties.

This is a clear indication of the power of the DC during this period. As mentioned earlier since the 1953 election the DC's strategy was to "occupy" the State. During this period it had come to control government, the bureaucracy and the public corporations. Its power was further aided by USA's support and by the weakness of a divided left nationally. The latter was further weakened in 1956 by the revelations made by Khrushchev about the nature of Stalin's rule in the USSR. Earlier, it was also stated that some forms of collaboration took place between government and opposition supported by the fact that the Communist party voted in favour of the majority of laws passed by the government during this period. While this is true, the housing and agricultural reforms and Italy's international policy reveal that on important matters the DC compromised very little on its strategy and ideology.

Threatening the Social Order. A third reason why the State did not support cooperatives is the fact that the State feared the rise of a movement which threatened the national and the international social order. In fact, during this period, La Lega did not support Italy's entry into NATO and the EEC. It was also in favour of the transformation of a capitalist society into a socialist society. This threat became more real since Italy had a large Communist

Party that La Lega supported. It is within this context that the then minister of the interior Scelba, used the police force against workers and cooperatives.[78] Fearing that La Lega would be a source of support for the Communists, he and his ministry embarked on a campaign of harassment in order to weaken those cooperatives which were regarded as an important social base of the PCI. Cooperatives were subject to strict inspections, were put under government appointed commissioners, and some were forced to go into liquidation.[79] This also discouraged people from joining or starting cooperatives. According to La Lega's president Cerreti, Scelba wanted to subordinate La Lega to the State by destroying its top 250 cooperatives.[80]

Limits to State Action. In spite of the discriminatory and violent actions by the State against them, La Lega's cooperatives still managed to survive during this period. As stated in Chapter four,[81] cooperatives managed to grow through intercooperative trading and by achieving economies of scale through the formation of consortia. This proves that in spite of hostility from the State expressed through government policies and the law enforcement agencies that tried to weaken La Lega's cooperatives, they could not destroy it as this would have meant violating the laws which legitimate the liberal democratic State. Secondly, further violence by the State on the cooperatives and the workers' movement could have led to sustained civil unrest which would have undermined the conditions for economic growth and access to revenue, vital for the existence of the State.

Another constraint on State action was the division of power between the central State and the local government. The latter has a number of roles to perform and manages at least 25% of public spending. Even during this period of high tension, local governments administered by left-wing coalitions, especially in the region of Emilia Romagna, supported cooperatives in a number of ways: land was given to agricultural cooperatives and housing cooperatives, public works were assigned to construction cooperatives and licences were granted to consumer cooperatives.

The government faced further constraints from the fact that a section of the cooperative movement supported two of its major coalition parties, the DC and the PSDI. For this reason the favourable cooperative law was maintained and the finance available through the BNL was also increased from 500 million lire to 7.5 billion lire. This was much less than what the whole cooperative sector demanded. However, the DC did not have to meet all of the financial requirements through the BNL, because the Catholic cooperatives could rely on its own rural and popular banks for credit. In addition, the DC controlled Federconsorzi, the most powerful agricultural institution in the country which helped provide credit, technical support and machineries to small farmers as well as the Catholic cooperative movement.

Thus, even in a period when the central State was hostile to cooperatives, there were a number of constraints imposed on the central State by the liberal democratic rules, the division of powers between the central and local government and by the cooperative movements supporting government parties which limited the damage it could inflict on La Lega. In addition to these constraints, La Lega's ability to organise into a united movement and the ability to count on political and social support, reduced the impact of a hostile State and ensured La Lega's survival.

Economic Crisis And Political Realignment: 1963-1980

The years between 1963 and 1980 were years in which great changes took place in Italy's economic, social and political arena. These changes increased the power of trade unions against private enterprises and that of left wing parties versus the DC. This realignment of political and economic forces led to changes at the economic and political level with important repercussions on the cooperative movement. The latter underwent continuous growth during these years and became a major economic player.

International Relations. International relations became less influential in Italian politics because of the better relations fostered between the superpowers and the changing policies of the PCI. Since the 1960s, under the policies known as "Détente", the tension between the two superpowers eased. In 1969 the Strategic Arms Limitation Talks (SALT) were held in Helsinki paving the way for less hostile relations between the USA and the USSR. The PCI also changed its attitude toward NATO and toward the EEC and by 1974 it accepted Italy's place within both institutions.[82]

The Economic Context. Another major change was the erosion of the economic and social conditions which created constant economic growth throughout the 1950s. By 1969 the low wage competitiveness of Italian goods had come to an end. A tightening labour market due to a high employment rate and emigration, and a well organised and united trade union movement, led to constant industrial conflicts and wage increases. Wages increased by 10.7% in 1962 and 14.7% in 1963. In 1969, a period known as the "Hot Autumn", the trade union movement won further wage increases, a shorter working week and automatic wage indexation.[83] In addition, the

"Workers' Statute" gave the trade unions power to nullify the discretionary powers of management at the shop floor level. This meant that the unions could control the pace and line of work procedures, the introduction of technology, work-force mobility and could veto layoffs. Thus, the unions won not only wage increases, but also control of the shopfloor which reduced the power of management to reorganise or restructure the workplace.[84]

Two international events further undermined Italian competitiveness. The US government reverted to a floating exchange rate and devalued the dollar by 9% in 1971 and by another 10% in 1973.[85] This reduced the competitiveness of Italian goods in the American market. In 1974, the oil crisis broke out, increasing the price of oil. This increased the costs of production throughout the world, but it effected Italy in particular because it was totally dependent on imported oil which was its prime source of energy.[86]

The Response by Italian Business. The consequences of the factors outlined above reduced the competitiveness of Italian businesses. As a result, the ability of businesses to self finance their activity was reduced from the 44% in 1960 to 15.4% in 1977.[87] Another indicator which reveals the difficulties that businesses were encountering, is the level of indebtedness. In 1978, a sample of 856 of the largest public and private enterprises showed a level of debt equal to 61.5% of their turnover.[88] Matters were made worse by the high level of industrial action and absenteeism. The automobile industry was particularly affected: for every 100 cars produced by FIAT, Opel produced 140 at the same costs; also the Alfa Romeo plant was producing between 350 to 500 cars a day instead of the 750 capacity.[89] This was happening when Italy was more than ever integrated in the world economy and facing competition from both the industrialised countries and the newly industrialised countries of Asia and South America.[90]

While the large businesses were becoming uncompetitive, small businesses were flourishing.[91] Some small businesses sprang up as a result of the decentralisation process initiated by large firms which preferred to subcontract some of the work to the smaller firms. Some of these small businesses had become competitive because they were non-unionised. This enabled them to evade a number of social security contributions and to exploit immigrant labour,[92] the large pool of unemployed and second job seekers.[93] Another segment of the small to medium size business sector competed by making use of their advantages in flexible production and their capacity for innovation. Others competed by cooperating with other businesses in areas known as "Industrial Districts". In these areas cooperation between firms enables those of small dimension to achieve economies of scale without losing their flexible advantage.[94]

State Intervention in the Economy. As the competitiveness of Italian business declined, the State was asked to play a different role to that played since 1945. As well as continuing to provide infrastructures, cheap energy and raw materials, State management of the economy now included measures such as: rescuing bankrupt firms and maintenance of excessive manpower in public firms.[95] IRI for instance, purchased 55 companies between 1971-1980 which employed 71,162 people. In all it now employed close to 500,000 people.[96] ENI did the same, and in 1971 GEPI was set up to rescue medium size enterprises.[97] These salvage operations damaged the economic viability of public corporations. Indeed, by 1978 for every 1,000 lire of turnover, they had accumulated 1,100 lire of debt, to the point that they were paying 10 billion lire per day to banks in interest. Furthermore, the State needed as much as 8% of the GDP to re-finance the State owned enterprises and their subsidiaries.[98] Thus, it had become clear that there were limits to what these holding companies could do to solve the economic problems facing Italy.

In addition to the holding companies, the State tried to solve the problem of unemployment by employing more people in the public administration and by encouraging early retirement. The public service employees increased from 1,592,000 in 1967 to 2,157,000 in 1978.[99] By 1978 pensioners numbered 12,600,000, of which 5 million were disablement pensions.[100]

However, the intervention of the State in the economy and the resurgence of the small and medium size firms did not stop the declining rate of economic growth. In fact, the average rate of GDP growth declined to 5.3% between 1963-1969, 4.3% between 1969-1973 and 2.8% between 1973-1980.[101] In addition to this, the level of tax evasion which occurred in the hidden economy and an inefficient tax system, were responsible for an estimated 20% of the taxes due being uncollected.[102] Thus the State's rising costs in public administration, social welfare and intervention in economy were not met by increased revenue. This led to a fiscal crisis of the State, thus explaining why the total government debt as a percentage of GDP rose from 36.9% in 1970 to 70.3% in 1982.[103]

The Erosion of the Christian Democratic Power. In spite of continuous high growth until 1963 and lower growth to 1980, many problems continued to exist in Italian society. The major concerns were the dichotomy between a prosperous North and a poor South, organised crime, lack of housing for urban workers and low income families, the quality of life in the large cities, inadequate education facilities, an unemployment rate which increased from 3.8% in 1963 to 7.7% in 1979 but was much higher among the youth, women and Southerners.[104] In addition, the emerging youth culture of the 1960s and secularisation of Italian society challenged many pillars of the established society. The youth movement challenged the hierarchical structures of society and demanded new forms of industrial democracy, self-management and a non alienating workplace.[105] Urbanisation and consumerism contributed to the creation of a predominantly urbanised[106] and secularised society. The now united and stronger trade unions were not only making demands in the workplace, but were also pressing for changes in the school, transport, retailing, health system and quality of life issues, especially in urban areas. These changes had a profound effect on the political system which until 1962 was dominated by the DC.

Throughout this period the basis of DC power was being eroded. The three pillars of its support were being undermined The Vietnam debacle and the economic problems faced by the US economy reduced the legitimacy that the US had in Italian society. Urbanisation, education and consumerism reduced the influence of the Catholic church. The successful referenda which legalised divorce and abortion in the mid seventies, and the reduced membership of a number of Catholic associations, was a clear indication of this trend.[107] In addition, the Encyclical "Vatican II" gave people the freedom to vote for a political party of their choice, further undermining the DC. Urbanisation also meant a lower number of people in the countryside was under the influence of the farmers' association, Coldiretti, which in the 1950s formed a powerful lobby group in the party.[108]

The national elections of 1976 confirmed that the voting power of the DC had weakened. Its share of the national vote was reduced from 48.5% in 1948 to 38.7% in 1976. In contrast, the Communist Party improved its position increasing its share of the national vote from 22.6% of 1953 to 34.4% in 1976. The Socialists had lost ground since 1953, declining from 12.7% to 9.6% in 1976.[109] To govern, the DC formed a coalition with the Socialist Party in 1963 with the intention of isolating the Communist party. This did not work. The election result of 1976 confirmed the popularity of the Communists and since the Socialists no longer wanted to form government with the DC, and the Communists were not in favour of a government of the left, the only option was a national solidarity government. Other factors, such as Italy's precarious position in the world economy and terrorist activities, also encouraged parties to come to an agreement.[110] This led to the formation of DC cabinet supported by the Communists for the period 1976-1979.

The changed balance of power between the political parties and the inability of the national State to solve the problems present in Italian society, led to a devolution of power within the State from the DC to other parties, including the PCI, and from the national State to regions and local councils. Considering that since the first regional elections held in 1970, Communists have always governed the regions of Emilia Romagna, Tuscany and Umbria, and that after the 1975 local elections, they also governed 51% of Italy's local councils representing 66% of the population, the Communists came to yield a lot of power at the sub-national level.[111]

This system of power sharing between political parties, the decentralisation of powers between the State and the sub-national governments, also included the business community and the trade unions. The banking system was structured to meet the needs of various business groups. Each business had access to a specialised bank: Artigiancassa for the artisans; Mediocredito Regionale for small and medium size businesses; Banca Commerciale and IMI for large businesses;[112] the cooperative branch of the BNL and the rural banks for the cooperative movement. The trade union movement shared in the spoils by having the privilege to nominate the administrators of INPS, the Social Security Department.[113]

State and Cooperatives 1963-1980. In the previous period prior to 1963, the State was hostile to La Lega because: it was dominated by the DC; it considered La Lega a threat to the national and international social order and because La Lega's cooperatives were basically small and locally based. Consequently, these were unable to create the economic growth and employment needed by the State to have access to revenue and to legitimate its role in society.

Between 1963 and 1980 these three discriminatory factors no longer existed. Firstly, the DC had lost its monopoly on power. Secondly, La Lega accepted Italy's place in the European Community and NATO. Furthermore, at the 1977 national conference on cooperation, La Lega's president clearly accepted the workings of a mixed economy and the liberal democratic system of government. Thus La Lega no longer threatened the national and international order.

Thirdly, La Lega and the cooperative sector had become more competitive. In 1976, it was estimated that the cooperative sector controlled 6% of the economy. During these years, La Lega had become a sophisticated organisation capable of providing cooperatives with a series of services in the area of finance, trade and administration improving the competitiveness of cooperatives. Despite mergers, the number of cooperatives increased from 7,735 in 1969 to 10,680 in 1976. The turnover produced by La Lega increased by a total of 403%, from 619 billion lire to 2,500 billion lire.[114] This compared favourably with the national average of 4.3% per annum between 1969-1973 and 2.8% between 1973-1980.[115]

The strength of La Lega is confirmed by evidence showing that between 1976 and 1980 cooperatives in the construction, manufacturing and service sector increased their value-added share of the turnover by 42%, while the national average was 18%; and they increased employment levels by 15% compared to a national average of 6%.[116] Another indicator of La Lega's strength is that it managed to convert into cooperatives 100 private enterprises between 1974-1978 saving 10,000 jobs.[117]

A further important aspect of La Lega in the 1970s, is the economic role it performed in times of economic crisis. In 1949, La Lega sought from the State financial aid, a percentage of public works and control of a percentage of imported food. In the late-1970s its programme sought to help the State solve some immediate problems caused by Italy's uneven economic development. In fact, it saw itself as an organisation playing a social role at a national level. Its programme included restructuring certain sectors of the Italian economy such as agriculture, urban planning, the distribution sector, and help to reduce the gap between Northern and Southern Italy. It also claimed to be capable of reducing inflation, which had reached 18% in 1975, by controlling food and housing prices.[118] The latter were built at prices which were between 30-40% lower than those built by private enterprises.[119]

The improved economic performance of La Lega, in addition to the new role it performed in the Italian economy, provided a number of benefits for the State. It increased the State's legitimacy because it contributed to the solution of important social and economic problems. Further, by taking over enterprises in crisis it saved the State social welfare expenditure on the unemployed as well as contributing to State revenue by paying company, incomes and other indirect taxes.

Summary 1963-1980. In summary the State's action in meeting cooperatives' needs between 1963 and 1980 was made in response to changes that had taken place in the economic, social and political sphere. These included:

- The realisation by the State that it could no longer rely on economic growth solely created by private business and State enterprises. This reduced the State's revenue base and with expenses increasing, it created a burgeoning public debt undermining its capacity to fulfil its role in society, thus undermining its legitimacy and its revenue base;

- The changes that took place in the relation of power between political parties led to power sharing arrangements at every level of the State (Parliament, Parliamentary Standing Committees, and public corporations). This allowed the left parties to influence the public policy-making process and to have access to State resources;
- One major policy change was the devolution of power from the national State to regions and local councils. Through this, the left wing parties were able to manage more resources at the local level and to initiate local economic development policies in a way which was more favourable to small and medium size enterprises including cooperatives;
- As well as benefiting from the changes that took place within the State and between political parties, changes within La Lega also increased its bargaining power *vis-à-vis* the State. During this period, La Lega developed into an organisation capable of contributing to economic growth and in solving some of the country's economic and social problems. This provided the State with revenue and in strengthening its legitimacy. The latter was also reinforced by La Lega's new policy toward the EEC and NATO. Another factor which influenced the State, was La Lega's increased social support resulting from a carefully constructed policy of alliances with small and medium size enterprises, good relations with the trade union movement, and the support it had from the 2.8 million members, giving a considerable amount of power when lobbying political parties and the State.

It is no surprise then that at both the national, regional and local level a number of measures were enacted favouring cooperative development in Italy. At the national level the State amended the cooperative laws providing further fiscal incentives and introducing members' loans to improve the financial capacity of cooperatives. Second, in 1971 it increased the funds available in the cooperative branch of the BNL from 30 to 100 billion, and in the same year it offered the three major central organisations a seat on the branch's board of directors. Third, by shifting public spending toward the social sector such as housing, schools and transport it benefited those cooperatives which operated in this area. Fourth, the State made available funds for job creation projects for young people.[120]

At the sub-national level, where most of the public spending takes place, cooperatives benefited from the combined regional and local policies which provided: low cost industrial parks; financial support; regulations favouring the growth of cooperatives in the housing and retail area; access to resources for cooperatives in the construction, health, service and cultural sector. All of which contributed to the improved performance of La Lega in the 1970s.[121]

Managing Growth in a Global Economy 1981-1991

The Political and Economic Context. National politics did not change a great deal in the 1980s. While the Communist Party began to lose votes and influence, the institutional reforms of the 1970s remained and the party system of power was unaltered. What did change was the power relation between the unions and business. The unions suffered two major defeats: in 1980, a month long workers' strike at the Fiat factory in Turin was ultimately lost, and in 1985, a national referendum to retain automatic wage indexation was defeated. Both of these decisions split the trade union movement with CISL and UIL more inclined to support the government which sided with business. Inevitably this led to lowering of real wages which became an important factor in private sector recovery.

Greater changes took place in Italy's relationship with the world economy. The 1980s symbolised an acceleration of the globalisation of the economy. National economies were increasingly more integrated and local markets were been penetrated by goods from all over the world.[122] Italy faced competition from the industrialised countries which competed in high-technology, high-value-added products and the emerging, newly industrialising countries, competing in low-technology, low-value-added goods taking advantage of their low wages[123] and low level of trade unionism.[124] Competition was further heightened by the declining rate of GATT tariff barriers which had been reduced to 5% by 1991, against the average rate of 40% in 1947.[125] In addition, the EEC was accelerating its economic integration by declaring its intention to abolish all trade barriers among member nations by 1993. The State and business responses to this situation highlighted both the vitality and weakness of the Italian economy.

Business Response to the 1980s. Private enterprise produced various responses to this crisis. The large enterprises took advantage of the divisions and the defeats incurred by the trade union and by a weaker Communist Party which had supported them. They introduced cost-saving measures by increasing the level of technology in the enterprise and the simultaneous reduction of the work-force.[126] Production was decentralised through subcontracting part of the work to smaller firms leading to a reduction in fixed costs and greater flexibility.[127] Productivity improved by increasing the number of working hours per person and by reducing conflicts between labour and management, leading to a substantial reduction in working hours lost. Their financial situation also improved. There was a higher use of risk capital obtained through the stock exchange[128] and a preference for medium and long term credit rather than short term credit.[129] In addition, both public and private large corporations sought cheaper credit abroad, something which small and medium size enterprises were unable to do.[130] The 1980s also saw the emergence of holding companies and a greater rate of mergers and acquisitions from large companies and holding groups.[131] As a consequence, economic power has been further consolidated in fewer hands. Bianchi notes that almost 50% of the companies listed on the stock exchange belong to nine industrial groups which control 80% of the shares.[132]

Small and medium size enterprises continued to flourish for the very same reasons that they did in the seventies. However, while the economic competitiveness of business did improve, many problems remained. In the 1991 annual Mediobanca report the largest 1,898 Italian companies revealed lower profits and a higher level of debt.[133] Another indicator of economic instability was that competitors were closing the gap in important areas such as textiles which accounted for 18.6% of total exports in 1988.[134] In this sector, Italy competes well on design and marketing, but is facing increasing competition from countries from Asia and Brazil who compete on low wages and are catching up on design. This has led a lot of textile firms either to move overseas or to invest overseas instead of at home.[135] Overall, the Italian economy based on small and medium sized firms faces increasing competition from much larger foreign firms and greater difficulty in expanding abroad.[136] Foreign companies have already acquired a large presence in the food and dairy industry, and are likely to move into other sectors of the economy.[137] Private enterprise's weakness is further reflected in the level of State subsidies which between 1981 and 1986 amounted to 4% of the GDP.[138] The fact that the State can no longer sustain this support, further weakens the Italian economy.

The Response by the State. The State's response during this period was restrained by a number of factors. The State faced further fiscal problems, a managerial crisis, it could not rely on the public holding companies to create growth like they did in the 1960s and 1970s, and furthermore, it faced a number of constraints from being a member of the EEC.

The fiscal crisis of the State grew worse in the 1980s. The financial problems were caused by: the inefficient use of public resources, pension payments amounting to 14% of GDP,[139] a hidden economy which in 1987 was estimated to be as high as 18% of the GDP,[140] and a total tax evasion totalling 270,000 billion lire for 1989 or 22.7% of the GDP.[141] By 1991, the overall effect had increased the public debt to 104% of the GDP.[142]

Consequently, the State could not go on subsidising the increased interventionist role of IRI and other public enterprises. Testimony of this is that during this period IRI reduced its work-force from 556,659 to 407,160 in 1991,[143] and sold off companies[144] and shares to balance its budget. However, in spite of this the State holding companies accumulated massive debts. In 1992 IRI had debts totalling 80,000 billion lire and ENI 36,000 billion lire.[145] This meant that public holding companies could no longer be relied upon to act as a counter cyclical force in the economy, nor could they bail out private enterprises in crisis.

Another weakness of the Italian State is the lack of managerial expertise. For instance environmental problems are not tackled promptly, infrastructures are left to deteriorate (the Italian railway system is slower than the French and the German), and money allocated for public works is not spent.[146] This has a deteriorating effect on the economy both in terms of efficiency and job creation. Unlike the 1950s and 1960s, when the State was able to plan and execute entire public works projects, now it is forced to work with the private sector because of its inefficiency and financial problems. This opens up opportunities for the private sector, including cooperatives, but it also places an extra financial and managerial burden on them.[147]

Another limitation to State action came from the restrictions imposed by the EEC. In 1979, Italy joined the European Monetary Union restricting its currency variation to a maximum of 6%. This was further reduced in January 1990 when Italy joined the narrow band that restricted variation to a maximum of 2.5%.[148] Further pressures on the Italian State have been imposed by the Maastricht treaty signed in 1991. This treaty expects each member nation to have a maximum budget deficit of 3% of the GDP, a total outstanding public debt of 60% of the GDP and an inflation rate within 1.5% of the lowest in the EEC.[149] With a public deficit of 104% and a budget deficit of over 10%[150] the only way Italy could reach these goals by 1996 is through massive spending cuts and increased taxes. Both of these measures will reduce domestic demand and virtually abandon the option to stimulate the economy. Further restrictions are imposed by EEC regulations prohibiting State discrimination in procurements contracts[151] and limiting the level of

State support for industries.[152] These combined EEC agreements and rules limit the freedom of the State to manage its national economy.

The combined problems faced by the State and private business in confronting the challenges posed by the world economy, have resulted in low growth rates and high unemployment. Italy experienced negative growth rates in the early 1980s. It later recovered to an average growth rate between 1983-1992 of 2.4% per annum.[153] This low growth rate did not absorb the work-force made redundant by the restructuring process. As a consequence, the manufacturing sector suffered a net loss of 700,000 jobs between 1982-1992.[154] During this period, the level of unemployment never fell below 10%. The inefficiencies of the Italian State are also evident when one considers that Italy spends less on research and development than the European average. Furthermore, in spite of the support received from EEC regional funds, the South has remained underdeveloped. A symbol of this crisis is Italy's decision to opt out of the European Monetary Mechanism in September 1993 leading to a series of devaluations to boost exports.[155]

The Response by Cooperatives. The relationship between the State and cooperatives should be set in the context of the problems confronted by the State and by the Italian economy. In respect of this, while the support received from political parties and from the regions and local councils continued to be crucially important for the development of cooperatives, as was the fact that cooperatives were no longer seen as threatening the national or international order, the most important factor which influenced the State during this period was the economic viability of cooperatives and the contribution they could make in solving the economic, welfare and social problems faced by the State in a changing world economy.

The contribution that cooperatives have made can be examined by analysing the following: the size of La Lega and the whole of the cooperative sector on a national basis; the quality of cooperative growth; the level of integration with the rest of the economy and La Lega's contribution in solving social problems.

Overall, in spite of continuous mergers and takeovers within La Lega, the number of cooperatives increased from 10,680 in 1976 to 12,889 in 1989. Membership increased from 2.8 million members to 4.18 million members and turnover from 2.5 trillion lire to 32.3 trillion lire. A closer analysis of La Lega that compares its economic power at a national, regional and sectoral level reveals the presence of a nationally important economic group of enterprises. On a national level, La Lega produced 2.73% of the national GDP and employed 3% of the national work-force. Statistics for the region of

Emilia Romagna for 1988 show that La Lega's cooperatives controlled 12.75% of the regional GDP, making them a crucial component for the region's economy.[156] Moreover, if the whole of the cooperative sector is considered, then its share of the GDP of Emilia Romagna is close to 25%[157] and the overall employment nationally rises to 6.5%.[158] Thus the first point to make is that La Lega and the cooperative sector, has become a crucial component of a region like Emilia Romagna and an important component of the national economy.

The quality of La Lega's cooperatives can be evaluated in a number of ways. It has become a leader in a number of sectors of the economy including construction, retail and agriculture. Some individual cooperatives such as Sacmi, CMC, La Ceramica, Coop Emilia Veneto, the wine group *Civ and Civ* and many others have become world market leaders. Indeed, by the mid-1980s the combined exports of La Lega's cooperatives became Italy's fourth highest export earner after Fiat, Montedison and Olivetti.[159] Further evidence of the quality of La Lega as an organisation is its ability to provide forms of horizontal and vertical integration which has improved the competitiveness of small and medium size cooperatives.

The level of integration is another factor which helps describe the contribution of La Lega in the national economy. As the case studies on the consortia and the individual cooperatives have shown, La Lega's cooperatives are very integrated with the rest of the economy. In the case of the construction cooperatives, Sacmi and the consumer cooperatives, they are providing either work for other small local firms or retail space for products produced from private enterprises. Thus lower growth in the cooperative sector will also mean lower demand for dependent private firms. Furthermore, in the construction sector in particular, cooperatives, private and State firms work together to outbid foreign competitors in the Italian and foreign markets. Both of these aspects make it difficult for the State to dismiss cooperatives' needs, as this would have negative consequences over the whole of the economy.

La Lega's social policy and its contribution in solving some social problems is another important element of La Lega's power to influence the State. Its activities in this area are many. La Lega's cooperatives have contributed to reducing inflation by keeping food prices and housing prices down.[160] They have been active in reducing unemployment by reinvesting over 90% of their surplus and by creating employment through the "Marcora" job creation scheme. Furthermore, they have employment policies that provide work for the disadvantaged such as the young, immigrants, and women re-entering the work-force.[161] Cooperatives have also put a great deal of effort in trying to create employment in Southern Italy through youth creation projects encouraged by the De Vito programme and by setting up a number of financial and managerial support structures to help cooperatives and small businesses in that region.[162] Cooperatives, like Edilter and Coop Sette, are planning, financing, building and managing city car parks on behalf of local councils, thus solving the cities' traffic problems without any financial outlay from the local council. Finally, with the approval of the local health authorities cooperatives provide some services to citizens saving the council administrative and other fixed costs.[163]

The above information clearly shows that cooperatives are helping the State overcome its financial and managerial deficiencies. In doing so they have contributed by helping the management of the economy, to reduce its welfare expenditure, to implement social employment policies, and to improve the quality of life. This economic source of power, in addition to the social power derived from a large membership and its relation to local economies and the support of political parties, were the main reason why the State continued to support La Lega in the 1980s and early 1990s.

The State responded to cooperatives' needs in a number of ways. First, it made changes to cooperative law facilitating self-finance capabilities by increasing the amount that could be invested as members' shares and loans; it made non-taxable the profits deposited in the indivisible reserves account, and in 1992 it allowed cooperatives to attract external shareholders. Second, it provided funds for employment creation projects such as the "Marcora Law" and "De Vito Law". Third, as the case studies have shown, the State provided cooperatives and consortia access to a variety of resources owned by the State. These included access to public works; funds to manufacturing and construction cooperatives through special State schemes promoting innovation and technology; funds from Ministries; technological collaboration with State owned Institutions such as the National Research Centre and Universities; cheap loans from the cooperative branch of the BNL; risk capital and managerial expertise from its banking sector (to leasing, factoring and banks of La Lega).[164]

Conclusion

The purpose of this chapter was to outline when and why the State supported cooperatives in Italy. It also distinguishes between the general characteristics of the Italian State and the nation-specific aspects that set it apart from its Western counterparts. This was followed by an historical analysis of

State/cooperative relations between 1943-1991. The findings from this chapter have indicated that the relationship between the State and cooperatives is a dynamic one. These changes have taken place when a series of related political, social and economic factors influenced the State. The findings indicate that the State is most likely to support cooperatives when a series of interrelated factors coincide. These are:

- The State is most likely to support cooperatives when it is in crisis. The Italian case indicates that the State increased its support given to cooperatives when it faced difficulties in managing the economy, in providing adequate welfare and in solving a number of social problems such as an underdeveloped South and unemployment. In this context, the cooperative sector contributed to economic growth providing revenue for the State and secondly, it helped solve social problems, thus strengthening its legitimacy *vis-à-vis* the people.
- The State is most likely to support cooperatives if they do not challenge the existing national social and economic order and the State's relations in the international order. The State was more willing to support La Lega when the latter accepted the workings of a mixed economy operating within a liberal democratic system, and an international order where Italy is part of a USA-led Western alliance and a full member of the EEC.
- A major factor which led the State to support cooperatives derived from the pluralist nature of the Italian State. The pluralist features include power sharing arrangements between political parties and between the national and the sub-national units of the State. The fact that La Lega had good relations with political parties of the left and good working relations with local authorities, enabled it to influence public policy at the national and local level and to have access to resources from all tiers of the State.
- The next major factor of why the State supported La Lega is to be found within La Lega. It slowly became a group of enterprises with substantial economic and political power as its level of membership, employment and turnover has indicated. This was further helped by La Lega's strategy of helping the State solve some of its most pressing problems and to become an integrated part of the economic and political system through a policy of alliances at the economic and political level.

The outcomes of this study on State-cooperative relations have two major implications for cooperative movements in other countries. The first lesson that can be learnt is the need to develop a political culture geared to understanding the powers of the State as a prerequisite for targeted political action. There is a clear indication that La Lega identified the major power centres of the State in political parties, sub-national governments, the Parliament, ministries (especially the Ministry for Labour) and public corporations. It also influenced the State through its own economic and social powers within and without the State. The findings show that La Lega influenced the State from within through its own members of Parliament, its alliance with political parties, and by having members sit on board of directors of the BNL and various regional institutions.

The second lesson that can be learnt from the strategy adopted by La Lega is to develop a continuous relationship with the State. This strategy can be defined as both collaborative and integrational. La Lega clearly understood the functions of the State in a modern capitalist society and sought to develop a collaborative relationship by promoting a strategy aimed at helping the State solve some of society's major problems. The policy to invest in Southern Italy, to construct low cost housing, to take over enterprises in crisis, to contain prices, are all part of this strategy. In addition, La Lega became an integral part of the State at the institutional level (it managed to elect its own Members of Parliament, it supported political parties, it was represented in various State and regional bodies). This was duplicated at the economic level through a range of alliances and collaboration between cooperatives, consortia and the State through the latter's own public corporations, research institutes, banks and local health authorities.

Notes

1 Norberto Bobbio, *The Future of Democracy: a Defence of the Rules of the Game*, Richard Bellamy (ed), University of Minnesota Press, Minneapolis, 1987, p.21. Yves Mény, Government and Politics in Western Europe: Britain, France, Italy and Germany, Oxford University Press, Second Edition, 1993, pp.1-8.

2 David Held, "Central Perspectives on the Modern State", in Gregor McLennan et al., *The Idea of the Modern State,* Open University Press, Milton Keynes, 1984, p.40.

3 Gustavo Gozzi, "Stato Contemporaneo", in Norberto Bobbio (ed), *Dizionario di Politica*, Utet, Torino 1990, pp.1105-1106. Gloria Regonini, "Stato del Benessere', in Norberto Bobbio (ed), *Dizionario di Politica*, Utet, Torino 1990, pp.1114-1118.

4 RC Birch, *The Shaping of the Welfare State*, Longman, London, 1984, pp.22-67.
5 Fabrizio Clementi et al., *Costituzione della Repubblica Italiana: il Testo, la Storia, la Spiegazione*, Avvenimenti Supplement, 1 Maggio 1991, pp.7-8.
6 Roberto Romano, *Nascita dell'Industria in Italia*, Editori Riuniti, Roma, 1984, p.92.
7 Valerio Castronovo, *L'Industria Italiana dall'Ottocento a Oggi*, Arnoldo Mondadori Editore, Milano, 1990, p.147.
8 Paul Furlong, "State, Finance and Industry in Italy", in Andrew Cox (ed), *State Finance and Industry: A Comparative Analysis of Post War Trends in Six Advanced Industrial Economies, Wheatsheaf Books*, Sussex, 1986, pp.143-148.
9 Romano, *op.cit.*, p.126.
10 Sylos Labini, *Le Classi Sociali Negli Anni Ottanta,* Laterza, Bari, 1986, p.22.
11 In 1950 the average tariff protection rate for Italian goods was 24%. See Martin Clark, *Modern Italy: 1871-1982*, Longman, London, 1984, p.350.
12 Between 1962 and 1971 the Lira was devalued by 50%. See Castronovo, *op.cit.*, *L'Industria Italiana dall'Ottocento ad Oggi*, p.321.
13 Patrizio Bianchi et al., "Privatisation in Italy: Aims and Constraints", *West European Politics*, Volume 11, October 1988, Number 4, pp.92-93.
14 Enrico Marro, "Ogni Cento Lire Quattro Alle Imprese", *Il Corriere della Sera*, 24 Settembre 1991, p.3.
15 Frederick Spotts and Theodor Wieser, *Italy:A Difficult Democracy*, Cambridge University Press, Cambridge, 1986, pp.129-137. Sabino Cassese, *Il Sistema Amministrativo Italiano*, Società Editrice Il Mulino, Bologna, 1983, pp.243-271.
16 Spotts and Wieser, *op.cit.*, pp.137-138.
17 Renzo Rosati and Roberto Seghetti, "Stato Padroncino", *Panorama*, 26 Luglio 1992, p.179.
18 Giorgio Galli, *Storia dei Partiti Politici Europei: Dal 1649 a Oggi*, Rizzoli, Milano, 1990, p.248.
19 Giuseppe Mammarella, *Italy After Fascism*, Mario Casalini Ltd, Montreal, 1964, pp.80-81.
20 Giuliano Procacci, *Storia Degli Italiani*, Editori Laterza, 1984, p.546. Note that the ex-Fascists also regrouped in a neo-Fascist party called the Italian Social Movement, but it has never received more than 7% of the national vote and has not had a major influence on Italian politics between 1945-1992.
21 Gianfranco Pasquino, "Partiti, Società Civile, Istituzioni e il Caso Italiano", *Stato e Mercato*, Numero 8, Agosto, 1983, pp.172-173.
22 A study of the Christian Democrats in 1966 revealed that it organised youth associations numbering 200,000 members, the Catholic trade union 2.4 million, Catholic Action 2.4 million, the Association of Catholic Workers (ACLI) 1 million, cooperatives 2 million, small landowners association (Coldiretti) 3.4 million, 60,000 school teachers, 100,000 activists, 1.4 million party members, plus it sold 2.3 million copies per week of newspapers and magazines. See Giorgio Galli, *Il Bipartitismo Imperfetto: Comunisti e Democristiani in Italia*, Mondadori Editore, Milano 1984, pp.197-198.
23 *Ibid.*, p.147.
24 Galli, *op.cit.*, *Storia dei Partiti Politici Europei: Dal 1649 a Oggi*, p.173.
25 Gianfranco Pasquino, "Italian Christian Democracy: A Party for all Seasons" in *Italy in Transition,* Peter Lange and Sydney Tarrow (ed), Frank Cass, London, 1980, pp.100-101.

26 Carlo Donolo, "Social Change and the Transformation of the State in Italy", in Richard Scase (ed), *The State in Western Europe*, Croom Helm, London, 1980, p.178.
27 Pasquino, *op.cit.*, "Italian Christian Democracy: A Party for all Seasons", pp.100-101.
28 Donald Sassoon, *Contemporary Italy: Politics, Economy and Society Since 1945*, Longman, New York, 1986, p.188.
29 For a good discussion on this see Raffaella Y Nanetti, *Growth and Territorial Policies: The Italian Model of Social Capitalism,* Pinter Publishers, London, 1988, Chapter Three.
30 Raphael Zarinski, "Italy", Peter H. Merkl (ed), *Western European Party Systems: Trends and Prospects*, Collier Macmillan Publishers, London, 1980, pp.144-146.
31 Sassoon, *op.cit.*, p.190.
32 Wolfgang Achtner, "The Italian Economic Mirage", *The Spectator*, 29 August 1992, p.16.
33 Sabino Cassese, "Hypothesis on the Italian Administrative System", *West European Politics*, Volume 16, Number 3, (July 1993), p.325.
34 Sassoon, *op.cit.*, Chapter 10.
35 Annarita Criscitiello, "Majority Summits: Decision-Making Inside the Cabinet and Out: Italy, 1970-1990", *West European Politics,* Volume 16, Number 4 (October 1993), pp.581-594.
36 Spotts and Wieser, *op.cit.*, p.148.
37 Joseph La Palombara, *Democracy Italian Style*, Yale University Press, New Haven, 1987, p.78.
38 Sabino Cassese e Rita Perez, *Istituzioni di Diritto Pubblico*, La Nuova Italia Scientifica, Roma, 1989, p.255.
39 Initially, regionalism lacked the support of the major parties. Other than the small Action Party and a small section of the Christian Democratic Party, the bulk of the Christian Democrats, Communists and Socialists were against it. The latter two feared that a decentralised State would have hampered the agrarian reform (redistribution of land to the peasants), and since they hoped to win the 1948 elections they continued to support a centralised State. After the 1948 elections when the DC won on a landslide 48% of the votes, the left parties supported the formations of regional governments to reduce the power of the DC. The latter resisted any sharing of power because regional elections would have given the Communists power in the centre of Italy in the regions of Tuscany, Emilia Romagna and Umbria. Bruno Dente, "Il Governo Locale", in Giorgio Freddi (ed), *Scienze dell'Amministrazione e Politiche Pubbliche,* La Nuova Italia Scientifica, Roma, 1989, pp.128-129.
40 Cassese, *op.cit.*, *Il Sistema Amministrativo Italiano*, p.163.
41 P A Allum, *Italy-Republic Without Government?*, Weidenfeld and Nicolson, London, 1973, pp.217-220.
42 Nanetti, *op.cit.*, p.96.
43 Robert H Evans, "Regionalism and the Italian City", in Michael C Romanos (ed), *Western European Cities in Crisis*, Lexington Books, Lexington, 1979, p.224.
44 Raphael Zariski, "Approaches to the Problem of Local Autonomy: The Lessons of Italian Regional Devolution", *West European Politics*, Volume 8, Number 3, July 1985, p.70.
45 Sassoon, *op.cit.*, p.210.
46 Gianni Carbonaro, "Le Politiche Pubbliche in Agricoltura", in Stefano Zan (ed), *Le Interdipendenze Organizzative in Agricoltura*, Regione Emilia Romagna, Bologna, 1987, pp. 41-58.
47 Spotts and Wieser, *op.cit.*, p.229.

48 Dente, *op.cit.*, p.156.
49 *Ibid.*, p.132
50 Dr Boselli, President of Emilia Romagna, speech given at the Regional Congress of La Lega of Emilia Romagna, Imola 20-21 March, 1991.
51 Bruno Dente, *op.cit.*, p.140.
52 Garzanti Editore, *Enciclopedia Del Diritto e Dell'Economia,* Milano, 1985, pp.1091.
53 Nanetti, *op.cit.*, Chapter 6.
54 For an overview of Emilia Romagna's Policies see Claudio Tolomelli, "Policies to Support Innovation in Emilia Romagna: Experiences and Prospects and Theoretical Prospects", in Enrico Ciciotti et al., *Technological Change in a Spatial Context,* Springer-Verlag, Berlin, 1989, pp.356-378. Leonardo Parri, "Politiche Locali per l'Innovazione Tecnologica: Rhone Alpes ed Emilia Romagna", *Stato e Mercato,* Il Mulino, Bologna, Aprile 1991, pp.77-116. Sebastiano Brusco, "The Emilian Model: Productive Decentralisation and Social Intergration", *Cambridge Journal of Economics,* 1982, 6, pp.167-184. For specific information on Ervet see Ervet, *Profilo e Strategie D'Intervento del Sistema Ervet,* Bologna, 1990; and Ervet, *Attività e Composizione del Sistema Ervet,* Bologna, 1990.
55 Philip Armstrong, Andrew Glyn and John Harrison, *Capitalism Since World War 2,* Fontana, London, 1984, p.90.
56 Paul Ginsborg, *A History of Contemporary Italy: Society and Politics 1943-1988,* Penguin Books, London, 1990, p.88.
57 *Ibid.*, p.99.
58 L Pestolazzi, *La Costituzione e lo Stato*, Editori Riuniti, Roma, 1975, p.207.
59 Valerio Castronovo, "Dal Dopoguerra a Oggi", in Renato Zangheri (et al.,) *Storia del Movimento Cooperativo in Italia*, Einaudi Editore, Torino, 1987, p.595.
60 *Ibid.*, pp.500-507.
61 John Earle, *The Italian Cooperative Movement*, Allen and Unwin, London, 1986, p.330.
62 Ginsborg, *op.cit*, pp.115-118.
63 Sassoon, *op.cit.*, p.37.
64 Castronovo, *op.cit.*, *L'Industria Italiana Dall'Ottocento a Oggi*, p.277.
65 Sassoon, *op.cit.*, pp.37-39.
66 Andrew Shonfield, *Modern Capitalism: The Changing Balance of Public and Private Power*, Oxford University Press, London, 1965, pp.184-185.
67 Clarke, *op.cit.*, p.330.
68 Sassoon, *op.cit.*, p.40.
69 Hermann Van Der Wee, *Prospects and Upheaval: The World Economy 1945-1980*, Penguin, Harmondsworth, 1987, p.50.
70 Ruggero Spesso, *L'Economia Italiana dal Dopoguerra ad Oggi*, Editori Riuniti, Roma, 1987, pp.53 and 97.
71 Castronovo, *op.cit.*, "Dal Dopoguerra a Oggi", p.623.
72 *Ibid.*, p.712.
73 There were three national authorities which provided public housing: INA-CASA (Institute of Public Housing); GESCAL (Authority for Workers Housing), IACP (Autonomous Institute for Popular Housing). See Ginsborg, *op.cit.*, p.247.
74 Giorgio Rochat (ed), *La Casa in Italia 1945-1980: alle Radici del Potere Democristiano*, Zanichelli Editore, Bologna, pp.17, 35, 58-59.

75 Giuseppe Mammarella, *L'Italia Contemporanea: 1943-1989*, Il Mulino, Bologna, 1990, p.149.
76 Guido Fabiani, "L'Agricoltura, Passato e Futuro", in *Profili dell'Italia Repubblicana*, Editori Riuniti, Roma, 1985, p.155.
77 Ginsborg, *op.cit.*, p.139.
78 Between 1948-1956, 15,835 persons in the province of Bologna alone were placed on trial for various offences against the public order. Some of these were placing posters on walls or even selling the Communist daily L'Unità. In 1960, during a demonstration against the newly formed centre right government the police fired on the protesters killing five persons. Pier Paolo D'Attorre, "La Politica", in Renato Zangheri (ed), *Bologna*, Laterza Editori, Bari, 1986, p.169. Nicola Lisanti, *Il Movimento Operaio in Italia: 1860-1980*, Editori Riuniti, Roma, 1986, p.109.
79 Earle, *op.cit.*, pp.31-32.
80 Castronovo, *op.cit.*, "Dal Dopoguerra a Oggi", p.665.
81 For further information discussed in this section, refer to Chapter four, pp. 86-88.
82 Donald Sassoon, "The Italian Communist Party's European Strategy", *Political Quarterly*, Volume 47, Number 3, July-September 1976, pp.253-275. Giorgio Amendola, "Speech at the Conference of Communist Parties of Capitalist Europe", in Peter Lange and Maurizio Vannicelli (ed), *The Communist Parties of Italy, France and Spain*, George Allen and Unwin, 1981, USA, p.307. Alfredo Reichlin, "Il PCI e L'Europa", *Rinascita*, Numero 47, Anno 32, 28 Novembre 1975, p.2.
83 The percentage of national income going to wage and salary earners increased from 57% in 1960 to 69% in 1970. Spesso, *op.cit.*, p.87.
84 Peter Lange and Maurizio Vannicelli, "Strategy Under Stress: the Italian Trade Union Movement and the Italian Crisis in Developmental Perspective", in Peter Lange et al., *Unions, Change and Crisis: French and Italian Union Strategy and the Political Economy 1945-1980*, George Allen and Unwin, London, 1982, p.126.
85 AG Kenwood and AL Lougheed, *The Growth of the International Economy: 1820-1980*, George Allen and Unwin, London, 1984, p.284.
86 For instance in 1980 Italy produced 2.2 billion kilowatts of alternative power energy compared to Switzerland 16.2, UK 33, GDR 38.4, and France 52.3. See Paolo Forcellini, "L'Industria tra Crisi e Terza Rivoluzione", in Ottavio Cecchi and Enrico Ghidetti (ed), *Profili dell'Italia Repubblicana*, Editori Riuniti, 1985, p.283.
87 Spesso, *op.cit.*, p.97.
88 Castronovo, *op.cit.*, *L'Industria Italiana dall'Ottocento ad Oggi*, p. 319.
89 *Ibid.*, pp.337-338.
90 In 1958 imports and exports accounted for 22% of the GDP, by 1974 this percentage had increased to 53.5%. Sasoon, *op.cit.*, *Contemporary Italy: Politics, Economics and Society Since 1945*, p.70.
91 Between 1971 and 1981 the number of enterprises employing less than 99 persons increased their share of employment in the manufacturing sector from 53.2% to 59.2%, those employing 100-499 persons decreased their percentage from 23.2% to 21.2 % (-2%), and those employing more than 500 persons had their share reduced from 23.6% to 19.65 (-4%). OECD Economic Surveys, *Italy* , Paris 1991, p.62.
92 For a survey of immigrant labour in Italy see Giuseppe Sciortino, "Immigration Into Europe and Public Policy: Do Stops Really Work?", *New Community*, 18 (10), pp.89-99.
93 Castronovo estimated that in all 7 million people were working in the hidden economy in Italy. See Castronovo, *op.cit.*, *L'Industria Italiana dall'Ottocento ad Oggi*, p.328.

94 See Charles F. Sabel, *Work and Politics: The Division of Labour in Industry*, Cambridge University Press, New York, 1982, pp.220-231; F Pyke (ed), *Industrial Districts and Inter-Firm Co-operation in Italy*, International Institute for Labour Studies, Geneva, 1990.
95 Patrizio Bianchi, "The IRI in Italy: Strategic Role and Political Constraints", *West European Politics*, Volume 10, April 1987, Number 2, pp.278-282.
96 Patrizio Bianchi, Sabino Cassese and Vincent Della Sala, "Privatisation in Italy: Aims and Constraints", *Western European Politics*, October 1988, Number 4, p.92.
97 GEPI rescued 205 companies between 1971 and 1990. OECD, *op.cit.*, p.79.
98 Castronovo, *op.cit.*, *L'Industria Italiana dall'Ottocento ad Oggi*, p.338.
99 *Ibid.*
100 Sassoon, *op.cit.*, *Contemporary Italy: Politics, Economy and Society Since 1945*, p.57.
101 Garzanti Editore, *op.cit.*, p.1263.
102 Donolo, *op.cit.*, pp.182-183.
103 Furlong, *op.cit.*, p.157.
104 Paolo Leon, "I Limiti della Politica Economica: né Stato, né Mercato", in Ottavio Cecchi and Enrico Ghidetti (eds), *Profili dell'Italia Repubblicana*, Editori Riuniti, 1985, p.340.
105 Jenny Thornley, "Workers Cooperatives and Trade Unions: the Italian Experience", *Economic Industrial Democracy*, Volume 4, London, 1983, p.331.
106 For instance in 1951 43% of the active population was engaged in agriculture, by 1971 this was reduced to 18% and by 1983 to 13%. Labini, *op.cit.*, p.22.
107 Catholic Action had three million members in the early 1950s but could only master 600,000 members by 1979. ACLI (the Association of Catholic Workers) also saw its membership decline from one million to 400,000. See Gianfranco Pasquino, *op.cit.*, "Italian Christian Democracy: a Party for All Seasons", pp.90-93.
108 Coldiretti is a small farmers' association. In its heyday it numbered more than 3 million members, 12,000 branches spread in the countryside and boasted that it elected up to 52 parlamentarians. Gianni Corbi, "Quella Fiat Agricola Targata Scudocrociato", *La Repubblica,* 21 May 1991, p.9.
109 Ginsborg, *op.cit.*, p.442.
110 Between 1969 and 1974, 50 people were killed and 351 injured during terrorist attacks attributed mainly to right wing forces. Left wing terrorists began killing just before the 1976 election, killing the ex Prime Minister Aldo Moro in 1978. M Brutti., "Sotto il Segno Dell'Emergenza", *Rinascita,* Numero 27, 12 Luglio 1986, p.37. Giorgio Galli, "Per Una Storia del Partito Armato", *Panorama*, 12 Novembre 1984, p.137.
111 Guido Martinotti, "Electoral Trends in Italy: The Cycle 1970-1985", *West European Politics*, April 1986, p.269.
112 Furlong, *op.cit.*, pp.160-163.
113 Cassese, *op.cit.*, "Hypothesis on the Italian Administrative System", p.319.
114 Castronovo, *op.cit.*, "Dal Dopoguerra ad Oggi", p.738. Vincenzo Galetti, *La Cooperazione in Italia*, Editori Riuniti, Roma, 1976, p.51.
115 Garzanti Editore, *op.cit.*, p.1263.
116 M D'Ambrosio and R Stefanelli, *La Cooperazione nell'Industria*, Editrice Cooperativa, Roma, 1983, p.75.
117 Robert Oakeshott, *The Case for Workers' Cooperatives*, Routledge and Kegan Paul, London, 1978, p.152.

118 See La Lega, "Per Una Politica di Piano", dalla Dichiarazione Programmatica della LNCM, Roma, 1962, in Walter Briganti (ed), *Il Movimento Cooperative in Italia 1926-1962, Editrice Cooperativa,* Roma, 1978, pp.372-376. La Lega, "La Linea della Lega al 28mo Congresso", in Walter Briganti ed., *Il Movimento Cooperativo in Italia 1963-1980*, Editrice Cooperativa, Roma, 1982, pp.134-151. Silvio Miana, "Proposte Programmatiche del Movimento Cooperativo", Relazione Introduttiva al 29mo Congresso della Lega (1973), in Walter Briganti (ed), *Il Movimento Cooperativo in Italia 1963-1980,* Editrice Cooperativa, Roma, 1982, pp.208-218.
119 Max Jaggi (et al.), *Red Bologna*, Writers and Readers, London, 1977, p.58.
120 For further information on these State measures refer to Chapter 4, pp.104-108.
121 For further information on these State measures refer to Chapter 4, pp.95-96.
122 Theodore Levitt, "The Globalisation of Market", *Harvard Business Review*, May-June 1983, Number 3, p.93.
123 In 1988, the average monthly wage stood at US $643 in Taiwan, $558 in Hong Kong, $401 in Singapore, $610 in Korea, $132 in Thailand, $129 in Malaysia, and $209 in Indonesia. See Walden Bello and Stephanie Rosenfeld, *Dragons in Distress: Asia's Miracle Economies in Crisis*, Penguin Books, London 1990.
124 The degree of unonism is very low, for instance only 14% of the workforce are union members in Hong Kong, Thailand (1.01%), Indonesia (4.08%), South Korea (7%), Malaysia (8.07%), Singapore (16%), Taiwan (17.03%). See Abe David and Ted Wheelwright, *The Third Wave: Australia and Asian Capitalism*, Left Book Club, 1989, pp.216-228.
125 *The Australian,* "Why Gatt Matters", 6 December 1993, p.9.
126 For instance Fiat sacked 23,000 workers in 1980. See Armstrong, *op.cit.,* p.380.
127 Benetton, a clothes manufacturer, employs fewer than two thousand workers and puts out four fifths of its business to a network of small firms. See *The Economist,* "Survey: Italy", May 26 1990, p.29.
128 The advantages of raising finance through issuing shares are: avoidance of having to pay interests, the freedom to pay dividends to shareholders only if the company makes a profit and then only if the executive decides that it is wise to do so (they may decide to reinvest it), and finally, shareholders are free to sell their shares at a profit if the company is viable. This is an enormous advantage that private companies hold over cooperatives. For a thorough and clear description on how companies raise money and various types of shares see Colin Howard, *Companies: What Are They And How They work*, Oxford, Melbourne, 1989.
129 Alberto Zevi, "La Strumentazione Finanziaria per le Imprese Cooperative", in *La Lega: La Questione Finanziaria e Lo Sviluppo Dell'Impresa Cooperativa,* Editrice Cooperativa, Roma, 1984, p.45.
130 Between 1977 and 1981 foreign borrowing as a proportion of external corporate financing increased from 7% to over 20%. See Paul Furlong, *op.cit.*, pp.155-156.
131 Between 1987 and 1989 alone the large Italian holding groups engaged in 308 operations which involved either mergers or acquisitions. Rossella Bocciarelli, "Rigore D'Europa", *L'Espresso*, 14 Ottobre 1990, p.167.
132 Patrizio Bianchi, "The Political Limits on European Economic Intergration", in Raffaella Nanetti and Raimondo Catanzaro (ed), *Italian Politics: A Review Volume 4*, Printers Publishers, London, 1990, p.46.
133 Raffaella Polato, "Foto di Gruppo con Imprese in Rosso", *Corriere della Sera*, 15 Ottobre 1992, p.27.
134 Istituto Nazionale di Statistica, *Introducing Italy*, Rome, 1990, p.43.

135 Between 1985-1992 Italian textile firms have bought controlling shares in 367 textile firms overseas. See *Panorama*, "Shopping per Forza", 7 Giugno 1992, p.193.
136 A good discussion on this theme is found in Patrizio Bianchi, *op.cit.*, "The Political Limits on European Economic Intergration", pp.36-57.
137 See Tullio Fazzolari, "Assalto Al Piatto", *L'Espresso*, 22 Gennaio 1989, pp.158-162. Antonio Macaluso, "Nestle si Mangia il Panettone", *Corriere della Sera*, 30 Luglio 1993, p.14.
138 Enrico Marro, *op.cit.*, p.3.
139 Robert Graham, "Italians Lose Golden Pensions", *Financial Times*, 11 July 1991, p.2.
140 *The Economist*, op. cit., "A Survey of Italy", 1993, p.16.
141 Maurizio Tortorella, *op.cit.,* p.53.
142 *The Economist*, *op.cit.*, "A Survey of Italy", 1993, p.20.
143 For the 1980 figures see the excellent article by Patrizio Bianchi, "The Iri in Italy: Strategic Role and Political Constraints", *West European Politics*, Volume 10, Number 2, April 1987, p.273. For the 1991 figures see, Renzo Rosati and Roberto Seghetti, "Stato Padroncino", *Panorama*, 26 Luglio 1992, p.182.
144 Between 1971 and 1980 IRI sold 18 companies and bought 55; between 1983-1985 Iri sold 20 and acquired only 1. See OECD Economic Surveys, *Italy*, Paris, 1989, p.52.
145 Enrico Marro, "Diecimila Miliardi per L'IRI", *Corriere della Sera*, 30 December 1993, p.17.
146 In Southern Italy usually 30% of the money allocated for public works is not spent. Gianfranco Franci, "Lavori a Rilento a Sud", *La Cooperazione Italiana*, Giugno-Luglio 1992, p.52.
147 Stefano Stanghellini, "L'Impresa di Costruzione Soggetto Innovativo nel Processo Produttivo delle Opere Complesse", Ecosfera (ed), *Le Imprese di Costruzione nel Mercato Europeo*, Il Sole 24 Ore, Milano, 1990, p.201.
148 *The Economist*, "Italy: a Survey", 26 May 1990, pp.5 and 11.
149 *The Economist*, *op.cit.*, "A Survey of Italy", 1993, p.21.
150 Robert Graham, "Doctor Subtle's Twin Pillars", *Financial Times*, 16 July 1992.
151 In 1990 the European Court of Justice declared illegal an Italian practice which obliged the State owned enterprises to buy 30% of its supplies from companies based in Southern Italy. See *The Economist*, *op.cit.*, "Italy: a Survey", 1990, p.20.
152 The EEC has been mounting pressure on the Italian State to reduce firm subsidies, see Enrico Marro, *op.cit.*, p.3.
153 *The Australian*, "Lucky Countries", January 1-2 1994, p.16.
154 Edoardo Marinelli, "La Crisi Pesa Sui Bilanci Industriali", *La Cooperazione Italiana*, Giugno-Luglio 1993, p.40.
155 *The Economist*, *op.cit.*, "Italy: a Survey", 1993, p.20.
156 For details of how the percentages were calculated see Chapter 1, Notes 10, 11 and 13.
157 Giancarlo Pasquini and Francesco Pagnetti, "Analisi della Legislazione Cooperativa in Emilia Romagna", *Rivista Della Cooperazione*, Nuova Serie, Numero 12, Luglio-Settembre 1982, pp.83-102.
158 Rino Petralia, "I Nostri Diritti", in Sandro Bonella (ed), *I Lacci di Gulliver:Deregulation e Movimento Cooperativo*, Editrice Cooperativa, Roma, 1986, p.140.
159 Castronovo, *op.cit.*, "Dal Dopoguerra ad Oggi", p.833.
160 In the eighties cooperatives built houses at costs 20%-30% lower than the market rate. Consumer prices of the consumer cooperative of Bologna, Coop Emilia Veneto, were 1.25%

below the national average and 2% below the average in Bologna. See Le Certificate, "Una Forza a Servizio della Qualita Urbana", *La Cooperazione Italiana,* Novembre/Dicembre 1988, p.147. For figures regarding the consumer sector see Coop Emilia Veneto, *Bilancio di Responsabilita Sociale 1990*, Bologna 1991, p.2.

161 See the case study on Coop Emilia Veneto in Chapter 8.

162 Laura Lupo, "I Pezzi della Rete del Mezzogiorno", *La Cooperazione Italiana*, Marzo 1990, pp.12-15.

163 See the case study on Spepcoop in Chapter 8.

164 For further information refer to Chapter 4, pp.104-108.

10 La Lega: a Solution to Cooperative Problems

The previous chapters have provided empirical information on the structure of La Lega and the contribution that the various component parts have made in improving the competitiveness of cooperatives. The purpose of this chapter is to define and evaluate the role of La Lega as an organisation. In doing so problems within the organisation will be identified and the course taken to overcome them will be analysed.

This chapter is divided in five parts. Part one will commence by synthesising the main features of La Lega as an organisation which have been identified in previous chapters. Part two will discuss La Lega's system of authority. Part three develops a concise definition of La Lega today. Part four is a discussion of the problems confronting La Lega. The final part will be an assessment of recent policy statements and organisational changes made by La Lega to solve its problems and to delineate a future path for cooperative growth.

The Main Features of La Lega

The main structural features of La Lega are the Central Association, the various consortia and cooperative owned conventional companies and individual cooperatives. In addition, La Lega has developed systemic features which have developed a level of economic integration between cooperatives from within a sector and within different sectors in which the large cooperatives play a central role.

The Central Association is present throughout the national territory through a decentralised structure comprising territorial and sectoral structures. It associates cooperatives from all sectors of the economy and provides them with a number of services. It provides guidance and cohesiveness by promoting shared values, a collaborative culture and by managing conflicts. It has given cooperatives a strategy which has led to the development of new sectors and successful business strategies. It has played an important role in promoting the interests of cooperatives versus the State at all levels of government. It has managed to promote new cooperatives in new economic sectors. It has successfully converted ailing private enterprises into cooperatives. It has also provided services such as legal and administrative skills, has negotiated industrial relations agreements, conducted research and supplied data from the EEC.

The second component of La Lega's structure is the various consortia and the financial companies. These organisations have given cooperatives the opportunity to achieve economies of scale and become highly competitive by providing them with loans or access to loans, lowering costs through common policies in purchasing goods and raw materials, in marketing, in bidding for public contracts, in engaging in research and development, and in getting wide ranging information about the markets in which they operate. They have also contributed in the creation of a cohesive cooperative sector by achieving operational interdependencies among cooperatives, by managing conflicts and by developing common strategies.

The third feature of La Lega, which is directly related to the role played by the consortia, is the level of economic integration between different cooperative sectors. Two sets of interconnecting sectors were identified. One is formed by the agricultural, manufacturing and the consumer sector, with the latter selling the food and goods produced by the other two, mainly from the agricultural sectors. The other is formed by the housing, the manufacturing and the construction cooperatives. In this case housing creates a demand for the construction cooperatives which in turn create a demand for the products made by the manufacturing cooperatives.

The fourth feature is the role played by the large cooperatives within the organisation. The large cooperatives provide most of the contractual power for the consortia. They also provided the bulk of the finance for Fincooper and Unipol Finance, especially the large consumer cooperatives. They provide La Lega with an image of competitiveness since they can compete with large private enterprises in Italy and abroad. Finally, they play a central role in La Lega's overall strategy of becoming a national public policy maker with the ability to solve some of the State's economic and social problems.

The discussion so far has identified four main features of La Lega and how each of these contribute in making cooperatives more competitive in the market place, and in giving the direction and maintaining cohesiveness. A major element of the success of La Lega has undoubtedly been its ability to keep its cooperative members united and to be able to get them to follow policy directions. The discussion so far has given a number of reasons which explain the ability of La Lega to maintain unity. The ability to create normative and operational interdependencies and the need for political representation have been undoubtedly elements of unity within La Lega. What needs to be further explored is the decision-making process. This will enable us to find out how La Lega further regulates the various components of the organisation and how it managed to get cooperatives to support the policy directions such as mergers and the policy of alliances. This is especially important because each cooperative is an autonomous unit in that cooperatives are free to join and leave La Lega. In fact, the majority of cooperatives in Italy are not members of any Central Association. A necessary underpinning of the decision-making process in any organisation is its system of authority. An understanding of the system of authority will provide an explanation of the decision-making process within La Lega.

La Lega's System of Authority: Directors and Political Parties

Authority is legitimated power, and through legitimation the ability of having a command executed by its subordinates.[1] In the case of La Lega the authority held by National Central Association over its decentralised territorial, sectoral and economic structures (consortia and companies owned by cooperatives) and the individual cooperatives comes from prestige, a common history and a political subculture spread throughout the movement. This type of authority can be classified as being weak as the individual cooperatives and the other structures have no formal obligation to support its decisions. Because of this, decisions are not made in a hierarchical manner, as each other structure is in itself autonomous. For instance, the authority of provincial and regional bodies comes from the member cooperatives of a particular area and not from the Central Association. Similarly, individual cooperatives derive their authority from their members. Thus for La Lega to develop a unitary policy a laborious consultation process must take place where decisions are debated in various bodies.[2] Lanfranco Turci, the ex-president of La Lega provided this account of how the Central Association gets the other structures and cooperatives to arrive at a decision. He states:

> ...our *Central Association* is not an hierarchical structure. It cannot have an hierarchical command over its cooperative members and the various associations and structures of La Lega. It can have a propositional role, a coordinating role, it may even be a business partner but the autonomy of the cooperative enterprise is always safeguarded. We can try to convince them in a thousand ways, we can use various channels of communications such as through the *Sectoral Associations*...but in the final

> analysis it remains an operation of persuasion and not a decision-making operation.[3]

In spite of lacking formal powers La Lega has managed to influence the strategies of the whole of the cooperative sector and that of individual cooperatives. The policy of alliances and the policy of mergers and concentration adopted in the sixties, were policies developed by the Central Association and later promoted within the cooperative sector. According to Zan, La Lega has managed to achieve this by coordinating the activity of its territorial structures, sectoral associations, economic organisations (consortia and other companies) and cooperative enterprises, through a system of "interlocking directorship". This means having the same directors, usually the presidents of cooperatives and/or political appointees, being present in more than one organisation.[4] This arrangement enabled them to provide a link between the various organisations which constitute La Lega and between them and the cooperatives, through which an "established order" in which decisions could be implemented is created. As mentioned earlier, since the various organisations comprising La Lega and the cooperatives are autonomous, these directors, in theory at least, could have made decisions autonomously from the other structures. Zan notes that their ambition to further their career and the political importance of maintaining a unitary movement are also factors impelling them to make decisions in accordance with the general guidelines provided by the Central Association.[5]

It is important to note that the decisions were not made in a hierarchical fashion within a process where the Central Association developed policies and the consortia and the cooperatives followed orders. The policies were developed jointly by the directors of the Central Association, the consortia and the cooperatives. Usually ideas are debated informally through personal relations and formally within the consortia, the sectoral associations, in special conferences and at regional and national conferences. However, a relation of power does exist between the Central Association, the consortia and the cooperatives. La Lega managed to implement the policies of mergers and the policy of alliances because in the 1960s it was the Central Association which possessed more human and financial resources than the cooperatives. This changed in the 1980s, and as it will be discussed later, it influenced the decision-making process of La Lega.

The second element of this "established order" is the role played by political factions. It is they which appoint the directors of the Central Association, the consortia and the companies owned by La Lega.[6] Because of this, political factions then play a very important role in the system of authority within La Lega. They provide unity between individual members and directors, and between cooperatives and La Lega. This is why it is often said that the legitimacy of La Lega comes from political parties. In reality, political parties appoint directors and then cooperatives and their members ratify their decisions. Thus the political parties act as the "ideological cement" and have played a major part in creating the established order through which La Lega has been able to unite and coordinate its members.

Defining La Lega: a Movement, a System or a Network?

In arriving at a definition of what is La Lega today it is worthwhile to discuss the debate within La Lega on how it has defined itself over the years. Since 1945, La Lega has defined itself as a movement, as a system of enterprises and more recently as a network of enterprises. Each of these terms implies a different relationship between the Central Association and its various structures and the individual cooperatives.

The term "movement" has been used from 1945 until the mid-1970s. It implies a cooperative sector strongly inclined towards solving the problems of its individual members and where cooperatives were a means to a political end: the transformation of a capitalist society into a socialist society. In this period the political goals were the primary concern of La Lega.[7]

The term "system" was coined at the 1987 congress. This term emphasises that La Lega's Central Association was a centre which governed its decentralised structures in an hierarchical manner and was able to make decisions on behalf of the individual cooperative enterprises.[8] In fact at times it was said to behave like a "holding company",[9] whilst some of its leaders claimed that it was a "mind complementary to that of the enterprise".[10] The case studies have shown that in the late-1980s this did not take place, as the consortia (CCC) and enterprises (SACMI, CMB, SPEPCOOP) delineated their own strategies. In fact, La Lega was already a system of enterprises between the late-1960s and 1970s when the legitimacy of political parties was very high, when political appointments were not questioned, when there was an homogeneous culture permeating La Lega and when the Central Association and the consortia had more knowledge and resources than the individual cooperatives. During this period the legitimacy of political parties, the cohesiveness of directors and the dependency of cooperatives on the Central Association and the consortia, ensured that the decisions made by the Central Association were carried out by the enterprises. The policy of mergers and alliances is a clear manifestation of this.

In 1991, La Lega was defined as a network of enterprises. A network denotes a relationship of exchange between two or more organisations. However, there are various degrees of networking. Each economic sector (eg consumer cooperatives) is a network where the cooperatives, the consortia and the regional and sectoral associations interact to produce common policies and to exchange resources. A greater form of interaction takes place between those sectors which engage in forms of intersectoral trade such as agriculture, manufacturing and consumer sector. Yet, even the cooperative Sacmi, which has a low level of inter-trade relations with La Lega's cooperatives, but invests in La Lega's financial structures and benefits from the cooperative law, is part of a network. These different levels of networking clearly reflects the reality of La Lega today.

The network also emphasises a different relationship between the enterprise and the Central Association. The decision-making within La Lega becomes a process in which the Central Association, the consortia network and the enterprises (especially the large enterprises) participate with their own strategies and plans.[11] However, in the final analysis, it is the enterprises which must make the final decisions regarding investments and business strategies. As the president Lanfranco Turci stated: "the old model of La Lega has ended...we can no longer propose decisions which are made externally to the enterprises, nor can we appeal to old ideological support."[12] Thus the major changes in the relationship between the cooperatives and La Lega are that cooperatives will have the final say over investment decisions and will have a greater input into the decision-making process. However, La Lega will still perform the role of representing the cooperative interest to society and the State and a coordinating and planning role on behalf of its cooperatives.[13] The latter role can still count on a system of authority which is based on political factions and interlocking directors.

Thus, while La Lega is not a holding company as it does not own the individual enterprises, it is also not a typical business association which simply lobbies the State and influences public opinion on behalf of its members. La Lega does everything a business association does, plus it also coordinates and plans the future strategies of the whole cooperative sector within an original network of relations established over the years. Thus La Lega could be defined as:

> An integrated network of cooperative enterprises comprising of many sub-networks at the sectoral and intersectoral level, which through a Central Association, articulated in decentralised territorial, sectoral and

economic structures, provides normative and operational interdependencies. Through La Lega's structures, which operate on a system of authority based on interlocking directorship and political factions, cooperative enterprises engage in a plurality of economic, commercial and political exchanges which improve their economic competitiveness in the market and their bargaining power when dealing with the State. The network also organises cooperatives of all sizes and all sectors, but it is one in which the large cooperatives from the consumer, construction and manufacturing sectors play an undisputed central role.

Limits Faced by La Lega

As an organisation La Lega faces five major problems which must be overcome if it is to function effectively, these are: problems with the system of authority, evidence of an incoherent strategy developing within the different structures of the Central Association, the persistence of territorial differences in size and economic strength, conflicts between large and small size cooperatives, and problems with the type of image cooperatives hold in society.

The system of authority has a number of problems which could disrupt the whole network. One major problem is that the decision-making process is often slow. This is caused by the conflictual relationship that exist between the political factions and the constant need to arrive at decisions based on consensus.[14] Second, the political factions have usually appointed generalists as directors on the various structures of the Central Association and the consortia at a time when specialist skills are needed. The lack of specialist skills weakens La Lega's capacity to provide adequate services to its cooperative members. This weakens the prestige of directors and the system of authority within La Lega.[15] As Zan has correctly noted, this leads to a crisis of representation as cooperatives begin to question and/or reject the decisions or proposals made by the Central Association.[16] This crisis is further exacerbated by the fact that political parties in Italy have a declining legitimacy.[17] The problems faced by political parties weakens the link between individual members and the political factions which operate within La Lega.

Another problem is the development of incoherent strategies within La Lega's structures. For instance, in the late 1970s La Lega wanted to make the regional territorial structures the main coordinating bodies of La Lega.[18] This has not eventuated. A report by La Lega of Emilia Romagna has found that most of the power in that region still lies with the provincial structures and with some of the more organised sectoral association. It also found that the most innovative ideas on how to best manage change are coming from the individual large cooperatives and not from the Central Association as was the case up to the 1970s. In addition, the report found that different regions and different cooperative sectors are managing change in original ways, indicating further that the development within La Lega is not uniform.[19] This indicates that the Central Association does not have the human resources to provide direction for the whole cooperative sector and that problems do exist with the system of authority.

Another problem developing is the conflict between the large and smaller cooperatives, with the latter accusing La Lega of concentrating their resources on large cooperatives. At the last congress in Bologna one small cooperative alleged that Fincooper did not even consider its application because the amount was too small. Other allegations state that large cooperatives receive the bulk of government projects secured by La Lega. There are a number of reasons why La Lega has placed more emphasis on large cooperatives. First, the large cooperatives are the backbone of the movement as the case studies on the consortia and the financial sector have clearly shown, thus the health of large cooperatives is vital for the success of La Lega's support network. Second, the increased competition coming from Italian and European firms has led La Lega to place more emphasis on economic and managerial matters and to concentrate on creating large competitive cooperatives. The small and medium size cooperatives have responded by organising themselves into a pressure group to further their interest within La Lega's structures and to encourage interfirm collaboration between small firms. One suggestion made by small and medium sized cooperatives is that La Lega at the provincial and regional level should have a separate structure to promote their specific needs.[20]

One of the limitations of La Lega is its inability to effectively reduce the divide between cooperative development in Northern and Southern Italy. While it has succeeded in increasing the number of cooperatives operating in Southern Italy as a percentage of the total number of cooperatives affiliated to La Lega from 5% in 1896 to 30.3% by 1986, (see Table 10.1), their share of the total turnover was only 6.3% in 1986. Indeed, in that same year Northern Italy produced 72% of the turnover and Central Italy 21.3%.[21] A more complete picture emerges when we consider that in 1989 the regions of Emilia Romagna (40.2%) and Tuscany (13.9%) between them produced 54.1% of the total turnover.[22] While cultural and environmental factors should be taken into account, such as the inefficiencies of local government and the lack of interfirm collaboration, the inefficiencies of La Lega's own territorial and sectoral structures are also a factor.[23] One inefficiency is a lack of human and capital resources to promote a strong economic cooperative sector on a national scale. However, this also suggests the limits faced by a decentralised structure like La Lega which operates within a weak system of authority.

Table 10.1 Geographic Distribution of La Lega's Cooperatives

	1896		1920		1976		1986[24]	
Area	No. of coops	% of Total	No. of coops	% of Total	No. of coops	% of Total	No. of coops	% of Total
North	183	72%	2169	69.3%	5,716	53.5%	7,015	43.9%
Centre	58	23%	449	14.4%	2,334	21.9%	4,128	25.8%
South	13	5%	513	16.3%	2,630	24.6%	4,845	30.3%
Total	254	100%	3131	100%	10,680	100%	15,988	100%

Sources: for 1896 see Maurizio Degl'Innocenti, *Storia Della Cooperazione in Italia,* Editore Riuniti, Roma, 1977, pp.126-128; For 1920 see Giuseppe Galasso, "Gli Anni Della Grande Espansione e La Crisi del Sistema", in Renato Zangheri (ed), *Storia del Movimento Cooperativo in Italia*, Giulio Einaudi Editore, Torino, 1987, p.248; For the years 1976 and 1986 see Orazio Pugliese (ed), *Il Sistema Cooperativo*, Marsilio Editori, Venezia, p.208.

A further problem confronting La Lega is to market the cooperative sector in society at large and to portray a favourable image as a cooperative organisation. A couple of reports indicate that La Lega is having problems in both. In 1983 a joint research was conducted by La Lega and a private firm Monitor to discover what people knew about the cooperative sector. In all 2,500 persons were interviewed. The research found was that a large number of interviewees knew La Lega as a powerful economic and political group of cooperatives. It also found that 37% of them preferred to work in a cooperative rather than a private enterprise and that 54.6% preferred to shop at a consumer cooperative. However, it was also found that 80% had no real knowledge of what cooperatives did, how they operated and whether they could solve some of their problems such as job creation or provision of services. Those 20% who did, had a vision of cooperatives as austere low wage enterprises. Whilst this was in part true, most medium to large size cooperatives paid good wages and provided good working conditions.[25] With this perception in the mind of people La Lega risked alienating most of the population, especially professionals, technicians and university graduates who by the 1980s sought high paid jobs and good career prospects.

Another research in this area was promoted in 1989 by the monthly magazine *La Cooperazione Italiana* and conducted by the private firm Imagerie. It entailed analysing 1,000 articles published on La Lega by national, local, party and economic newspapers. It was found that the length of articles were mostly short, written by unknown journalists, there were hardly any in-depth articles nor any interviews of La Lega's directors. They appeared mainly in June-July during the summer breaks when, perhaps the papers were short on news. The themes covered were mainly to do with economic growth (31.6%), business strategies (25.5%), politics (26.6%) and social functions such as interest paid on dividends and number of members (17.3%). What was missing were themes such as democratic management, collective ownership, acts of solidarity, relation with local economy, and possible potential of cooperative sector in the economy.[26]

A number of factors could explain why the media publishes certain information. The privately owned media would not be inclined to promote the idea of collective ownership or democratic management as it challenges the fundamentals of a capitalist society. Media owned by political parties too concentrates on political matters, hence many articles in the Communist daily paper *l'Unità* talks about political factions. However, La Lega is also to blame. Its own monthly magazine, *La Cooperazione Italiana,* during 1990, published hardly any articles on democratic management or on some of the social functions of cooperatives. It too concentrated mainly on economic matters, business strategies, and public policy. Only in 1993 has it started a debate on the mission of cooperatives in the 1990s and is debating issues like ethics, democratic management, solidarity etc.[27]

This inability to portray a realistic picture of cooperatives causes many problems in the public perception of what cooperatives are. Fabrizio Gerbella emphasised this problem when he said: "people and policy makers think that cooperatives are either a community non-profit organisation or a profit-making enterprise no different than private enterprises, both of which are wrong." This may have a negative influence on public policy makers who are not aware of the full potential of the cooperative sector. Evidence of this is the following statement made by the newly appointed director of the cooperative section of the Ministry of Labour, Maurizio Polverari, who said "...we are aware that in Italy there are approximately 100,000 cooperatives employing 500,000 persons, but we do not have a true picture of the real dimension and the full potential of the cooperative sector".[28]

Recent Developments: Overcoming the Problems

The practical problems identified throughout the 1980s were at the centre of a debate within La Lega which culminated with a release of a discussion document by the national executive in late 1990, and continued at the 1991 national, regional and provincial congresses. The outcome of that debate, the changes made to the cooperative law in 1992 and subsequent events have led to a number of significant decisions being made which are attempting to solve some of the problems confronting La Lega.

One of the outcomes involved redefining the relationship between the large enterprises and the Central Association. This had ramifications on the system of authority and on the overall strategies of La Lega. The 1991 congress and the 1992 cooperative law confirmed the importance of the Central Association. The validity of the Central Association in representing the interests of cooperatives *vis-à-vis* the State, in being able to mediate conflicts between cooperatives, in providing a number of administrative and information services and in coordinating the activities of cooperatives from different sectors was confirmed.[29] Its coordinating role was further enhanced by the decision made by the 1992 law to set up a solidarity fund, funded from 3% of the profits from every registered cooperative, which could be used to set up cooperatives in new economic sectors or to increase cooperative development in Southern Italy.

The most significant change however, is the power relationship between the Central Association and the large cooperative enterprises. The 1990 discussion document redefined this relationship. The large cooperatives will now have the responsibility to contribute and to monitor the strategic decisions made in conjunction with the Central Association and the consortia network. The document further stated that it is the responsibility of the large enterprises to give guidance to the whole sector in which they operate.[30] This increase in power of the large enterprises was recently manifested at the companies Unipol Finance and the cooperative bank Banec where the largest cooperative shareholders, the consumer cooperatives, replaced the previous directors who were appointed by the political factions, with the presidents of two consumer cooperatives.[31]

This wider role played by the large cooperatives has influenced La Lega's system of authority. While the political factions and interlocking directorship are still the backbone of the system, the political factions are not as powerful as before. The appointments of directors at Unipol Finance and Banec by the cooperatives is a clear example of this. In addition, in future, specialist managers are to be appointed on the basis of merit and could be recruited from the cooperative, private and State enterprises.[32] It should be noted that the directors appointed at Unipol and Banec are also members of a political faction. However, in being appointed by the enterprise, the directors' legitimacy comes from the enterprise and not the political faction. Thus, a change in the relation of power has taken place.

The changes in the relationship between the Central Association and the enterprise may also provide the basis for a more coherent strategy to develop. If the large enterprises are given more responsibility in the policy-making process then once a decision is made it has a better chance of being implemented. The possibility of developing a more coherent strategy has also been enhanced by the decision made by the general council of La Lega in November 1989 to include in the national executive the presidents of the four largest cooperative sectoral associations (consumers, private retailers, production and labour, and agriculture).[33]

The relationship that should develop between cooperative firms was another topic discussed at the 1991 congress. It was suggested that the relationship between firms should take into account economic and social goals. The 1991 congressional document indicated that the relationship should develop on the basis of solidarity and economic convenience. All things being equal, cooperatives should support other cooperatives as long as this does not reduce their economic competitiveness.[34] Again the emphasis is on economic competitiveness. This is a response to the loss of competitiveness experienced by cooperatives in the early 1980s and to the many occasions when large cooperatives were called on to rescue other cooperatives even though it may not have been economically viable.

The 1990 discussion congress also addressed the "image" problems encountered in previous years within a discussion of the broader goals of cooperation in a modern society. La Lega released a mission statement for the 1990s which contained a number of important points. First, the importance of creating competitive enterprises which could compete in the world market was emphasised. Second, it stressed the social role of cooperatives which is to develop a capacity to solve people's problems such as work, food, housing, health, and improve the general quality of life. Third, it outlined that a major part of the cooperative mission is to expand democracy in the workplace. Fourth, the overall political strategy of the cooperative sector was defined as one whose task is to expand economic democracy and to continue its alliance with artisans and small businesses, but also be open to all progressive large State and private businesses.[35] The 1992 legislation complemented the mission statement. It supported economic competitiveness by introducing forms of external shareholders with voting and non voting rights and it supported the social goals by introducing the solidarity fund and the certification of budgets for large enterprises.[36] This mission statement is an important step in convincing the public that cooperatives are a different form of enterprise than conventional firms and non-profit organisations, while at the same time accepting an economic imperative.

Conclusion: La Lega in Perspective

To understand the changes that are taking place within La Lega it is important to place them in perspective. The changes that have recently been made are a product of the dynamic relationship that exists between cooperatives, La Lega, political parties, the State and the world economy. Today's problems are caused by the inability of the Central Association and the economic structures of La Lega to change according to the needs of the different types of cooperative enterprises. However, La Lega has shown a remarkable ability to identify and to solve these problems. The changes made so far aim at giving cooperatives more power in the decision-making process and at reducing the power of factions. This should produce a more cohesive policy making process in which the cooperatives, the economic structures and the Central Association are equal partners. Considering the success of La Lega as a network of enterprises, gradual reforms seem to be more appropriate than radical ones. In the future, La Lega's success will still depend on its ability to maintain intersectoral unity, to develop suitable and adaptable economic structures and to maintain a culture which is geared to achieving economic efficiency and social goals. This is the strength of the network:

> To be a network does not mean mediating one's interests, but providing an intelligent strategy which is capable of conciliating the principles of solidarity with those of economic convenience, by making sure that convenience will not lead only to enterprise interests and, vice-versa, that solidarity will not be practised at the expense of enterprise convenience.[37]

Notes

1 Max Weber, "Legitimation, Authority and Bureaucracy", from Max Weber, The Theory of Social and Economic Organisation, Free Press, 1947, pp.328-340; in D S Pugh (ed), Organisational Theory, Penguin, Second Edition, 1987, pp.15-27.
2 Stefano Zan, *La Cooperazione in Italia: Strutture, Strategie e Sviluppo della Lega Nazionale delle Cooperative e Mutue*, De Donato, Bari, 1982, p.328.
3 *Sistema*, "Publico Privato e Cooperativo: Protagonisti di un Nuovo Rapporto fra Programmazione, Ambiente e Sistemi Imprenditoriali", Lega delle Cooperative dell' Emilia Romagna, Bologna, Anno 1, Numero 4, Ottobre 1989, p.23.
4 Stefano Zan, "The Management of Entrepreneur Associations: the Case of the National League of Cooperative and Mutual Aid Societies", Paper Presenter at the Joint Session of the European Consortium for Political Research, in the Workshop on "Markets, Politics and Associations: The Case of Consumer Welfare in the Public, Private and Cooperative Sectors", Held at Rimini, Italy, 1988, p.8.
5 Zan, *op.cit.*, *La Cooperazione in Italia: Strategie e Sviluppo della Lega Nazionale delle Cooperative e Mutue*, p.337.
6 For information on how political factions bargain for power see Chapter 5, p.129.
7 Roberto Calari, *Autonomia e Collateralismo del Movimento Cooperativo nella Provincia di Bologna dal 1945-1962. La Lega Provinciale delle Cooperative tra Economia e Politica nel Secondo Dopoguerra*, Tesi di Laurea, Facoltá di Scienze Politiche, Università degli Studi di Bologna, 1989, p.221.
8 Onelio Prandini, "Relazione Introduttiva", in *Societa, Economia Impresa: La Proposta Cooperativa*, Atti del 32mo Congresso della Lega, Roma 6-10 Maggio 1987, pp.23-24. See also Gildo Campensato, "Lega, Tanta Voglia di Capitalismo Popolare", *L'Unità,* 4 Aprile 1991.
9 Walter Dondi, "Nuova Coop: Né Fiat né Holding", *L'Unità,* Martedì 28 Novembre, p.11.
10 Walter Dondi, "Cervello Complementare", in *Lega Senza Frontiere*, L'Unità, 16 Giugno 1989, p.24.
11 Stefano Zan, "Il Quadro Concettuale di Riferimento", in Stefano Zan (ed), *Le Interdipendenze Organizzative in Agricoltura*, Regione Emilia Romagna, Bologna, 1987, pp.27-31.
12 Guido Campensato, *op.cit.*
13 Francesco Boccetti, "Relazione del Presidente", 5o Congresso Lega Emilia Romagna, Imola, 20-21 Marzo 1991, pp.23-27.
14 An example of this was the infighting that took place after the European elections of 1989 when the political factions wanted to renegotiate the composition of the national executive. Walter Dondi, "Lega, Psi-Pri all'Attacco di Turci", *L'Unità,* 20 Luglio 1989. *La Repubblica*, "Alla Lega i Socialisti all'Attacco Decidono di Bocciare i Conti '89", 20 Luglio 1989, p.35.
15 Zan, *op.cit.*, *La Cooperazione in Italia: Strategie e Sviluppo della Lega Nazionale delle Cooperative e Mutue*, p.368.
16 Zan, *op.cit.*, "The Management of Entrepreneurial Associations: The Case of the National League of Cooperatives and Mutual Aid Societies", p.9.
17 Political corruption, high level of public mismanagement and control over the State's institutions are the major factors which have reduced the legitimacy of parties in Italy. The effect of this are: lower party membership, higher level of absenteeism, and the use of referendums promoted by cross party alliances to force political changes.

18 Luigi Rosafio, "Relazione Introduttiva", *Conferenza Nazionale D'organizzazione Montecatini 1986*, Editrice Cooperativa, Roma, 1987, p.31.
19 Lega Regionale Emilia Romagna,"Analisi Qualitativa: le Radici dell'Organizzazione", in *Analisi Sulla Organizzazione della Lega Emiliano-Romagnola,* Bologna, 1988, p.34.
20 *Krasis*, "Documento Unitario delle Piccole e Medie Imprese della Federcoop di Bologna in Preparazione del 23mo Congresso Lega", Roma, Anno 2, Numero 1, 1991, p.3.
21 Orazio Pugliese (ed), *Il Sistema Cooperativo*, Marsilio Editore, Venezia, 1987, p.212.
22 The total turnover of these two regions amounts to 17,518 billion lire which is 54.1% of the 32,381 billion lire turnover of La Lega as a whole. For the figures on Emilia Romagna see Emanuel Danieli (ed), *Le Imprese Cooperative: Trend 1982-1989*, Editrice Emilia Romagna, Bologna, 1990, p.10. For statistics on Tuscany see *La Cooperazione Italiana*, "La Qualità Sociale Come Obbiettivo", Aprile 1993, p.10.
23 Michele Balboni notes that the level of information and knowledge regarding several State laws which support enterprise development varied from province to province. See Michele Balboni, "Finanza: Il fai da te è Perdente per un Sistema di Imprese", in Francesco Garella (ed), *Il Movimento, il Sistema, La Rete: Un Decennio di Cambiamenti nelle Imprese Cooperative*, Editrice Emilia Romagna, Bologna, 1991, p.193.
24 Please note that the author took these figures from the General Register which usually contains a margin of error of about 26% (for an explanation on this see Appendix B).
25 Roberto Malucelli, "Gli Italiani e le Coop", *La Cooperazione Italiana*, Gennaio 1984, pp.10-16.
26 Virgilio Chelli, "La Lega allo Specchio", *La Cooperazione Italiana*, Giugno 1990, pp. 20-23.
27 See the January-February 1993 issue of *La Cooperazione Italiana* which deals with "Ethics and Economy, Values and the Cooperative Enterprise" and the May 1993 issue on "Work and the Social Economy: Reasons to Cooperate".
28 Costanza Fanelli, "Il Futuro del Lavoro nell'Economia Sociale", *La Cooperazione Italiana*, April 1993, p.12.
29 La Lega, *Documento Politico per il 33mo Congresso Nazionale 1991,* Roma, 1990, pp.30-31.
30 *Ibid.*, p.19.
31 The two representatives are Gastone Notari, vice president of the consumer cooperative Toscana Lazio who became the director of Unipol Finance and Mario Zucchetti, the vice president of the consumer cooperative Coop Estense of Emilia has become director of Banec.
32 La Lega, *op.cit.*, *Documento Politico 33mo Congresso Nazionale 1991,* p.29.
33 Walter Dondi, "In Lega Tutti D'Accordo: Cambiare", *L'Unità,* 29 Novembre 1989, p.14.
34 La Lega, *op.cit.*, *Documento Politico 33mo Congresso Nazionale 1991*, p.29.
35 By progressive businesses is meant all those businesses which do not practice exploitative working relations, do not evade taxes, protect the environment, invest in the enterprise, those which compete in the open market as against those who have monopolies. La Lega, *op.cit.*, *Documento Politico: 33mo Congresso Nazionale Roma 1991*, pp.20 and 27-28.
36 See Gazzetta Ufficiale della Repubblica Italiana, *Nuova Norme in Materia di Societa Cooperative*, Roma, 31 Gennaio 1992. See also Sandro Bonella, "Finalmente Cittadine del Mercato", *La Cooperazione Italiana*, Gennaio 1992, pp.4-9.
37 La Lega, *op.cit.*, *Documento Politico 33mo Congresso Nazionale*, p.29.

11 Conclusion

The objective of this work was to identify the factors which led to the formation and growth of cooperatives associated with La Lega. In order to set this research within the broader field of cooperative studies, the question of whether cooperatives were a failed alternative was discussed. The main characteristics of a cooperative enterprise were analysed and a brief comparison with private enterprises was made. Then the cooperative movements of Britain and Mondragon and worker capitalist firms were analysed and contrasted. It was concluded that the ICA and Mondragon enterprises can be regarded as being cooperatives, where worker capitalist firms and ESOPs are essentially profit making, non-democratic firms.

What also emerged from this analysis is that cooperative experiences are a product of a nation's history and a product of cultural, economic and political circumstances. Thus each cooperative sector should be best seen as nation specific.

The comparison of the British and the Mondragon experience also showed that there is a range of factors which can lead to the success or demise of cooperatives which operate in capitalist systems. That the Mondragon experience has been so successful over a thirty year period, the revival of cooperatives since the 1970s, the inability of market dominated economies to create full employment and to satisfy some people's needs in terms of economic democracy and quality of life issues, is a clear indication that cooperatives can still be regarded as a viable alternative.

The main problems faced by cooperatives were then identified and ways to overcome them were canvassed. The analysis centred upon discussing seven problems which hinder the development of cooperatives: entrepreneurial, finance, managerial and specialist competencies, internal limits to growth, discrimination, constraints on takeovers, place of cooperatives in the economy. The findings demonstrated that caution should be exercised when analysing these problems. It was revealed that those problems identified through purely neo-classical theoretical models had little relevance to cooperatives as they actually operate. It was also found that it is important to note when the research was conducted and place it in its proper temporal and historical setting. In addition, the size of cooperatives, the specific enterprise culture and at times discrimination from the State have hindered the development of cooperatives. Once again, these findings were nation specific and should be treated with caution. The discussion then identified ways of overcoming the various problems. In particular, cooperative support structures and support from the State were identified as means capable of helping cooperatives overcome these problems. While Cornforth's categorisation has its limits, it was found to be a good tool of analysis regarding the viability of cooperative enterprises in a market economy.

This work was set against this background and sought to discover the factors which enabled cooperatives in Italy to overcome these obstacles and develop into a substantial cooperative sector. The methodology used to explore this was both historical and analytical by seeking to analyse the interrelationship that evolved between the State, the cooperative support structures and the individual cooperative enterprises between 1945 and 1992. An historical analysis of La Lega from 1886 until 1992 provided the general background. This was followed by an analysis of La Lega's Central Association, consortia network and financial structures. Then four case studies provided evidence demonstrating how cooperatives from different sectors of the economy managed change over a period of time. This was followed by a theoretical analysis of the Italian State and a historical analysis of the relationship between the State and cooperatives during the period 1945-1992. The final chapter defined and evaluated the role of La Lega.

Factors Contributing to the Success of La Lega

The study found that the following eleven factors have each significantly contributed to the success of La Lega. They are summarised as follows:

1. Legislation

The cooperative legislation has been an important contributor to the success of cooperatives. It encouraged both the economic viability of cooperatives and the maintenance of its ideals. The law requires that both dividends on shares and bonus payments are limited, thus guaranteeing that the majority of profits were re-invested in the cooperative. It also required that cooperatives could not be converted to private enterprises by not tying shares to the assets of the enterprises and forbidding the sale of shares to the public.[1] It also required that the social character of the cooperative was maintained. Cooperative rules such as limiting the return on capital, one person-one vote, limiting the number of non-members and the establishment of a solidarity fund all reinforced the cooperative ideals.

2. La Lega's Central Association: Territorial and Sectoral Associations

These structures have provided four major contributions to the success of cooperatives. Firstly, they have maintained cohesiveness within the network of enterprises. This was accomplished by promoting shared values, a collaborative culture and by mediating conflicts between cooperatives. Secondly, they have successfully promoted the interests of cooperatives to the State. This was achieved by direct lobbying, by promoting a parliamentary lobby group, by electing its own parliamentarians and having its own representatives in a number of governmental institutions. Thirdly, they have provided a number of services in the areas of administration, research and planning. Fourthly, they have promoted new cooperatives and organised cooperatives to diversify and be active in different sectors of the economy.

3. Consortia

The development of consortia is a distinctive feature of La Lega. The consortia have basically been responsible for permitting the individual cooperatives to improve their market competitiveness by pooling resources together and by providing them with some of the functions that they could not provide on their own. Through the consortia, cooperatives have achieved economies of scale, have reduced the costs of raw materials through bulk buying or other contractual arrangements, have won public contracts, have marketed their products and have had access to new technology. Consortia have also provided cooperatives with technical and managerial expertise, further improving their chances of survival and growth when competing with large enterprises. They have also maintained unity within the network by managing conflicts and by distributing work among all members. Finally, have also been instrumental in promoting intersectoral trade. Such trade is a major characteristic of La Lega's cooperatives and a major reason for their success.

4. Intersectoral Trade and Collaboration

Intersectoral trade within the cooperative sector has been very important to the competitiveness of cooperatives. Linkages between the housing, manufacturing and the construction sector and the agricultural, manufacturing and consumer sector were arranged by the consortia Acam and

Coop Italia respectively. This created a cooperative market which was instrumental for the growth of cooperatives. Intersectoral collaboration among cooperatives from various sectors has been important to establish consortia like Fincooper and Icie and many conventional companies owned by cooperatives of which Unipol Finance and Unipol Insurance are the most important.

5. *Financial Support*

Financial support is organised through Fincooper, Unipol Finance and a range of other minor institutions. These provided loans directly to cooperatives. They also arranged for cooperatives to receive loans from State owned banks through contractual agreements. They have reduced the need to raise finance by providing rental properties, leasing and factoring services. Further, Finec provides risk capital. In addition, a number of financial services such as consultancy, foreign transactions, feasibility studies, investment analysis and market research have also been provided.

6. *Policy of Alliances*

The policy of alliances delivered political and economic benefits. The alliances between La Lega and political parties, trade unions, small business, artisan and other cooperative associations were instrumental in pressuring the State to act on behalf of cooperatives. In economic terms, alliances made at the consortia and enterprise level with private and State enterprises improved the economic competitiveness of cooperatives by providing them with extended access to knowledge, managerial expertise, risk capital, and access to public works and new markets.

7. *Large Cooperatives*

Another factor in the success of La Lega's cooperatives is the influence and role of the large cooperatives operating in various sectors of the economy. The large cooperatives contributed in a number of ways. First, they provided the consortia Acam and Coop Italia, with the contractual power needed to bargain for lower prices, and, the consortium CCC, with the knowledge and expertise needed to win large scale public contracts. Secondly, they have been the major source of finance for the financial organisations of La Lega. Thirdly, they are the main component of La Lega which gives credibility to strategy of solving some of the country's economic and social problems.

8. Managing Change

The four cooperative case studies demonstrated that to survive and grow it is imperative to manage the changes that take place at the economic, political and social level. Cooperatives did this by developing a coherent business strategy supported by a suitable organisational structure and culture. Some of the strategic changes undertaken were product diversification, market diversification, mergers, joint ventures and flexible production. Organisational changes included the development of a decentralised structure, a professional management team with specialised skills and the creation and ownership of subsidiaries. The main cultural changes included the development of an entrepreneurial culture geared to economic growth and high level of personal investment, higher wage differentials and an acceptance of cooperating with small and medium sized businesses and the middle class. The case studies also demonstrated the complexities involved in developing a strategy at the enterprise level while still being part of a network of enterprises and the different levels of integration developed by the different enterprises with the network.

9. The State

This research placed a major emphasis on the role of the State. The State has contributed enormously to the success of the movement. Six major areas of intervention can be identified. Firstly, the State has provided tax incentives which have helped cooperatives to finance their operations and encouraged the formation of cooperatives. Secondly, the combined regulatory powers of the State at the national, regional and local levels have contributed to the growth of La Lega's consumer sector. Thirdly, the national and local government have provided cooperatives with access to resources in the form of land for agricultural and housing cooperatives and public works for construction cooperatives. Fourthly, the State initiated many job creation programmes at the local and regional level contributing to cooperative formation in many sectors of the economy. Fifthly, the State has provided finance to cooperatives in the forms of loans, grants and risk capital. Finally, State banks and research institutions have provided knowledge and managerial expertise. In all, while there have been periods of State inertia and hostility toward the cooperative sector, it has been a major factor in the success of the movement.

10. Culture

Culture refers to a system of beliefs and values which have been shaped by history and collective experience. It also implies a way of thinking, of solving problems and forms of human relations. So far many aspects of the culture have already been mentioned, this section synthesises them into six groupings, all of which are important Firstly, the cooperative movement has developed a culture which maintains a balance between economic goals and social responsibility toward the individual, the enterprise, the cooperative sector and the community. Secondly, cooperatives have developed a culture geared toward economic growth. Thirdly, cooperatives have shown the ability to work in a unified movement. Fourthly, the research has shown cooperatives to have a remarkable ability to adapt to changing circumstances: the move towards an interclassist alliance, to higher wage differentials, and worker entrepreneurs are all evidence of this. Fifthly, they have cultivated a culture of collective ownership. Finally, a culture of persistence permeates the movement. By this is meant a determination to expand the cooperative sector without a rigid adherence to past principles and practices at the expense of the survivability of the enterprise. The persistence of Fincooper to succeed after having experienced initial difficulties, the changes which were made to the consortia system, the persistence to invest in Southern Italy, the creation of large enterprises through a policy of mergers, the introduction of higher level of remuneration for members' shares and of external ownership are all aspects of this cultural trait.

11. Political Factors

Political factors include political action and policies of La Lega on behalf of its members and their ideals. Since its formation, La Lega has always been at the forefront of political activity. The contribution it made to the anti-Fascist resistance movement, the support it gave to the policy to decentralise the State, its policy toward social issues like housing, child care, employment creation in Southern Italy are all aspects which forged an identity linking cooperatives with the people. All of these have made cooperatives an easily identifiable and familiar feature of the Italian economy and a legitimate member of the community.

Original Contribution to the Field of Cooperative Studies

This work has made a number of original contributions to the field of cooperative studies. One major contribution is that it has provided an in-depth historical analysis of how La Lega's cooperatives have managed to survive and grow within a market economy by analysing original sources and by making use of empirical evidence gathered from case studies of cooperatives and consortia.

It has also given a detailed understanding and analysis of the working of La Lega as an organisation. Its various parts were identified and analysed. A definition of La Lega as a network of enterprises was given. Further, an explanation of the decision-making process was made, identifying the system of authority centred on interlocking directorships and political factions as its main components.

Another major contribution has been the analysis of the Italian State in relation to the cooperative movement. This study identified the major nation specific characteristics of the Italian State and then provided empirical evidence to demonstrate why the State acted as it did and when is it most likely to act on behalf of cooperatives. It was found that the State is most likely not to support cooperatives when the private and State sector can provide economic growth, when the government is hostile to cooperatives, when the State has enough revenue to fulfil its functions and when the cooperative sector is economically weak and challenges the legitimacy of the State. Alternatively, it was found that the cooperative sector received a more favourable response from the State when the latter faced a fiscal and managerial crisis, when the private and State sector could no longer guarantee economic growth, when power was distributed between political parties and other tiers of government at a territorial level; at a time when La Lega (and the rest of the cooperative sector) was economically strong, did not challenge the legitimacy of the State and contributed in solving some of the country's economic and social problems.

This study also has the merit of providing a methodology which examines the relationship between the State, individual cooperatives and the cooperative support structures. This method can become a tool for analysis to examine the histories and evolution of other cooperative sectors around the world.

It has been demonstrated that a large cooperative sector can grow from within market economies which operate in liberal democratic political systems. It has also shown that it can become an important and integrated part of the economic system co-existing with the private and State sector by developing a policy of collaboration and competition based on commercial needs and not ideological opposition.

Implications for other Cooperative Movements

In considering the implications of this study on cooperative movements, it is important to remember that this study was set in a country which is governed by a liberal democratic political system and operates under a capitalist mixed economy. Thus, the comparison is directed at cooperatives which operate under similar political and economic systems and consequently are likely to face similar obstacles when competing in the market. As with the Mondragon case, it is impossible to transplant the experience of one country to another in its entirety. However, it is important to distinguish between what can be regarded as universally applicable and what is not Given that cooperatives operate in similar economic and political systems, in my opinion, other cooperative movements can adopt some of the following factors which have made La Lega successful: the cooperative legislation; the support structures; finding a cultural balance between the needs of the individual, the enterprise, the cooperative movement and the community; the strategy of developing political and economic alliances to influence the State; the importance of developing a concept of what the State is, how it can help cooperative development and how it can be influenced.

However, there are also nation specific factors which are difficult to reproduce. A number of these factors which have contributed to the success of La Lega include the strong anti-capitalist culture derived from the Catholic, Socialist and the Liberal Socialist traditions, the power of political parties in society and in the State, the decentralised nature of the Italian State and, finally, the complexities of La Lega's organisational structure. These are all nation specific factors and are difficult to reproduce in another country in their entirety.

Wider Societal Implications

The evidence provided by this study is a clear indication both of the ability of cooperatives to survive over an extended period and of the valuable contribution they can make to society.

A major area where this cooperative model could be used is in regional economic development. Today local economies have to compete in a deregulated world market where the mobility of capital to maximise profits causes great hardships and economic insecurity to local communities. La

Lega's economic model can overcome this problem. The cooperative legislation and the fact that enterprises are collectively owned makes it impossible for firms to relocate in other countries. This also ensures that profits are re-invested in the cooperative enterprises. La Lega's network of organisations is also a good way for small to medium size firms to overcome obstacles they face in the market, thus improving their capacity to compete in local and world markets. Further, local economies have a better chance of surviving in global markets if firms adopt the culture of La Lega's cooperatives which have continually invested not only in their own enterprise, but also when possible, in other established enterprises and banks operating in the local economy.

The second major societal contribution is favouring a redistribution of wealth and a more egalitarian society. The fact that cooperatives are collectively owned and that individuals do not own the assets, but only the nominal sum invested, ensures that the wealth produced is used by future generations and the local community. Further, the lower wage differentials practised by La Lega's cooperatives also ensure that wealth differentials are reduced. This contribution made by cooperatives at the enterprise level could complement those government policies which, through a progressive taxation system and policies aimed at increasing the social wage (lower housing and transport costs etc), have in the past tried to redistribute wealth in favour of the disadvantaged.

This cooperative model can also make a good contribution in job creation projects. La Lega has shown remarkable success in creating cooperatives by taking over private enterprises (Marcora Law) and by promoting cooperatives formed by young people (De Vito Law). This supports La Lega's credentials as a job creating organisation. This evidence is a clear indication that new enterprises have a better chance of succeeding if they belong to a network of enterprises which can provide finance, managerial services, and develop trade relationships between firms.

A new business ethic is another contribution that cooperatives make to society. The economy is dominated by private businesses whose primary concern is to make profit. The pursuit of profit has no boundary and capital will travel all over the world for the highest possible return. History suggests that to these businesses, individuals and local communities are secondary concerns. This is not to propose that all private businesses behave in the same way. They do not, but generally this explanation can be accepted as the norm rather than the exception. In contrast, cooperatives provide the basis for a new business ethic which pursues: non-speculative profit; shows concern for individuals who work in them by providing good salary and working conditions; and supports the local community by re-investing profits in the enterprise and the local economy and by spending a portion of profits in solidarity initiatives for the benefit of economic, social and cultural activities. This type of behaviour has the possibility of transforming enterprises from merely being seekers of private wealth accumulation to enterprises which balance economic and social considerations.

Concluding Remark

The experience of La Lega has shown that cooperatives can not only survive but flourish in a capitalist market over long periods of time and that they can contribute to the amelioration of many social and economic problems. The fact that this model, as was the case with Mondragon, cannot be reproduced in its entirety, should not necessarily lead to a pessimistic conclusion about the economic viability of a cooperative sector in other countries. Instead, the evidence points to the more optimistic conclusion that different cooperative development models can lead to successful results. It is a matter of developing a cooperative model which suits a country's specific historical, political, social and economic environment.

Notes

1 The 1992 law allows voting shares to be sold to the public as long as they do not exceed 25% of the voting rights, thus not changing the thrust of the previous law.

Appendices

Appendix A Information on Case Studies

Cooperatives Case Studies

1. *ALTERCOOP*

Year Founded:	1985
Sector:	Service Sector (Paper Wholesalers, Recycling, Bill Posters, Cleaning)
Turnover:	3 Billion Lire
Employment:	25 Full Time and 45 Part Time

2. *ALVEO*

Year Founded:	1986
Sector: Service:	(Environmental Planning and Control)
Turnover:	300 Million Lire
Employment:	12

3. *COOP EMILIA VENETO*

Year Founded:	1975
Sector:	Retail
Turnover:	700 Billion Lire
Employment:	2,361

4. *COOPERATIVA MURATORI E BRACCIANTI DI CARPI*

Year Founded:	1977
Sector:	Construction
Turnover:	331 Billion Lire
Employment:	1,033

5. *COOPERATIVA MURATORI & CEMENTISTI DI RAVENNA*

Year Founded:	1901
Sector:	Construction
Turnover:	507.9 Billion Lire
Employment:	3,792

6. *COMITALIA*

Year Founded:	1987
Sector:	Service (Removalists)
Turnover:	N/A
Employment:	23-25

7. *SACMI*

Year Founded:	1919
Sector:	Manufacturing
Turnover:	335 Billion Lire
Employment:	651

8. *SPEPCOOP*

Year Founded:	1979
Sector:	Service (Health)
Turnover:	7.7 Billion Lire
Employment:	800, of whom 150 employed Part Time

Consortia Case Studies

9. *ACAM*

Year Founded:	1960
Sector:	Construction and Manufacturing
Turnover:	1,183 Billion Lire
Employment:	45 in Head Office plus others in 13 other branches

10. *COOP ITALIA*

Year Founded:	1968
Sector:	Retail
Turnover:	N/A
Employment:	110

11. *CONSORZIO COOPERATIVE COSTRUZIONI*

Year Founded:	1912
Sector:	Construction
Turnover:	2,359 Billion Lire
Employment:	N/A

12. *CORTICELLA*

Year Founded:	1948
Sector:	Manufacturing (Pasta, Bread, Four Milling)
Turnover:	142.6 Billion Lire (1989)
Employment:	417

13. *GIGLIO*

Year Founded:	1934
Sector:	Agriculture
Turnover:	480 Billion Lire
Employment:	280 in Head Office of Reggio Emilia

14. *FINCOOPER*

Year Founded:	1969
Sector:	Finance
Turnover:	Lending capacity of 550 Billion Lire plus 250 billion lire held in reserve
Employment:	N/A

15. *ICIE*

Year Founded:	1972
Sector:	Service (Research & Technology)
Turnover:	N/A
Employment:	N/A

16. *UNIPOL*

Year Founded:	1963
Sector:	Finance
Turnover:	2,725 Billion lire
Employment:	3,100

Appendix B Registered Cooperatives in Italy

The Italian cooperative movement is quite large, however exact figures are difficult to give for a variety of reasons. The first statistical evidence of the cooperative sector is that provided by the law courts where cooperatives have to first register to begin operating. According to the law courts register, in 1989 there were 159,723 cooperatives in Italy. Most of them were housing cooperatives (66,902), but most importantly 36,194 were producer cooperatives.[1] However, some of these cooperatives never got started and many are regarded as bogus cooperatives, so these figures should be treated cautiously.[2]

A more reliable statistical source is the Schedario Generale (General Register) kept by the provincial Prefects. This office registers all cooperatives which are eligible to receive legal benefits under national laws and which are also periodically inspected by the State authorities or the Central Associations to which they are associated.[3] In 1989 there were 105,050 cooperatives registered in the General Register (see Table B1). However, while all of these are genuine cooperatives, the statistics contain a margin of error. The error is caused by the Ministry of Labour's inability to inspect every cooperative each year. Therefore the actual number is lower than that given by the statistics for the following reasons: many cooperatives register but never get started, many have gone into liquidation since registering and others have either merged or were taken over by other cooperatives. In fact, the actual figure given by the general register minus 20% is the actual size of the cooperative sector.[4]

Another interesting aspect of these statistics is that 49,596 cooperatives are members of four cooperative Central Associations (see Table B2). These associations are: La Lega which has 17,451 member cooperatives; the Confederazione 24,261 members; the Associazione 5,105 members; the last and smallest is UNCI (National Union of Italian Cooperatives) with 2,779 affiliated cooperatives.[5] Once again these figures are not correct. Considering that for the same year La Lega declared 12,889 cooperatives,[6] 4,562 less than those attributed to La Lega by the General Registry, there is a margin of error of 26%.

Table B.1 Number of Registered Cooperatives by Sector

Year	1951	1961	1971	1976	1981	1984	1989
Consumer Cooperatives	2,930	4,686	4,423	4,212	4,442	4,874	4,696
Production & Worker Coops	4,572	4,684	4,626	5,893	11,203	14,563	21,199
Agricultural Cooperatives	1,891	4,960	9,282	11,287	14,808	16,136	17,306
Housing Cooperatives	3,602	16,659	28,983	38,684	48,794	51,278	45,784
Transport Cooperatives	154	288	458	732	984	1,079	1,129
Fishing Cooperatives	164	433	494	564	725	794	850
Mixed Cooperatives	1,018	1,790	2,066	2,980	7,027	9,519	14,086
Total	14,331	33,500	50,332	64,352	88,383	98,353	105,050

Source: For 1951-1984 see: Silvia Gherardi, "Worker Takeovers: The Italian Experience", in *Analysis of the Experiences and Problems Encountered by Worker Takeover of Companies in Difficulty or Bankrupt,* Main Report, Commission of the European Communities, Luxembourg, 1987, p.162. For 1989 see Ministero del Lavoro e della Previdenza Sociale, *Statistiche della Cooperazione,* Roma, 1990, Table 3.

Table B.2 Membership of Cooperative Associations by Sector, 1989

	Consumer	Worker	Agri-culture	Housing	Trans-port	Fishing	Mixed	TOTAL
CCI	1,623	4,118	6,922	7,472	213	437	3,476	24,261 (48.9%)
Lega	2,014	4,725	2,910	5,102	248	157	2,295	17,451 (35.2%)
AGCI	173	1,111	680	2,575	102	86	378	5,105 (10.3%)
UNCI	55	491	431	1,498	9	25	270	2,779 (5.6%)
Total	3,865	10,445	10,943	16,647	572	705	6,419	49,596

Source: Ministero del Lavoro e della Previdenza Sociale, *Statistiche della Cooperazione*, Roma, 1990, Tables 6-9.

Appendix C Exchange Rates

Table C.1 Foreign Exchange Rate (in Lire) 1945-1992

Currency									
	1945	1946	1947	1949	1971	1972	1973	1974	1975
US $	100	225	350	625		583	562	650	684
AUS $	n/a	n/a	n/a	n/a		710	909	869	865
	1976	1977	1978	1979	1980	1981	1982	1983	1984
US $	875	871	830	804	931	1,200	1,370	1,655	1,936
AUS $	960	1,004	963	898	1,100	1,376	1,346	1,501	1,608
	1985	1986	1987	1988	1989	1990	1991		
US $	1,678	1,351	1,169	1,305	1,271	1,130	1,151		
AUS $	1,161	898	853	1,119	1,114	876	880		

Source: For exchange rates of Lira to US $ for the period 1945-1947 see Donald Sassoon, *Contemporary Italy: Politics, Economics and Society Since 1945*, Longman, New York, 1986, p.25; For the period 1950-1991 see International Monetary Fund, *Annual Report of Exchange Restrictions*, Washington, DC, 1950-1991. For exchange rates of La Lira to AUS $ see *The Australian*, December 27-31, 1972-1983 and *Corriere della Sera*, December 27-31, 1984-1991.

Notes

1 Ministero del Lavoro e della Previdenza Sociale, Statistiche della Cooperazione, Roma, 1990, Table 4.
2 A good discussion on this is provided by John Earle, *The Italian Cooperative Movement*, Allen and Unwin, London, 1986, pp.63-67.
3 See Chapter 4 for information on benefits made available to cooperatives from the State.
4 John Earle noted that in 1984 out of 98,353 cooperatives registered 19,351 were being liquidated which amounts to 19.7% of the total. John Earle, *op.cit.*, pp.64-65.
5 Ministero del Lavoro e della Previdenza Sociale, *op.cit.*, Tables 6-9.
6 See Chapter 4, Table 4.2, p.102.

Glossary

Basevi Law

This law was enacted in 1947 and it provided the general guidelines for cooperatives. The most salient features include: democracy based on the one vote, one person principle; limited return on shares invested; provision for the distribution of profits of which not more than 20% could be used to increase members' income, at least 20% had to be deposited in the reserve fund with the remainder either spent on social or charitable activity or be deposited in the reserve fund; in the event of dissolution any net assets had to be devoted to a public fund; white collar workers could not exceed 4% of the work-force; finally the law also made provisions for cooperatives to receive tax concessions ranging from 25% for consumer cooperatives to 100% for agricultural cooperatives.

Central Association

Along with the individual cooperatives and the various consortia, the Central Association makes up the structures that collectively form La Lega. The Central Association is comprised of two main structures: the territorial support structures organised at a national, regional and in Emilia Romagna, also at the local level; and the sectoral associations organised at a national and regional level. The former represents cooperatives from all sectors, the latter represents cooperatives from a particular sector only. The role of the Central Association is to represent cooperative interests *vis-à-vis* the State and society, to supervise their activity, to provide services, to promote new cooperatives and to guide and coordinate the policies of the whole network of enterprises.

Consortium

A consortium is an organisation formed by cooperatives to improve their market competitiveness. The consortium enables cooperatives to achieve this by pooling resources together and by providing some of the functions that the individual enterprises are not able to provide on their own. Some of the benefits of operating through a consortium are: achieving economies of scale, reduced costs of raw materials through bulk buying or contractual arrangements, winning public contracts, marketing cooperative products and to have access to new technology and technical and managerial expertise. They have also maintained unity within the network by managing conflicts and by promoting intersectoral trade.

Cooperative Companies

This term refers to conventional companies owned by individual cooperatives which are part of, and operate on behalf of, La Lega's network of enterprises.

De Vito "Youth Law"

This law became operational in 1986 to create youth employment in Southern Italy. It provides grants for up to 60% of the start up capital needed and for the initial administrative costs. It also makes available low interest loans covering 30% of the initial costs at 30% of the market rate payable over 10 years.

Law of 1992

The major innovation made by this law was the introduction of external voting and non voting shares, with the former never exceeding more than 30% of the voting power of the general assembly. It also increased the amount that could be lent as "members' loans" to 80 million lire for agricultural and producer cooperatives and 40 million lire for other cooperatives. The amount which could be lent as "members' shares" was also increased to 120 million lire for producer and agricultural cooperatives and 80 million lire for other cooperatives.

Marcora Law

This law came into operation in 1987 and had two basic objectives. First it made available a special fund to facilitate the conversion of private enterprises in crisis into cooperatives with grants not exceeding the equivalent of three years' wages. Second it set up another fund to provide cooperatives with low interest loans for the purpose of 1) increasing productivity through the introduction of technology and organisational innovation; and 2) for the purpose of maintaining employment by restructuring or reconverting their plant. Loans for the second fund ranged from 200 million to two billion lire payable between 8-10 years. Interest rates charged were between 25% to 50% lower than the market rate.

Members' Loans

First introduced in 1973, these are investments which members make with the cooperative aided by favourable tax laws. In reality they are similar to bank accounts allowing members to withdraw their money at any time. A limit on the amount of money each member can invest also applies. In 1973 this was set at 10 million lire for all cooperatives except agricultural and producer cooperatives whose members could lend up to 17 million lire. Since 1992 members can lend up to 40 and 80 million lire each respectively. The maximum interest rate payable on the loans cannot exceed the rate payable to government bonds or postal bonds by more than 2.5%. The State charges a flat tax rate of 12.5% on interest received, which is half the amount it charges on interest received from conventional bank accounts.

Member' Shares

Investments made by individual members kept in individual accounts which can be withdrawn upon leaving the cooperative or when retiring. These shares are not tied to assets and are not transferable. There is a limit on the amount a member can invest and a limit also on the interest paid yearly. In 1947 the maximum amount which each member could invest was set at 500,000 lire and the maximum interest payable set at 5%. Since 1992 members are allowed to invest up to 80 million lire in all cooperatives except producers and agricultural cooperatives whose members can invest up to 120 million lire. The interest payable is similar to that payable to members' loans.

Mini Reform of 1971

This law made a number of slight changes to the Basevi Law of 1947. It increased the amount that each member could invest as shares from 500,000 lire to 4 million lire for agricultural and producer cooperatives and to 2 million lire for other cooperatives. It increased the percentage of white collar workers from 4% to 12% of the total work-force for agricultural and producer cooperatives and from 4% to 8% for the remainder of cooperatives. It also excluded consortia from paying company tax.

Visentini Law of 1983

The Visentini law increased the maximum amount of money which could be held in shares to 30 million lire for producer and agricultural cooperatives and to 20 million lire for other cooperatives. It increased the rate of interest payable on members' shares from a maximum of 5% to a maximum of 2.5% above the rate payed by postal and government bonds, as well as allowing the cooperative to use profits to increase members' shares as long as it did not exceed 10% of the existing amount. It also increased the amount which members could lend to the cooperative as "members' loans" from 17 million lire to 40 million lire for producer and agricultural cooperatives and from 10 million to 20 million lire for other cooperatives. The level of white collar workers was increased to 20% and cooperatives were allowed for the first time to hold shares in limited companies.

Bibliography

Primary Sources

Acam, *Assemblea di Bilancio: Elementi Statistici*, a cura del Servizio Informatico Aziendale, Bologna, 28 June 1991.

ACAM, *Assemblea di Bilancio: Relazione della Presidenza*, Bologna, 28 June 1991.

Associazione Regionale Cooperative di Abitazione, Per una Gestione Produttiva dei Beni Immobili di Proprietà Pubblica, Editrice Emilia Romagna, Bologna, 1990.

Associazione Nazionale Cooperative dei Consumatori, *La Cooperazione Italiana di Consumatori*, Roma, 1990.

Luciano Bernardini, *L'Offerta Riformatrice del Sistema Lega*, Relazione D'apertura del Vice Presidente della Lega Luciano Bernardini al Convegno "Condizioni per lo Sviluppo dell'Imprenditorialitá: la Riappropriazione Sociale del Rischio", La Lega Nazionale delle Cooperative e Mutue, Roma, 1988.

Francesco Boccetti, *Lega e Cooperazione: Cittadini nell'Economia, Imprenditori nella Società,* Relazione Del Presidente al 5o Congresso Regionale dell'Emilia Romagna, Imola 20-21 March 1991.

Dr Boselli, President of Emilia Romagna, speech given at the Regional Congress of La Lega of Emilia Romagna, Imola 20-21 March, 1991.

Walter Briganti (ed), *Il Movimento Cooperativo in Italia 1854-1925: Scritti e Documenti*, Editrice Cooperativa, Roma, 1982.

Walter Briganti (ed), *Il Movimento Cooperativo in Italia 1926-1962: Scritti e Documenti*, Editrice Cooperativa, Roma, 1982.

Walter Briganti (ed), *Il Movimento Cooperativo in Italia 1963-1980: Scritti e Documenti*, Editrice Cooperativa, Roma, 1982.

Walter Briganti (ed), "L'Articolo 45. La Relazione e La Discussione", in *Il Movimento Cooperativo In Italia, 1926-1962,* Editrice Cooperative, Roma, 1978, pp.162-188.

Alessandro Brusca, *Qualità, Ricerca, Innovazione: Nuove Sfide per le Imprese Cooperative*, ICIE, Roma, May 1991.

Centro di Documentazione sulla Storia del Movimento Cooperativo, *Dati Statistici sul Movimento Cooperativo di Bologna e Provincia 1968-1989,* Bologna 1991.

Centro di Documentazione sulla Storia del Movimento Cooperativo, *Dati Statistici Sul Movimento Cooperativo Regione Emilia Romagna 1977-1987*, Bologna, 1991.

Centro di Documentazione sulla Storia del Movimento Cooperativo, *Il Movimento Cooperativo in Emilia Romagna 1990: Consistenza, Settori, Adesioni (Dati Assoluti e Percentuali)*, Bologna, 1991.

CMB, *Bilancio Consuntivo 1990: Relazione del Consiglio di Amministrazione*, Carpi, 1990.

Confederazione Nazionale dell'Artigianato, *La Risorsa-Futuro per L'Artigianato e la Piccola Impresa*, Bologna, 1991.

Confederazione Nazionale dell' Artigianato, "Profilo Quantitativo dell'Artigianato e Della CNA dell'Emilia Romagna", (information given at the 5th regional Congress of CNA in Emilia Romagna), Bologna, 1991.

Consorzio Provinciale delle Cooperative di Produzione e Lavoro, Notiziario Numero 1, 31 January 1977, p.3.

Consorzio Cooperative Costruzioni, *Assemblea di Programmazione: I Punti Fondamentali della Relazione*, Bologna, 1982.

Consorzio Cooperative Costruzioni, *Assemblea di Programmazione: Divisione Tecnica Note Sulla Programmazione 1982,* Bologna 1982.

Consorzio Cooperative Costruzioni, *Seconda Conferenza Finanziaria Consortile: Note per la Discussione*, Bologna 1982.

Coop Emilia Veneto, *Bilancio Economico 1990*, Bologna, 1991.

Coop Emilia Veneto, *Bilancio di Responsabilità Sociale 1990*, Bologna 1991.

Cooperativa Muratori e Cementisti, *Bilancio Consuntivo 1989*, Ravenna, 1990.

Cooperativa Muratori e Cementisti, *Bilancio Consuntivo 1990*, Ravenna, 1991.

La Cooperazione Italiana, "Rapporto sulla Imprenditoria Cooperativa a Confronto con le Imprese Private", July -August 1990, pp.17-40.

Corticella, *Corticella Information Booklet,* Bologna, 1990.

Ente Delta Padano, *Venticinque Anni di Cooperazione*, Bologna, 1976.

Federazione di Bologna del PDS, *Elezioni Amministrative 1990*, Bologna 1990.

Fincooper, *Bilancio Consuntivo 1 July 1988-30 June 1989,* Bologna, 1989.

Gazzetta Ufficiale della Repubblica Italiana, *Nuove Norme in Materia di Società, Cooperative*, Legge 31 January 1992, n.59.

Giglio, *Relazione del Consiglio di Amministrazione al Bilancio 1985*, Reggio Emilia, 1986.

Giglio, *Relazione del Consiglio di Amministrazione al Bilancio 1986*, Reggio Emilia, 1987.

Giglio, *Relazione del Consiglio di Amministrazione al Bilancio 1987*, Reggio Emilia, 1988.

Giglio, *Relazione del Consiglio di Amministrazione al Bilancio 1988*, Reggio Emilia, 1989.

Giglio, *Relazione del Consiglio di Amministrazione al Bilancio 1989*, Reggio Emilia, 1990.

Giglio, *Relazione del Consiglio di Amministrazione al Bilancio 1990*, Reggio Emilia, 1991.

Icie, *Innovazioni nelle Imprese Cooperative,* Lega Nazionale delle Cooperative e Mutue, Roma, May 1991.

Intercoop, Information Booklet, Rome, 1987.

Krasis, "Documento Unitario delle Piccole e Medie Imprese della Federcoop di Bologna in Preparazione del 23o Congresso Lega", Roma, Anno 2, Numero 1, 1991, p.3.

La Lega Emilia Romagna, *Atti del Primo Congresso Regionale della Lega Nazionale Cooperative e Mutue dell' Emilia Romagna,* Bologna, 8-9 November 1973.

La Lega Emilia Romagna, *Atti del Secondo Congresso Regionale della Lega Nazionale Cooperative e Mutue dell' Emilia Romagna,* Bologna, 20-22 December 1977.

La Lega Emilia Romagna, *Atti del Terzo Congresso Regionale della Lega Nazionale Cooperative e Mutue dell' Emilia Romagna*, Bologna, 20-22 April1982.

La Lega Emilia Romagna, "Analisi Qualitativa: le Radici dell' Organizzazione", in *Analisi Sulla Organizzazione della Lega Emiliano-Romagnola,* Bologna, 1988.

La Lega Emilia Romagna-Dipartimento Economico Finanziario, *Le Imprese Cooperative: Trend 1982-1989*, Editrice Emilia Romagna, Bologna, 1991.

La Lega Emilia Romagna, *La Gestione delle Risorse Umane e le Relazioni Industriali nelle Imprese Cooperative*, Editrice Emilia Romagna, Bologna, 1991.

La Lega Emilia Romagna, *Rete di Servizi Finanziari*, (Information Brochure) a Cura del Dipartimento Finanziario, Bologna, 1991.

La Lega Federazione Provinciale delle Cooperative di Bologna, *Documenti del 7mo Congresso Provinciale*, 7-8 June 1952, Bologna.

La Lega Federazione Provinciale delle Cooperative di Bologna, *Documenti del 8mo Congresso Provinciale*, 28-30 May 1954, Bologna.

La Lega Federazione Provinciale delle Cooperative di Bologna, *Documenti del 9mo Congresso Provinciale*, December 1958, Bologna.

La Lega Federazione Provinciale delle Cooperative di Bologna, *Documenti del 10mo Congresso Provinciale*, 7-10 February 1962, Bologna.

La Lega Federazione Provinciale delle Cooperative di Bologna, *Documenti del 11mo Congresso Provinciale*, Bologna, 1966. .

La Lega Federazione Provinciale delle Cooperative di Bologna, *Documenti del 12mo Congresso Provinciale*, Bologna, 1970.

La Lega Federcoop Bologna, *Appunti sul Rapporto tra Pubblico e Privato*, Bologna, 1991.

La Lega Federcoop Bologna, *Rapporto Economico delle Imprese Cooperative della Federcoop di Bologna 1987-1989*, Bologna, 1991.

La Lega Nazionale delle Cooperative, "Statistica della Cooperazione 1902", in Walter Briganti (ed), *Il Movimento Cooperativo in Italia 1854-1925: Scritti e Documenti*, Editrice Cooperativa, Roma, 1982, pp.193-200.

La Lega Nazionale delle Cooperative e Mutue, "Delibere del 22mo Congresso della La Lega Nazionale delle Cooperative e Mutue", in Walter Briganti (ed), *Il*

Movimento Cooperativo in Italia 1926-1962, Editrice Cooperativa, Roma, 1978, pp.256-259.

La Lega Nazionale delle Cooperative e Mutue, "A Dieci Anni dalla Liberazione", dalla Relazione Morale al 24mo Congresso, in Walter Briganti (ed), *Il Movimento Cooperativo in Italia 1926-1962*, Editrice Cooperativa, Roma, 1978, pp.309-329.

La Lega Nazionale delle Cooperative e Mutue, "Per Una Politica di Piano", (Dalla Dichiarazione Programmatica della LNCM, Roma, 1962), in Walter Briganti (ed), *Il Movimento Cooperativo in Italia 1926-1962,* Editrice Cooperativa, Roma, 1978, pp. 372-376.

La Lega Nazionale delle Cooperative e Mutue, "Dati Statistici Relativi alle Cooperative Mutue e Consorzi aderenti alla Lega Nazionale delle Cooperative e Mutue al 31 December 1967", in Walter Briganti (ed), *Il Movimento Cooperativo in Italia 1963-1980,* Editrice Cooperativa, Roma, 1982, pp.93-107.

La Lega Nazionale delle Cooperative e Mutue, "La Linea della Lega al Ventottesimo Congresso", in Walter Briganti (ed), *Il Movimento Cooperativo in Italia 1963-1980,* Editrice Cooperativa, Roma, 1982, pp.134-151.

La Lega Nazionale delle Cooperative e Mutue, *Il Dirigente dell'Impresa Cooperativa*, Editrice Cooperativa, Roma, (no date).

La Lega Nazionale delle Cooperative e Mutue, *La Politica dei Quadri nel Movimento Cooperativo*, Editrice Cooperativa, Roma, 1984.

La Lega Nazionale delle Cooperative e Mutue, *La Questione Finanziaria e lo Sviluppo dell'Impresa Cooperativa,* Editrice Cooperativa, Roma, 1984.

La Lega Nazionale delle Cooperative e Mutue, *Conferenza Nazionale D' Organizzazione*, Editrice Cooperativa, Roma, 1986.

La Lega Nazionale delle Cooperative e Mutue, *I Lacci di Gulliver: Deregulation e Movimento Cooperativo*, Editrice Cooperativa, Roma, 1986.

Lega Nazionale delle Cooperative e Mutue, *Lega*, Roma, 1987.

La Lega Nazionale delle Cooperative e Mutue, *Società, Economia, Impresa; la Proposta Cooperativa*, Atti del 32mo Congresso della Lega, May 1987, Roma.

La Lega Nazionale delle Cooperative e Mutue, *Il Sistema Lega di Fronte All'Innovazione Finanziaria*, Roma, 1988.

La Lega Nazionale delle Cooperative e Mutue, "Analisi Qualitativa: le Radici dell'Organizzazione", In *Analisi Sulla Organizzazione della Lega Emiliano Romagnola*, Unpublished Document, Bologna, 1988.

La Lega Nazionale delle Cooperative e Mutue, *Cento Profili di Imprese di Produzione e Lavoro,* Roma, 1988.

La Lega Nazionale delle Cooperative e Mutue, *Cooperazione e Relazione Industriali: dal Conflitto al Governo dei Processi*, Roma, 1988.

La Lega Nazionale delle Cooperative e Mutue, *Ottavo Congresso Nazionale delle Cooperative di Produzione e Lavoro,* (6-7 December 1988), Edizioni delle Cooperative di Produzione e Lavoro, Roma, 1989.

La Lega Nazionale delle Cooperative e Mutue, "Intesa Politica e Programmatica per Rinnovare La Lega", *La Cooperazione Italiana*, December 1989, pp.28-33.

La Lega Nazionale delle Cooperative e Mutue, *Strategie Imprenditoriali in Emilia Romagna: Dalle Reti Locali Alle Reti Globali*, La Lega, Bologna, 1989.

La Lega Nazionale delle Cooperative e Mutue, *Il Sistema Finanziario della Lega delle Cooperative*, Bologna, 1990.

La Lega Nazionale delle Cooperative e Mutue, *Documento Politico: 33mo Congresso Nazionale Roma 1991*, Roma 1990.

La Lega Nazionale delle Cooperative e Mutue, *Principali Indicatori del Movimento Cooperativo Lega*, Roma, 1991.

Roberto Malucelli, Relazione Introduttiva, *Ottavo Congresso Nazionale delle Cooperative di Produzione e Lavoro, 6/7 December 1988,* Associazione Nazionale delle Cooperative di Produzione e Lavoro, Roma, 1989, pp.13-23.

Ministero del Lavoro e della Previdenza Sociale, *Atti Prima Conferenza Nazionale della Cooperazione Italiana*, Volume 1, Roma, 1977.

Ministero del Lavoro e della Previdenza Sociale, *Atti Prima Conferenza Nazionale della Cooperazione Italiana*, Volume 2, Roma, 1977.

Ministero del Lavoro e della Previdenza Sociale, *Atti Prima Conferenza Nazionale della Cooperazione Italiana*, Volume 3, Roma, 1977.

Ministero del Lavoro e della Previdenza Sociale, *Statistiche della Cooperazione Italiana del 1975*, Roma, 1975.

Ministero del Lavoro e della Previdenza Sociale, *Statistiche della Cooperazione Italiana del 1979*, Roma, 1979.

Ministero del Lavoro e della Previdenza Sociale, *Statistiche della Cooperazione Italiana del 1983*, Roma, 1983.

Ministero del Lavoro e della Previdenza Sociale, *Statistiche della Cooperazione Italiana del 1989*, Roma, 1989.

Agostino Ottani, "Introductory Speech Given at the VII Provincial Congress of Bologna June 1952", in La Lega Provinciale di Bologna, *Atti del VII Congresso Provinciale, 7-8 June 1952*, Bologna.

Rino Petralia, *Movimento Cooperativo: Prospettive e Problemi*, Lega Nazionale Cooperative e Mutue, Roma, 1988.

Onelio Prandini, "Relazione Introduttiva al 32o Congresso della Lega", *Atti del 32mo Congresso: Società, Economia e Impresa Cooperativa,* La Lega, Roma, 1987, pp.15-47.

Renato Ascari Raccagni, "Speech Given at the First National Conference on Cooperatives Held in Rome in 1977"; in Ministero del Lavoro e della Previdenza Sociale, *Atti della Prima Conferenza Nazionale sulla Cooperazione Italiana*, Primo Volume, Roma, 1978, pp.71-79.

Alieri Rodiero, personal correspondence, 30 June 1992.

Alieri Rodiero, personal correspondence, 25 August 1992.

Luigi Rosafio, Relazione Introduttiva, in La Lega, *Conferenza Nazionale dell'Organizzazione,* Montecatini, Editrice Cooperativa, 1986, pp.9-40.

Pietro Rossi, Lecture Delivered at the Conference "Organizzazione e Controllo dei Gruppi", Sala dei Convegni della Coop Emilia Veneto, Bologna, 13 June 1991.

Agostino Rota, "Introduzione", in CGIL-Emilia-Romagna, Seminario Interno sulla Cooperazione Italiana, Centro Studi Sindacali Ca Vecchia, Bologna, 11 December 1986.

Mauro Saccenti, personal correspondence, 11 March 1993.

Sacmi, *Sacmi, un Nome su cui Contare: 1919-1989*, Bologna, 1989.

Sacmi Group, *Consolidated Balance Sheet 1991*, Sacmi, Imola, 1991.

Sinnea, *Retribuzione Flessibile, Lega Nazionale delle Cooperative e Mutue*, Bologna, 1989.

Sintesi del Sistema, "Fincooper: Strumento Finanziario della Lega", March 1990.

Sintesi del Sistema, "Factorcoop, Coopfond e i Nuovi Strumenti: La Rete di Vendita dei Fondi Comuni", Bologna, Numero 1-2, Anno 2, 1990, pp.7-8.

Sistema, "Publico Privato e Cooperativo: Protagonisti di un Nuovo Rapporto fra Programmazione, Ambiente e Sistemi Imprenditoriali", Lega delle Cooperative dell' Emilia Romagna, Bologna, Anno 1, Numero 4, October 1989, pp.16-23.

Sistema, "Spepcoop: Budget 1990, Operatività e Formazione", May 1990, p.9.

Sistema, "I Principali Servizi che Svolge la Spep", May 1990, p.10.

Alessandro Skuk, *Relazione al 17mo Congresso della Federcoop di Bologna*, Handwritten Document, Bologna, 1991.

SMP srl, *Strategie Evolutive delle Imprese Cooperative e Nuovo Rapporto Pubblico/Privato*, Documento Presentato alla Conferenza "Pubblico e Privato: fra Difficile ed Indispensabile un Rapporto Utile allo Sviluppo dell'Emilia-Romagna e Dell'Intero Paese", Parma, April 1991.

Vincenzo Tassinari, *45a Assemblea Generale Ordinaria: Relazione del Presidente del Consiglio di Amministrazione*, 20 June 1991, Coop Italia, Bologna.

Lanfranco Turci, *La Lega Verso il Cambiamento,* (Relazione del Presidente alla Riunione del Consiglio Generale), La Lega Nazionale delle Cooperative e Mutue, Roma, 10 February 1988.

Unipol, *Unipol Insurance Information Booklet,* Bologna 1990.

Valerio Valeriani, "Il Prestito da Soci nelle Cooperative di Consumo dell'Emilia Romagna", *Lettera E.F.*, a cura del Dipartimento Economico Finanziario-Lega Emilia Romagna, Numero 3, February 1991, pp.1-6.

Cristina Venturoli, "Il Socio dell' Impresa Cooperativa come Prestatore di Lavoro: Fondamento e Ragione della Tutela Sindacale", in CGIL - Emilia Romagna, *Seminario Interno sulla Cooperazione Italiana*, Centro Studi Sindacali Ca Vecchia, Bologna, 11 Dicembre1986.

Onofrio Zappi, Documento di Idee per il Servizio Programmazione, Unpublished Document, Bologna 1991.

Carlo Zingaretti, personal correspondence, 22 April1992.

Secondary Sources

Peter Abell, "The Viability of Industrial Producer Co-operation", in Colin Crouch, and Frank Heller (eds), *International Yearbook of Organisational Democracy*, John Wiley and Sons, London, 1983, pp.73-103.
Wolfgang Achtner, "The Italian Economic Mirage", *The Spectator*, 29 August 1992, pp.14-17.
AGCI, *AGCI Dopo Trenta Anni*, Ravenna, 1990.
Gianni Agnelli, *Intervista sul Capitalismo Moderno*, Laterza, Bari, 1983.
Howard Aldrich and Robert N Stern, "Resource Mobilization and the Creation of US Producers Cooperatives, 1835-1935", *Economic and Industrial Democracy*, Volume 4, 1983, pp.371-406.
Dino Alfieri, "Il Fascismo e la Cooperazione", *La Cooperazione nell'Italia Fascista*, Milano 1929, in Walter Briganti (ed), *Il Movimento Cooperativo in Italia 1926-1962: Scritti e Documenti*, Editrice Cooperativa, Roma, 1978, pp.40-43.
P.A. Allum, *Italy-Republic Without Government?*, Weidenfeld and Nicolson, London, 1973.
Giorgio Amendola, "Speech at the Conference of Communist Parties of Capitalist Europe", in Peter Lange and Maurizio Vannicelli (eds), *The Communist Parties of Italy, France and Spain*, George Allen and Unwin, 1981, USA, pp.307-308.
Gabriella Ammassari, "Obiettivi Possibili per un Mercato Difficile", *La Cooperazione Italiana*, December 1992, pp.34-36.
Eugenio Arbizzani, "Verso Una Nuova Gestione degli Interventi Complessi", *La Cooperazione Italiana*, October 1991, pp.76-78.
Philip Armstrong, Andrew Glyn and John Harrison, *Capitalism Since World War Two,* Fontana, London, 1984.
AROC, *Organizzare L'Autogestione,* I Quaderni di Quarantacinque, Editrice Emilia Romagna, Numero 2, 1987.
The Australian, "Why GATT Matters", December 6 1993, p.9.
The Australian, "Lucky Countries", January 1-2 1994, p.16.
Riccardo Azzolini e Patrizia Di Monte, "L'Impresa Cooperativa: Regolamentazione Legislativa e Problemi Economici", in *Pubblico e Privato: Secondo Rapporto CER-CENSIS sull'Economia Italiana*, Edizione del Sole 24 Ore, Milano, 1987, pp.109-136.
Anna Avitabile (et al.), *Cooperare e Competere*, Feltrinelli, Milano, 1986.
Chris Axworthy, *Worker Cooperatives in Mondragon, the U.K. and France, Some Reflections*, Occasional Papers, Centre for the Study of Cooperatives, Saskatchewan, Canada, 1985.
Chris Axworthy and Terry Phalen, *Cooperative Growth and Survival: Two Viewpoints*, Cooperative College of Canada, Volume 4, Number 5, 1986.

Chris Axworthy and David Perry, *Worker Cooperatives and Worker Ownership: Issues Affecting the Development of Worker Cooperatives in Canada*, Occasional Papers, Centre for the Study of Cooperatives, University of Saskatchewan, Canada, 1988.

Enzo Badioli, "Nell' Epoca delle Multinazionali", *Rivista della Coperazione*, Numero 5, October-December, 1980, in Walter Briganti (ed), *Il Movimento Cooperativo in Italia 1963-1980*, Roma, 1982, pp.413-423.

Gianni Baget-Bozzo, "Pensiero Sociale Cristiano", in Norberto Bobbio (ed), *Dizionario Di Politica*, TEA, Torino, 1990, pp.779-783.

Gerardo Baione, "La Funzione delle Strutture Politico Sindacali", in *I Lacci di Gulliver: Deregulation e Movimento Cooperativo*, Editrice Cooperativa, Roma, 1986, pp.71-78.

Gerardo Baione, "Il Peso dell'Associazionismo nella Distribuzione in Italia", *Bianco e Bruno*, Anno 3, January-February, 1991, Bologna, p.5.

Michele Balboni, "L'Impresa Cooperativa: Aspetti Legislativi e Fiscali", in Francesco Carella (ed), *Il Movimento, Il Sistema, La Rete: Un Decennio di Cambiamenti nelle Imprese Cooperative*, Editrice Emilia Romagna, Bologna, 1991, pp.39-68.

Michele Balboni, "Finanza: Il Fai da Te è Perdente per un Sistema di Imprese", in Francesco Garella (ed), *Il Movimento, il Sistema, La Rete: Un Decennio di Cambiamenti nelle Imprese Cooperative*, Editrice Emilia Romagna, Bologna, 1991, pp.189-196.

Michele Balboni, "Indagine Annuale sul Credito e Sulla Gestione Finanziaria nelle Cooperative Lega", in Francesco Garella (ed), *Il Movimento, Il Sistema, la Rete: Un Decennio di Cambiamenti Nelle Imprese Cooperative*, Editrice Emilia Romagna, 1991, pp.219-241.

Frediano Baldi, "Evergomma", in AROC (ed), *Organizzare L'Autogestione,* I Quaderni di Quarantacinque, Bologna, 1987, pp.98-105.

Godfrey Baldocchino, "A War of Position: Ideas on a Strategy for Worker Cooperative Development", *Economic and Industrial Democracy*, Volume 11, 1990, pp.463-482.

Giuseppe Banchieri, *Elementi di Storia e Principi della Cooperazione Italiana*, Editrice Cooperativa, Terza Edizione, Roma, 1981.

Ivano Barberini, "Quando i Consumatori Fanno Impresa Insieme", *La Cooperazione Italiana,* October 1986, pp. 231-234.

Alberto Basevi, "L'Istituto di Credito alla Cooperazione", in Walter Briganti (ed), *Il Movimento Cooperativo in Italia 1854-1925*, Editrice Cooperativa, Roma, 1982, pp.229-230.

Paul Bate and Neil Carter, "The Future for Producers' Cooperatives", *Industrial Relations Journal*, Volume 17, Number 1, Spring 1986, pp.57-70.

Eric Batstone, "Organisation and Orientation: A Life Model of French Cooperatives", *Economic and Industrial Democracy*, Volume 4, 1983, pp.139-161.

Giuliano Bellezza, *La Comunità Economica Europea*, Editori Riuniti, Roma, 1980.

Lorenzo Bellicini, "Mercati, Dinamiche e Strutture del Settore delle Costruzioni Europeo", in Ecosfera (ed), *Le Imprese di Costruzione nel Mercato Europeo*, Il Solc 24 Ore, Milano, 1990, pp.15-52.

Walden Bello and Stephanie Rosenfeld, *Dragons in Distress: Asia's Miracle Economies in Crisis*, Penguin Books, London 1990.

Ugo Bellocchi, "Mille Banche per il Popolo", *Storia Illustrata*, July 1986, 118-125.

Giuseppe Belotti, "La Posizione della CCI", *L'Italia Cooperativa*, Roma, 19 February 1949, in Walter Brigante (ed), *Il Movimento Cooperativo in Italia 1926-1962*, Roma, 1978, pp.225-231.

Mario Bello, "I Progetti ci Sarebbero ma, Ovviamente, Mancano i Soldi", *L'Unità*, 21 July 1989.

Benito Benati, "Sacmi", in *Organizzare L'Autogestione*, AROC (ed), I Quaderni di Quarantacinque, February 87, Bologna, 1987, pp.80-86.

Joan Bennett, *Producer Cooperatives: A Case for Market Protection*, Discussion Paper Number 11, Centre for Research in Industrial Democracy and Participation, University of Glasgow, 1984.

Paola Bergonzoni, "Una Scelta Europea per Crescere Ancora", *La Cooperazione Italiana*, June-July 1991, p.38.

Enrico Berlinguer, "Riflessioni Sull'Italia Dopo I Fatti Del Cile", originally published in *Rinascita*, 28 September 1973, 5th and 9th October 1973, in Luciano Gruppi (ed), *Il Compromesso Storico*, Editori Riuniti, Roma, 1977, pp.266-286.

Katina V Berman, "The United States of America: A Cooperative Model for Worker Management", in Frank H Stephen, (ed), *The Performance of Labour Managed Firms*, MacMillan Press, London, 1982, pp.74-98.

Giorgio Bettini, "Una Crescita nella Democrazia", *La Cooperazione Italiana*, October 1986, pp.282-283.

Giorgio Bettini, "Un' Unica Rete fra Credito e Cooperazione", *La Cooperazione Italiana*, October 1986, pp.289-291.

Giorgio Bettini, "Un'Impresa del Nostro Tempo", in *La Cooperazione Italiana*, October 1986, pp.265-267.

Giorgio Bettini, "Una Strategia per Stare sul Mercato", *La Cooperazione Italiana*, October 1986, pp.284-285.

Giorgio Bettini, "L'Impresa come Strategia e Organizzazione", *La Cooperazione Italiana,* October 1986, pp. 318-320.

Giorgio Bettini, "La Sacmi di Imola: Servire il Mercato in Modo Completo", *La Cooperazione Italiana*, March 1991, pp.102-103.

Mauro Bianchi et al., "La Cooperazione Italiana di Servizio in Emilia Romagna", in A Carbonaro and S Gherardi (eds), *I Nuovi Scenari Della Cooperazione in Italia: Problemi di Efficacia, Efficienza e Legittimazione Sociale*, Franco Angeli, Milano, 1987, pp.17-68.

Patrizio Bianchi, "The Iri in Italy: Strategic Role and Political Constraints", *West European Politics*, Volume 10, Number 2, April 1987, pp.269-290.

Patrizio Bianchi, Sabino Cassese and Vincent della Sala, "Privatisation in Italy: Aims and Constraints", *West European Politics*, Volume 11, Number 4, October 1988, pp.278-282.

Patrizio Bianchi, "The Political Limits on European Economic Intergration", in Raffaella Y Nanetti and Raimondo Catanzaro (eds), *Italian Politics: A Review,* Volume 4, Printer Publishers, London, 1990, pp.36-57.

RC Birch, *The Shaping of the Welfare State*, Longman, London, 1984.

Joseph R Blasi, Perry Mehrling and William Foote Whyte, "The Politics of Worker Ownership in the United States", in Colin Crouch and Frank Heller (eds), *Organisational Democracy and Political Processes*, John Wiley and Sons, Chichester, 1983, pp.637-654.

Joseph Raphael Blasi and Douglas Lynn Kruse, *The New Owners: The Mass Emergence of Employee Ownership in Public Companies and What it Means to American Business,* Harper Business, USA, 1991.

Peter M Blau, "Theories of Organisations", *International Encyclopedia of the Social Sciences*, MacMillan and Free Press, USA, 1968, pp.297-305.

Norberto Bobbio, *The Future of Democracy: a Defence of the Rules of the Game,* Richard Bellamy (ed), University of Minnesota Press, Minneapolis, 1987.

Norberto Bobbio, "Pluralismo", in Norberto Bobbio et al., (eds), *Dizionario di Politica*, UTET, Torino 1990, pp.789-794.

Francesco Boccetti, "Introduzione", in *Le Imprese Cooperative: Trend 1982-1989*, Osservatorio Economico Finanziario della Lega Regionale dell' Emilia Romagna, Editrice Emilia Romagna, 1991, pp.5-7.

Rossella Bocciarelli, "Rigore D'Europa", *L'Espresso*, 14 October 1990, pp.167-169.

Franco Bojardi, "Cooperazione Reggiana e Tradizione Riformista", in Angelo Vardi (ed), *Emilia-Romagna Terra di Cooperazione*, Eta/Analisi, Bologna, 1990, pp.161-172.

Guido Bonfante, "La Legislazione Cooperativistica", in Giulio Sapelli (ed), *Il Movimento Cooperativo in Italia: Storia e Problemi*, Einaudi Editore, Torino, 1981, pp.191-253.

Sandro Bonella, "Finalmente Cittadine del Mercato", *La Cooperazione Italiana*, January 1992, pp.4-5.

Arnold Bonner, *British Cooperation: the History, Principles, and Organisation of the British Cooperative Movement*, Cooperative Union Limited, Manchester, 1961.

Sven Ake Book and Kaj Ilmonen, "Problems of Contemporary Cooperatives: Consumer Cooperatives in Sweden and Finland 1960-1980", *Economic and Industrial Democracy*, Volume 10, 1989, pp.499-515.

Sergio Bozzi, President of CNA, "Piccoli ma Forti e Vogliamo Contare", Interviewed by Virgilio Chelli, in *La Cooperazione Italiana*, April1989, pp.27-29.

Keith Bradley and Alan Gelb, *Cooperation at Work: The Mondragon Experience,* Heinemann Educational Books, London, 1983.

Keith Bradley and Alan Gelb, *Worker Capitalism: The New Industrial Relations*, Heinemann Educational Books, London, 1983.

Keith Bradley and Alan Gelb, "Cooperative Labour Relations: Mondragon's Responses to Recession", *British Journal of Industrial Relations*, Volume XXV, Number 1, March 1987, pp.77-97.

Walter Briganti, "Introduzione", in Walter Briganti (ed), *Il Movimento Cooperativo in Italia:1926-1962*, Editrice Cooperativa, Roma, 1978, pp.1-34.

Walter Briganti (ed), "L'Articolo 45. La Relazione e La Discussione", in *Il Movimento Cooperativo In Italia, 1926-1962,* Editrice Cooperative, Roma, 1978, pp.162-188.

Sebastiano Brusco, "The Emilian Model: Productive Decentralisation and Social Intergration", *Cambridge Journal of Economics,* Number 6, 1982, pp. 167-184.

M. Brutti, "Sotto il Segno dell'Emergenza", *Rinascita*, Numero 27, 12 July 1986, pp.36-38.

Franco Buzzi, "Il Caso CMC", in Anna Avitabile (et al.), *Cooperare e Competere*, Feltrinelli Editore, Milano, 1986, pp.37-50.

Roberto Calari, *Autonomia e Collateralismo del Movimento Cooperativo nella Provincia di Bologna dal 1945-1962. La Lega Provinciale delle Cooperative tra Economia e Politica nel Secondo Dopoguerra*, Tesi di Laurea, Facoltà di Scienze Politiche, Università degli Studi di Bologna, 1989.

Gildo Campensato, "Lega, Tanta Voglia di Capitalismo Popolare", *L'Unità* , 4 April1991.

Canevari et al., "L'Articolo 45. La Relazione e la Discussione", in Walter Briganti (ed), *Il Movimento Cooperativo in Italia 1926-1962*, Editrice Cooperativa, Roma, 1978, pp.162-188.

Vittorio Capecchi, "A History of Flexible Specialisation in Industrial Districts in Emilia Romagna", in Frank Pyke (et al.), *Industrial Districts and Inter-Firm Co-Operation in Italy*, International Labour Organisation, Geneva, 1990, pp.20-36.

Ann Capling and Brian Galligan, *Beyond the Protective State*, Cambridge University Press, Cambridge, 1992.

Gianni Carbonaro, "Le Politiche Pubbliche in Agricoltura", in Stefano Zan (ed), *Le Interdipendenze Organizzative in Agricoltura*, Regione Emilia Romagna, Bologna, 1987, pp.41-58.

Francesco Carella, *Il Movimento, Il Sistema, la Rete: Un Decennio di Cambiamenti nelle Imprese Cooperative*, Editrice Emilia Romagna, Bologna, 1991.

Vittorio Casarini, "Cooperative e Gruppi di Società: L'Esperienza della CMB", in Roberto Genco (ed), *Cooperative e Gruppi di Società: Le Nuove Dimensioni dell' Organizzazione Mutualistica*, Editrice Emilia Romagna, Bologna, 1990, pp.150-153.

Sabino Cassese, *Il Sistema Amministrativo Italiano*, Il Mulino, Bologna, 1983.

Sabino Cassese, "Hypothesis on the Italian Administrative System", *West European Politics*, Volume 16, Number 3, (July 1993), pp.316-328.

Sabino Cassese e Rita Perez, *Istituzioni di Diritto Pubblico*, La Nuova Italia Scientifica, Roma, 1989.

Valerio Castronovo, "Dal Dopoguerra ad Oggi", in Renato Zangheri, Giuseppe Galasso e Valerio Castronovo, *Storia del Movimento Cooperativo in Italia 1886-1986,* Giulio Einaudi Editore, Torino, 1986, pp.497-848.

Valerio Castronovo, *L'Industria Italiana Dall'Ottocento a Oggi*, Mondadori Editore, Milano, 1990.

Cavina Mauro, "I Problemi Organizzativi e Gestionali nell'Impresa Cooperativa", in *La Lega della Cooperative di Fronte alle Trasformazioni, le Modificazioni Strutturali dell"Economia: il Nuovo Rapporto Produzione-Ambiente*, La Lega-Convegno Dei Dirigenti e dei Quadri, Bologna, 3 July 1985, pp.113-123.

Centro Servizi Quasco, *Rapporto sulle Opere Pubbliche in Emilia Romagna nel 1990*, Regione Emilia Romagna, Bologna, March 1991.

Le Certificate, "Intervista con Pietro Verzelletti", *La Cooperazione Italiana,* November-December 1988, pp.36-38.

Le Certificate, "Unipol Assicurazioni", *La Cooperazione Italiana*, November-December 1988, pp.42-43.

Le Certificate, "Intervista con Fabio Carpanelli", *La Cooperazione Italiana,* November-December, 1988, pp.52-53.

Le Certificate, "Intervista con Dante Fantini", *La Cooperazione Italiana,* November-December, 1988, pp.68-69.

Le Certificate, "Produttività e Dimensione Aziendale in Aumento", *La Cooperazione Italiana,* November-December, 1988, pp.97-99.

Le Certificate, "Intervista con Enrico Gualandi", *La Cooperazione Italiana,* November-December, 1988, pp.116-117.

Le Certificate, "In Crescita Costante la Direzione Aziendale", *La Cooperazione Italiana,* November-December, 1988, pp.135-137.

Le Certificate, "Intervista con Pietro Rossi", *La Cooperazione Italiana*, November-December, 1988, pp.138-139.

Le Certificate, "Una Forza a Servizio della Qualità Urbana", *La Cooperazione Italiana,* November-December 1988, p.147.

Alfred Chandler Jn, *Strategy and Structure: Chapters in the History of the American Industrial Enterprise,* Anchor Books, New York, 1966, (first Published by MIT, 1962).

Virgilio Chelli, "La Lega allo Specchio", *La Cooperazione Italiana,* June 1990, pp.20-25.

Virgilio Chelli, "Se lo Stato si Mette in Cooperativa", *La Cooperazione Italiana,* August-September 1991, pp.4-7.

Giuseppe Chiarante, *La Democrazia Italiana*, Editori Riuniti, Roma, 1980.

Gerardo Chiaromonte, *Le Scelte della Solidarietà Democratica*, Editori Riuniti, Roma, 1986.

Zeffiro Ciuffoletti, "Dirigenti e Ideologie del Movimento Cooperativo", in Giulio Sapelli, *Il Movimento Cooperativo in Italia: Storia e Problemi*, Giulio Einaudi Editore, Torino 1981, pp.89-190.

Martin Clark, *Modern Italy 1871-1982,* Longman, London, 1982.

Tom Clarke, *Contrasting Theories of Cooperative Production*, Discussion Paper 7, Centre for Research in Industrial Democracy and Participation, University of Glasgow, April 1983.

Alasdair Clayre (ed), *The Political Economy of Cooperation and Participation: A Third Sector*, Oxford University Press, Oxford, 1980.

Alasdair Clayre, "Some Aspects of the Mondragon Cooperative Federation", in Alasdair Clayre (ed), *The Political Economy of Co-Operation and Participation*, Oxford University Press, 1980, pp.171-173.

Fabrizio Clementi (et al.), *Costituzione della Repubblica Italiana: il Testo, la Storia, la Spiegazione*, Avvenimenti Supplement, 1 May 1991.

GDH Cole, *A Short History of the British Working Class Movement 1789-1947*, George Allen and Unwin Ltd, London, 1948.

Maurizio Cocchi, "Dieci Anni di Spep: Una Cooperativa nel Sistema Sociale e Sanitario", *Sistema*, May 1990, pp.7-10.

Giuseppe Codisposti, "Esigenze e Strumentazioni Finanziarie per le Cooperative nel Settore Distributivo", in La Lega (ed), *Il Sistema Lega di Fronte all'Innovazione Finanziaria,* Stampa Nuova Grafica Fiorentina, Firenze, 1988, pp.267-273.

Piero Collina, "Finec", in Lega Nazionale delle Cooperative e Mutue, *Il Sistema Finanziario di Fronte all'Innovazione Finanziaria*, Roma, 1988, pp.70-73.

Stefania Conti, "La Ricostituzione della Lega: 1943-1948", in Fabio Fabbri (ed), *Il Movimento Cooperativo Nella Storia D'Italia 1854-1975*, Feltrinelli Editore, Milano, 1979, pp.317-346.

Comune di Bologna, *Indirizzi ed Obbiettivi di Programmazione Economico-Finanziaria per la Formazione del Bilancio Annuale 1991 e del Bilancio Pluriennale 1991-1993 del Comune di Bologna*, Bologna, 1990.

Cooperatives Research Unit, *Mondragon Cooperatives - Myth or Model*, The Open University, Milton Keynes, 1982.

La Cooperazione Italiana, Intervista con Giancarlo Brunello, "Una Crescita nella Democrazia", October 1986, pp.282-283.

La Cooperazione Italiana, Intervista con Italico Santoro, "Ai Soci L'Onere della Decisione", April 1989, pp.50-51.

La Cooperazione Italiana, Intervista con Alessandro Brusca, "Primo: Cambiare la Testa dei Manager", December 1989, pp.61-63.

La Cooperazione Italiana, "Energia: Un Ponte tra Ricerca e Azienda", December 1989, pp.74-75.

La Cooperazione Italiana, "Turci: Non Cerchiamo Solo il Business", December 1989, pp.6-7.

La Cooperazione Italiana, "La Parte del Leone la fa il Pubblico", December 1989, p.71.

La Cooperazione Italiana, "I Meccanismi della Legge", 4 April 1989, p.23.

La Cooperazione Italiana, "Il Testo Integrale Dell' Accordo Coop Sindacato", May 1990, pp.10-12.

La Cooperazione Italiana, "Fondi su Misura per i Soci Coop", June 1990, pp.54-55.

La Cooperazione Italiana, "Rapporto sulla Imprenditoria Cooperativa a Confronto con le Imprese Private", July-August 1990, pp.17-48.

La Cooperazione Italiana, "Mercato Dinamico Aperto alle Coop", September 1990, pp.53-54.

La Cooperazione Italiana, "La Cassaforte Coop", October 1990, p.81.

La Cooperazione Italiana, "Un Sensore che Segnala come Cambiano le Coop", October 1991, pp.46-47.

La Cooperazione Italiana, "Nuova Struttura Europea a Favore del Dettaglio", November 1991, p.26.

La Cooperazione Italiana, "Tra Coop e Ferrovie un Rapporto Speciale", December 1991, p.9.

La Cooperazione Italiana, "Iniziativa del Conad per il Terzo Mondo", January 1992, p.18.

La Cooperazione Italiana, "Compagnie alla Sfida della Professionalità", February March 1992, pp.56-57.

La Cooperazione Italiana, "Un Libro per Realizzare una Scuola in Senegal", April 1992, p.31.

La Cooperazione Italiana, "Servizi Integrati Contro la Concorrenza", April 1992, pp.60-61.

La Cooperazione Italiana, "Dieci Progetti per Cambiare il Volto Delle Imprese", August-September 1992, pp.40-41.

La Cooperazione Italiana, "Il Business Plan è la Prima Cosa", October 1992, p.57.

La Cooperazione Italiana, "La Qualità Sociale Come Obbiettivo", April 1993, pp. 10-11.

Gianni Corbi, "Quella Fiat Agricola Targata Scudocrociato", *La Repubblica,* 21 May 1991, p.9.

Chris Cornforth et al., *Developing Successful Worker Cooperatives*, Sage Publications, London, 1988.

Chris Cornforth, "The Role of Support Organisations in Developing Worker Cooperatives: A Model for Promoting Economic and Industrial Democracy?", in Gyorgy Szell (et al.)., *The State, The Trade Unions and Self Management*, Walter De Gruyter, Berlin, 1989, pp.105-124.

Chris Cornforth, "The Role of Managers in Worker Cooperatives", in *Yearbook of Cooperative Enterprise 1989,* Plunkett Foundation, Oxford, 1989, pp.13-22.

Chris Cornforth and Alan Thomas, "Cooperative Development: Barriers, Support Structures and Cultural Factors", *Economic and Industrial Democracy,* Volume 11, 1990, pp.451-461.

Corriere della Sera, "Parmalat, un Giglio delle Coop nell'Occhiello di Tanzi", 26 March 1992, p.27.

Costruire, Le Classifiche 1990, Milano, November 1990.

Andrew Cox, "State, Finance and Industry", in Andrew Cox (ed), *State, Finance and Industry*, Wheatsheaf Books, Bristol, 1986, pp.1-59.

Bernard Crick, *Socialism*, Open University Press, Milton Keynes, 1987.

Annarita Criscitiello, "Majority Summits: Decision-Making Inside the Cabinet and Out: Italy, 1970-1990", *West European Politics,* Volume 16, Number 4 (October 1993), pp.581-594.

Raffaele Cuccurullo and Dora Jacobelli, "Finanza Locale e Settoriale", in Lega Nazionale delle Cooperative e Mutue, *Il Sistema Lega di Fronte all'Innovazione Finanziaria,* Firenze, 1988, pp.230-239.

M. D'Ambrosio, Renzo Stefanelli, *La Cooperazione Italiana nell'Industria,* Editrice Cooperativa, Roma, 1983.

Moreno D'Angelo, "Annibale ha Varcato le Alpi", in *Consumi e Società*, Anno 5, Numero 3, May-June 1991, pp.14-18, 31-32.

Emanuel Danieli, "L'Impresa Cooperativa Definizione e Tipologia", in Francesco Garella (a cura di), *Il Movimento, Il Sistema, la Rete: Un Decennio di Cambiamenti Nelle Imprese Cooperative,* Editrice Emilia Romagna, Bologna 1991, pp.16-38.

Emanuel Danieli (ed), *Le Imprese Cooperative: Trend 1982-1989*, Editrice Emilia Romagna, Bologna, 1991.

Pier Paolo D'Attorre, "La Politica", in Renato Zangheri (ed), *Bologna*, Editori Laterza, Bari, 1986, pp.63-190.

Pier Paolo D'Attorre, "Solidarietà, Innovazione, Impresa: La Cooperazione Ravennate", in Angelo Varni, *Emilia Romagna Terra di Cooperazione*, Eta/Analisi, Bologna 1990, pp.93-105.

Abe David and Ted Wheelwright, *The Third Wave: Australia and Asian Capitalism,* Left Book Club, Sutherland, 1989.

Ettore Dazzara, "La Questione Finanziaria e lo Sviluppo dell'Impresa Cooperativa", in La Lega, *La Questione Finanziaria e lo Sviluppo dell'Impresa Cooperativa*, Editrice Cooperativa, Roma, 1984, pp.13-31.

Renato De Bertoli, "Foncooper: Adeguare la Normativa e le Risorse ai Reali Bisogni", in *La Cooperazione Italiana*, January-February 1993, (Supplement: Legge 49/85 "Marcora" Stato di Attuazione e Nuove Proposte), pp.4-7.

Massimo Degli Esposti, "Le Coop D'Europa Fondano Holding delle Assicurazioni", *Il Sole 24 Ore*, 18 November 1989.

Maurizio Degl'Innocenti, *Storia della Cooperazione in Italia*, Editori Riuniti, 1977.

Maurizio Degl' Innocenti, "Geografia e Struttura della Cooperazione in Italia", in Giulio Sapelli, *Il Movimento Cooperativo in Italia: Storia e Problemi*, Giulio Einaudi Editore, Torino 1981, pp.3-88.

Maurizio Degl'Innocenti, "Le Origini della Cooperazione in Emilia Romagna", in Angelo Varni (ed), *Emilia Romagna Terra di Cooperazione*, Eta/Analisi, Bologna 1990, pp.21-35.

Bruno Dente, "Il Governo Locale", in Giorgio Freddi (ed), *Scienze dell'Amministrazione e Politiche Pubbliche,* La Nuova Italia Scientifica, Roma, 1989, pp.123-169.

Giuseppe de Rita, *La Cultura del Sociale nell'Impresa Cooperativa*, Club '87, Bologna, 1989.

Viviana D'Isa, "Il Valore Primario della Risorsa Uomo", *La Cooperazione Italiana*, October 1986, pp.308-310.

Viviana D'Isa, Intervista con Valerio Veltroni, "L'Universo Cooperativo Attraverso L'Immaggine", *La Cooperazione Italiana*, October 1986, pp.305-307.

Viviana D'Isa, "La Strada Ripida dei Bottegai in Coop", *La Cooperazione Italiana*, October 1986, pp.239-242.

Viviana D'Isa, "Servizi Integrati per Stare in Europa", *La Cooperazione Italiana*, April1989, pp.42-44.

Viviana D'Isa, "Una Mano allo Stato", *La Cooperazione Italiana*, April1989, pp.38-45.

Viviana D'Isa, "Negozi a Misura di Consumatore", *La Cooperazione Italiana*, May 1990, pp.40-42.

Viviana D'Isa, "Per Crescere Occorre un Partner", *La Cooperazione Italiana,* May 1990, pp.38-40.

Viviana D'Isa, "Marcora, Una Buona Legge che ora va Potenziata", *La Cooperazione Italiana*, October 1991, p.38.

Viviana D'Isa, "Un Sistema di Imprese Verso il Mare Aperto", *La Cooperazione Italiana*, January 1992, p.27.

Viviana D'Isa, "Per Farle Crescere Ci Vuole il Tutor", *La Cooperazione Italiana*, October 1992, p.59.

Peter Donaldson, *Economics of the Real World*, Penguin, Third Edition, London, 1988.

Walter Dondi, "È Appena Iniziato il Viaggio di Cipputi", *La Cooperazione Italiana*, April1989, p.35.

Walter Dondi, "Cervello Complementare", in *Lega Senza Frontiere*, L'Unità, 16 June, 1989, pp.22-24.

Walter Dondi, "Cecop e Euroc", in *Lega Senza Frontiere*, L'Unità, 16 June 1989, p.30.

Walter Dondi, "Lega, Psi-Pri all'Attacco di Turci", *L'Unità* , 20 July 1989.

Walter Dondi, "A Bologna si Ricuce lo Strappo", *L'Unità,* 26 November 1989.

Walter Dondi, "Nuova Coop: né Fiat né Holding", *L'Unità,* 28 November 1989.

Walter Dondi, "In Lega Tutti D'Accordo: Cambiare", *L'Unità*, 29 November 1989, p.14.

Walter Dondi, "L'Unipol Assicura L'Europa. Obbiettivo: i Paesi dell'Est", *L'Unità,* 15 December 1989, in *Unipol Press*, 16 January 1990, p.12.

Walter Dondi, "Debutta Coopfond, Venderà ai Piccoli Risparmiatori", *L'Unità,* 31 March 1990, p.15.

Walter Dondi, "Nella Hit Parade della Grande Distribuzione Entra il Supercolosso dell'Adriatico", in *L'Unità,* 11 May 1991.

Walter Dondi, "Fincooper Punta alla Leadership in Banec", *La Cooperazione Italiana*, February-March 1992, pp.54-55.

Walter Dondi, "Compagnie alla Sfida della Professionalità", *La Cooperazione Italiana*, February-March 1992, pp.56-57.

Walter Dondi, "Unipol Finanziaria ha Messo Ordine", *La Cooperazione Italiana*, February-March 1992, pp.58-59.

Carlo Donolo, "Social Change and Transformation of the State in Italy", in Richard Scase (ed), *The State in Western Europe*, Croom Helm, London, 1980, pp.164-196.

The Economist, "A Survey of Italy", May 26 1990.

The Economist, "A Survey of Italy", June 26 1993.

John Earle, *The Italian Cooperative Movement: A Portrait of La Lega Nazionale delle Cooperative e Mutue*, Allen and Unwin, London, 1986.

John Earle, "Italy's Sacmi", *Worker CO-OP*, Volume 10, Number 1, Summer 1990, pp.24-26.

Edilfornaciai, *Pietra su Pietra: La Storia dell'Edilfornaciai*, Video Cassette, Bologna, 1990.

Finn Aage Ekelund, *Cooperatives and Social Democracy: Elements of the Norwegian Case*, Occasional Papers, Centre of Cooperatives Studies, University of Saskatchewan, May 1986.

David Ellerman, *Worker Ownership: Economic Democracy or Worker Capitalism?,* Industrial Cooperative Association - School of Management, Boston College, March 1985, pp.1-15.

Bruno Enriotti, "Turci: alla Lega ci Vuole Glasnost", *L'Unità*, 19 June 1989.

Ervet, *Profilo e Strategie D'Intervento del Sistema Ervet*, Bologna, 1990.

Ervet, *Attività e Composizione del Sistema Ervet,* Bologna, 1990.

Robert H Evans, "Regionalism and the Italian City", in Michael C Romanos (ed), *Western European Cities in Crisis*, Lexington Books, Lexington, 1979, pp.215-231.

Giuseppe Fabbri, "La Scommessa della Promozione", *La Cooperazione Italiana,* October 1986, pp.321-232.

Guido Fabiani, "L'Agricoltura, Passato e Futuro", in *Profili dell'Italia Repubblicana*, Editori Riuniti, Roma, 1985, pp.145-166.

Costanza Fanelli, "Il Pacchetto Coop", in *La Cooperazione Italiana,* September 1990, pp.25-28.

Costanza Fanelli, "Il Futuro del Lavoro nell'Economia Sociale", *La Cooperazione Italiana*, April 1993, p.12-13.

Connell M Fanning and Thomas McCarthy, "A Survey of Economic Hypotheses Concerning the Non-Viability of Labour-Directed Firms in Capitalist Economies", in Sune Jansson and Ann-Britt Hellmark, (eds), *Labor-Owned Firms and Workers' Cooperatives*, Gower, Aldershot, 1986, pp. 7-50.

Teresa Farnetti, *Fattori di Successo delle Imprese Cooperative*, Franco Angeli, Milano, 1989.

Tullio Fazzolari, "Assalto Al Piatto", *L'Espresso,* 22 January 1989, pp.158-162.

Enzo Forcella, "Le Confessioni di Mancini", *La Repubblica*, 22 August 1989, p.8.

Paolo Forcellini, "L'Industria tra Crisi e Terza Rivoluzione", in Ottavio Cecchi and Enrico Ghidetti (eds), *Profili dell'Italia Repubblicana*, Editori Riuniti, 1985, pp.261-288.

R Forte, "Il Secondo Congresso della Confederazione Cooperativa Italiana", *La Rivista della Cooperazione*, Roma, October-December 1947, in Walter Briganti (ed), *Il Movimento Cooperativo in Italia 1926-1962*, Edizione Cooperativa, Roma, 1978, pp.190-193.

Gianfranco Franci, "Il Vantaggio delle Coop non Partire Favorite", *La Cooperazione Italiana*, September 1990, pp.8-13.

Gianfranco Franci, "Lavori a Rilento a Sud", *La Cooperazione Italiana*, June-July 1992, p.52.

Paul Furlong, "State, Finance and Industry in Italy", in Andrew Cox (ed), *State, Finance and Industry*, Wheatsheaf Books, Brighton, 1986, pp.142-171.

Mario Gabbi e Alberto Terzi, *Il Manager Cooperativo,* Edizioni Sipiel, Milano, 1989.

Pasquale Gagliardi, "The Creation and Change of Organisational Cultures: a Conceptual Framework", *Organization Studies*, 1986, 7/2, pp.117-134.

John Kenneth Galbraith, *Almost Everyone's Guide to Economics*, Penguin, Harmondsworth, 1978.

Giuseppe Galasso, "Gli Anni della Grande Espansione e La Crisi del Sistema", in Renato Zangheri (ed), *Storia del Movimento Cooperativo in Italia*, Giulio Einaudi Editore, Torino, 1987, pp.219-496.

Vincenzo Galetti, *Cooperazione: Forza Anticrisi,* Feltrinelli, Milano, 1975.

Vincenzo Galetti, *La Cooperazione in Italia,* Editori Riuniti, Roma, 1976.

Vincenzo Galetti, "Intervento", *Atti della Prima Conferenza Nazionale della Cooperazione Italiana*, Primo Volume, Roma, 1977, pp.90-100.

Giorgio Galli, *Il Bipartismo Imperfetto*, Mondadori Editore, Milano, 1984.

Giorgio Galli, "Per Una Storia del Partito Armato", *Panorama,* 12 November 1984, pp.133-159.

Giorgio Galli, *Storia dei Partiti Politici Europei: Dal 1649 a Oggi*, Rizzoli, Milano, 1990.

Giuliana Ricci Garotti, "La Cooperazione in Emilia Romagna nel Periodo Fascista", in Angelo Varni (ed), *Emilia Romagna Terra di Cooperazione,* Eta/Analisi, Bologna, 1990, pp.37-45.

Giuliana Ricci Garotti, "Il Movimento Cooperativo Bolognese e la Federazione Cooperative e Mutue dal Secondo Dopoguerra agli Anni Cinquanta", in Federazione Provinciale delle Coperative e Mutue di Bologna e Il Centro Documentazione sulla Storia del Movimento Cooperativo (ed), *L'Unione dei Mille Strumenti*, Editrice Emilia Romagna, Bologna, 1991, pp.185-224.

Garzanti Editore, *Enciclopedia Del Diritto e Dell'Economia,* Milano, 1985.

Roberto Genco, *Cooperative e Gruppi di Società: Le Nuove Dimensione dell'Organizzazione Mutualistica*, Editrice Emilia Romagna, Bologna, 1990.

Pietro Gentilucci, "Cooperservice il Segreto di un Successo", *La Cooperazione Italiana*, May, 1992, pp.30-33.

Guido Gerosa, "I Notabili al Parlamento", *Storia Illustrata*, July 1987, pp.83-88.

Silvia Gherardi, "Worker Takeovers: The Italian Experience", in *Analysis of the Experiences and Problems Encountered by Worker Takeover of Companies in Difficulty or Bankrupt,* Main Report, Commission of the European Communities, Luxembourg, 1987, pp.160-192.

Silvia Gherardi and Attilio Masiero, "The Impact of Organisational Culture in Life Cycle and Decision Making Process in Newborn Cooperatives", in *Economic and Industrial Democracy,* Sage, London, Volume 8, 1987, pp.323-347.

Gianni Giadresco, *Dai Magliari Ai Vu Cumpra*, Rubettino Editore, Soveria Mannelli, 1988.

Paul Ginsborg, *A History of Contemporary Italy: Society and Politics 1943-1988*, Penguin Books, London, 1990.

Il Giornale della Banca, "Voglia di Mercato", September 1989, in *Unipol Press*, 16 January 1990, pp.16-17.

Mauro Gori, "Per un Nuovo Rapporto tra Pubblico e Privato", *La Cooperazione Italiana*, August-September 1991, pp.7-9.

Gustavo Gozzi, "Stato Contemporaneo", in Norberto Bobbio (ed), *Dizionario di Politica*, UTET, Torino 1990, pp.1103-1112.

Robert Graham, "Italians to Lose Golden Pensions", *Financial Times*, July 11 1992, p.2.

Robert Graham, "Doctor Subtle's Twin Pillars", *Financial Times*, July 16 1992.

Antonio Gramsci, *Prison Notebooks*, Edited and Translated by Quintin Hoare and G. Narell Smith, International Publishers, New York, 1971.

Edward S. Greenberg, "Producer Cooperatives and Democratic Theory: the Case of the Plywood Firms", in Robert Jackall and Henry M. Levin (ed), *Worker Cooperatives in America,* University of California Press, Berkeley, 1984, pp.171-214.

Donald Hay and John Vickers, "The Economics of Market Dominance", in Donald Hay and John Vickers (eds), *The Economics of Market Dominance,* Basil Blackwell, Oxford, 1987, pp.1-60.

Brian W Head, "State and Economy: Theories and Problems", in BW Head (ed), *State and Economy in Australia,* Oxford University Press, Melbourne, 1983, pp.22-54.

David Held, "Central Perspectives on the Modern State", in Gregor McLennan (et al.), *The Idea of the Modern State,* Open University Press, Milton Keynes, 1984, pp.29-79.

Eric Hobsbawn, *The Italian Road to Socialism: an Interview with Giorgio Napolitano*, Translated by John Cammet and Victoria De Grazia, Lawrence Hill and Company, Westport Connecticut, 1977.

Mark Holmstrom, *Industrial Democracy in Italy*, Gower, Aldershot, 1989.

Colin Howard, *Companies: What Are They and How They Work*, Oxford University Press, Melbourne, 1989.

Ettore Iami, "Dove Compriamo Pesce? Anche dalla Montagnosa Svizzera", *L'Unità* , 21 July 1989, p.18.

ICOM, *ICOM: a Description of the Industrial Common Ownership Movement*, London, 1975.

Kaj Ilmonen, "Movement, Organisation and Identity", *Kooperativa Studier*, 1990, pp.48-62.

Istituto Nazionale di Statistica, *Introducing Italy*, Rome, 1989.

Istituto Nazionale di Statistica, *45 Anni di Elezioni in Italia 1946-1990*, Roma, 1991.

Istituto di Studi Cooperativi "Luigi Luzzatti", *Cooperazione ed Autogestione in Italia ed in Jugoslavia*, Editrice Cooperativa, Roma, 1986.

Max Jaggi et al., *Red Bologna*, Writers and Readers, London, 1977.

Sune Jansson and Ann-Britt Hellmark (eds), *Labor-Owned Firms and Workers' Cooperatives*, Gower Publishing Co., Aldershot, 1986.

Peter Jay, "A Cooperative Economy", in Alasdair Clayre (ed), *The Political Economy of Cooperation and Participation*, Oxford University Press, Oxford, 1980, pp.9-45.

Keith Jefferis and Alan Thomas, "Measuring the Performance of Worker Cooperatives", Cooperative Research Unit, Open University, Milton Keynes, 1985.

Keith Jefferis and Chris Cornforth, "Worker Cooperatives in Britain: a Review of the Literature", unplublished document, Milton Keynes, 1989.

Derek C Jones and Jan Svejner, "Participation, Profit Sharing, Worker Ownership and Efficiency in Italian Producer Cooperatives", *Economica*, Volume 52, Number 208, November 1985, pp.449-466.

Chalmers Johnson, *Miti and the Japanese Miracle*, Stanford University Press, 1982.

John E Jordan, "A System of Interdependent Firms", in Sune Jansson and Ann-Britt Hellmark (eds), *Labor-Owned Firms and Workers' Cooperatives*, Gower Publishing Co., Aldershot, 1986, pp.105-116.

AG Kenwood and AL Lougheed, *The Growth of the International Economy 1820-1980*, George Allen and Unwin, London, 1984.

Len Krimerman and Frank Lindenfeld (eds), *When Workers Decide: Workplace Democracy Takes Root in North America*, New Society Publishers, Philadelphia, 1992.

Len Krimerman and Frank Lindenfeld, "Changing Worklife: Grassroots Activism Takes a New Turn", in Len Krimerman and Frank Lindenfeld (eds), *When Workers Decide: Workplace Democracy Takes Root in North America*, New Society Publishers, Philadelphia, 1992, pp.5-8.

Paolo Sylos Labini, *Le Classi Sociali negli Anni Ottanta*, Laterza, Bari, 1986.

Peter Lange, "Crisis and Consent, Change and Compromise: Dilemmas of Italian Communism in the 1970s", in Peter Lange and Sydney Tarrow (ed), *Italy in Transition,* Frank Cass, London, 1980, pp.110-132.

Peter Lange and Maurizio Vannicelli, "Strategy Under Stress: The Italian Union Movement and the Italian Crisis in Developmental Perspective", in Peter Lange (et al.), *Unions, Change and Crisis: French and Italian Union Strategy and the Political Economy, 1945-1980*, George Allen and Unwin, London, 1982, pp.97-206.

Joseph La Palombara, *Democracy Italian Style*, Yale University Press, New Haven, 1987.

David Laylock, *Cooperative-Government Relations in Canada: Lobbying, Public Policy Development and the Changing Cooperative System*, Centre for the Study of Cooperatives, Sasketchewan, 1987.

Felice Lenti, "Unipol: La Rossa in Nero", *La Repubblica,* 5 January 1990, in *Unipol Press,* 16 January 1990, Number1/2, pp.1-2.

Paolo Leon, "I Limiti della Politica Economica: né Stato, né Mercato", in Ottavio Cecchi and Enrico Ghidetti (eds), *Profili dell'Italia Repubblicana*, Editori Riuniti, 1985, pp.331-350.

Adriano Leonardi, "Il Fincooper Punto D'Appoggio del Nuovo Disegno Finanziario", in La Lega, *La Questione Finanziaria e Lo Sviluppo dell'Impresa Cooperativa*, Editrice Cooperativa, Roma, 1984, pp.88-98.

Aurelio Lepre, "La Rivoluzione del Voto", *Storia Ilustrata*, July 1987, pp.88-92.

Gad Lerner, "Meglio Craxi che Mai", *L'Espresso*, 27 August 1989, pp.14-17.

Henry M Levin, "ESOPs and the Financing of Cooperatives", in Robert T Jackall and Henry M Levin (eds), *Worker Cooperatives in America*, University of California Press, Berkeley, 1984, pp.245-256.

Theodore Levitt, "The Globalization of Markets", *Harvard Business Review*, May-June 1983, Number 3, pp. 92-102.

Nicola Lisanti, *Il Movimento Operaio in Italia: 1860-1980*, Editori Riuniti, Roma, 1986.

Lars Lindkvist and Ann Westenholz (eds), *Employee Owned Companies in the Nordic Countries: A Summary*, Nordic Council of Ministers, Copenhagen, 1987.

Charles Lindblom, *Politics and Markets,* Basic Books, Inc., Publishers, New York, 1977.

Charles Lindblom, "Comment on Manley", *The American Political Science Review*, Volume 77, June 1983, pp.384-386.

Virginia Lori, "Europa Sociale", in *Lega Senza Frontiere*, Editrice L"Unità, 16 June 1989, pp.18-20.

Nino Lucantoni and Filippo Vita, "Un'Alleanza per L'Ambiente", *La Cooperazione Italiana,* May 1991, pp.13-53.

Laura Lupo, "I Pezzi della Rete", *La Cooperazione Italiana*, March 1990, p.15.

Antonio Macaluso, "Nestle si Mangia il Panettone", *Corriere della Sera*, 30 July 1993, p.14.

Telesio Malaspina, "Obbiettivo Mirafiori", *L'Espresso* 14 January 1990, in *Unipol Press,* Bologna, 16 January 1990, p.3.

Roberto Malucelli, *Cooperativa Muratori Cementisti di Ravenna 1901-1915*, Grafiche Galeati, Imola, 1978.

Roberto Malucelli, "Gli Italiani e le Coop: Indagine Monitor Demoskopea Lega", *La Cooperazione Italiana,* January 1984, pp.10-16.

Giuseppe Mammarella, *Italy After Fascism*, Mario Casalini Ltd, Montreal, 1964.

Giuseppe Mammarella, *L'Italia Contemporanea: 1943-1989*, Il Mulino, Bologna, 1990.

Claudia Mancina, *La Famiglia,* Editori Riuniti, Roma, 1981.

Ernest Mandel, "Self-Management Dangers and Possibilities", *International*, Volume 2, Number 4, Winter/Spring, 1975, pp.3-9.

Sandro Mangiaterra, "Vento del Sud", *Panorama*, 30 August 1992, pp.134-138.

JJ March and HA Simon, *Organisation,* Wiley, New York, 1958.

Maurizio Maggi, "Il Giallo dell'Estrogeno", *L'Espresso*, 3 September 1989, p.140.

Edoardo Marinelli, "Una Legge dai Buoni Esiti che va Potenziata e Sviluppata", in *La Cooperazione Italiana*, January-February 1993, (Supplement:Legge 49/85 "Marcora" Stato di Attuazione e Nuove Proposte), pp.3-4.

Edoardo Marinelli, "La Crisi Pesa Sui Bilanci Industriali", *La Cooperazione Italiana*, June-July 1993, pp.40-42.

Marco Marini e Chiara Cavallaro, "Miliardi Ben Spesi", *La Cooperazione Italiana,* April1989, pp.18-21.

Enrico Marro, "Ogni Cento Lire Quattro Alle Imprese", *Il Corriere della Sera*, 24 September 1991, p.3.

Enrico Marro, "Nasce il Silico in Abruzzo", *Corriere della Sera*, 9 May 1992, p.29.

Enrico Marro, "Diecimila Miliardi per L'IRI", *Corriere della Sera*, 30 December 1993, p.17.

Giancarlo Martelli, "Come Unire le Forze Senza Perdere Identità", *La Cooperazone Italiana*, February-March 1992, p.65.

Giancarlo Martelli, "Un Matrimonio che Porterà Giglio in Borsa", *La Cooperazione Italiana*, June-July 1992, pp.17-18.

Daniele Martini, "Il Business è Servito", *Panorama*, 7 June 1992, pp. 187-189.

Guido Martinotti, "Electoral Trends in Italy: The Cycle 1970-1985", *West European Politics*, April 1986, pp.253-281.

Vittorio Marzocchi, "Un Patrimonio da Valorizzare", *La Cooperazione Italiana,* October 1986, pp.296-297.

Vittorio Marzocchi, "Di Qua e Di Là dell'Atlantico", *La Cooperazione Italiana,* October 1986, pp.298-290.

Sandro Massarelli, "Radiografia dei Microsettori", *La Cooperazione Italiana,* January 1992, p.35.

Gregor McLennan, "Capitalist State or Democratic Polity? Recent Developments in Marxist and Pluralist Theory", in Gregor McLennan, David Held and Stuart Hall (eds), *The Idea of the Modern State*, Open University Press, Milton Keynes, 1984, pp.80-109.

Giuseppe Mazzini, "Lavoro e Capitali nelle Stesse Mani", in Walter Briganti (ed), *Il Movimento Cooperativo in Italia 1854-1925*, Editrice Cooperativa, Roma, 1982, pp.26-29.

Gary Mead, "Profile: Mondragon Cooperative Movement", *Financial Times*, 24 November 1993, p.29.

James E Mead, "The Theory of Labour Managed Firms and Profit Sharing", *The Economic Journal*, Volume 82, March 1972, pp.402-428.

Christopher B Meek and Warner P Woodworth, "Technical Training and Enterprise: Mondragon's Educational System and its Implications for Other Cooperatives", *Economic and Industrial Democracy,* Sage, London, Volume 11, 1990, pp.505-528.

Mariella Melchiorri, Intervista con Vladmiro Lecca, "Una Struttura per lo Sviluppo", *La Cooperazione Italiana*, October 1986, pp.301-302.

Mariella Melchiorri, intervista con Marco Bulgarelli e con Alessandro Busca, "Dalla Ricerca All'Impresa Coop", *La Cooperazione Italiana,* October 1986, pp.311-315.

Giovanni Melis, *Il Bilancio D'Esercizio Nell'Economia Dell'Impresa Cooperativa*, Cedam, Padova, 1983.

Mary Mellor et al., *Worker Cooperatives in Theory and Practice,* Open University Press, Milton Keynes, 1988.

George Melnyk, "Future Directions for Worker Cooperatives: a Postscript", in Jack Quarter and George Melnyk (eds), *Partnership in Enterprise: The Worker Ownership Phenomenon*, Black Rose Books, Montreal, 1989, pp.192-199.

Michele Menichella, "Goria Sblocca i Fondi all'Agricoltura e il Cipe Distribuirà 2,700 Miliardi", *Il Sole 24 ORE*, 20 July 1991, p.3.

Yves Mény, *Government and Politics in Western Europe: Britain, France, Italy and Germany*, Oxford University Press, Second Edition, 1993.

Silvio Miana, "Proposte Programmatiche del Movimento Cooperativo", (Relazione Introduttiva al Ventinovesimo Congresso della Lega, 1973), in Walter Briganti (ed), *Il Movimento Cooperativo in Italia 1963-1980,* Editrice Cooperativa, Roma, 1982, pp.208-217.

Renato Midoro, *Gli Strumenti per il Finanziamento delle Cooperative,* Editrice Cooperativa, Roma, 1984.

Peter Milford, "Worker Cooperatives and Consumer Cooperatives: Can They Be Combined?", in Sune Jansson and Ann-Britt Hellmark (eds), *Labor-Owned Firms and Worker Cooperatives,* Gower, Aldershot, 1986, pp.117-139.

David Miller, "Market Neutrality and the Failure of Cooperatives", *British Journal of Political Science*, Number 11, 1981, pp.309-329.

Ralph Miliband, *State in Capitalist Society*, Quartet Books, London, 1973.

François Mitterrand, "Un'Idea Antica di cui l'Europa ha Bisogno", in *La Cooperazione Italiana*, December 1989, pp.16-17.
Giovanni Montanari, *La Cooperativa Muratori e Cementisti di Ravenna Durante il Fascismo 1926-1945,* Feltrinelli, Milano, 1986.
J Carroll Moody and Gilbert C Fite, *The Credit Union Movement: Origins and Development 1850-1970*, University of Nebraska Press, Lincoln, 1971.
Roy Morrison, *We Build the Road as We Travel,* New Society Publishers, Philadelphia, 1991.
David Morris, "Mondragon: Cooperative at Work", *Co-op America Quarterly*, Winter 1992, p.6.
Mario Moruzzi, *I Comunisti e La Cooperazione Italiana*, De Donato, Bari, 1981.
Melissa a Moye, "Mondragon: Adapting Cooperative Structures to Meet the Demands of a Changing Environment", *Economic and Industrial Democracy*, Volume 14, 1993, pp.251-276.
Massimo Mucchetti, "I Retroscena del Grande Boom", *L'Espresso*, 24 December 1989, in *Unipol Press,* 16 January 1990, Number 1/2, pp.5-6.
Chloe Munro, *The Financing of Worker Cooperatives*, CRU Monograph Number 8, The Open University, Milton Keynes, 1988.
Robin Murray, "Withering Heights: Social Ownership in a Changing World", *New Socialist*, April 1987, pp.41-45.
Niels Mygind, "From the Illyrian Firm to the Reality of Self-Management", in Sune Jansson and Ann-Britt Hellmark (eds), *Labor-Owned Firms and Workers' Cooperatives*, Gower, Aldershot, 1986, pp.73-104.
Raffaella Y Nanetti, *Growth and Territorial Policies; the Italian Model of Social Capitalism*, Pinter Publishers, London, 1988.
Giorgio Napolitano, "Intervento", *Atti della Prima Conferenza Nazionale della Cooperazione Italiana,* Ministero del Lavoro e della Previdenza Sociale, Secondo Volume, Roma, 1977, pp.115-116.
Tommasini Nazzareno, "Crescere Cambiando", in *Consumi e Società,* Anno 5, Numero 3, May-June 1991, pp.20-30.
Mariella Nejrotti, "La Lunga Notte dell'Era Fascista", *La Cooperazione Italiana*, October 1986, pp.181-188.
OECD Economic Surveys, *Italy*, Paris, 1989.
OECD Economic Surveys, *Italy*, Paris, 1991.
Robert Oakeshott, *The Case for Workers' Cooperatives*, Routledge and Kegan Paul, London, 1978.
Robert Oakeshott, *Workers as Entrepreneurs: Two Striking Success Stories From Italy,* Partnership Research Limited, London, March 1990.
Claus Offe and Volker Ronge, "Theses on the Theory of the State", *New German Critique*, Number 6, Fall 1975, pp.137-147.
Nazario Sauro Onofri, "Rinasce La Cooperazione Italiana Bolognese", in Federazione Provinciale delle Cooperative e Mutue di Bologna e il Centro Documentazione sulla Storia del Movimento Cooperativo (ed), *L'Unione Dei Mille*, Editrice Emilia Romagna, Bologna, 1991, pp.45-184.

Pier Luigi Orvieto, "Trent'Anni sulle Vie del Mondo", *La Cooperazione Italiana*, October 1986, pp.292-295.

Ida Ossi, "Euro Sportello Targato Lega", *La Cooperazione Italiana*, June 1990, pp.37-41.

Robert Owen, *A New View of Society and Other Writings*, JM Dent and Sons, London, 1927.

Francesco Pagnetti, *Le Cooperative di Produzione e Lavoro,* Editrice Cooperativa, Roma, 1987.

Angelo Panebianco, *Political Parties: Organisation and Power,* Cambridge University Press, Cambridge, 1988.

Rita Pareschi, "Progetti dal Lavoro Integrato", *La Cooperazione Italiana*, October 1990, pp.61-63.

Leonardo Parri, "Politiche Locali per l'Innovazione Tecnologica: Rhone Alpes ed Emilia Romagna", *Stato e Mercato*, Il Mulino, Bologna, April1991, pp.77-116.

Giancarlo Pasquini, "La Cooperazione Italiana fra Imprese Cooperative: La Formazione del Sistema Consortile", *Rivista della Cooperazione Italiana*, October-December 1981, pp.43-50.

Gianfranco Pasquino, "Partiti, Società Civile, Istituzioni e il Caso Italiano", *Stato e Mercato,* Numero 8, August 1983, pp.170-205.

Gianfranco Pasquino, "Italian Christian Democracy: A Party for all Seasons", in *Italy in Transition,* Peter Lange and Sydney Tarrow (eds), Frank Cass, London, 1980, pp.88-109.

Giacomo Patasso, "Comprata L'Italia, Ora Compriamo gli Italiani", *Avvenimenti*, 14 March 1990, pp.8-13.

Rob Paton, *Reluctant Entrepreneurs*, Open University Press, Milton Keynes, 1989.

Claudio Pellegrini, "Italian Industrial Relations", in Greg J Bamber and Russel D Lansbury (eds), *International and Comparative Industrial Relations*, Allen and Unwin, Sydney, 1987, pp.121-141.

Marco Pelliconi, "Uomini e Strutture della Cooperazione Imolese" in Angelo Varni (ed), *Emilia-Romagna Terra di Cooperazione*, Eta/Analisi, Bologna, 1990, pp.119-133.

Nida Peretti, "Quattro Paradossi di Un'Impresa", *Sistema*, May 1990, p.7.

Piergiovanni Permoli, "Quando la Coop era Ancora Bambina", *La Cooperazione Italiana*, October 1986, pp.121-123.

Charles Perrow, "Organisational Goals", *International Encyclopedia of the Social Sciences*, MacMillan and Free Press, USA, 1968, pp.305-310.

Paolo Perulli, "Industrial Flexibility and Small Firm Districts: The Italian Case", *Economic and Industrial Democracy,* Sage, London, Volume 11, 1990, pp.337-354.

Victor Pestoff, "The Dilemma Facing Swedish Consumer Cooperatives; Can Members, Markets, Authorities and Employees all be Optimised", in Colin Crouch and Frank Heller (eds), *Organisational Democracy and Political Processes*, John Wiley and Sons Ltd, Chichester, 1983, pp.433-453.

L Pestolazzi, *La Costituzione e lo Stato*, Editori Riuniti, Roma, 1975.

Rino Petralia, "I Nostri Diritti", in La Lega, *I Lacci di Gulliver: Deregulation e Movimento Cooperativo*, Editrice Cooperativa, Roma, 1986, pp.131-145.

Patrizia Pirazzoli, "Retribuzione Variabile nella Cooperazione Italiana: Bilancio di un Esperimento in Corso", *La Cooperazione Italiana*, May 1990, pp.56-60.

Peter R Pitegoff and Deborah Groban Olson, "ESOP Tax Benefits", in Len Krimerman and Frank Lindenfeld (eds), *When Workers Decide: Workplace Democracy Takes Root in North America*, New Society Publishers, Philadelphia, 1992, pp.288-289.

Arnaldo Plateroti, "Da Coop Italia a Coop Europa", *Consumi e Società,* Anno 5, Numero 3, May-June 1991, pp.12-13.

Panorama, "Shopping per Forza", 7 June 1992, p.193.

Gianfranco Poggi, *The State: its Nature, Development and Prospects*, Polity Press, Cambridge, 1990.

Onelio Prandini, *La Cooperazione Italiana: Organizzazione, Storia e Futuri Sviluppi del Movimento Cooperativo*, Editori Riuniti, Roma, Second Edition, 1986.

Giuliano Procacci, *Storia Degli Italiani*, Editori Laterza, Bari, 1984.

Frank Pyke (ed), *Industrial Districts and Inter-firm Co-operation in Italy*, International Institute for Labour Studies, Geneva, 1990.

Orazio Pugliese, *Il Sistema Cooperativo*, Marsilio Editori, Venezia, 1987.

Jack Quarter and George Melnyk (eds), *Partners in Enterprise: The Worker Ownership Phenomenon*, Black Rose Books, Montreal, 1989.

Jack Quarter, "Worker Ownership: One Movement or Many", in Jack Quarter and George Melnyk (eds) *Partners in Enterprise: the Worker Ownership Phenomenon,* Black Rose Books, Montreal, 1989, pp.1-31.

Jack Quarter, "Starting Worker-Owned Enterprises: Problems and Prospects", in Jack Quarter and George Melnyk (eds), *Partners in Enterprises: the Worker Ownership Phenomenon*, Black Rose Books, Montreal, 1989, pp.33-58.

Jack Quarter, "Workers of the World", in *Economic and Industrial Democracy,* Volume 13, Number 2, May 1992, pp.277-281.

Regione Emilia Romagna, *Sistema Metropolitano Policentrico*, Bologna, 1985.

Regione Emilia Romagna, *Programma Regionale di Sviluppo (1986-1988)*, Bologna 1986.

Regione Emilia Romagna, *Consuntivo del Programma Regionale di Sviluppo 1986-1988: Note e Tabelle di Sintesi*, Bologna, 1989.

Regione Emilia Romagna, *Consuntivo del Programma Regionale di Sviluppo 1986-1988: Note Elaborate dai Settori,* Bologna, 1989.

Regione Emilia Romagna, *Piano Territoriale Regionale*, Bologna 1990.

Regione Emilia Romagna, *Vent'Anni di Elezioni Regionali in Emilia-Romagna: Il Rinnovo del Consiglio Regionale dal 1970 al 1990*, Bologna, 1991.

Regione Emilia Romagna, *Repertorio delle Medie e Grandi Strutture di Vendita al Dettaglio per il 1990*, Bologna, 1991.

Gloria Regonini, "Stato del Benessere", in Norberto Bobbio (ed), *Dizionario di Politica*, Utet, Torino 1990, pp.1114-1118.

Alfredo Reichlin, "Il PCI e L'Europa", *Rinascita*, Numero 47, Anno 32, 28 November 1975, pp.1-2.

La Repubblica, "Alla Lega i Socialisti all'Attacco: Chiedono di Bocciare i Conti '89", 20 July 1989.

Aldo Ricci, "I Problemi Lasciati Aperti dalla Piccola Riforma", Walter Briganti (ed), *Il Movimento Cooperativo in Italia 1963-1980,* Editrice Cooperativa, Roma, 1982, pp.188-189.

Rinascita, *Il PCI e la Svolta del 1956,* Rinascita Supplement, Roma, 1986.

John Robbins, "The Cooperative Alternative: The Revival of a Democratic Ideal in Industry", *The Journal of Industrial Relations*, March 1982, pp.3-18.

Giorgio Rochat (ed), *La Casa in Italia 1945-1980: Alle Radici del Potere Democristiano*, Zanichelli Editore, Bologna, 1980.

Paliva Romagnoli, Intervista con Stefano Zan, "Italia Modello Unico", in *La Lega Senza Frontiere,* L'Unità Supplement, 16 June 1989, pp.48-49.

Carlo Romanelli, *Raccontare Un'Impresa: Cambiare per Restare se Stessi*, Cooperative Muratori e Braccianti di Carpi, Carpi, 1988.

Roberto Romano, *Nascita dell'Industria in Italia*, Editori Riuniti, Roma, 1984.

Di Romarin, "Dal Nostro Inviato Speciale", *La Cooperazione Italiana*, October 1986, pp.125-147.

Renzo Rosati and Roberto Seghetti, "Stato Padroncino", *Panorama*, 26 July 1992, pp.178-182.

Corey Rosen, "ESOPs: Hype or Hope", in Len Krimerman and Frank Lindenfeld (eds), *When Workers Decide: Workplace Democracy Takes Root in North America*, New Society Publishers, Philadelphia, 1992, pp.184-187.

Pietro Rossi, "La Strategia della Coop di Consumatori", in *Sintesi del Sistema*, May 1990, p.13.

Joyce Rothschild-Whitt, "The Collectivist Organisation: An Alternative to Rational-Bureaucratic Models", *American Sociological Review*, Volume 44, 1979, pp.509-527.

Charles F. Sabel, *Work and Politics: The Division of Labour in Industry*, Cambridge University Press, New York, 1982.

Maria Silvia Sacchi, "Latte Concentrato", *Panorama*, 7 June 1992, p.191.

Edda Saccomani, "Fascismo", in Norberto Bobbio (et al.) (ed), *Dizionario di Politica*, Tea/Utet, Torino 1990, pp.365-374.

Stefano Sacconi, "Da Quel Sogno del Vecchio Cassina", *La Cooperazione Italiana,* October 1986, pp.274-281.

Giulio Sapelli, *Il Movimento Cooperativo in Italia: Storia e Problemi,* Einaudi Editore, Torino, 1981.

Giulio Sapelli, "Introduzione", in Carlo Romanelli, *Raccontare Un'Impresa: Cambiare per Restare se Stessi'*, Cooperativa Muratori e Braccianti di Carpi, Carpi, 1988.

Giulio Sapelli e Stafano Zan, *Costruire L'Impresa: La Cooperativa Muratori e Cementisti di Ravenna dal 1945 al 1972*, Il Mulino, Bologna, 1991.

Donald Sassoon, "The Italian Communist Party's European Strategy", *Political Quarterly*, Volume 47, Number 3, July-September 1976, pp.253-275.

Donald Sassoon, *Contemporary Italy: Politics, Economics and Society Since 1945*, Longman, New York, 1986.

Stefania Schipani, "Strumenti che Aprono la Porta ai Capitali", *La Cooperazione Italiana*, February-March 1992, pp.46-47..

Giuseppe Sciortino, "Immigration Into Europe and Public Policy: Do Stops Really Work?", *New Community*, 18 (10), pp.89-99.

Roberto Seghetti, "Leggina Continua", *Panorama*, 16 February 1992, p.155.

Philip Selznick, *TVA and the Grass Roots*, Harper & Row Publishers, New York, 1966.

Andrew Shonfield, *Modern Capitalism: The Changing Balance of Public and Private Power*, Oxford University Press, London, 1965.

Alberto Sisto, "Un Tabù che si Chiama Ricerca", *La Cooperazione Italiana*, December 1989, pp.54-60.

Alberto Sisto, "Manager Più Mobili col Nuovo Contratto", *La Cooperazione Italiana*, February-March 1993, pp.70-71.

Spazio Impresa, "Costruire una Rete di Servizi per l'Azienda del Sud", 2 April 1991, p.21.

Spazio Impresa, "Golfo: La Lega Interverrà in Kuwait", 7 May 1991, p.17.

Ruggero Spesso, *L'Economia Italiana dal Dopoguerra ad Oggi*, Editori Riuniti, Roma, 1980.

Federick Spotts and Theodore Wieser, *Italy: A Difficult Democracy*, Cambridge University Press, Cambridge, 1986.

Paolo Spriano, *The Occupation of the Factories*, Pluto Press, London, 1975.

Stefano Stanghellini, "Le Grandi Imprese Nazionali Nella Competizione Europea", Ecosfera (ed), *Le Imprese di Costruzione nel Mercato Europeo*, Il Sole 24 Ore, Milano, 1990, pp.117-172.

Stefano Stanghellini, "L'Impresa di Costruzione Soggetto Innovativo nel Processo Produttivo delle Opere Complesse", Ecosfera (ed), *Le Imprese di Costruzione nel Mercato Europeo*, Il Sole 24 Ore, Milano, 1990, pp.173-208.

Renzo Stefanelli et al., *L'Autogestione in Italia: Realtá e Funzione della Cooperazione Italiana*, De Donato, Bari, 1975.

Carla Straini, "Una Nuova Legge 'Marcora' per Snellire le Procedure e Allargare le Aree di Intervento", in *La Cooperazione Italiana*, January-February 1993, (Supplement:Legge 49/85 "Marcora" Stato di Attuazione e Nuove Proposte), pp. 16-17.

Filippo Strati, "Gli Strumenti di Politica Attiva del Lavoro Aventi per Soggetto L'Autogestione", in *I Nuovi Scenari della Cooperazione Italiana in Italia: Problemi di Efficienza, Efficacia e Legittimazione Sociale*, A cura di A. Carbonaro e S. Gherardi, Franco Angeli, Milano, 1988, pp.315-348.

Dennis Swann, *The Economics of the Common Market*, Penguin, Harmondsworth, Fifth Edition, 1985.

Nadia Tarantini, "Il Prodotto è Svestito", *La Cooperazione Italiana,* June 1990, pp.28-29.

Nadia Tarantini, "Come si Costruisce la Qualità Totale", *La Cooperazione Italiana*, June 1990, pp.30-32.

Nadia Tarantini, "Bue Stressato fa Cattiva Bistecca", in *La Cooperazione Italiana*, May 1991, p.31.

Angelo Tasca, "Gli Attacchi del Fascismo alla Cooperazione", *Nascita e Avvento del Fascismo*, Quarta Edizione, Bari 1972, in Walter Briganti (ed), *Il Movimento Cooperativo in Italia 1854-1925: Scritti e Documenti*, Editrice Cooperativa, Roma, 1982, pp.249-253.

F W Taylor, "Scientific Management", in DS Pugh (ed), *Organisation Theory: Selected Readings*, Penguin Books, London, pp.157-176.

Alan Thomas, "Financing Worker Cooperatives in EC Countries", in *Annals of Public and Cooperative Economics*, Volume 61, Number 2-3, April-September 1990, pp.175-212.

Henk Thomas and Chris Logan, *Mondragon: An Economic Analysis*, George Allen and Unwin, London, 1982.

Keith Thompson, "The Serpent in the Supermarket's Paradise", *European Management Journal*, Volume 10, Number 1, March 1992, pp.112-118.

Jenny Thornley, *Workers' Cooperatives: Jobs and Dreams,* Heinemann Education Books, London, 1981.

Jenny Thornley, "Workers' Cooperative and Trade Unions: the Italian Experience", *Economic and Industrial Democracy,* Sage, London, Volume 4, 1983, pp.321-344.

Palmiro Togliatti, *Il Partito: Scritti e Discorsi*, PCI Publication, 1973.

Palmiro Togliatti, "Rapporto all'Ottavo Congresso del Pci", in *Il PCI e la Svolta del 1956*, Rinascita Supplement, Editrice L'Unitá, Rome, 1986, pp.49-101.

Massimo Tognoni, "Marcora: da Aziende in Crisi a Cooperative Efficienti", in *Quarantacinque*, Anno XI, July-August 1989, pp.36-37.

Massimo Tognoni, "La Ricetta è una Sola: Integrazione tra Pubblico e Privato", in *Spazio Impresa*, Editrice l'Unitá, 2 April1991, p.19.

Claudio Tolomelli, "Policies to Support Innovation in Emilia Romagna: Experiences and Prospects and Theoretical Prospects", in Enrico Ciciotti (et al.), *Technological Change in a Spatial Context,* Springer-Verlag, Berlin, 1989, pp.356-378.

Nazareno Tomassini, "Crescere Cambiando", *Consumi e Società,* Anno V, Numero 3, May-June, 1991, pp.19-30.

Luca Torrealta, "I Mattoni di Carpi", *Il Manifesto*, 11 December 1990, p.2.

Maurizio Tortorella, "Tutto Castello e Bottega", *Panorama*, 4 October 1992, p.53.

Roberto Tremelloni, "Per Una Statistica Della Cooperazione 1915-1921", in Walter Briganti (ed), *Il Movimento Cooperativo in Italia 1854-1925: Scritti e Documenti*, Editrice Cooperativa, Roma, 1982, pp.278-287.

Eric Trist, "A Concept of Organisational Ecology", *Australian Journal of Management,* Volume 2, Number 2, October 1977, pp.161-175.

L'Unità, *Lega Senza Frontiere,* June 1989.

L'Unità, "Edilter Leader nelle Costruzioni", 30 November 1989, p.28.

L'Unità, "Nel 1993 a Bologna ... un Nuovo Centro Commerciale", 1 July 1991, p.16.

L'Unità, "Sul Nome di Turci Presidente La Lega Ritrova la Sua Unanimità", 12 April 1991.

L'Unità, "Giglio", 1 May 1991, p.15.

L'Unità, "Una Rete per il Mercato", 8 June 1991, p.22.

Maurizio Valentini, "Sogni Proibiti", *L'Espresso*, 14 October 1990, pp.162-165.

Hermann Van Der Wee, *Prospects and Upheaval: The World Economy 1945-1980*, Penguin, Harmondsworth, 1987.

Jaroslav Vanek, "The Basic Theory of Financing Participatory Firms", Working Paper Number 27, Cornell University, Department of Economics, Ithaca, July 1971, in Jaroslav Vanek (ed), *Self Management: Economic Liberation of Man*, Penguin Books, Harmondsworth, 1975, pp.445-455.

Angelo Varni (ed), "ACAM, un Consorzio Nazionale per L'Approvvigionamento, da Trent'Anni al Servizio delle Imprese Associate", *Emilia Romagna Terra di Cooperazione*, ETA/Analisi, Bologna, 1990, p.318.

Angelo Varni (ed), "Camst: Una Grande Associazione di Idèe per la Ristorazione Italiana", in *Emilia Romagna Terra di Cooperazione*, ETA/Analisi, Bologna, 1990, p.324.

Angelo Varni (ed), "Il Coop Italia", *Emilia Romagna Terra di Cooperazione*, Eta/Analisi, Bologna, 1990, pp.264-365.

Angelo Varni, (ed), "Coop Emilia Veneto: Tanti Soci Consumatori in Grado di Intervenire nella Vita e nelle Scelte Cooperative", in *Emilia Romagna Terra di Cooperazione*, Eta-Analisi, Bologna, 1990, p.369.

Angelo Varni (ed), "Giglio Leader Mondiale nel Commercio del Parmiggiano Reggiano", in *Emilia Romagna Terra di Cooperazione*, Eta/Analisi Bologna, 1990, p.399.

Angelo Varni (ed), "Granarolo Felsinea CERPL un Ruolo di Primo Piano in un Settore Strategico Nazionale", *Emilia Romatgna Terra di Cooperazione*, Eta/Analisi, Bologna, 1990, p.401.

Angelo Varni (ed), "Unipol: La Compagnia d' Assicurazioni del Mondo del Lavoro", in *Emilia Romagna Terra di Cooperazione*, Eta/Analisi, Bologna, 1990, p.425.

Angelo Varni (ed), "La Banca Cooperativa dell' Emilia Romagna: Importante Realtà Presto su Scala Regionale", in *Emilia Romagna Terra di Cooperazione*, Eta/Analisi, Bologna, 1990, p.427.

Giuseppe Campos Venuti, "Bilancio della Legge 167", in Giorgio Rochat (ed), *La Casa in Italia 1945-1980: Alle Radici del Potere Democristiano*, Zanichelli, Bologna, 1980, pp.185-190.

Pietro Verzelletti, "Il Ruolo della Lega delle Cooperative nel Nuovo Scenario Economico", in La Lega Nazionale delle Cooperative e Mutue, *Il Sistema Lega di Fronte All'Innovazione Finanziaria,* Roma, 1988, pp.19-30.

Simona Vettraino, "L'Impresa Cooperativa Vuol Dire Stabilità. E per il Futuro?", *Spazio Impresa*, 2 April1991, p.21.

Pierpaolo Vichi, *La Cooperativa Muratori Cementisti di Ravenna 1916-1926*, Grafiche Galeati Imola, 1981.

Roberto Vighi, "La Resistenza e il Maltolto", in Walter Briganti(ed), *Il Movimento Cooperativo Italiano, 1926-1962*, Editrice Cooperativa, Roma, 1978, pp.115-121.

Andrew Vincent, "Conceptions of the State", in Mary Hawkwsworth and Maurice Kogan (eds), *Encyclopedia of Government and Politics*, Routledge, London, 1992, pp.43-55.

Giuseppe Vitale, "L'Integrazione nei Consorzi", in *L'Autogestione in Italia: Realtà e Funzione della Cooperazione Italiana*, De Donato, Bari, 1975, pp.73-98.

Benjamin Ward, "The Firm in Illyria: Market Syndicalism", *The American Economic Review*, Volume XLV11, June 1958, Number 3, pp.566-589.

Sydney and Beatrice Webb, "Special Supplement on the Cooperative Movement", *The New Statesman,* May 30, 1914, pp.1-31

Sydney and Beatrice Webb, "Special Supplement on Cooperative Production and Profit Sharing", *The New Statesman*, February 14 1914, pp.1-34.

Max Weber, "Legitimation, Authority and Bureaucracy", from Max Weber, *The Theory of Social and Economic Organisation*, Free Press, 1947, pp.328-240; in DS Pugh (ed), *Organisational Theory*, Penguin, London, Second Edition, 1987, pp.15-27.

Linda Weiss, "Regional Economic Policy in Italy", in Colin Crouch and David Marquand (eds), *The New Centralism: Britain Out of Step in Europe?*, Basil Blackwell, Oxford, 1989, pp.109-124.

William Foote Whyte and Kathleen King Whyte, *Making Mondragon: the Growth and Dynamics of the Worker Cooperative Complex,* New York, ILR Press, 1991.

Frank L Wilson, *European Politics Today: The Democratic Experience*, Prentice Hall, New Jersey, 1990.

Ma Jesus Zabaleta, "Mondragon: Un'Esperienza Integrata", in Anna Avitabile (et al.), *Cooperare e Competere*, Giangiacomo Feltrinelli Editore, Milano, 1986, pp.18-30.

Vera Zamagni, "L'Economia", in Renato Zangheri (ed), Bologna, Editori Laterza, Bari, 1986, pp.245-314.

Luca Zan, *l'Economia dell'Impresa Cooperativa*, Utet Libreria, Torino, 1990.

Stefano Zan, *La Cooperazione in Italia: Strutture, Strategie e Sviluppo della Lega Nazionale Cooperative e Mutue*, De Donato, Bari, 1982.

Stefano Zan, "Tipologia delle Cooperative", *L'Impresa*, Aprile, 1983, pp.13-19.

Stefano Zan, "Il Quadro Concettuale di Riferimento", in *Le Interdipendenze Organizzative in Agricoltura*, Regione Emilia Romagna, Bologna, 1987, pp.17-40.

Stefano Zan (A Cura di), *Le Interdipendenze Organizzative in Agricoltura,* Assessorato Agricoltura e Alimentazione della Regione Emilia-Romagna, Bologna, 1987.

Stefano Zan, *The Consumer Entrepreneur: New Synergies Among Needs, Society and Business Strategies*, Report Presented to Coop Emilia Veneto, Sala dei Convegni, Bologna, 1987, pp.1-16.

Stefano Zan, "The Management of Entrepreneur Associations: the Case of La Lega Nazionale delle Cooperative e Mutue", Paper Presented at the Joint Session of the European Consortium for Political Research, held in Rimini on 5-10 April 1988 for the Workshop on Markets, Politics and Associations: The Case of Consumer Welfare in the Public, Private and Cooperative Sectors.

Stefano Zan, "Gli Effetti Antisistemici del Collateralismo Pluralista", in *Quarantacinque*, Anno 11, Numero 9, September 1989, p.23.

Renato Zangheri, "Nascita e Primi Sviluppi", in Renato Zangheri (ed), *Storia del Movimento Cooperativo in Italia*, Giulio Einaudi Editore, Torino, 1987, pp.5-218.

Illio Zani, "Le Casse Rurali: Problemi Legislativi e di Prospettiva", in La Lega Nazionale delle Cooperative e Mutue, *Il Sistema Lega di Fronte all'Innovazione Finanziaria*, Roma, 1988, pp.173-177.

Raphael Zariski, "Italy", Peter H. Merkl (ed), *Western European Party Systems: Trends and Prospects*, Collier Macmillan Publishers, London, 1980, pp.123-151.

Raphael Zariski, "Approaches to the Problem of Local Autonomy: The Lessons of Italian Regional Devolution", *West European Politics*, Volume 8, Number 3, July 1985, pp.64-81.

Alberto Zevi, "La Strumentazione Finanziaria per le Imprese Cooperative", in La Lega, *La Questione Finanziaria e lo Sviluppo dell'Impresa Cooperativa*, Editrice Cooperativa, Roma, 1984, pp.41-55.

Alberto Zevi and Carla Strani, "Le Esperienze, le Prospettive della CFI", in La Lega delle Cooperative e Mutue: Dipartimento Finanziario, *Il Sistema Lega di Fronte All'innovazione Finanziaria*, Firenze, 1988, pp.194-197.

Alberto Zevi, "The Financing of Cooperatives in Italy", in *Annals of Public and Cooperative Economy*, Volume 61, Number 3, April-September 1990, pp.353-365.

Alberto Zevi, "Uno Strumento Valido da Sfruttare Meglio", *La Cooperazione Italiana*, October 1991, p.40.

Alberto Zevi, "Una piu Ampia Partecipazione dei Lavoratori Anche in Imprese non in Crisi", in *La Cooperazione Italiana*, January-February 1993, (Supplement: Legge 49/85 "Marcora" Stato di Attuazione e Nuove Proposte), p. 18.

Nicola Zotti, *Lega Nazionale delle Cooperative: La Sua Storia, La Sua Immaggine, La Sua Politica*, Editrice Cooperativa, Roma, 1983.

Nicola Zotti, *La Cooperazione Italiana di Consumatori*, Editrice Cooperativa, Roma, 1983.

Index